Praise for
The Ideal of Culture: Essays

"Gone are the days, . . . [Epstein] writes, when 'stability, solidity, gravity, a certain weight and aura of seriousness suffused public life.' Although 'in our egalitarian age,' cultural elitism is damned, Epstein happily champions 'the best that has been thought and said.'"

—*Kirkus Reviews*

"Epstein's work is . . . thoughtful and playful . . . a rarely found combination of . . . light, energy, and grace. . . . He parses . . . the delights, the irritations, and the many mysteries of life. . . . He's neither right-wing nor left-wing, but the entire bird . . . (one of the requirements of wisdom being the ability to distinguish a moral crusade from a racket.)"

—Larry Thornberry, *American Spectator*

"*The Ideal of Culture* . . . seems, in its insistence on essential verities in an age of great flux, just the right book for our historical moment. . . . As more than one Epstein fan has noted, he seems to have read everything . . . [with] effortless intelligence."

—Danny Heitman, *Christian Science Monitor*

"The release of a major collection of Joseph Epstein's essays stands as something of an event in the world of belles-lettres. . . . Epstein . . . is not merely someone with a feeling for words. He has the breadth of knowledge, wide perspective, and the mix of shrewdness and prudence that a great commentator must."

—Jonathan Leaf, *Modern Age*

"Masterful writing from Joseph Epstein. . . ."

—Julia McMichael, *Seattle Book Review*

Praise for
Wind Sprints: Shorter Essays

"I am purring, chortling and cursing my way through [Wind Sprints]. Cursing, because [the] wit, . . . erudition, . . . elan, panache, and . . . *je ne sais quoi* is just too depressing. There's treasure in every sentence. It's like spoon-eating caviar. I may have a stroke, but what a way to go."

—Christopher Buckley, author of *Thank You for Smoking*

"A master of the essay form returns with a collection of brief pieces spanning nearly 20 years. . . . Another subtitle might have been *Healthful Snacks*, for these bite-size pieces are both enjoyable to ingest and good for you."

—*Kirkus Reviews* (Starred Review)

"Witty, common-sensical, civilized, reliably pleasure-giving, Epstein is solace."

—Patrick Kurp, *Anecdotal Evidence*

"In *Wind Sprints*, his latest collection of essays, Joseph Epstein confesses to literary tippling—sampling bits of prose while in the supermarket line, during television commercials, or even in traffic. . . . He excels at lively, instructive, and often funny essays that sometimes run to 10,000 words. The only complication in starting them is that they're so charming and chatty that one cannot easily put them down. A reader who begins an Epstein piece behind the wheel is likely to be stalled on the freeway for a very long time."

—Danny Heitman, the *Christian Science Monitor*

"It has long been implausible to argue that there's a more engaging essayist on the planet than Epstein. . . . There are 143 pieces in *Sprints*, with almost no repetition of subject. Perhaps because of the length of these pieces, Epstein takes on fewer literary questions and deals with more small, quotidian matters, though in ways to demonstrate that almost anything can be dealt with intelligently, and in an entertaining way."

—Larry Thornberry, the *American Spectator*

"This collection is the perfect introduction to the erudite and entertaining work of a prolific essayist. . . . Noted writer Joseph Epstein offers a smorgasbord of wit in the collection *WIND SPRINTS: SHORTER ESSAYS*."

—Peter Dabbene, *FOREWORD REVIEWS*

"Epstein (emeritus lecturer of English, Northwestern University), a frequent contributor to the *WALL STREET JOURNAL*, *COMMENTARY*, and the *WEEKLY STANDARD*, is acclaimed for his witty, perceptive, and occasionally contentious essays, which he began during his editorship (1974–97) of *AMERICAN SCHOLAR*."

—Lonnie Weatherby, *LIBRARY JOURNAL*

"The 143 essays in Epstein's entertaining new collection . . . are compulsively readable. . . . Epstein shows himself capable of writing engagingly at that brief length on just about any topic that strikes his fancy. . . . The essays are peppered with personal memories and quotes from literature and punctuated with bursts of humor—Epstein likens a bandleader's bellow to that 'of a man who has just been pushed off a cliff'—and they abound with pleasures that belie their brevity."

—*PUBLISHERS WEEKLY*

"In the 143 short essays, Epstein discusses his reading habits, language snobbery, his love of khakis and good ol' fashioned shoe shines, the need for a word to describe someone who is more than an acquaintance but less than a friend, the rise of hot dog prices, and the demise of the high five. . . . Generally acknowledged as one of America's foremost essayists, Epstein's short pieces are delightful and infuriating, endearing, and aggravating."

—Sean West, *SAN FRANCISCO BOOK REVIEW*

Praise for
A Literary Education and Other Essays

"Epstein follows up ESSAYS IN BIOGRAPHY (2012) with another collection of provocative and beguiling thought pieces. The range of his curiosity is exhilarating."

—*PUBLISHERS WEEKLY*

"[In *A LITERARY EDUCATION*] prolific essayist, biographer, and novelist Epstein . . . delivers . . . lots of erudition . . . and . . . fun."

—*KIRKUS REVIEWS*

"Erudite, penetrating, and decisive . . . Epstein's delivery is filled with thorough analysis, delightful allusions, and outright laughs. . . ."

—Peter Dabbene, *FOREWORD REVIEWS*

"Maybe it's time for a 'Joseph Epstein Reader' that would assemble the best work from his previous books for old and new fans alike. In the meantime, *A LITERARY EDUCATION* inspires hope that Mr. Epstein's good run [referring to the author's 24 books] isn't over just yet."

—Danny Heitman, *WALL STREET JOURNAL*

"[This is a] wonderful book of summer reading that's [also] . . . good for the cold, gray days ahead. . . . [Epstein is] a man of his time and above his time. . . ."

—Suzanne Fields, *WASHINGTON TIMES*

"Joseph Epstein turns out the best essays—of the literary or familiar kind—of any writer on active duty today. . . . Those who've reviewed Epstein's work over the years . . . praise his humor, his erudition, his vast learning, and his elegance. . . . Epstein's writing, like most French desserts, is very rich stuff."

—Larry Thornberry, *AMERICAN SPECTATOR*

"Epstein's . . . *A Literary Education and Other Essays* . . . is his 24th book. This volume confirms that Epstein is not only the greatest living American literary critic, but also the country's foremost general essayist. He is, almost singlehandedly, holding aloft the flame for what used to be the honorable calling of 'the man of letters.'"

—John Podhoretz, *Commentary*

"[Epstein] writes sentences you want to remember. . . . His essays are troves of literary reference and allusion, maps between centuries, countries, genres. . . . [They] have personality and style, yes, but they also have something to say, and that's the pivotal distinction between Epstein and his bevy of imitators. . . . What's more, his wit is unkillable. . . ."

—William Giraldi, *New Criterion*

"Epstein is an essayist of the old school—learned, productive, and available to many occasions. A man gifted with a wit both cutting and self-deprecating, and an easy command of the many syntactic variations of the periodic sentence, he also has a fearless willingness to assert a view—and this, as any reader of the essay knows, is the drive wheel of the whole business, never mind if that view is widely shared or unpopular."

— Sven Birkerts, *Los Angeles Review of Books*

Praise for
Essays in Biography

"Erudite...eloquent...opinionated...edifying and often very entertaining."

—*Publishers Weekly*

"The acclaimed essayist . . . presents a provocative collection of essays that [is] . . . guaranteed to both delight and disconcert."

—*Kirkus Reviews*

"[He] brings to biography a genius of discernment."

—*Choice*

"Mr. Epstein's essays are brilliant distillations. . . . "

—Carl Rollyson, *Wall Street Journal*

"*Essays in Biography* . . . is smart, witty and a pleasure to read."

—Jonathan Yardley, *Washington Post*

"This . . . collection of biographical essays . . . [is] unabashedly personal, and flavored throughout by a wit that never stays in the background for long. [What Epstein calls a] 'heightened sense of life's possibilities' is . . . what a reader may take away."

—*Boston Globe*

"Joseph Epstein['s] . . . style and wit make his subjects come alive. . . . [He is] the dean of contemporary essayists."

—*Washington Times*

"Epstein is a gifted storyteller, a discerning critic, and a peerless stylist. . . . It's fair to say that a variety of over-used adjectives—witty, urbane, intelligent—are in this case quite appropriate."

—*Weekly Standard*

"[Joseph Epstein is] one of the few living writers whose every book I try to read promptly. He is never—really never—less than a pure thoughtful joy."

—Brian Doherty, Senior Editor, *Reason*

"Epstein writes suave, free-wheeling, charged essays."

—Robert Fulford, *National Post*

"[Joseph Epstein's] personal mission statement, apparently, is to instruct and delight. . . . This is a book you can pick up and skip around in with pleasure and profit."

—Christopher Flannery, *Claremont Review of Books*

Gallimaufry

Gallimaufry

A Collection of Essays, Reviews, Bits

Joseph Epstein

Also by Joseph Epstein

Charm: The Elusive Enchantment (2018)

The Ideal of Culture: Essays (2018)

Where Were We?: The Conversation Continues,
with Frederic Raphael (2017)

Wind Sprints: Shorter Essays (2016)

Frozen in Time (2016)

Masters of the Games: Essays and Stories on Sport (2015)

A Literary Education and Other Essays (2014)

Distant Intimacy: A Friendship in the Age of the Internet,
with Frederic Raphael (2013)

Essays in Biography (2012)

Gossip: The Untrivial Pursuit (2011)

The Love Song of A. Jerome Minkoff: And Other Stories (2010)

Fred Astaire (2008)

In a Cardboard Belt!: Essays Personal, Literary, and Savage (2007)

Friendship: An Exposé (2006)

Alexis de Tocqueville: Democracy's Guide (2006)

Fabulous Small Jews (2003)

Envy (2003)

Snobbery: The American Version (2002)

Narcissus Leaves the Pool: Familiar Essays (1999)

Life Sentences: Literary Essays (1997)

With My Trousers Rolled: Familiar Essays (1995)

Pertinent Players: Essays on the Literary Life (1993)

A Line Out for a Walk: Familiar Essays (1991)

The Goldin Boys: Stories (1991)

Partial Payments: Essays on Writers and Their Lives (1988)

Once More Around the Block: Familiar Essays (1987)

Plausible Prejudices: Essays on American Writing (1985)

Middle of My Tether: Familiar Essays (1983)

Ambition: The Secret Passion (1980)

Familiar Territory: Observations on American Life (1979)

Divorced in America: Marriage in an Age of Possibility (1974)

The essays in this book were previously published
in journals and anthologies. Original publication
information can be found on page 467.

Axios Press
PO Box 457
Edinburg, VA 22824
888.542.9467   info@axiosinstitute.org

Library of Congress Cataloging-in-Publication Data

Names: Epstein, Joseph, 1937- author.
Title: Gallimaufry : a collection of essays, reviews, bits / Joseph Epstein.
Description: Edinburg, VA : Axios Press, [2020] | Includes index. |
Identifiers: LCCN 2020014033 (print) | LCCN 2020014034 (ebook) | ISBN 9781604191288
    (hardcover) | ISBN 9781604191295 (ebook)
Classification: LCC PS3555.P6527 A6 2020 (print) | LCC PS3555.P6527 (ebook) | DDC
    814/.54--dc23
LC record available at https://lccn.loc.gov/2020014033
LC ebook record available at https://lccn.loc.gov/2020014034

For
HUNTER LEWIS
Ideal publisher

Gallimaufry: A confused jumble or medley of things

Contents

Bits & Pieces

Edward Redux

Introduction

WE LEARN FROM HERODOTUS, in his account of Solon's meeting with Croesus, king of Lydia and at the time thought to be the world's richest man, that, in Solon's words, "You should count no man happy until he dies." With all due respect to Solon, I count myself, at least as of the moment, if not among the happiest then among the more fortunate of men. Allow me to set out some of the reasons.

I have not had to go into an office for work since 1970. I was given a university teaching job without possessing any advanced degrees. I was appointed editor of a magazine on which I had no fund-raising responsibilities and on which two able sub-editors in an office nine hundred miles away did most of the detail work, the heavy-lifting, while I was given most of the credit. And, to top it off, I have been allowed to publish sixteen, with this book seventeen collections of my essays and occasional writings.

These writings have, moreover, had more than their share of praise. Some of this praise has been public, but much of it has come from appreciative readers who have found in one or another scribble of mine echoes in their own hearts, and have written to tell me about it. Apart from pleasure in the work itself, the greatest reward for any writer is the appreciation of intelligent readers. Those who have written to me have been kindly, gracious, and generous about my literary efforts. Perhaps the most amusing bit of praise I have ever received came from a man named Steve Straus, who wrote: "Coming across one of your pieces is like finding a $20 bill."

While counting my blessings, I need to include the small number of magazine editors who over the years have continued to seek out my writing. By allowing me to indulge my own interests, and in some cases anticipating those interests, these editors have keep me steadily at work. These interests meanwhile have over the years grown not more specialized but wider, ranging, as I note from the table of contents of this book, from Theodor Mommsen to P. G. Wodehouse, from Alcibiades to Big Bill Tilden, from Denis Diderot to Jewish jokes.

The good (if personal) news, then, is that I have had the luck to find congenial places to publish and an intelligent audience for my writing; the bad news is that I often feel that my kind of writing is coming at what might be the end of a long and distinguished line, one that begins with Plutarch, moves along to Montaigne, Joseph Addison, William Hazlitt and Charles Lamb, Thomas Macaulay, Max Beerbohm, and George Orwell—the line of the general, often biographical, essay. In the current day what might be called "the general interest" is being swamped by politics. So many magazines once given over almost entirely to general subjects—*Harper's, The Atlantic, The New Yorker*, and others—devote more and more space to political topics. General interest is everywhere being trumped by partisan political interests.

I have myself been accused of being a political writer, which I don't believe I am. True, in this book you will find essays on political correctness, the perils of the meritocracy in America, the decay of the contemporary university, and more. In so heatedly political an atmosphere as ours, one cannot avoid engaging with politics, at least not entirely. Still, as a man without a theory of government, or strong opinions on foreign policy, or much in the way of knowledge about economics, I continue to prefer to believe that I am only political enough to protect myself from the politics of others.

Along with the dominance of politics in the intellectual and cultural life of our time, there has been that most mixed of all mixed blessing, the Internet, which has taken its toll on literary culture and on literacy itself. The great battle of the day is not the culture war, or the uncivil skirmishes between political parties, but what I think of as the serious conflict between pixels and print, with pixels increasingly dominant.

By pixels I refer to reading and writing on phones, computers, kindles, tablets, watches, and other mechanical devices.

The two, pixels and paper, I have come to believe, engender distinctly different modes of cognition. One reads pixels, as they are chiefly meant to be read, quickly, skimmingly, chiefly for information. That is no doubt why, when one feels one has the information one needs online, one's hand twitches on one's cursor and one is ready to scroll down, to be done and gone. Reading pixels one doesn't often notice style, rhythm, wit, all those individual touches a careful writer puts into his work, certainly not in the same way one reads on paper. Something there is insubstantial, ephemeral, impermanent about writing that appears in pixels.

Reading a book or magazine, even a newspaper, one is usually in repose, becalmed, pensive. One notes interesting turns of phrase, striking metaphors and similes, the architecture of well-made sentences, all things that tend to pass unnoticed in pixels. On paper one sometimes returns to reread key passages, or pauses to make a note, or lightly sidelines an arresting phrase. Not so with pixels, which have now taught people to read differently, and, since one learns to write from reading, pixels also figures to change the way people will write, which seems, potentially, a serious subtraction, a sadness if not a shame.

Still, there remains—one likes to think there will always remain—a saving remnant. Whether this remnant is of 20,000, 50,000, or more than a 100,000 people cannot be known. But those readers who find the time for, and take pleasure in, serious books and magazines are out there I know, and I am immensely grateful to have to heard from my share of them.

Part One

Essays & Reviews

The Bookish Life

(2018)

THE VILLAGE IDIOT of the *shtetl* of Frampol was offered the job of waiting at the village gates to greet the arrival of the Messiah. "The pay isn't great," he was told, "but the work is steady." The same might be said about the conditions of the bookish life: low pay but steady work. By the bookish life, I mean a life in which the reading of books has a central, even a dominating, place. I recall some years ago a politician whose name is now as lost to me as it is to history who listed reading among his hobbies, along with fly-fishing and jogging. Reading happens to be my hobby, too, along with peristalsis and respiration.

Like the man—the fellow with the name Solomon, writing under the pen name Ecclesiastes—said, "Of the making of many books there is no end; and much study is a weariness of the flesh." So many books are there in the world that no one can get around to even all the best among them, and hence no one can claim to be truly well-read. Some people are merely better-read than others. Nobody has read, or can read, everything, and by everything I include only the good, the beautiful, the important books.

THE FIRST QUESTION IS "How can one tell which books qualify as good, beautiful, important?" In an essay of 1978 called "On Reading Books: A Barbarian's Cogitations," Alexander Gerschenkron, a Harvard economist of wide learning, set out three criteria: A good book must be interesting, memorable, and rereadable. This is as sensible as it is unhelpful. How can one know if a book is interesting until one has read it; memorable until time has or has not lodged it in one's memory; rereadable until the decades pass and one feels the need to read it again and enjoys it all the more on doing so?

Not much help, either, is likely to be found in various lists of the world's best books. In 1771 a man named Robert Skipwith, later to be Thomas Jefferson's wife's brother-in-law, asked Jefferson to compile for him a list of indispensable books. Jefferson obliged with a list of 148 titles, mostly Greek and Roman classics, and some intensely practical treatises, among them a book on horse-hoeing husbandry. The *Guardian* not long ago published a list of the world's one hundred best nonfiction books in English, and while nearly every one seemed eminently worthy, one could just as easily add another hundred books that should have been on such a list, and this does not include all the world's splendid works of fiction, drama, and poetry, and not merely in English alone. In 1960, Clifton Fadiman, then a notable literary critic, produced a work called *The Lifetime Reading Plan*, a work of 378 pages, which I have chosen never to read, lest it take up the time I might devote to a better book.

Such lists reveal a yearning for a direct route to wisdom. Brace yourself for the bad news: None is available. If one wanted to establish expertise in a restricted field—economics, say, or art history, or botany—such a list might be useful. But for the road to acquiring the body of unspecialized knowledge that sometimes goes by the name of general culture, some-times known as the pursuit of wisdom, no map, no blueprint, no plan, no shortcut exists, nor, as I hope to make plain, could it.

BOOKISH, which sounds a bit like Jewish, is the word I use to describe lives that are dominated by books. I grew up in a home proudly Jewish but not in the least bookish. I don't believe we even had a dictionary in our apartment during the years I was growing up. The only books I can recall are a few volumes of a small-format, dun-colored, red-trimmed Funk & Wagnalls encyclopedia that my father acquired through newspaper subscription. Both my parents were well-spoken, my paternal grandfather in Montreal published three books in Hebrew whose cost was underwritten by my father, and my mother was a near genius in her accurate judgment of other people, but reading books takes time, and neither of my parents found time for them.

As a young boy, I didn't find much time for books, either. Sports were all that interested me, and sports took up all four seasons of the year. I read only the sports pages in the *Chicago Daily News,* and I read lots of comic books, including classic comic books, which were useful for giving book reports in school. The first book that genuinely lit my fire—no surprise here, it was a sports book—was John R. Tunis's *All-American.* So enamored was I of the novel that I took out my first library card so that I could read the rest of Tunis' sports novels.

The next four years I spent as an entirely uninterested high-school student. Shakespeare's *Julius Caesar*, George Eliot's *Adam Bede*, a few essays by Ralph Waldo Emerson, all offered as part of the required school curriculum, none of them so much as laid a glove on me. Willa Cather, a writer I have come to admire as the greatest twentieth-century American novelist, chose not to allow any of her novels put into what she called "school editions," lest young students, having to read her under the duress of school assignments, never return to her books when they were truly ready for them. She was no dope, Miss Cather.

Only after I had departed high school did books begin to interest me, and then only in my second year of college, when I transferred from the University of Illinois to the University of Chicago. Among the most beneficial departures from standard college fare at the University of Chicago was the brilliant idea of eliminating textbooks from undergraduate study. This meant that instead of reading, in a thick textbook, "In his *Politics* Aristotle held . . . ," or "In *Civilization and Its Discontents* Freud argued . . ." or "In *On Liberty* John Stuart Mill asserted . . . ," students read the *Politics, Civilization and Its Discontents, On Liberty*, and a good deal else. Not only read them, but, if they were like me, became excited by them. Heady stuff, all this, for a nineteen-year-old semi-literate who, on first encountering their names, was uncertain how to pronounce Proust or Thucydides.

Along with giving me a firsthand acquaintance with some of the great philosophers, historians, novelists, and poets of the Western world, the elimination of that dreary, baggy-pants middleman called the textbook gave me the confidence that I could read the most serious of books. Somehow it also gave me a rough sense of what is serious in the way of reading and what is not. Anyone who has read a hundred pages of Herodotus senses that it is probably a mistake—that is, a waste of your finite and therefore severely limited time on earth—to read a six-hundred-page biography of Bobby Kennedy, unless, that is, you can find one written by Xenophon.

WHAT IS THE TRUE POINT of a bookish life? Note I write "point," not "goal." The bookish life can have no goal: It is all means and no end. The point, I should say, is not to become immensely knowledgeable or clever, and certainly not to become learned. Montaigne, who more than five centuries ago established the modern essay, grasped the point when he wrote, "I may be a man of fairly wide reading, but I retain nothing." Retention of everything one reads, along with being mentally impossible, would only crowd and ultimately cramp one's mind. "I would very much love to grasp things with a complete understanding," Montaigne wrote, "but I cannot bring myself to pay the high cost of doing so. . . . From books all I seek is to give myself pleasure by an honorable pastime; or if I do study, I seek only that branch of learning which deals with knowing myself and which teaches me how to live and die well." What Montaigne sought in his reading, as does anyone who has thought at all about it, is "to become more wise, not more learned or more eloquent." As I put it elsewhere some years ago, I read for the pleasures of style and in the hope of "laughter, exaltation, insight, enhanced consciousness," and, like Montaigne, on lucky days perhaps to pick up a touch of wisdom along the way.

The act of reading—office memos, newspaper articles on trade and monetary policy, and bureaucratic *bumpf* apart—should if possible never be separable from pleasure. Twenty or so years ago there was a vogue for speed-reading. ("I took a speed-reading course and read *War and Peace* in twenty minutes," Woody Allen quipped. "A book about Russia, isn't it?") But why, one wonders, would you wish to speed up an activity that gives pleasure? Speed-reading? I'd as soon take a course in speed-eating or speed-lovemaking. Yet the notion of speed generally hovers over the act of reading. "A real page-turner," people say of certain novels or biographies. I prefer to read books that are page-stoppers, that cause me to stop and contemplate a striking idea, an elegant phrase, an admirably constructed sentence. A serious reader reads with a pencil in hand, to sideline, underline, make a note.

Nor, I suspect, is the bookish soul likely to read chiefly on a Kindle or a tablet. I won't go into the matter of the aesthetics of book design, the smell of books, the fine feel of a well-made book in one's hands, lest I be taken for a hedonist, a reactionary, and a snob. More important, apart from the convenience of Kindles and tablets—in allowing for enlarged print, in portability if one wants to take more than one or two books along when traveling—I have come to believe that there is a mysterious but quite real difference between words on pixel and words in print. For reasons perhaps one day brain science will reveal to us, print has more weight, a more substantial feel, makes a greater demand on one's attention, than the pixel. One tends not to note a writer's style as clearly in pixels as one does in print. Presented with a thirty- or forty-paragraph piece of writing in pixels, one wants to skim after fifteen or twenty paragraphs in a way that one doesn't ordinarily wish to do in print. Pixels for information and convenience, then, print for knowledge and pleasure is my sense of the difference between the two.

I have heard many stories of intelligent people deriving much pleasure from listening to books, serious books, on their smartphones or other devices. I wish them joy of it, for I cannot find any. Many years ago, a number of my own books were put on something then called "books on tape." Ordinarily I would have thought this a lovely ego sandwich, walking or driving about the city listening to my own words spoken by a (doubtless) out-of-work actor. On the contrary, I found I couldn't bear it. This stranger's reading rhythms were far from the rhythms I had put into my sentences; his pronunciations were sometimes off; listening to him I felt chiefly a sense of intrusion. Besides, listening to someone read, not just one's own but any serious writing, doesn't allow one to linger, go back to reread, ponder an interesting passage. Reading and listening to someone else reading are two widely, I should even say wildly, different things.

In the risky generalization department, slow readers tend to be better readers—more careful, more critical, more thoughtful. I myself rarely read more than twenty-five or thirty pages of a serious book in a single sitting. Reading a novel by Thomas Mann, a short story by Chekhov, a historical work by Theodor Mommsen, essays by Max Beerbohm, why would I wish to rush through them? Savoring them seems more sensible. After all, you never know when you will pass this way again.

A GREAT HELP in leading the bookish life is to recognize that as a reader, you might be omnivorous, but you can never be anywhere near omniscient. The realization removes a great deal of pressure. Some of this pressure derives from the claim of recent years that there is a much wider world than the Western one most of us grew up and were educated in. If one is not to be thought parochial in one's interests, the argument holds, one is responsible for knowing not Western culture alone but also the cultures of the Far and Near East. Yet when I think of all I haven't read in or about Western culture, I am perfectly prepared to take a pass on Islam, Hinduism, Shintoism, Buddhism, and the rich store of Chinese Confucian and contemplative literature. These and more will have to wait until I have read Pindar, Terence, Hume's *History of England*, Taine, Zola, and a few hundred other such items, not to speak of the books I should like to reread. They'll have to wait, it begins to look, until the next life, which, I like to think, will surely provide a well-stocked library. If it doesn't, I'm not sure I want any part of it. Hell of course will have a library, but one stocked exclusively with science fiction, six-hundred-odd page novels by men whose first name is Jonathan, and books extolling the 1960s.

Rereading is a subject on its own. How many books you have read when young seem less impressive when you are older! The books of Ernest Hemingway and Henry David Thoreau are two instances that jump to mind for me. Hemingway's code of manliness and Thoreau's plea to simplify our lives both seem so much balderdash, fustian, rodomontade. Ralph Waldo Emerson left me cold as a kid and even colder now. While other books that one was less impressed with when young—Willa Cather's is my example here—now seem richly complex, deep, indispensable. Some of the best of all books are those one loved when young and finds even better in later life. Marguerite Yourcenar's novel *Memoirs of Hadrian* is such a book for me. The *frisson* afforded by rereading is the discovery not only of things one missed the first time round but of the changes in oneself.

When I was in grammar school, in the sixth grade, our class had a visit from a woman from the Chicago Public Library. She came to inform us, in a sanctimonious voice, that books will "take us to unknown shores, bring us treasures hitherto undreamed of. Yes, boys and girls," she said, "books are your friends." Marcel Proust, of all people, would have agreed, with a single proviso. He believed that books were in some ways better than friends. "In reading," he held, "friendship is suddenly brought back to its first purity." Unlike with friends, we spend time with books only because we truly wish to be in their company. We never have to ask what they thought of us. Clashes of egotism have nothing to do with the bookish relationship. Perhaps best of all, when we tire of books, unlike tiring of friends, we close them and replace them on the shelf. Friendship with books, Proust felt, though it may be one-way, is nonetheless an unselfish friendship.

READING MAY NOT be the same as conversation, but reading the right books, the best books, puts us in the company of men and women more intelligent than ourselves. Only by keeping company with those smarter than ourselves, in books or in persons, do we have a chance of becoming a bit smarter. My friend Edward Shils held that there were four modes, or means, of education: that in the classroom, that through superior newspapers and journals, that from the conversation of intelligent friends, and that obtained from bookstores and especially used bookstores. The so-called digital age, spearheaded by Amazon, is slowly putting this last-named mode out of business. With its ample stock, quick delivery, and slightly lower prices, Amazon is well on its way to killing the independent bookstore. But the owners of these stores are not the only losers. Readers, too, turn out to be ill-served by this bit of mixed progress that Amazon and other online booksellers have brought.

I have seen used bookstores described as places where you find books you didn't know you wanted. I recently went into a neighborhood used bookstore just to browse, and came out with two books I hadn't, until I had them in my hands, known I'd wanted: Lesley Chamberlain's *Nietzsche in Turin* and Barry Strauss's *The Battle of Salamis*. I regularly make such unexpected discoveries. A few years ago, in another used bookstore, in its classics section, I came upon a book titled *Rome and Pompeii* by a writer I had never heard of named Gaston Boissier (1823–1908). I opened it, was pleased by the few passages I scanned, and bought it. I have subsequently read two other of Boissier's books, *Roman Africa* and *The Country of Horace and Virgil,* both of which gave much satisfaction. Without coming upon Boissier in a shop, holding his book in my hands, examining it, I should have missed out on a splendid writer.

As you will have gathered, correctly, I am far from a systematic reader. I read only books on subjects that interest me, and my interests tend to rove all over the intellectual and aesthetic lot. These interests tend to come in phases, sometimes resulting in reading binges. Not uncommonly a broad general subject will absorb my interest—the history of Rome, the Austro-Habsburg Empire, the *belle epoque*—and I find much of my reading devoted to it. Within the last few years, for example, caught up in a passion for all things Roman, I read Sallust, lots of Cicero, a great deal of Livy, some Appian, Polybius, Plutarch, Tacitus, Seneca, Pliny the Younger, Suetonius, Edward Gibbon, Theodor Mommsen, Ronald Syme, and more. I read all this not to gain mastery over the subject but for pleasure and what I hope is the occasional insight into human nature across a vast stretch of time that reading about Rome brings. I know no better ways to spend my days.

66 I HATE TO READ NEW BOOKS," William Hazlitt began an essay called "On Reading Old Books." He closes the same essay with a brief listing of many of the books he would still like to read: Lord Clarendon's *History of the Grand Rebellion,* Guicciardini's *History of Florence,* the plays of Beaumont and Fletcher, the speeches in Thucydides, *Don Quixote* in the original Spanish, and more. Reading that list, I immediately feel an intellectual kinship with Hazlitt.

I cannot say that I hate to read new books; since I write a few of them, this would put me in an awkward position. But as one grows older and recognizes that one's time isn't infinite, one is more likely to choose to read the three volumes of Mommsen's *History of Rome* over the five volumes of Robert Caro's *The Years of Lyndon Johnson,* the poetry of Wallace

Stevens over that of John Ashbery, the novels of Marcel Proust over those of Jonathan Franzen.

We all live in the contemporary world, but that doesn't mean that we have to restrict our reading to that world, which is doubtless already too much with us. "The art of not reading is a very important one," Schopenhauer wrote.

> It consists in not taking an interest in whatever may be engaging the attention of the general public at any particular time. When some political or ecclesiastical pamphlet, or novel, or poem is making a great commotion, you should remember that he who writes for fools always finds a large public. A precondition for reading good books is not reading bad ones: for life is short.

I know of no better advice for taking a pass on just about everything on the *New York Times* best seller list.

IF YOU HAPPEN TO BE IN SEARCH of an example of the word "desultory," allow me to offer my own current reading. On or near my bedside table I have bookmarks in the following books: Paul Johnson's little book on Mozart, John Aubrey's *Brief Lives,* A. J. P. Taylor's *The Habsburg Monarchy, 1809–1918,* William Rothstein's *Men & Memories, 1872–1938,* and Robert Burton's 1,381-page *Anatomy of Melancholy.* I've twice before made a run at Burton's book, but it now begins to look as if I may have to finish reading it in the next life. In my bathroom astride the back of the commode sits Ernst Pawel's *The Labyrinth of Exile: A Life of Theodor Herzl,* André Maurois's *Byron,* and the *Journal de L'Abbé Mugnier.* (As for reading in the bathroom, one of the highest compliments I have had came from a reader of a magazine I edited when he told me that he took it to the bathroom.) Elsewhere round my apartment, I have bookmarks in studies of Catullus and Alcibiades, a recent biography of Brutus, G. K. Chesterton's *Saint Francis of Assisi, The Reflections and Maxims of Luc de Clapiers, Marquis of Vauvenargues,* two slender volumes on Proust by Princess Marthe Bibesco, and Cornelius Nepos's *Lives of Eminent Commanders.* If you can make sense of this jumble of subjects, yours is a keener mind than mine.

Which brings me to the clutter that books can bring into a home. *Books Do Furnish a Room* is a truism as well as the title of the tenth novel in Anthony Powell's twelve-volume *Dance to the Music of Time* novel cycle, but it needs to be added that books can also take over a room—and not one room alone. Harry Wolfson, the Harvard scholar and philosopher, is said to have used both his refrigerator and oven to store books. I tell you this so your feelings shouldn't be hurt if, had you happened to have known him, Professor Wolfson failed to invite you to dinner.

I have myself twice sold off large numbers of my books. I had hoped to keep my own collection of books within respectable bounds—down, say, to the two or three hundred of the books I most love—but have found that impossible. I also instituted a failed policy of telling myself that for every book I brought home, I would get rid of one already in my possession. Meanwhile, over the years, I seem to have acquired two thousand or so books. Publishers and people send me books. Like an incorrigible juvenile delinquent who can't stay out of pool halls, I wander into used bookshops and do not often emerge empty-handed. Books in my apartment continue to multiply. Some of them, I suspect, do it overnight, in the dark, while I am asleep.

A S A BOOK ACCUMULATOR, I am a piker next to Edward Shils, who in a capacious three-bedroom apartment in Chicago had a library of roughly 16,000 volumes, in three languages, all of them serious, with another 6,000 books stored in a house he kept at Cambridge in England. In one of the two bathrooms in his Chicago apartment, Edward had bookshelves built over and above the bath and commode. No flat surface in his apartment, including his dining room table, was uncovered by books (or magazines or papers).

I am Edward Shils's literary executor, and in his will he noted that he wished his personal library to go to Hebrew University in Jerusalem. When I wrote to a former student of his, himself now a teacher at Hebrew University, to inform him of this bequest, he called back to say that, though he was touched by Edward's sentiment, the library at Hebrew University couldn't find the space for so many books, nor the money—he estimated it at $100,000—needed to ship and catalogue them, but would accept a few hundred or so books that they would set out on shelves under his name. I eventually sold the bulk of the books to a private dealer, for the sum of $166,000, which went into Edward's estate, but I also felt a touch of sadness that this great personal library, reflecting a powerful thinker's intellectual autobiography, would now be broken up.

Nietzsche said that life without music is a mistake. I would agree, adding that it is no less a mistake without books. Proust called books "the noblest of distractions," and they are assuredly that, but also more, much more. "People say that life is the thing," wrote Logan Pearsall Smith, "but I prefer reading." In fact, with a bit of luck, the two reinforce each other. In *The Guermantes Way* volume of his great novel, Proust has his narrator note a time when he knew "more books than people and literature better than life." The best arrangement, like that between the head and the heart, is one of balance between life and reading. One brings one's experience of life to one's reading, and one's reading to one's experience of life. You can get along without reading serious books—many extraordinary, large-hearted, highly intelligent people have—but why, given the chance, would you want to? Books make life so much richer, grander, more splendid. The bookish life is not for everyone, nor are its rewards immediately evident, but at a minimum taking it up you are assured, like the man said, of never being out of work.

Body without Soul

(2020)

I AM NOT ALTOGETHER INCURIOUS, but one entity about which I have over the years shown little curiosity is my own body. Until recently I could not have told you the function of my, or anyone else's, pancreas, spleen, or gallbladder. I'd just as soon not have known I have kidneys, and was less than certain about their exact whereabouts, apart from knowing that they reside somewhere in the region of my lower back. About my entrails, those yards of intestines winding through my body, the less I knew about them the better, though I have always liked the sound of the word duodenum. About the cells and chromosomes, the hormones and microbes crawling and swimming about in my body, let us not speak.

For better *and* worse, these deficiencies in my knowledge have been cleared up, at least for the nonce, by a splendid book by Bill Bryson called *The Body, A Guide for Occupants*. The book is an account of human parts, both inside and out, and what is known and still not known about them; it catalogues the diseases and mechanical failures to which these parts are heir; establishes a pantheon of heroic medical researchers and a rogues' gallery of quacks; sets out some of the differences between humans and other mammals and between the male and female of our own species— and it does all this in a highly fluent, often amusing, never dull manner.

The whole is informed by a point of view that is ironical yet suffused with awed appreciation for that endlessly complex machine the human body.

In the first hundred pages of *The Body* one learns that there are microbes in one's belly button, the average adult touches his face sixteen times an hour, the number of human facial expressions ranges between 4,100 and 10,000, tears come in three varieties, the human eye can distinguish between 2.5 million and 7.5 million colors, humans choke more easily than any other mammal, people who have had their tonsils removed when young may have a 44 percent greater risk of heart attack later in life, one of the inventors of the lobotomy won the Nobel Prize for Medicine in 1949, and Leonardo's "Mona Lisa" has no eyebrows. Scores of such items float through the book.

But above all this and more rich factual matter—the number of heart beats in a lifetime (up to 2.5 billion), famous stutterers, "the complicated hydraulics of male erection," the world's tallest human being (Robert Wadlow, at 8'11"), the world's oldest human being (Jean Louise Calumet, who lived to be 122, and quit smoking only at 117) the removal of Samuel Pepys' gall stone (but not Montaigne's), the many functions of the liver (which does everything, Bill Bryson tells us, but kick extra points)— reading *The Body* naturally throws one back on thoughts about one's own body. The book has caused me to feel that, on balance, I have been fairly fortunate in my own body. I have no serious deformity, suffer no chronic illness of any seriousness, have arrived in my eighties in relatively decent health, though, an old joke has it, one definition of a healthy person is someone who has not had a recent medical examination.

A few qualifications. In 1997, at the age of sixty, I had bypass heart surgery. My immune system is apparently not all it should be. (The immune system's task, Bill Bryson writes, is "to identify anything in the body that shouldn't be there, and if necessary, kill it.") Some years ago, I had been diagnosed, probably mistakenly, with Crohn's disease. I was given the steroid Prednisone to cope with Crohn's, a steroid that caused something called avascular necrosis in my right hip, which had me on a cane for a few months and ended my career as a high-B racquetball player. In the medical fashions of the day, as a young child I had my tonsils removed, and I was not breast-fed (an activity that was thought *déclassé*, or peasanty, by middle-class women of that day). I recall having chicken pox but not measles. I had a brief bout of ringworm when in the sixth-grade, which meant I had to wear a hat for several weeks in school. More recently I have been found to have low-grade Celiac Disease, so that I have had to go on a gluten-free diet, on which from time to time I happily cheat.

I nearly forgot that a few years ago I had something called bulbous pemphigoid—a term always to be pronounced with one's best imitation of W. C. Fields—that entailed a blistering on my chest and legs. I was twice misdiagnosed about it, first by a dermatologist who suggested I get rid of my mattress, then by another who had me standing in my under-shorts in a cabinet under ultra-violet lights. The man who got it right, a dermatologist named Alan Lasser, was admirably candid on the subject of the shakiness of dermatology generally.

On the other, more vigorous hand, I have had no allergies. I avoided venereal disease. (At headquarters company, Fifth Armored Division, Fort Hood, Texas, in 1959 we were offered something called a good-conduct holiday if the company could go a full month with no car accidents or reported cases of venereal disease. We never got the holiday.) I managed to evade diabetes, a disease that often afflicts many of my co-religionists. (A Frenchman, a German, and a Jew are lost in the desert: "I am thirsty, and must have wine," exclaims the Frenchman. "I am thirsty and must have beer," cries out the German. "I am thirsty and must have diabetes," says the Jew.) I have never been overweight. (" . . . more people on earth [today] suffer from obesity," Bryson reports, "than from hunger.") I have thus far escaped being among those 800,000 Americans who annually have joint-replacement surgery. I smoked cigarettes—never less than a pack a day—between the ages of sixteen and thirty-nine without apparent detriment. I've never required the too-often dubious services of a psychotherapist. I have been allowed to keep a respectable amount of hair atop my head, most of it now grey and white, though hair long ago departed my legs and arms. If we live long enough, it has been said, we go out of the world as we entered it: hairless, toothless, babbling.

Sexist dog that I am, I am pleased to have been born male. Men on average may die younger than women, but they escape the inconvenience of menstruation and later the psychological adjustment of menopause. Bill

Bryson reports that 80 percent of autoimmune diseases occur in women, though men "get Parkinson's more often and commit suicide more, even though they suffer less from clinical depression." The cruncher of course is childbirth, which I am delighted never to have had to undergo. No more difficult than defecating a pumpkin is a description of childbirth that refuses to depart my memory. After describing the pain of child-birth, Bryson writes: "If ever there was an event that challenges the con-cept of intelligent design, it is the act of childbirth."

Owing to the complications and pain of childbirth, one learns from *The Body,* Caesarian births are on the increase, with a third of births in America now being done by C-section, and 60 percent of these done not for medi-cal reasons but out of convenience. The complication here, Bryson notes, is that those born by C-section "have substantially increased risks for type 1 diabetes, asthma, celiac disease, and even obesity and an eightfold greater risk of developing allergies." He adds that in the current day, one in seven couples currently seek help in conceiving, an exercise that I, with two sons born before I was twenty-five and a former chairman of my neighborhood Unplanned Parenthood Committee, am pleased to have evaded. A friend who went through fertility therapy years ago likened it to being a field-goal kicker: "You're called into the game at odd times," he said.

So, I personally have less complaint than wonder at that extraordinary carapace of flesh and bone that is the body. I feel sorry for those who drew a less ordinary carapace than mine, who go through life feeling repug-nance for their own bodies. I think of heavyset young women who each morning confront the fact that they loathe the thickness of their legs; or those, men and women both, who find their own facial features dis-pleasing. So many things can go wrong in the composition of the human face, the construction of the human body. Then there are the people who are wracked with allergies, or burdened with brittle bones, or—dirtiest trick of all—mentally unbalanced or askew. The human body, though the standard issue contains 206 bones and roughly 600 muscles, is highly, one is inclined to say wildly, various.

Begin with the varying size of the thing. At O'Hare Airport I once found myself standing next to Wilt Chamberlain, then playing with the Los Angeles Lakers, and felt I did not come up much higher than his belt buckle. I am, if I stand up very straight, 5'7." (Humphrey Bogart was 5'8," Fred Astaire somewhere between 5'7" and 5'9"; two differently charming men whose work required they wear a hairpiece.) I have never considered not being taller a serious—you will pardon the expression—shortcoming. Had I been taller I might have gone beyond playing on my high-school frosh-soph basketball team to play on the varsity. When young I might also have pursued taller girls. But I can think of no further, no serious disadvantage my modest height conferred.

The world over my lifetime meanwhile seems to be growing taller and taller. When I was a kid, basketball players of more than 6'3" were *ipso facto* ill-coordinated, klutzy. Now men like LeBron Davis and Kevin Durant, at 6'8" and 6'9" respectively, move more gracefully on the basketball court than I ever did. Rod Laver and Kenny Rosewall, two of the top tennis players of my youth, were both 5'7," while five of today's top-ten ranked tennis players are over 6'5." Football players are currently not only taller but, with several 300-pound linemen and 250-pound running backs commonplace in college and pro football, wider. Major-league pitchers under 6'3" are rare. Among civilians walking the streets in my college neighborhood, more and more tall young women are about; Asian men, whom one is used somehow to thinking of as smallish, seem so no longer. I don't believe I've lost any height while aging, but somehow in recent years walking the streets I've begun to feel smaller.

In humans, as in cars and other machines, parts wear out. I've already mentioned the high number of hip, knee, and other joint replacements, most of them done on older people. Back pain is a common complaint as we age. Arthritis is perhaps a less common yet still fairly frequent problem. (I have a touch of it myself, in my left thumb.) Eyesight dims. (I have had cataract surgeries in both eyes.) Hearing becomes less sharp. (A common complaint among people over seventy is the noisiness of contemporary restaurants.) As for sleeping, which Bill Bryson refers to as "the most mysterious thing we do," for most older people sleep ceases to become the continuous, purely restful exercise it was in earlier years, but is generally interrupted two, three, four times during the night, in good part owing to the loss of elasticity in the bladder as one grows older. "Getting much," among men my age, no longer refers to sex but to sleep.

"Cancer," Bryson reports, "is above all an age thing. Between birth and the age of forty, men have a just one in seventy-one chance of getting cancer and women one in fifty-one, but over sixty the odds drop to one in three for men and one in four for women." With the cancer comes the complications of radiation, the nightmare of chemotherapy. At what age does one decide to forego treatment and give up the ghost. A gastro-enterologist I used on occasion to see one day showed me a letter from a patient, a man of seventy-one, who had decided to forego any efforts to stave off his recently discovered stomach cancer, preferring death to treatment. He had, he wrote in the letter, "had enough of life."

Then there is Alzheimer's, which has come to serve, incorrectly, as a general rubric for all forms of dementia. Alzheimer's apparently cannot be specifically diagnosed until post-mortem, though Bill Bryson notes that "Alzheimer's accounts for between 60 and 70 percent of all dementia cases." Apart from a sloppy or painful death, dementia is the perhaps the greatest dread of old age. To lose it, to go ga-ga, to join the multitudes— "some fifty million people around the world," according to Bryson, suffer dementia—who can no longer remember the names or recognize the faces of their own children is the horror of horrors.

Bill Bryson maintains that the threat of dementia can be reduced by healthy diet, moderate exercise, abstinence from smoking and heavy drinking. He also claims that "the more education you have had the less likely you are to get Alzheimer's," adding that "having an active and questing mind" helps even more. Would it were so! The wife of a dear friend of mine, a man possessed of as active and questing a mind as I have known, once reported to me that she had a call from the owner of a nearby bookstore café that her husband, whose mind was clearly vanishing into dementia, was stealing cookies. She told the café-owner to run a tab. Later when my friend had to be put into a nearby institution for the demented, his wife, on a visit, noted a good deal of straw on the floor of the institution's dining room. When she asked about it, she was told that it was there because there had been barn-dancing the night before. "Did my husband participate?" she asked. She was told he did and seemed to enjoy it greatly. I can more easily imagine Field Marshall Rommel or Charles de Gaulle barn-dancing than I can my dignified dear friend. A different brain, clearly, had come to inhabit his body.

"Your brain," Bill Bryson writes, "is you. Everything else is just plumbing and scaffolding." Of the various activities of the brain, that of memory seems most mutable, especially as one grows older. Memory seems so arbitrary, so oddly selective, often so disappointing. In the past few days, I could not call up the last name of a woman who once did me a great deal of harm, nor of the Cubs pitcher Kerry Wood, nor that of Antonio Vivaldi. During the same time I recalled vividly the name and face of Merle Scurry, the prettiest girl in my kindergarten class at Eugene Field School in 1942, and the ditty accompanying the radio commercial for Prell Shampoo. Calling up proper names is chief problem many people my age. "What was the name of that actor in the movie whose title I forget?" is a question a friend of mine not long asked at lunch. Do these fairly regular memory lapses, as seems natural to wonder, mark onset of dementia? I prefer to think not, but, such are the mysteries of the mind, who knows?

One of the few subjects associated with the body that Bill Bryson does not touch on is hypochondria, or abnormal fear of one's health joined to the fear that one has a serious disease. I have heard it said that hypochondriacs tend to live longer than those without this mental affliction, if only because they so regularly visit physicians. The older one gets, though, the more likely is hypochondria not only to kick in and seem not at all nutty but rather sensible. The greater one's age, after all, the higher are the odds that one will be struck down by one devastating blow or another. Forty percent of Americans, Bill Bryson reports, will over their lifetimes have had cancer, sixty percent visited by dementia, while heart attack remains the primary cause of death. That soreness in one's left arm—does it suggest a heart attack waiting in ambush? The blemish on one's right shoulder—might it be lymphoma, or mylenoma, or one of those other mellifluous-sounding but quite deadly skin cancers. As for that slight irregularity of one's bowel movements—colon, or stomach cancer perhaps? Why not? At seventy-five and beyond, one waits for both shoes to fall, or at any rate I have.

"We now die more from non-communicable than from contagious disease," Bill Bryson writes. We die more frequently, in other words, from genetic inheritance—"The best way to ensure longevity," according to George Bernard Shaw, "is to pick your parents"—or from poor self-maintenance. Self-maintenance chiefly means exercise and diet. As it happens, I hold with neither. I have friends my age who still run 5K races, do one-hand push-ups, dozens of chin-ups; others who still play singles tennis. My only exercise, apart from a bit of stretching and shoulder rolls in the shower and putting my trousers on standing up, is walking about on errands.

According to a study cited by Bryson, "someone who sits for six hours or more per day" qualifies as a couch potato. Most days I sit for more than twelve hours. Adding up the time I sit reading or at my desk writing or in a comfortable chair reading, or on the couch watching baseball games or English detective shows in the evening, I qualify as a couch potato with oak-leaf cluster. But why, my thinking is, be jogging round the block or working up a sweat on a NordicTrack, destroying what remains of the cartilage in my knees, when I could be comfortably sitting on my duff reading the stories of Nikolai Lesko or the essays of David Hume.

As for diet, in recent years I, having forsaken all health foods, eat what I like. Wild and crazy guy that I am, this includes at least one hard-boiled egg a day, ice cream whenever it is on offer, and red meat no fewer than twice a week. "The most popular vegetable in America by a very wide margin," Bill Bryson notes, "is the french fry," and I have my share of those, too. Lest I make myself sound braver than I am, I do take four different vitamins, and a statin to cut down my cholesterol. But with only one prescription drug (the statin), I am, among those my age, rather abstemious. Many among my contemporaries are on five or six prescriptions. "We rarely know, for instance," Bill Bryson writes, "what happens when various medications are taken in combination." A friend told me that Tom Wolfe when at Johns Hopkins for a general check-up revealed that he was on thirteen different pills. The physicians at Hopkins told him to cut out any eight.

Life spans round the world have increased just as deaths at childbirth have decreased. Cancer survival rates have improved. According to a study cited by Bryson, medicine has accounted for roughly 20 percent of these improvements; improved sanitation, diet, and healthier working conditions have been more important. The rich—no surprise here—live longer than others. But Americans—a surprise here—have a greater death rate

than the Australians, the English, the Germans, and the French, owing no
doubt to poor diet, stress, and death through ill-health and violence among
the poor.

Spinoza claimed that "the free man thinks of nothing less than death."
But, then, Spinoza (1632–1677) lived only to the age of forty-five, so what
did he know? Montaigne (1533–1592), who lived to nearly sixty, felt that
if we are to "banish the strangeness of death," we "should always keep the
image of death in our minds and in our imagination." If one has had the
good fortune to reach one's eighties, the subject of death becomes insistent and questions that arise from this insistence are how much longer
will one live and how long one would wish to live? We have no control
over the answer to the first question, obviously, but we can at least theo-
rize upon the second question.

Everyone, surely, would like to continue living as long as life is good.
But when does it cease to be good? When pain vastly outweighs pleasure. When one feels a serious slippage in one's mental prowess. When
one can no longer do many of the things one loves and still wants to
do. (My father, who lived to ninety-two, regretted more than anything
else his loss of independence when in the last year or so of his life he
required care-givers.) As for myself, I should like to remain alive as long
as I continue to find the world the same richly complex, endlessly puz-
zling, vastly amusing place I have always found it.

Chicago, Then and Now

(2018)

THE BIG NEWS OUT OF CHICAGO, city of my birth and upbringing, is murder. According to a reliable website called Hey Jackass! during 2017, someone in Chicago was shot every 2 hours and 27 minutes and murdered every 12 hours and 59 minutes. There were 679 murders and 2,936 people shot in the city. This, for those who like their deviancy defined down, is an improvement over 2016, when 722 people were murdered and 3,658 shot. The overwhelming preponderance of these people, victims and murderers both, are black, and the crimes committed chiefly in black neighborhoods on the city's south and west sides. Many of the murders were among the sorts of gangs long familiar in Chicago, which over the years has seen the Egyptian Cobras, the Blackstone Rangers, the Disciples, and the Conservative Vice Lords, among many others. According to a 2008 Department of Justice report, something like 100,000 members of up to 75 gangs were operating in the city. Gang involvement in drug trafficking has upped the stakes and intensified the violence in many of the city's black neighborhoods.

Who to blame for this wretched, hideous, and genuinely barbarous situation? The city's police, its politicians, its schools, its black leadership, contemporary black culture—all have come in for their share of accusations. But then Chicago has a rich tradition of murder. As early as

1910, the city led the nation in homicides and was known as the murder capital of the country. Much of the violence then and through the years of Prohibition was committed by organized crime. As late as the 1950s, when you told people you were from Chicago, they not uncommonly pretended to hoist a tommy gun and rat-a-tat-tatted away in reference to the bloody days of Al Capone & Co.

Chicagoans long took a certain pride in this criminal tradition. Never called the Mafia, organized crime in Chicago was generally referred to as the Syndicate or the Mob or the Outfit, and sometimes just the Boys. So big was the Syndicate presence in Chicago that at least one of the local television news channels kept a special correspondent, a man named John Drummond, to cover Mob news. Organized crime often led off a news broadcast or garnered a front-page headline, as when Allen Dorfman, an adviser to the Teamsters' Jimmy Hoffa and an all-around fixer, was gunned down in the parking lot of the Lincolnwood Hyatt. Mob figures—Tony "Big Tuna" Accardo, Sam Giancana, Joseph Lombardo— were celebrities, known throughout the city. A juicy bit of gossip was when Mob guys showed up to play golf at the Tam O'Shanter Country Club. Best, sound advice had it, to let them play through.

I myself, in the early 1970s, ran into a few of the Mob figures at the Riviera Club, where I sometimes played racquetball. Gus Alex, said to have been head of Mob gambling and prostitution in Chicago, was among them, and I remember locker-room discussions in which they expressed amazement at America's dithering in Vietnam. The strong should never take any crap from the weak; "blow the bastards to hell" was their view. The Mob influence reached all the way down to high schools, where football parlay cards—beat the spread on three college games and win $6 on a $1 bet—were always available. An Italian customer of my father's told him that if he ever had a cash-flow problem, the Boys were ready to help out.

Jews in the chiefly Italian Mob tended to play administrative roles. Jake "Greasy Thumb" Guzik, a Galician Jew, was the Syndicate's legal and financial adviser from the Capone days through the middle 1950s. Jewish bookies were not uncommon in Chicago. My mother's older brother, "Lefty Sam" Abrams, was one. He eventually owned a few points in the Riviera in Vegas. I may best establish my uncle's social standing by mentioning that

Sinatra was at his granddaughter's wedding. After her brother's funeral, my mother, peering into his closet, counted 27 ultrasuede jackets.

In our neighborhood lived a man named Maury "Potsy" Pearl, a Jewish bookie whose bodyguard drove his son, a friend of my younger brother's, to school every day. A friend of mine's father, a borax man who had scored heavily in the aluminum-awning business, made the mistake of dabbling in boxers, which meant connecting to the Syndicate, which controlled the sport, with the result that one day he found himself pursued simultaneously by the FBI and a brute named "Milwaukee Phil" Alderisio. People in the Chicago of those days took a certain pride in their often tenuous connections to the Mob.

The Mob today seems to have retreated to the point of oblivion in Chicago. Prostitution and gambling, its two chief sources of income, have dried up. Gambling is now available on the Internet, and, with the advent of the pill and the sexual revolution, nice girls have all but put prostitutes out of business. The illicit big money these days is in drugs, and the trade is monopolized by drug lords working out of Latin America and the Chicago gangs who serve as their distributors. One is hard-pressed to name any prominent Mob members in current-day Chicago because, one gathers, there are none.

B Y THE TIME OF MY BIRTH in Chicago in 1937, "the city of the big shoulders," in Carl Sandburg's phrase, had developed a considerable slouch. Not that there was ever much truth in Sandburg's sentimental poem of 1914, but in my boyhood there was at least still a Chicago stockyards, and on warm summer nights, with a wind blowing in from the south, even in my far north side neighborhood of Rogers Park one could smell the abattoir roughly a hundred blocks away. One of the standard grammar-school trips, one which I am not at all sorry somehow to have missed, was to the stockyards, where tons of dead animal flesh and entrails were on view and where large men stunned cows with sledgehammers before slaughtering them.

Chicago was nothing if not a reality instructor. Political idealism never really came alive in this city. By the 1930s, the Irish were in firm control of city hall, their machine nicely lubricated by patronage, corruption, and organized crime. Edward J. Kelly was mayor from 1933 to 1947; he was followed by Martin H. Kennelly and then the 21-year term of Richard J. Daley. With a brief pause for the negligible mayoralties of Michael Bilandic, Jane Byrne, and Harold Washington, Richard M. Daley (*le fils*, as he was never known), served as mayor of Chicago for 22 years, bringing us up to the less than impressive tenure of Rahm Emanuel.

My father, with more than a light touch of irony, used to say of Chicago aldermanic elections: "Strange, a man putting out a quarter of a million dollars to get a job that pays $20,000 a year. It doesn't make sense." The only person who mattered politically in Chicago when I was a kid was your precinct captain; he might get you a parking permit or out of jury duty or some jerseys for your kid's baseball team. In Chicago, the game of politics was fixed, locked in. My mother, who was never guilty of reading a word about politics in the *Chicago Daily News* and later the *Sun-Times*—Colonel McCormick's isolationist *Tribune* was not allowed in our apartment—dispensed with my father's irony on the subject of Chicago politicians. Raising her coffee cup, little finger bent, she remarked: "They're all thieves, you know." No one so far has proven her wrong.

The Chicago of my boyhood was an intensely Catholic city. Ask someone where he lived and he was likely to answer with the name of his parish (St. Nicholas of Tolentine, St. Gregory's). Catholic culture was everywhere in the country a hundred-fold stronger then than now, and the Catholic atmosphere was especially strong in Chicago owing to its large populations of Irish, Italians, and Poles. So Catholic did the place seem—with priests in cassock, nuns in habit everywhere part of the cityscape—that as a young boy I took Catholicism and Christianity to be coterminous. The Bing Crosby movies of those years—*Going My Way* (1944), *The Bells of St. Mary's* (1945)—reinforced this sense of Catholic omnipresence. A now-forgotten actor named Pat O'Brien made a living playing a priest in the movies. How many cinematic murderers he prayed for while accompanying them on their way to the gallows or electric chair would be difficult to calculate.

In the courtyard building on Sheridan Road to the north of ours lived the Cowling family. The father, Sam Cowling, did a regular comic bit called "Fiction and Fact from Sam's Almanac" on the then immensely popular national radio show called *Don McNeill's Breakfast Club*. Sam's beautiful wife was named Dale, the same name, older moviegoers will recall, as Roy Rogers's wife. Their boys, Sam Jr. (who was my age) and Billy, both went to St. Jerome's, thence to Loyola Academy, and thence to Jesuit Georgetown University, though they probably could have gotten into Harvard, Yale, or Princeton. Catholicism of their kind has vanished from American life.

Among Chicago's many sobriquets—Windy City, Second City, City on the Make, City That Works—the City of Neighborhoods had the highest truth quotient when I was growing up. So geographically stratified by ethnicity and race was Chicago that a kid had only to tell where he lived than you knew his ethnic heritage, his family's income, and whether the family ate in the dining room or kitchen, his father in a collar or in his undershirt. Apart from going into the Loop to shop at Marshall Field's or Carson Pirie Scott or to Wrigley Field for a Cubs or Bears game, there was no reason to leave the friendly confines of one's neighborhood. The neighborhood contained everything—church or synagogue, schools public and parochial, shops, like-minded neighbors—one might possibly require. If our family hadn't had cousins living in the far south side neighborhood of Roseland, I might never have known Chicago had a south side until I was in my adolescence.

Ethnicity and race were the organizing principle behind Chicago neighborhoods. Greeks, Italians, Poles, Irish, Jews all wished to live among their own, and they did so. Our own neighborhood of West Rogers Park, to which we moved in 1947 from Rogers Park along Lake Michigan, was changing from white-collar gentile to ascending middle-class Jewish. My father bought a two-flat, and our renters, living on the second floor, were the Andersons, Mr. and Mrs. Anderson and Mrs. Anderson's unmarried sister, Edna, all then in their late 50s. Mr. Anderson worked at a nearby bank. Mrs. Anderson spent the day in housecoat and curlers, dressing shortly before her husband returned home. The only words of Mrs. Anderson's I can recall, and the family lived above us for more than a decade, are: "Mr. Anderson gets a nice lunch at the bank." What they thought of us invading Jews I do not know. "There goes the neighborhood" would not be a wild guess.

West Rogers Park was roughly 30 percent Jewish when we moved in, but soon the balance shifted to well over 60 percent. Devon (pronounced Dih-vonne) Avenue, the main shopping hub in West Rogers Park, quickly became markedly Jewish in character. Within an area of eight-or so blocks, there were three Jewish delis and three Chinese restaurants (one, the Pekin House, had an owner who over the years served so many Jews that he began to dress and look Jewish himself). The two men's stores—Turner Brothers and Aidem & Dess (the latter featuring color-coordinated window displays)—were Jewish-owned, and so was the high-line women's shop called Seymour Paisin, where shoppers were offered a cocktail while trying on clothes. Later a Jewish bakery and a shop selling K-rations (kreplach, knish, kugel, kasha) moved in. All very happy and *heimish*.

O NE OF THE MARKED CHANGES in Chicago in recent decades has been in the character of its neighborhoods. West Rogers Park, for example, has become largely South Asian. Today on a Saturday night Devon Avenue resembles nothing so much as Mysore or some other provincial Indian city. Tamil is heard everywhere. Women walk about in saris, men in white cotton kurtas and trousers, young boys in cricket sweaters. Sikh turbans are not uncommon. Stores sell live chickens, also goat meat. Cellphone shops have chargers available that work in electrical outlets on the other side of the world. Sari shops are abundant. Asian vegetables are on offer at the greengrocer's, and Indian restaurants predominate.

Along with the East Indians in current-day West Rogers Park live Haredi, or ultra-orthodox, Jews—chiefly farther west, past California Avenue. Ner Tamid, the conservative synagogue from which I was barmitzvahed in 1950, is out of business. West Devon is now rife with orthodox synagogues, Jewish day schools, and yeshivas. There are kosher butchers, religious bookstores, bakeries, and most of it closed on *Shabbos*.

Many of the old Chicago neighborhoods have undergone gentrification. A notable example on the north side has been Andersonville. A once rather drab neighborhood of working-class Swedes and Germans, it is known today as Mandersonville, home to older gays and lesbians—as opposed to the younger Boystown, the city's second gay neighborhood, farther south, around Belmont and Broadway, a place much more go-go. Years ago I wrote a short story in which a woman in the Andersonville restaurant called M. Henri remarks to her lunch companion that in the old days when Jews and blacks moved in people used to say, "There goes the neighborhood"; now, when gays move in, they say, "Here comes the neighborhood." And so it has been with Andersonville, which is filled with pleasant restaurants and interesting shops, has a striking absence of people begging on its streets, very little crime, and modest houses and apartment buildings carefully kept up—a splendid instance of progress without disruption.

One sees this gentrification throughout the city in such neighborhoods as Ravenswood (where Rahm Emanuel lives), Roscoe Village, Lake View, Bucktown, Logan Square, Wicker Park. Entirely new neighborhoods have been created, too, such as South Loop and West Loop. South Loop in my youth was a skid row with a sprinkling of light industry. West Loop, another skid row, which back then had only dreary bars and no restaurants or nightlife of any sort, is now the center of *au courant* dining in Chicago. Both South and West Loop are now populated chiefly by the young. Much more than in the past, Chicago seems a city for the young, a place where to be in, say, one's early 30s seems ideal.

Hyde Park, the neighborhood of the University of Chicago, an enclave of intellectual life surrounded by black neighborhoods on three sides, remains much the same despite a rather energetic program of interventionist urban renewal in the 1950s and early '60s led by a man named Julian H. Levi, which left the neighborhood's main shopping streets bereft. Saul Bellow, a longtime resident of Hyde Park, once told me that they ought to erect a statue to Julian Levi for his urban renewal efforts—and then blow it up. In my student days at the university in the middle 1950s, Hyde Park was already a slightly dangerous neighborhood, and the Midway Plaisance, a strip of land between the south end of the campus and the black neighborhood of Woodlawn, was known as Apache territory.

The sweeping changes that have done most to alter the human topography of Chicago have been the decline of the city's heavy industry and the increase in its black and Hispanic populations. Chicago lost some 411,000 factory jobs between 1947 and 1982, or roughly 60 percent of its total. The stockyards closed, the steel mills followed, stores went under, real income went down. More and more whites moved out to the sub-urbs, and Chicago lost its place as the nation's second-largest city to Los Angeles. Chicago today is roughly one-third black, one-third Hispanic, and one-third white. The city's working-class character is gone.

Not surprisingly, blacks more than any other group were hurt by the reduction of factory jobs. The city's 26 black neighborhoods (defined by having a 75 percent or more black population) were further affected by the destruction, through urban renewal, of two mammoth public-housing complexes, the Robert Taylor Homes on the near south side and Cabrini-Green on the western edge of the near north side. This caused many already trouble-burdened black families—fatherless, unem-ployed, with delinquent kids—to move into already struggling black neighborhoods.

In my youth, blacks—Negroes as they then were—played scarcely any obvious, or perhaps I should say visible, role in Chicago. Then as now the city was highly segregated, with blacks living almost exclusively in the south side section of town known as Bronzeville. As a small boy, the only black person I came in contact with was the sweet-natured Emma, who came to clean our apartment on Tuesdays, and died there one day.

At six or seven years old, I made the mistake of reciting to my father the poem that begins "Eeny, meeny, miny, moe." In a rare fit of fury, he gave me a strong lecture on the parallel pasts of persecution of blacks and Jews, and underscored how Jews were the last people who should be prejudiced against blacks. A man who backed up his sentiments with his actions, my father had a black secretary and blacks were predominant among the eight or ten people who made costume jewelry in his one-floor factory in a five-story building on North Avenue. (The building is now the site of a glitzy gym in the youthful Wicker Park neighborhood.)

In that earlier day, whites could go into black neighborhoods much more easily—that is to say, more securely—than blacks could go into white ones. I was one of six adolescent Jewish boys who one night drove into the heart of Bronzeville to sample the bordello services of Iona Sat-terfield, the ex-wife of Bob Satterfield, the heavyweight whom I saw knocked out in the second round by Ezzard Charles in 1954 at Chicago Stadium. Larry Goldenberg parked his father's maroon and white Buick

Roadmaster at the curb at 4246 South St. Lawrence in front of Iona's apartment without giving its or our safety a second thought.

Going into certain tough Italian or German neighborhoods was much more daunting. After a game against Waller High School, our mainly Jewish Senn High School basketball team was ambushed and beaten up by young Brando-ish thugs. Playing against Amundsen High School, we heard anti-Semitic chants coming from the stands.

T HE DEMOCRATIC MACHINE remains in power in Chicago, though not so firmly or all-pervasively as in earlier decades. Some years ago, the political scientist Milton Rakove pointed out the non-ideological character of the machine in Chicago, which was chiefly interested in keeping its members in power, things under control, and the financial rewards of patronage rolling along. Keeping things under control, alas, has also meant keeping blacks segregated, or so argues the historian Andrew J. Diamond in a recent book called *Chicago on the Make.*

Diamond's attack on the Daleys, *père et fils*, is that they didn't merely ignore black neighborhoods in Chicago but actively worked against their advance by keeping them strictly segregated. The Dan Ryan Expressway, he holds, was built to slow black incursion into the white neighborhoods of the southwest side. The campus of the University of Illinois at Chicago was placed where it was, on the southwestern edge of the Loop instead of in Humboldt Park where it might have uplifted the Puerto Rican neighborhood, to keep west side blacks from moving closer into the Loop. The Daleys did this, Diamond argues, through strategically planned urban-renewal projects, through capturing anti-poverty funds from federal programs and putting them to their own uses, and through their extensive efforts to build up the Loop, encourage tourism, and protect the city's wealthier neighborhoods: Streeterville, Lincoln Park, Lake Shore Drive. The result was blacks segregated in hyperghettos and the hegemony of what Diamond calls "neoliberalism." Neoliberalism, the great villain of *Chicago on the Make*, is defined by a Berkeley political scientist named Wendy Brown as "a rationality extending a specific formulation of economic values, practices, and metrics to every dimension of human life"— or, in other words, as putting monied interests before human ones.

The deterioration of most black neighborhoods in Chicago is not up for argument. Ridden with crime, without amenities, lacking even necessities (many are "food deserts," a term denoting the absence of supermarkets or even convenience stores in some of them), the general desolation of these neighborhoods is such that, Diamond reports, "the Mexican aversion to settling in and around black neighborhoods—an aversion shared by Chicago's next largest Latino group, Puerto Ricans—was so strong that by 2000 Chicago displayed the highest degree of segregation between blacks and Latinos among the hundred largest cities in the United States." The black west side, long ago the home of much of the city's Jewish population before its migration to the north side and thence to the plush suburbs of the North Shore, saw 28 blocks all but destroyed by fire after the black riots following the 1968 assassination of Martin Luther King Jr. These blocks have never been rebuilt.

If blacks once seemed all but invisible in my Chicago, today they are ubiquitous. Turn on the local news, a depressing experience in itself, and all too many nights one will be greeted by the sight of a black woman weeping because of the death by shooting of a son, or grandson, in a gang killing, or of a young daughter having been hit by a stray bullet. A picture of the dead boy or girl, often in high-school graduation cap and gown, will appear, and an uncle or aunt or older sibling comes on to attest to the sweetness and promise of the deceased. The killers are seldom apprehended, for the understandable reason that neighborhood residents are terrified of retaliation if they turn them in. Then there are the news items about carjackings, muggings on the El for cellphones, stolen cars crashed into Michigan Avenue shops in jewelry robberies, and groups of black youth storming into the Gap and other such shops to grab jeans or other items.

Diamond lays the blame for the hell that most of Chicago's black neighborhoods have recently become on Richard M. Daley. While mayor, Diamond argues, Daley's "public relations team made sure to use every gang incident to claim that gangs rather than the mayor's policies were to blame for the two main problems African-Americans had been complaining about for years: defective schools and brutal cops." Chicago police animosity toward blacks, which included "Red Squads" used to disrupt earnest efforts at community organization, supplies a leitmotif in *Chicago on the Make*. The author also characterizes the large number of blacks and Latinos appointed to Richard M. Daley's cabinet as, using Michael Katz's phrase, "the management of marginalization." Diamond is no easier on Rahm Emanuel, Daley's successor, calling him "Mayor 1%."

A month or so ago, after a particularly brutal weekend of gang killings in Chicago's Englewood neighborhood, I heard a black man, an angry resident of the neighborhood, shout at a television reporter, "They better get some programs down here fast." What "programs," I wondered, did he suppose would seriously help? In *Great American City* (2012), a book about contemporary Chicago, Robert J. Sampson made the argument, based on a vast arsenal of social-science research, that troubled neighborhoods have their greatest chance of maintaining order through community organization. Sampson argues, in the less-than-convincing language of contemporary social science, which always seems to set reality off at a comfortable distance, that "whether through the enhancement of age-graded mentorship and monitoring of adolescent activities as a form of collective efficacy, increasing organizational opportunity for citizen participation in decision making, or enhancing the legitimacy of government institutions that have eroded trust among those served, we need a surgical-like attention to repairing or renewing existing structures rather than simply designing escape routes."

To have organization one needs leadership, and part of the problem in Chicago is that black leadership has been—I can think of no more kindly word for it—dismal. Most black politicians and clergy appear to have been in business for themselves. Beginning with William Dawson, a black alderman who sold himself to the Richard J. Daley machine, through the never-camera-shy Jesse Jackson and the disappointing Senator Carol Moseley Braun to the Black Panther-turned-congressman Bobby Rush, no one has emerged to organize and lead Chicago's black population out of the wilderness of their increasingly crime-infested neighborhoods, where drug trafficking, high unemployment, and disproportionate poverty rates reign and seem unlikely soon to decline.

The recent black protest movements seem irrelevant in the face of such misery. Even Diamond is dubious about the efficacy of the Black Lives

Matter movement to accomplish more than traffic jams and attracting television cameras. He mentions that a Pew Trust study found "only 15 percent of Hispanics and 14 percent of whites claimed to strongly support" the Black Lives Matter movement. In 2016 and 2017, of the nearly 1,500 killings in Chicago, 22 involved the police, the target of Black Lives Matter. Not many people, and no putative black leaders, meanwhile, have stood up to ask why, if black lives truly matter, black-on-black gang murders have been allowed to arrive at the horrendous level they have.

E**ARLY IN** *CHICAGO ON THE MAKE,* Andrew Diamond refers to the "culturization of politics," which he describes as "the transfer of political acts and events onto the terrain of culture, where they become disassociated from questions of structure, power, and, ultimately, political mobilization." On the penultimate page of his book, he again notes that many whites are "still invested in cultural explanations of poverty in the other [that is, black] Chicago." The cultural, as opposed to the political, argument holds that while admitting the toll of racial discrimination in the past, something has meanwhile gone deeply wrong with urban black culture.

The argument is scarcely news. As long ago as 1965, Daniel Patrick Moynihan published his "The Negro Family: The Case for National Action," which when it first appeared was greeted with derision by nearly everyone, black and white, on the left. In his report, Moynihan argued that the gap between black and other groups was widening owing chiefly to the breakdown of the black nuclear family. Too few black fathers were on the scene and this, even more than continued discrimination by race, was chiefly responsible for the wretched conditions in which too many blacks in America found themselves. In a crucial, and much excoriated, sentence, Moynihan wrote: "The steady expansion of welfare programs can be taken as a measure of the steady disintegration of the Negro family structure over the past generation in the United States."

Whatever the flaws in the cultural argument—and not least among them is the fear that it can lapse into racism with its implication that black culture (and hence blacks themselves) is inherently inferior—few people are likely to note any valuable advances in that culture over the past 60 years. Compare Nat Cole to Jay-Z, Duke Ellington to Chance the Rapper, or the brilliant essays of the young James Baldwin to the racial tirades of Ta-Nehisi Coates and the sense of the regress of black culture—from one of elegance and pride to soaking in victimization—is staggering, saddening, depressing in the extreme.

Meanwhile, political correctness makes any meaningful criticism of the new black culture from outside all but impossible, if only by keeping the country's best minds from addressing the subject. Toward the close of his career George Kennan thought about turning his interests from foreign policy to domestic problems but found himself unable to do so, he noted in his *Diaries* in 1975, "when one of the greatest of the problems is the deterioration of life in the great cities and when one of the major components of the problem this presents is the Negro problem, which is taboo." Those black writers—Shelby Steele, Thomas Sowell, William Julius Wilson—who think outside the victimhood box are repudiated for doing so.

Every newly arrived immigrant group has in darker moments thought itself, however briefly, victimized, but by now too many American blacks have so clung to the notion that victimhood itself has become the center of their sense of themselves and has all but usurped any other identity. They have been encouraged in this victimhood script for decades and decades, first by liberals and now by progressives, to the point where it could be argued that the left generally has contributed as heavily to the condition of contemporary blacks as lingering racism. In fact, encouragement in the belief that all black problems are at root owing to racism is certain to keep blacks in their place, and might itself just be the ultimate racism.

Chicago is today two cities, one gentrified and grand, the other devastated and despairing, both within a single municipal boundary. The situation is intolerable. Something has got to be done, and, complex, difficult, and arduous as the task is, if it is one day to get done, however great the goodwill of many whites in the city, the black population of Chicago will, like every racial and ethnic group before it, have to do it pretty much on its own.

Jewish Jokes

(2018)

66 "OW ODD OF GOD / TO CHOOSE THE JEWS," a scrap of verse by the English journalist William Norman Ewer, has over the years had many answering refrains. "Not odd, you Sod / The Jews chose God" is one; "What's so Odd / His son was one" is another; and a third goes "This surely was no mere whim, / Given that the *goyim* annoy 'im." But the central mystery remains: God chose the Jews for what, exactly? After reading Jeremy Dauber's *Jewish Comedy: A Serious History*, an excellent new survey of Jewish humor from the Old Testament through Adam Sandler, some might say that God chose the Jews to convey jokes, write sitcoms and comic movies, and publish novels peopled chiefly by clownish anti-heroes.

Citing a Pew Research Center study titled "A Portrait of Jewish Americans," Dauber reports that "42 percent of respondents felt that 'having a good sense of humor' was part of 'being Jewish in America today,' 14 percent more than being 'part of a Jewish community' and 23 percent more than 'observing Jewish law.'" In other words, at the heart of being Jewish, in the minds of a preponderant number of American Jews, is comedy. How did this minority people produce so much humor, so many Jokey Jakeys?

The Old Testament, to put it gently, is not notable for humor. As Dauber notes, the first of its paucity of laughs is given to Sarah, wife of the 100-year-old Abraham, who informs her she is to have his child. Dauber early considers, and frequently harkens back to, the book of Esther, which he cites as "the first work to feature the joyful celebration and comic pleasure that comes with an anti-Semite's downfall and the frustration of that form of persecutory intent." After a recent rereading, I must report that the book of Esther is less than uproarious. But the book does record a resounding Jewish victory, and such victories, until the advent of the Israel Defense Forces, were only slightly less rare for the Jews than Super Bowl appearances for the Cleveland Browns.

Humor has not been without its dreary analysts and theorists. Along with so much else, Freud got the impulse behind comedy wrong, arguing that a joke is chiefly an act of aggression. He did, though, as was his wont, make a number of useful observations while coming to his false conclusion. "I do not know," he wrote apropos of the Jews, "whether there are many other instances of a people making fun to such a degree of their own character."

Their often-ambiguous place in the world has given Jews a great deal to think about and, having taken thought, subsequently to joke about. Jeremy Dauber divides this body of humor into seven categories, devoting a chapter to each. His categories are:

1. Jewish comedy is a response to persecution and anti-Semitism.
2. Jewish comedy is a satirical gaze at Jewish social and communal norms.
3. Jewish comedy is bookish, witty, intellectual allusive play.
4. Jewish comedy is vulgar, raunchy, and body-obsessed.
5. Jewish comedy is mordant, ironic, and metaphysically oriented.
6. Jewish comedy is focused on the folksy, everyday, quotidian Jew.
7. Jewish comedy is about the blurred and ambiguous nature of Jewishness itself.

Every decent book on comedy should at a minimum include several good jokes, a criterion by which both Freud's *Jokes and Their Relation to the Unconscious* and Henri Bergson's *Laughter: An Essay on the Meaning of the Comic* notably fail. So does Arthur Koestler's *The Act of Creation*. Even a bad book on comedy, one with the most improbable theories, is partially saved by a few good jokes, so that it "shouldn't," as the punchline from an old Jewish joke has it, "be a total loss." Jeremy Dauber, recognizing that analyzing comedy is a mug's game, along with being one of the quickest known paths to boredom, lards—or should I say "schmaltzes"?—his text with several splendid jokes within his seven categories.

Of Dauber's categories, anti-Semitic jokes have never been in short supply ("What is the ultimate Jewish dilemma: Ham—on Sale!"). Jokes about anti-Semites, though, tend to be richer, like the one about the drunk at the bar who three times offers to buy drinks for the house, each time excluding from his generosity "my Israelite pal at the end of the bar." When the Jew asks the drunk what he has against him, the drunk answers, "You sank the *Titanic*." The Jew replies, "I didn't sink the *Titanic*, an iceberg sank the *Titanic*." After belching daintily, the drunk responds: "Iceberg, Greenberg, Goldberg—you're all no damn good."

I USED TO FANCY a definition of the Jews as "just like everyone else, only more so." But more needs to be said if one is to understand Jewish humor—not the jokes but the impetus driving the humor. I should say this derives from the split social personality of Jews, their simultaneous feeling of resentment at not being entirely in the mainstream of ordinary life joined to their disdain for the vapidity of that life, thus linking a sense of inferiority to one of superiority. Jeremy Dauber notes that there are essentially three kinds of Jewish jokes: "jokes that showcase particular Jewish conditions or circumstances, jokes that highlight particular Jewish sensibilities, and jokes that feature particular Jewish archetypes."

Dauber sets out the various theories of humor. These include the incongruity theory, the relief (of tension) theory, and the congruity theory. There is also the Jewish superiority theory and, thrown in at no extra charge, the lachrymose theory of Jewish history (the joke here is that the theme of every Jewish holiday is "We suffered, we survived—let's eat!"). Dauber also considers the comedy of Jewish novelists and storytellers—S. Y. Abramovitch, Sholem Aleichem, and I. L. Peretz; Bellow, Malamud, and Roth (the Hart, Shaffner & Marx of American literature, as Bellow derisively called them); Bruce Jay Friedman, and others. Dauber's comments on these writers are necessarily scant, but then to have given this aspect of his subject full attention would have swollen his book and diverted him from his main task.

More interesting are Dauber's pages on Jews and the movies. Two of the best comic directors—Ernst Lubitsch and Billy Wilder—were Jewish. Perhaps the most amusing comment in *Jewish Comedy* is about the movie *Gentleman's Agreement*, a movie that attacks anti-Semitism, a comment made not by a Jew but by Ring Lardner Jr., who said the moral of the film was that "you should never be mean to a Jew because he might turn out to be a Gentile." Dauber brings up earlier movies that were "de-Semitized," or made less Jewish, by Hollywood studio moguls—the Jewish Sam Goldwyn, Louis B. Mayer, and others—lest they not find ready recognition and acceptance with non-Jewish audiences. No movie, though, could be more Jewish than Mel Brooks's *The Producers* (1967). That it could be made at all, let alone come to be considered a classic, is a sign of how deeply Jewish humor has permeated American culture.

T HE LIVELIEST PAGES in *Jewish Comedy* are those on which Dauber take up Jewish jokes within his categories. These include rabbi jokes, *schnorrer* (or beggar) jokes, *schlemiel* and *schlimazel* jokes, *shadkhn* (or matchmaker) jokes, Jewish American Princess jokes, Nazi jokes, even Holocaust jokes. A nice selection of Jewish curses—"May your bones be broken as often as the Ten Commandments"—is also provided. The most politically incorrect of such jokes are Jewish women jokes, which play on the stereotypes of the nagging, over-caring, overbearing disapproving Jewish mother (portrayed brilliantly years ago by Elaine May in one of the Nichols and May skits); the Jewish American Princess ("What does a JAP make for dinner?" "Reservations, of course."); Jews and cosmetic surgery (Dorothy Parker said that Fanny Brice's rhinoplasty was a case of "cutting off her nose to spite her race"); the domineering wife (when a boy returns home from school to announce that he is to play a Jewish husband in the school play, his mother sends him back to tell the teacher he wants a speaking part); and the extravagant wife ("A thief stole my wife's purse with all her credit cards. I'm not going after him. He's spending less than she does.")

Perhaps the *summa* of Jewish women jokes has Goldberg, walking along the beach, who picks up a bottle out of which emerges a genie, offering him one wish. Goldberg wishes for world peace. The genie tells him that he gets that wish a lot and hasn't had much success in fulfilling it. Perhaps he'd like to try another wish. Very well, Goldberg says, then he would like more respect from his wife, for her to provide the occasional home-cooked meal, perhaps allow him sex every other fiscal quarter. The genie pauses, then says, "Tell me, Goldberg, what precisely do you mean by peace?"

Several pages in Jeremy Dauber's book are given over to Jewish standup comics, a group in the modern era never in short supply. (The title of the world's shortest book, no one will be surprised to learn, is *Famous German Stand-Up Comics*.) The roster of notable Jewish comedians includes Mickey Katz, Belle Barth, Jack Benny, George Burns, Henny Youngman, Joe E. Lewis, Oscar Levant, Phil Silvers, Jack E. Leonard, Myron Cohen, the Marx Brothers, the Three Stooges, Milton Berle, Sid Caesar, Buddy Hackett, Don Rickles, Shecky Greene, Jerry Lewis, Lenny Bruce, Mort Sahl, Sam Levenson, Allan Sherman, Mel Brooks, Joan Rivers, Jackie Mason, Woody Allen, Larry David, Jerry Seinfeld, Albert Brooks, Sarah Silverman, and more. The minor league for many of these older comedians, the place where they honed their skills, was the Borscht Belt in the Catskills, whose resort audiences of mostly New York Jews provided one of the most knowing and toughest of all audiences going, so tough that Joey Adams, quoted by Dauber, remarked that "when you bomb in the mountains, it's like a concentration camp with sour cream."

Some of these comedians worked Jewish—told Jewish jokes, did greenhorn accents, used Yiddishisms—others not. Another division among Jewish comedians is between the safe and edgy, a few of the latter going over the edge itself into dangerous political or sexual territory (Mort Sahl, Lenny Bruce) or into simple bad taste. Larry David's specialty on his own show *Curb Your Enthusiasm* is to walk right up to the line of bad taste and then cross it, not to everyone's amusement. Mel Brooks worked the line of bad taste and got away with it; recall *Blazing Saddles* with its flatulence campfire scene and Yiddish-speaking American Indians. Interviewed in 2001 by Mike Wallace for *60 Minutes* when *The Producers* was reincarnated as a Broadway show, Brooks ignored Wallace's first question to ask him what he paid for his wristwatch; instead of answering Wallace's second question, Brooks rubbed Wallace's lapel between his thumb and forefinger and asked what the jacket he was wearing set him back. Playing on the stereotype of the vulgar, money-crazed Jew, Brooks, somehow, came off as lovable.

Lenny Bruce spoke of putting "the jargon of the hipster, the argot of the underworld, and Yiddish" together in his act. I saw him one evening in an east side New York movie theater—he had not long before lost his cabaret license owing to his generous use of obscenity—doing a bit in which a Jewish nightclub owner is attempting to persuade a Puerto Rican busboy to service sexually Sophie Tucker, the grand old lady of show business, who is appearing at the club and who is presumed to be an insatiable nymphomaniac. They go back and forth, the Puerto Rican busboy and the Jewish owner, the latter arguing and pleading, the former stalwart in his refusals, until finally the busboy exclaims, "She is an old woman, Mr. Rosenberg, I don't care how much you pay me, I won't [a slight pause here] *schtup* [word drawn out] her." The joke, of course, is not only in the premise of Sophie Tucker's low needs, but also in the young Puerto Rican's reverting to Yiddish to close the argument.

Perhaps the edgiest of contemporary Jewish comedians is Sarah Silverman, who in one of her bits, quoted by Dauber, claimed it was neither the Romans nor the Jews who killed Christ but the blacks. In another, not in *Jewish History* but in some of her shows, Silverman plays a faux-naïve Jewish American Princess, whose niece tells her that she learned in school that Hitler killed 60 million Jews during the Holocaust. Silverman corrects her niece: "I think he's responsible for killing 6 million Jews." And she said, "Oh yeah, 6 million, I knew that. But seriously, I mean, what's the difference?" "Uh, the difference is 60 million is unforgivable." In another bit Silverman plays a ditzy woman in her early 30s, childless, her biological clock running, who recounts how inconvenient at various earlier stages in her life it would have been to have had a child, and concludes, "The best time to have a baby is when you're a black teenager." How Silverman has been able to tell such politically incorrect jokes and not been stoned to death is an interesting question.

Jewish Comedy seeks to be comprehensive, to touch all aspects of its subject, from the Old Testament through the Talmudic canon through the past century and up-to-the-moment comedy, and all in under 300 pages (not counting endnotes). Dauber does an impressive and fairly complete job of it. Some things, inevitably, are more lightly touched than others. Talmudic humor is among them. The humor of Jewish intramural rivalry—the snobbery obtaining among Eastern, German, and Sephardic Jews—is another. All I remember from a novel read decades ago, whose title and author's name are lost to me, is that what separates Sephardic Jews from all others, apart from their extravagant genealogical pretensions, is that no Sephardic Jew can stand gefilte fish. German Jews were known by Eastern Jews as *yekkes*, meaning jackets, or suit jackets, which German Jews in their formality were said never to remove. The stereotype made possible the joke that holds the difference between a *yekke* and a virgin is that a *yekke* remains a *yekke*.

Of television comedy, Dauber takes up, among others, Norman Lear, Larry David, and Jerry Seinfeld. Lear's most memorable show, *All in the Family*, featured the rebarbative Archie Bunker, who tossed off anti-Semitic, racial, and reactionary remarks and could only have been created by a Jewish liberal, which Lear, still working at 95, remains. Larry David was of course one of the principal writers for *Seinfeld*, a show whose Jewish content I think Jeremy Dauber may overemphasize. He calls the character Elaine Benes, played by Julia Louis-Dreyfus, "a classic example of the Jewish American princess," which she is not, and he suggests that Jewishness was central to the show in a way that doesn't ring true, even though Jerry's parents are stereotypically Jewish and so is the character George Costanza and his family. (Jerry Stiller, who plays Frank Costanza, remarked that the Costanzas were "a Jewish family living under the witness protection program under the name Costanza.") Yet not Jewishness but heightened selfishness and a refusal to accept adulthood seem to me the twin comic engines that kept the show humming along for nearly a decade.

A category that Dauber might have added to his other seven is that of jokes about Jewish assimilation and Jews sliding away from Judaism and their Jewishness generally. This would include all those jokes about nose jobs and name-changing. Perhaps the subtlest of these jokes is the one about the three rabbis who over lunch discover that all of them have a problem with mice in their synagogues. The first rabbi recounts that he called in an exterminator, but without great success. The second rabbi tells that he set tens of mousetraps around his synagogue, but when one of the traps went off it greatly disturbed the service and he had to remove them all. The third rabbi, however, announces that he found a solution by buying a 25-pound wheel of Stilton cheese that he set on the *byma*, or altar, whereupon 68 mice suddenly appeared. When asked how that got rid of the problem, the rabbi replies, "I *bar mitzvahed* all 68. They never returned."

At the close of his book, Dauber mentions the possibility that the end of the era of Jewish comedy may be near. Political correctness figures eventually to take its toll on Jewish comedy, as it does on all humor. The greenhorn accent, often central to the telling of Jewish jokes, is unknown to (because unheard by) generations of younger Jews. The art of joke-telling itself, a form of oral short story, seems everywhere in decline.

My own view is that Jewish humor will continue as long as the reigning note behind Jewish jokes continues to be the belief, everywhere confirmed, that out of the crooked timber of humanity nothing entirely straight can be made, that human nature in all its nuttiness does not change, and that the greatest fool of all—he could be mayor of Chelm, that legendary Jewish town of fools—is he who thinks it can.

Short Attention Span

(2017)

ANY OF US are born with attributes that slightly, sometimes greatly, set us apart: unusual strength, musical or artistic ability, skill with numbers, mental quickness, good looks. My own two attributes have been excellent physical coordination and a short-attention span. The latter has been much more decisive than the former in the development of my character, my outlook, and my general good fortune in life.

The physical coordination useful to me chiefly as a boy on athletic fields made a genuine contribution to my early, quite possibly too high, estimate of myself. I was a grammar-school shortstop, a quarterback, a point guard. I was too small to play high-school football and played basketball only at the level of the frosh-soph team. I also lettered on my high-school tennis team. But I continued to think myself a shortstop, quarterback, point guard—and, in the deepest recesses of my mind, perhaps I still do.

As for my short attention span, only recently have I come to appreciate the benefits it has bestowed on me. The notion of a short attention span has been getting bad press in recent years. The text, the tweet, the cursory e-mail beginning "Hi," and much more in contemporary life have been subject to regular harangues on the part of older generations. But this is ahistorical. Long before the dawning of the Age not of Aquarius but of the Digital, one felt attention spans generally were already diminishing, even at the highest reaches of intellectual life.

In universities after the 1960s, lecture courses were often replaced by those dominated by classroom discussions. Quarterly magazines that once allowed articles of eight and ten thousand words began to tell their writers to keep it to three to five thousand, with photographs and pull-out quotes added. Descending to the more middlebrow, popular door-stopper novels of nine-hundred and more pages of the kind James Michener used regularly to produce—*Hawaii, Texas, Alaska*—today would not get off the press. In an earlier time a blockbuster movie—*Gone with the Wind, Gandhi, The Godfather Part II, Lawrence of Arabia*—was allowed to run three or even four hours, whereas now any movie that runs over the standard two-hour limit courts commercial disaster.

To return from the gross national attention span to my own short attention span, allow me to delimit just how short it is, or isn't. For one thing, it is not in any way debilitating. Nor does it show up in that old Jewish condition known as *schpilkes*, or needles in the pants. I appear calm and concentrated enough. A short attention span has in no way made my life especially disorderly: I pay my bills on time, can read (slowly) lengthy books, and arrive well before the polls close. No, my short attention span chiefly reveals itself in an antipathy to boredom and a genuine worry about boring others, of which more later, if by then you are not yourself already bored by this essay.

My short attention span has made it impossible for me to concentrate full-time on serious money making. My father was a moderately successful businessman, and a place in his business, with respectable emoluments certain, awaited me. But I sensed, even in my adolescence, that, however ample the financial rewards, I could never have kept at it. To this day I cannot read financial reports even about the fate of my own money without my eyeballs turning to isinglass, and instead search out the bottom line amidst all the bumpf, and walk away ignorant about how such profits or losses I have enjoyed or suffered over the past month or fiscal quarter had come about. I suppose I could, a pistol at my head, learn the stock market, but to do so I should have to forget about reading such works as Mommsen's four-volume *History of Rome*, and the sacrifice doesn't seem worth it. (A more capacious mind than mine could doubtless do both, but then one can't have everything.) I am not in any way above money, nor unaware of the pleasures in accruing it, the prestige of possessing it, the delight in spending it. I just can't bring myself to think about it for long or in anything like the concentrated way earning vast quantities of it apparently requires.

Along with business, a career in medicine or in law was never remotely available to me. With wealthier and more foolhardy parents supplying a trust fund that would have put me nicely out of the money wars, I might have gone on to become a *flaneur*, the more elevated version of a playboy, or a connoisseur of some minor division of visual art while living in London or Paris. But even here my short attention span would have got in the way.

No, in the end, as in the beginning, there was nothing for it for me but to become a writer, for one of the surest routes to becoming a writer, or so after some consideration I have discovered, is to be fit to do nothing else. In my case, a writer meant, specifically, an essayist, that butterfly among literary workers, flying from subject to subject, as butterflies do from flower to flower. Montaigne, William Hazlitt, Charles Lamb, Max Beerbohm, H. L. Mencken, the great essayists, were, I do believe, short-attention-span men, butterflies all.

Turning to fiction in my forties, I found the short story, that form favored both by short-attention-span writers and readers alike. On a few occasions I have been asked if I wouldn't like to write a novel. My answer is that I would indeed, a family chronicle, spanning three or four generations, played out against a rich European history—the Diaspora *shtetl* days, the Russian Revolution, the Second World War—a novel on the model of I. J. Singer's *The Brothers Ashkenazi*! Given my attention span, though, the likelihood of my doing so is roughly equivalent to that of my winning next year's NBA slam-dunk competition.

The shortness of my attention span prevented me, as a writer, from ever concentrating heavily on a single subject, becoming an expert, an authority. Instead I flitted, as I continue to flit, from subject to subject as my interests of the moment direct, having over the years written books on

Divorce, Ambition, Snobbery, Envy, Friendship, Gossip, most recently Charm—books that, once having been written, exhausted my interest in their subjects.

In a story of Stefan Zweig's called "Buchmendel" I came upon the following, to me, fascinating sentence: "Jacob Mendel was the first to reveal to me in my youth the mystery of absolute concentration which characterizes the artist and the scholar, the sage and the imbecile; the first to make me acquainted with the tragical happiness and unhappiness of complete absorption." Have I ever known such absorption? Yes, but for no more than two or three hours. Just now I am absorbed in writing this essay, but I shall soon be called away from it to run an errand, lunch will follow, and then perhaps I'll watch a bit of the Cubs-Brewers game later in this weekend afternoon.

Many years ago, in a biography of Hannah Arendt, I read that every afternoon, in her Upper West Side apartment, Miss Arendt set herself down on her couch and thought for an hour. About just what she thought wasn't mentioned. One assumes it was about one or another of the great general philosophical problems, or a question of historical interpretation, or something to do with a book on which she was currently at work. Whatever the case, there each afternoon she was, on her couch, on her back, for one hour, thinking.

I tried it. I intended to concentrate on finding a solution for the knotty problem in a composition on which I was at work, but the prospect of that night's dinner with friends at a restaurant in Chinatown arose. Regrets over two different girls I should but failed to have courted in high school 30 years before cropped up. The dreary season of the Chicago Bears brought a fleeting shot of depression. Did it bode ill that an editor to whom I'd sent a story, usually so prompt in response, was taking more than two weeks to get back to me about it? The mind, the rabbis tell us, is a great wanderer. They didn't know the half of it. With only eight minutes of my scheduled hour spent, I got up off the couch and forgot the entire enterprise, taking comfort in remembering that Sidney Hook once told me that Hannah Arendt, despite her panoply of German classical learning, was wrong about everything important. Too much time on the couch perhaps, thinking at too abstract a level, putting, one might say, the Descartes before the horse.

Over the years I have been able to find jobs that allowed my short attention span to work to my advantage. As a young man, I slipped into editing jobs on general magazines and on an encyclopedia—butterfly work if ever there was any—then later was hired to teach at a university in a job where, since I neither had any advanced degrees nor wished for tenure, it was understood that I needn't show any pretensions to the concentrated mental work called scholarship. These various jobs allowed me to essay away, so to say, writing early in the day, or late into the night, on subjects that engaged my interest at that moment. I seem to have produced seventeen such books of these intellectual wanderings. People with short attention spans do not necessarily lack energy. Only lengthy concentration.

THE ADVANTAGES OF A SHORT ATTENTION SPAN extend well beyond my work, or so-called professional, life. I find I am unable to brood, at least for long, on public events. I marvel, for example, at the man who is currently the president of our country—how did we come to this fallen state?—but I do not allow his current residency on Pennsylvania Avenue to disturb my sleep or enjoyment of meals, pleasure in friends, and general amusements.

Nor does my short attention span permit me to dwell lengthily on international sadness. Such sadness is of course never in short supply—in the forms of famine, floods, raging fires, political tyrannies—but this, somehow, does not stop me from each morning checking the Major League Baseball standings. I am not without my political passions, but they flicker, and I keep a perennially cold place in my heart only for those Jews who do not find Israel morally as good as they think themselves. I consult the headlines in the daily press, usually online, but find myself quickly dropping away from the copy that appears beneath them. Whether this is owing to short attention span or cynicism about getting at the truth of public matters in the press is less than clear. Like Malcolm Muggeridge, "I'd rather read about John F. Kennedy's *amours* than what his speech-writers wrote for him to say or how his public image comported itself."

I have had my share of personal grief—divorce, death in the family, heart surgery, and the rest—yet I find my short attention span has not allowed me to sustain for long the depression that such events usually bring on.

Here perhaps is to be found the greatest reward of having a short attention span: the avoidance of long bouts of gloom. I do not say that I smiled through these sad events, only that I could not stay depressed for anywhere near what I suspect is the regulation time. Might this be that I am ultimately a shallow person? Or might it instead be that, as I prefer to think, I have always found the world an amusing place, and refuse to be long deterred from this view, whether from political or personal sadness.

Anyone who has read this far will scarcely be surprised to learn that I have never been in psychotherapy. I have never considered it. I do not gainsay therapy and its powerful recent ally psychopharmacology; it has helped bring people out of the hellish throes of schizophrenia and other wretched psychoses. I have known people who claim to have had their lives changed much for the better owing to it; even someone who averred that it saved his life. I might consider psychotherapy myself if the sessions were reduced from fifty to, say, ten minutes, and the fees cuts proportionately.

As the chief emotion of capitalism is greed, that of socialism envy, the chief emotion of those of us with short attention spans is, as I have suggested, boredom, or more precisely the fear of both lapsing into boredom or purveying it. Easily bored myself, I live in modest but real fear of boring others.

As a college teacher for more than thirty years, I never walked into a classroom without at least a touch of trepidation. My fear was that I would put my students through the excruciating tedium that most of my time in classrooms as a student entailed for me. I also early came to learn that anyone who thinks he is a good teacher, like anyone who thinks he is charming, probably isn't. Giving a talk or lecture to larger audiences naturally intensified this same trepidation. This fear was not without a basis in history.

Many years ago, I received a call from the chairman of the English department at Dennison University in Ohio informing me that a book of mine had been chosen as the main text for the English course required by the freshman class of 800 or so students. The attached string was that I had to appear in person to give a talk, for which I would be given an additional modest fee.

My talk was given in a church and my audience was made up almost exclusively of freshman students. I had expected more faculty to attend.

The title of my talk, a survey of literary groups in history, was "Is There a Literary Life Before Death," which I thought vaguely amusing. My first paragraph, meant to hook the audience and bring it over to my side, was larded with what I thought a few delicious witticisms. As soon as I delivered this paragraph, I could tell by the deadening response, the nonplussed look on the kids' faces, that it had sailed blithely over the heads. And I had twenty-two more pages of the talk to give.

I prattled on, nobody in the audience smiling or laughing in the proper places. I didn't look back at the large crucifix behind me, for fear Jesus, in his infinite sympathy, might be weeping. I was living a short-attention-span-man's nightmare, boring the pajamas off 800 young people, though causing them to long for their pajamas might be closer to it. I felt as if I were walking through the Loop in Chicago, at noon, on a cold but busy day, wearing nothing but loafers. As I turned down my twenty-second page, I was accorded the faintest possible applause, and the students, grumbling, filed out.

Which of the following seven fairly serious flaws, none of them among the seven deadly sins, would you least like to be accused of: being vulgar, selfish, tasteless, prejudiced, ignorant, humorless, or dull? For me dullness would be the roughest, and that was the agony of the Denison lecture. They found me dull.

In part, I dread being thought dull because I am a writer and thus implicitly pledged to be at least moderately interesting—though I can, on request, name a dozen or so contemporary writers of some fame who have all failed to live up to the pledge. But also because I think being boring is a social flaw that goes to a serious want of self-awareness. "Try to be a person on whom nothing is lost," declared Henry James in his essay "The Art of Fiction," and to be dull is, if one thinks about it, to be a person on whom just about everything is lost.

THE QUESTION, one I have been skirting round till now, arises if having a short attention span comes to little more than being someone without much depth, a person who is too shallow to concentrate for long on anything of substance. The Talmudic tradition doesn't allow for a short attention span, and neither does the scientific. Difficult to think of a first-line philosopher with a short attention span, or even imagine a good accountant with one. Let us, please, not speak of a surgeon with a short attention span.

Might it be that a short attention span is in fact part of the mental equipment required of the intellectual, that *boulevardier* of ideas? Isn't any figure who needs the freedom to roam—out of evading boredom or of giving way to curiosity or because of the proclivities of temperament—essentially a short-attention-span man got up in fox's clothing? The fox I have in mind is, specifically, the fox in Archilochus's famous (made so by Isaiah Berlin, another short-attention-span man) formulation, who "knows many things, [while] the hedgehog knows one big thing?" For the true fox, as for the short attention span man generally, no one thing alone is worth knowing if it means giving up so many other things worth exploring, however superficially.

The narrator in Stefan Zweig's story notes that only through observing this Mendel, a bibliophile of prodigious memory, did he "first become aware of the enigmatic fact that supreme achievement and outstanding capacity are only rendered possible by mental concentration, by a sublime monomania that verges on lunacy." (Wallace Stevens, in the "The Emperor of Ice Cream," refers to those "lunatics of one idea.") That monomania and its accompanying lunacy are, for better and worse, unavailable to those of us with short attention spans. The great monomaniacs—Darwin, Marx, Freud—leave their mark and have their powerful influence, though in the case of Marx and Freud that influence has long been on the wane and the mark begun to seem a blurry if not a black one. The short attention span man, meanwhile, plugs along, seeking primarily to amuse himself and anyone else who cares to read or listen to him. What he does may be ultimately negligible, but he wouldn't have it any other way. It's not, after all, as if he has any choice.

Intellectual Marines
in Little Magazines

(2008)

M Y TITLE DERIVES from "Under Which Lyre, A Reactionary Tract for the Times," the 1946 Harvard Phi Beta Kappa poem by W. H. Auden. The subject of the poem is a war over the form education ought to take, conducted by Hermes and Apollo, two major gods of Olympus. The pertinent stanza runs:

> Lone scholars, sniping from the walls
> Of learned periodicals,
> Our facts defend,
> Our intellectual marines,
> Landing in little magazines
> Capture a trend.

As for "Our intellectual marines/Landing in little magazines," witty though those lines are, their meaning may well be too greatly camouflaged, I fear, to be understood by anyone born after 1970. Does the phrase "little magazine" ring clear, I wonder? Do people any longer have a confident grasp of what constitutes an "intellectual," especially now that we have that new phenomenon, someone called "the public intellectual," who seems to be anyone who speaks grammatically and can write the Op-ed piece or do the political talk shows.

Little magazines earned their adjective—little—from their circulation, which was invariably small. The circulation was small because the content was pitched high and the readership was felt to be elite, a readership passionately interested in literature, music, art, politics, culture—and interested at a high level of seriousness.

These magazines have a long—and continuing—history. In Czarist Russia, these same magazines are referred to by no less a figure than Anton Chekhov as the "thick magazines," for which, as a young man Chekhov found himself pleased to write, after beginning his career doing hack work for a larger but less intelligent readership. Earlier, in the first decades of the nineteenth century, they were a mainstay of intellectual life in England, where such magazines as the *Edinburgh Review, Blackwoods,* the *Quarterly Review,* the *Westminster Review,* and others ran the writings of such now canonical writers as William Hazlitt, Samuel Taylor Coleridge, William Wordsworth, Sydney Smith, William Cobbett, and Thomas Carlyle. When John Stuart Mill reviewed a new book about America by a young Frenchman named Alexis de Tocqueville, he did so in the October 1840 issue of the *Edinburgh Review.* Lord Macaulay reviewed books at great length in such journals. He claimed that his own and all other such articles had a life of roughly six weeks after their appearance in print, and of course, as we now know, he was quite wrong. George Eliot began writing for the *Westminster Review* in 1850 and signed on as an assistant editor of that journal in 1851.

In the twentieth century, T. S. Eliot founded and edited a little magazine, the *Criterion,* which was begun in 1922; he remained at the helm as editor until its demise in 1939. The magazine never had as many as 1,000 subscribers, yet was, as we know, of great cultural import. Along with much of his own immensely influential literary criticism, Eliot published his poem *The Wasteland* in it, which appeared concurrently in the *Dial,* an American little magazine, one of whose editors was Marianne Moore and which published so many of the key poets of the modernist movement in America and Europe as well as much pertinent social criticism. In France, such magazines as the *Revue du Deux Mondes,* the *Journal du Debats,* and the *Nouvelle Revue Francais* are coterminous with the history of French literature and intellectual life. I could go on—and on and on—but it is by now already plain that, without such magazines, the artistic and literary history of the past two centuries would look very different.

Defining an intellectual is slightly more complicated. It's made so by a confusion of vocabulary. Alongside "intellectual," there exist such terms as "intelligentsia" and "intellect." The language, as Flaubert, that great wrestler with words, once said, is "inept." "Intellect" speaks to one's general intelligence and ratiocinative power; "intelligentsia," originally a Russian word, refers to people who earn their livings with their minds—engineers, say, or lawyers or upper-bureaucrats.

An intellectual is rather different. He is a generalist, someone with more than a single or even dual specialty. He is someone much taken with ideas, their formulation, dissemination, and (less often) consequences. He is a grand amateur, someone distinguished by a certain cast of mind, a style of thought, wide-ranging, playful, curious, excited by ideas almost for their own sake. Daniel Bell defined an intellectual as "a specialist in generalizations" and "someone who asks if something works in practice, does it also work in theory?" If I had to cite pure types of the intellectual in recent centuries, I would choose Voltaire for the eighteenth century, John Stuart Mill and the Tocqueville for the nineteenth, and George Orwell for the twentieth. Susan Sontag may be the purest type of the intellectual in our day, for better *and* worse, I hasten to add.

The scholar tries to deepen every subject he touches, the artist attempts to elevate every subject he touches. (T. S. Eliot said about Henry James that "he had a mind so fine no idea could violate it," by which he meant that James was interested in truths above the level of mere ideas.) The intellectual attempts to wider the discussion—to turn the criticism of literature or art or the movies or politics into broader statements about the culture generally.

Which brings me to the higher journalism, which might, to some, sound an oxymoron rather like an honest used-car dealer. Even as described by its most impressive practitioners, journalism has had a non-serious side that may well be its most attractive side. H. L. Mencken, in *Newspaper Days,* notes that, when he was eighteen, he was faced with the decision of going to college or going to work for a newspaper. There really wasn't, Mencken averred, any serious choice. Mencken, who as editor of the *American Mercury* later became something of a higher journalist himself, wrote:

> At a time when the respectable bourgeois youngsters of my generation were college freshmen, oppressed by simian soph-omores and affronted with balderdash daily and hourly by chalky pedagogues, I was at large in a wicked seaport of half a million people [Baltimore, that is], with a front seat at every public show, as free of the night as of the day, and getting earfuls and eyefuls of instruction in a hundred giddy arcana, none of them taught in schools. . . .

> I was laying in all the worldly wisdom of a police lieutenant, a bartender, a shyster lawyer, or a midwife. And it would certainly be idiotic to say that I was not happy.

This is putting the best, because the most amusing, face on the low side of journalism. Yet what could be high, let alone "higher" about journalism, *mere* journalism, as it is sometimes called. Balzac, who wrote brilliantly about the perfidies of journalism in *Lost Illusions,* said of the journalist that one of his grandest pleasures was "the vengeful witticism." He makes plain in that novel that the "Press never runs any risk," whereas those who govern "stand to lose everything." Tolstoy, in a letter of 1871, called journalism "an intellectual brothel from which there is no retreat." By the twentieth century, the reputation of journalists hadn't greatly improved. Karl Kraus, the acidic Viennese wit, once defined a journalist as "someone who, given time, writes worse." They haven't had a very good press, journalists.

What gives the higher journalism its standing is that, insofar as it is able, it has removed itself from the epiphenomena of the everyday. The higher journalism is writing about literature, art, music, politics, culture that always appears first in journals, or in the non-news sections of a small number of newspapers with national pretensions. Its authors have been men and women often initially trained as news journalists, but whose talents have driven them beyond that rather narrow calling. One thinks here of the early staff of the *New Yorker:* James Thurber, Joseph Mitchell, A. J. Liebling, all of whom began as beat reporters writing for smaller town newspapers and ended up in the purlieus of literature itself. Edmund Wilson, the doyen of American literary critics in the twentieth century, used to call himself a journalist, chiefly because his work invariably appeared in such journals as the *New Republic* (of which he served as literary editor), the early *Vanity Fair,* and, beginning in the 1940s, the *New Yorker.*

Before higher education became as commonplace as it now is, a great many novelists also began on newspapers, and the role of American writers who did so is a highly honorable one; it includes: Mark Twain, William Dean Howells, Stephen Crane, Theodore Dreiser, Willa Cather (who first went to the University of Nebraska), Ben Hecht, Ernest Hemingway. "Genius," a character in Henry James's novel *The Tragic Muse* says, "is only the art of getting experience fast, of stealing it, as it were." Then perhaps more so than now, the newspaper was felt to be a fine training ground for a novelist, permitting him to get outside his social class and see the world in both its high and low, public and private, aspects in a way that perhaps no other job did. Newspaper work allowed one to get experience faster—in Henry James's formulation—than any other job.

But working on a newspaper, especially working as a reporter, was also felt to be a young man's game. If one were a reporter beyond the age of forty—with the possible exception of being a foreign correspondent—one was felt to be pushing it.

Then, too, not everyone had the taste or temperament for the roiling waters of the daily tumult that is called "the news." As a character in Evelyn Waugh's novel *Scoop* puts it: "Look at it this way. News is what a chap who doesn't care much about anything wants to read. And it's only news until he's read it. After that it's dead."

Working the higher journalism was also a way of breaking into print for writers who were still young and hadn't fully developed their talents—a way to try themselves out in print. We have the record of a case very much in point in the instance of Virginia Woolf. Like George Orwell (another writer of the higher journalism), Virginia Woolf clearly preferred to think herself a novelist—an artist, above all—but it is by no means clear whether she wasn't more impressive in writing the essays, reviews, and articles that, in her hands, eventually constituted the higher journalism practiced at a very high power.

We have a fairly full record of Virginia Woolf's breaking into print doing higher journalism provided by her diaries. She began doing so in 1904, at the age of 22. At the time she was still Virginia Stephen, daughter of Sir Leslie Stephen, the English man of letters and original editor of *The National Dictionary of Biography*.

Soon after the death of her father, in February 1904, Virginia Woolf plunged into her second major breakdown, this one accompanied by her first suicide attempt. She was pulled out of her deep funk by the offer of the great historian of the medieval world, Frederick Maitland, to help him with his work on her father's biography, by marking those passages from her parents' letters that she thought he might quote and by filling in for him an account of her father's last years. She found the work reinvigorating. Soon her friend Violet Dickinson arranged for her to be invited to write for the women's section of the *Guardian*. She published book reviews in its issues of December 7 and 14 and an essay on the Brontes' parsonage at Haworth in that of December 21, 1904. She began making money through her writing. "She had lost her mother. She had lost her father," the editor of her diaries writes. "But she had found work."

Balzac notes that most people who go into the literary life suffer a disabling disproportion between desire and will power. Not Virginia Woolf. Her work in journalism was often bothersome, but, despite her fragile mental condition, she never lost control of it. Along with her writing for newspapers, she began giving lectures at Morley College, an evening institute in South London for working people, on ancient history and on English history, both of which she got up through wide reading. She also wrote for the English *National Review* and for a magazine called *Academy & Literature*. She hoped for a connection with the London *Times Literary Supplement*—"If I am taken on by the *Times*" she writes in her diary, "I shall think myself justified"—and this soon came about.

Presently, in her diary, she is complaining, rather like an old pro, about the conditions of writing for editors. ("Wrote at my review, which is difficult because of the space allowed, only 600 words & many things to put into it.") She does not like to be edited: "Home - & bought the *Academy*, with what purports to be my article in it; but my blood as an author boils; name is changed, half cut out, words are put in & altered, & this hotch potch signed Virginia Stephen." She is sent books she knows nothing about. ("It is hard work reviewing when you don't know the subject," she notes.) Great thick novels are no bargain either: "Another book from the *Times*—a fat novel, I'm sorry to say. They [the *Times*] pelt me now." She is asked to review Henry James's *The Golden Bowl.* ("Henry James I hope to finish tonight—the toughest job I have had yet.") She has work rejected. The *Times Literary Supplement* returns a review, its editor, Bruce Richmond, apologizing, adding that "a professional historian is needed" for the book in question; "it goes," she notes in her diary, "in the wastebasket." She writes "that all this time given up to reviewing rather bothers me," but she also likes—actually, needs—the money it brings in. She is hooked, and even though she will soon spend more and more time on writing her novels, she never abandons her criticism and essays, her journalism—what I am calling her higher journalism.

A small but distinguished list of novels about working at the higher journalism would include Balzac's great *Lost Illusions,* George Gissing's *New Grub Street,* and Wilfred Sheed's *Office Politics,* which is about life on a political weekly in New York. Balzac's is much the most impressive of these books. It views journalism, which in the France between the end of the empire and 1830 was deeply corrupt, as a trap away from which anyone with serious artistic intentions or even a modest desire to live a life of honor will steer clear. Balzac himself knew this terrain from the inside, for he wrote for the little magazines, *les petits journaux,* of the 1820s, and was himself the editor and proprietor of Parisian periodicals. His novel also offers very specific advice on how to write the theatrical review or criticism of a novel that will bring the greatest credit to the person writing the review or criticism. One of the veteran journalists in *Lost Illusions* instructs the novel's hero, Lucien Rubempré, to begin by complimenting a work, be sure to quote foreign writers throughout your piece, subtly show the dangerous tendencies in the work, put a sprinkling of wit into your argument, add a touch of vinegar for seasoning, end on a note of pity for the poor misguided author, yet finally hold out a bit of hope for his improvement. This formula, set down by Balzac in 1840, could be successfully put to use today.

Gissing's novel, *New Grub Street,* is easily the most depressing of the novels to take up the higher journalism as its subject. George Gissing is the author of what I believe is untopably the saddest line in all of literature, which is about a man and his wife trying to grub out a living doing journalistic odd jobs. "They had three children," Gissing wrote, "all happily buried." Grub Street refers to the former name of a London street in the ward of Cripplegate, which was, Samuel Johnson reports, "much inhabited by writers of small histories, dictionaries, and temporary poems; whence any mean production is called *grubstreet.*"

Gissing's own life was markedly sad. Born in 1857, the son of a pharmacist, he was, as a boy, the very type of the good student, winning scholarships to not quite the best schools. He was in one such institution—Owens College in Manchester—when, at nineteen, he fell in love with a seventeen-year-old prostitute, which, just about put paid to his career. He stole from the college library to help this young woman, was caught, and sent off to jail for a month. He later married her, and tried, unsuccessfully, to reform and redeem her. She eventually died of alcoholism. Gissing meanwhile soldiered on, briefly working at intellectual journalism, writing his dark novels, and tutoring private students, work that he much resented.

New Grub Street is set in the late nineteenth and early twentieth centuries at the time of the rise number of magazines and of the growth in the number of writers to fill them up. In 1800 there were said to be 500 writers in England; by 1900, the number rose to more than 9,000. The spread of education and literacy had had a large hand in bringing this about; but a new kind of reader had arisen, half-educated but very earnest, what we should today perhaps call middlebrow readers. And all sorts of magazines set out to satisfy the demands of this reader.

One sees, even as far back as *New Grub Street,* what we have today begun to call the effort of dumbing down. The idea behind this effort is increasingly to service the reader, not to incite writers to greater heights. Briefer is always thought better, and one of the novel's secondary characters, a man named Whelpdale, dreams of beginning a magazine in which no single piece of writing will be longer than two inches. In his novel Gissing, perhaps the first person to do so, anticipated what the Marxists would call the commodification of literature, though he was himself no Marxist and would doubtless have hated so barbarous a word as "commodification." But what Gissing did know was that there was something deeply against the spirit of literature in the attempt to use it to please large and rather artificially created audiences.

In *New Grub Street* Gissing posed, in starkest terms, the question of the integrity of the writer. "The theme of the novel is the tragedy of the intellectual worker," as V. S. Pritchett put it. The tragedy is that circumstances everywhere force such a writer to compromise his integrity. "Art must be practiced as a trade," says the ambitious wife of the sad hero of this novel. But it can't be—at least serious art cannot be. A mark of the relentless darkness of this novel is that every character in it who struggles to retain his integrity goes under; and every character who cheerfully abandons it, or for whom integrity simply doesn't exist as an issue, wins through to happiness. It's all bad news, the news George Gissing brings in *New Grub Street*.

But now before the depression grows too great, let the Gissing (like the kissing) stop, while I take a wide, perhaps almost a bipolar, mood swing, and ask you to contemplate a young man, an undergraduate in his junior year at the University of Chicago. He is not from a particularly bookish home, himself half—make that a quarter—educated, with an inchoate but nonetheless heated desire one day to become a writer. His education at the University of Chicago, quite good in so many ways, has, if anything, frustrated this desire. He has read scarcely anything but great books for the past three years—much of it Greek and Roman (in English): vast quantities of Plato and Aristotle—so that Edward Gibbon's *Decline and Fall of the Roman Empire* has come to seem almost light reading.

He knows, our young man does, that this is first-class stuff, the very best, yet the discouragement comes with the realization that he has been set an impossible standard. The issues, questions, problems set out in his reading are too grand for him to hope to deal with in any writing of his own, especially at the age of twenty; while he recognizes the grandeur of the prose styles set before him—Benjamin Jowett's Plato, Thomas Hobbes's Thucydides, Edward Gibbon's confident, irony-laden cadences—he sees no point in attempting to imitate them, for their rhythms, their diction, their syntax are not his, nor can they ever be. Greatness in literature, while it can inspire, can also, if one wishes to write oneself, be daunting, deadly daunting.

Then one day this young man—you will have guessed by now that he is me—stops, quite by happenstance, in the periodical room of the William Raney Harper Library, where I discovered several racks of magazines that I knew neither from my home or from the plethora of newsstands that still dotted the city. Thickish, many of them turn out to be quarterlies, though some are monthlies. *Partisan Review, Kenyon Review, Hudson Review, Yale Review, Sewanee Review, Virginia Quarterly Review*—lots in the world to review, it appeared—were among their titles; there were also magazines called *Accent, Epoch, Poetry, Commentary,* and a very elegant British magazine, *Encounter,* that had only recently begun publication. Then there were the weeklies: the *New Republic,* the *Nation,* the *National Review, Commonweal.* These magazines published some poems and stories, but essays and reviews of books were at the center of their interest. Some could bore the pajamas off a coma victim; but a few were filled with things that I found of immediate, passionate, and, as it would turn out, permanent interest. I find it difficult to do justice to the deep pleasure I then found in these magazines, but will say here only that it was of the highest intensity, like the discovery of sex or oysters.

Education is a very disorderly business. It proceeds by stops and starts, with accident generally playing a larger part than plan. Education is available through five institutions, or agencies: schools, libraries, new and particularly used bookshops, conversations with intelligent friends, and intellectual magazines. For me, who never flourished in the classroom, bookshops and intellectual magazines were the key elements, with magazines the more important of the two.

Serious intellectual interest, for me, commenced in the periodical room of the William Raney Harper Library. Some of the names I came across in the pages of the intellectual magazines I found there were European and already vaguely known to me from my general reading: André Malraux, Ignazio Silone, Bertrand Russell, F. R. Leavis, Arthur Koestler. (It was the late 1950s, and Americans still existed in a condition of cultural inferiority vis-à-vis Europe.) Others—a vast number of others—I encountered for the first time: Lionel Trilling, Isaiah Berlin, Philip Rahv, Sidney Hook, Hugh Trevor-Roper, Richard Crossman, Saul Bellow, Harold Rosenberg, Hannah Arendt, Goronwy Rees, Gertrude Himmelfarb, Leslie Fiedler, Clement Greenberg, James Baldwin, Delmore Schwartz, Randall Jarrell, Raymond Aron, Robert Lowell, Irving Howe, Mary McCarthy, E. H. Gombrich. Reading these writers introduced me to still others—Vassarion Belinsky, Paul Valéry, Max Beerbohm, and more, and to scores of subjects of which I had been previously ignorant. And so, owing to these magazines, the net of my intellectual acquaintance grew wider and wider. This was education by a procedure I think of as exfoliation: with one thing opening onto another, an endless unfolding, to the very end of one's days.

Some of the writers for *Partisan* and *Kenyon Reviews, Commentary,* and *Encounter* were academics. But a larger number—and for me some of the most attractive—had no academic connection, and were pure intellectuals.

An intellectual, as I came to learn through reading the higher journalism—and to expand a bit on my earlier definition—is someone taken up with general ideas. He is almost never a specialist, let alone an expert. The intellectual was also more freelance, both in spirit and in fact, than the academic. He tended to be engaged—*engagé,* in the French word—with the life of his time and wrote only about what stirred him.

A man named Robert Warshow, who died at the age of 37 and who wrote for *Partisan Review* and *Commentary* (and was an editor of the latter), provides a stellar instance of the intellectual and his essay "The Gangster as Tragic Hero," is an excellent example of the *modus operandi* of the pure intellectual at work. In this essay, in roughly 3,000 words, Warshow sets out to discover the true meaning of gangster movies and the source of their attraction to us. He does not so much argue as assert his case, and what he asserts is that inherent in our pleasure in gangster movies is an element of sadism: in watching them, he writes, "we gain the double satisfaction of participating vicariously in the gangster's sadism and then seeing it turned against the gangster himself." But the deeper significance of these movies, according to Warshow, lies in the way they encapsulate what he called "the intolerable dilemma" we all feel about success. The gangster, in brief, is "what we want to be and what we are afraid we may become." And so the effect of the gangster movies "is to embody this dilemma in the person of the gangster and resolve it by his death. The dilemma is resolved because it is his death, not ours. We are safe; for the moment, we can acquiesce in our failure, we can choose to fail."

Here is a writer, Robert Warshow, who possesses no specialized knowledge, or even any extraordinary fund of personal experience. He does what he does with no other aid than the power of his mind. He has seen the same movies we all have seen, but he happens to have seen more in them than many of us perhaps ever recognized was there. The late Edward Shils, a man who thought a great deal about intellectuals, wrote: "This interior need to penetrate beyond the screen of immediate concrete experience marks the existence of the intellectual in every society." A precise definition, that, of Robert Warshow at work.

Other writers for these magazines made plain that a higher standard of judgment could be called into play than that of the marketplace. You can't argue with success, an old bromide had it, but few things seemed more worth arguing with to the writers of the higher journalism. Dwight Macdonald was a writer for *Partisan Review, Commentary, Encounter,* and, later, the *New Yorker,* whose specialty was that of gatekeeper— another function of the higher journalism—by which I mean sifting out the genuine from the ersatz in culture. Macdonald wrote rollickingly funny pieces on such then commercially successful projects as the new English translation of the Bible and Encylcopaedia Britannica's *Great Books of the Western World,* titling his essay on the latter "The Book of the Millennium Club."

Brilliance seemed the first requisite to writing for the little magazines. Lionel Trilling, through sheer percipience, took literary criticism to its next level, discovering the terror in the poetry in Robert Frost, the emptiness in American realistic fiction, the tragic vision implicit in the works of Sigmund Freud. Mary McCarthy, one of the many demolition experts at work in those days, exploded the reputations of Tennessee Williams and J. D. Salinger. Others wrote about politics, popular culture, visual art—often in a polemical spirit, always in an authoritative way.

One of these writers, Edmund Wilson, whom I never met, became much more important to me than any teacher I ever had. In his book of 1921, *Axel's Castle,* Wilson had introduced literary modernism—as represented by such writers as James Joyce, T. S. Eliot, Gertrude Stein, Yeats, and others—to Americans with literary interests. What he did for me and for a great many people of my generation was acquaint us, through his reviews and essays, to a vast number of writers, American and international, that we might never have known without him. He also gave us a model of a literary life as something professional, manly, cultivated, entirely admirable.

I had read bits of Marx—"The Communist Manifesto," "The 18th Brumaire"—at the University of Chicago, but in the intellectual magazines Sidney Hook, once the foremost American exponent of Marxism and an astonishingly impressive polemicist, took on still vital Communism's proponents, not least among them Bertrand Russell. Russell in those days was arguing that it was better to be Red than Dead. After their battle in print, in a New York weekly called the *New Leader,* I decided it was better to be Hook than Russell, whom Hook had rendered, at least in the political realm, intellectually red and dead both.

If reading the higher journalism of that day made one politically an anti-Communist, culturally it left one, immitigably, irredeemably, a highbrow. Clement Greenberg in a famous essay, "Avant-Garde and Kitsch," eviscerated *kitsch,* that empty simulacrum of genuine culture which Greenberg viewed as false experience and faked sensations, watered down, "destined," as Greenberg put it, "for those who, insensitive to the values of genuine culture, are hungry nevertheless for the diversion that only culture of some sort can provide."

Apart from the discrete opinions one might pick up there, what excited me about the higher journalism, as I encountered it from these intellectual marines in their little magazines, was that it made a solid connection between the life of the mind and the world. Hilton Kramer, recounting his own early encounter with the magazine *Partisan Review* put this point, retrospectively, with a nice precision that almost perfectly mirrors my own experience:

> For certain writers and intellectuals of my generation . . .
> drawn to *PR* in the late forties and early fifties . . . it was more
> than a magazine, it was an essential part of our education,

as much a part of that education as the books we read, the visits we made to museums, the concerts we attended, and the records we bought. It gave us entree to modern cultural life—to its gravity and complexity and combative character—that few of our teachers could match (and these few were likely to be readers or contributors to *PR*.) It conferred upon every subject it encompassed—art, literature, politics, history, current affairs—an air of intellectual urgency that made us, as readers, feel implicated and called upon to respond. If later on, we began to question the perfect confidence that *PR* seemed to bring to its pronouncements on every issue, and to understand its style of apodictic authority—well, that too was an essential part of our education.

What I read in these magazines was more lively, had more dash, more *brio*, than other writing I had hitherto known, with the exception of that of H. L. Mencken.

Their contributors had a taste for risky generalization, which is one way that knowledge outside the scientific realm sometimes advances. What was going on in the pages of these magazines, near as I could determine, was an attempt to penetrate what was going on behind the surface of the culture, to grasp the "true gen," to use the phase Ernest Hemingway used for the real lowdown. It seemed a swell, a superior game, I thought, and one I myself wished myself one day to play.

I continued to read these magazines through the end of my college days. Living in New York after college, I hunted down back issues of them in old bookshops. Such became my dependence upon them that I snuck them into my footlocker as an enlisted man going through basic training in the US Army, at the possible penalty (never paid) of having to do lengthy sessions of KP, for one wasn't supposed to have any reading matter at all, but I found I couldn't quite live without them.

While in the Army—working as a typist of physical examinations in a recruiting station in Little Rock, Arkansas—I wrote and sent off my own first contribution to the *New Leader*. The piece was called "Letter from Little Rock" and had a fairly high quotient of pretentiousness; my memory of it is that every third paragraph began "In any event" and the phrase "to be sure" was hauled out to insert before only my most dubious statements.

But I have not yet forgot the purity of joy I felt upon having this piece accepted. My guess is that the one event in his career no writer ever forgets is his first acceptance. In a *Backward Glance,* Edith Wharton tells of one day going through the mail to discover that she had poems—her first submissions to magazines—accepted by three different editors. All she could do to work off her excitement, she reports, was lift her longish skirt, and run up and down the grand staircase of her family's New York mansion. All I could do was several times sneak into the bathroom at the recruiting station on Main Street in Little Rock, remove my letter from my shirt pocket, unfold it, read it yet again, close my eyes—we did not yet have the high five or the Yes gesture—and say to myself that I was now a contributor to a magazine to which Sidney Hook, Diana Trilling, Leslie Fielder, and others had contributed. I was twenty-two, felt myself a member of the club, and very proud.

Perhaps this is the place to underscore that not everything about the higher journalism is high. After my letter of acceptance from the *New Leader* and after receiving my two free contributor's copies, I awaited my fee for the piece. Two weeks went by, then three, and sometime during the fourth week I decided to write to the editor, a man I had never met named S. M. Levitas, a Russian emigré, a former Menshivik, an early opponent of Stalin, and a man (I subsequently learned) who smoked two packs of cigarettes a day without ever buying any. I also learned that his sub-editors used to come to him for a raise and leave his office with only a review copy of a novel. "Dear Mr. Levitas," I wrote, "There have been a number of mail thefts in the building in which I live, and I wonder if your check for my essay, 'Letter from Little Rock,' might have been stolen. May I ask you to look into this for me?" Within the week, he wrote back: "Dear Mr. Epstein, You are a young man and are apparently unaware that the truth has no price tag. The *New Leader* does not pay its contributors. But I am here to encourage you to do more writing."

Not all higher journalism was done for nothing, but in the 1940s, '50s, and through the early '60s, unless one wrote for the *New Yorker* or *Esquire* (itself, in those years, a highly suspect thing to do, thought to be selling out), one might receive at best a few hundred dollars for an article or short story. *The American Scholar,* in the early 1970s, paid $250 for an essay, $50 for a book review or a poem. As recently as fifteen or so years ago, I was paid $180 for a short story by the *Hudson Review.* More recently I received a check for $50 from *Sewanee Review* for a memorial tribute to a friend, the poet John Frederick Nims. One wrote the higher journalism, then, not for the money, but for the need to have one's say and to say it to a small but select audience.

Audience was a decisive element. Writing in the journals that published the higher journalism, one didn't have to talk down—or, in the current phrase, dumb down—but said things as best one knew how to say them. Later, when I came occasionally to write for *Harper's* or *The Atlantic,* I often found I couldn't give to subjects the same complexity or subtlety of thought or even shared humor that are permitted in, say, *Commentary* or the *Hudson Review*, or that I assumed my readers could handle when for a time I edited another such magazine, *The American Scholar.*

Here I want to interject that I thought this matter of audience was ordered better in England than America. In the early sixties, when I worked in New York, I began to read the English weeklies, the *Spectator,* the *New Statesman,* and the *Listener* (this last published by the BBC). English writers of the higher journalism didn't—as Americans writers often seem to do—waste much time in their writing teaching and (worse) preaching. The English writers were without condescension; even if they happened to be dons, they never wrote down; they assumed that, though you may not have possessed the specific information they did on a perhaps arcane subject— the Alexandrian Library, the Dreyfus Affair—you were, nonetheless, in a rough general way, quite as well educated as they. And if you weren't, then it was incumbent upon you to become so, my dear fellow, lest you miss out on a very good game—one involving intellectual suavity in the discussion of politics and culture of a kind that leads to deeper penetration, perhaps even wisdom, about the ways of men and women in the world.

On the matter of becoming educated enough to play the game, I soon found that I was one of those people who was getting his education in public. Once I had begun publishing in the intellectual journals I had made a valuable connection at the *New Republic*, whose literary editor, a man named Bob Evett, generously sent me books to review—other journals began asking me to write for them. Lest I make all this seem effortless, I had better insert here that I worked very hard on even what might seem the most negligible piece of writing—my efforts came, I believe to less than fifty cents an hour—for I always wanted to do it right, to leave, somehow or other, an impress. I was, I fear, too egotistic to settle for less.

I recall once being asked by an editor if I would like to review *My Past and Thoughts,* the memoirs of Alexander Herzen, about to appear in a four-volume edition. I said I would be pleased to do so. When I got off the phone, I went directly to an encyclopedia to find out who exactly Alexander Herzen was. For the same place—*Book World,* which then appeared in New York, Chicago, and San Francisco—I reviewed, in my twenties, Bertrand Russell's autobiography and Thomas Mann's letters. Intellectually ambitious, if not downright chutzpaical, I wrote about almost anything that was offered to me; and the only time I recall failing on a book-review assignment was a piece on Arthur Koestler's *The Act of Creation,* the first half of which was an analysis of humor, the second— well out of my depth—an attempt to show how the same methodology Koestler used to analyze jokes was at the heart of discovery in modern biology. I report all this not out of any sense of braggadocio, but instead to show that one of the ways of becoming highly intelligent is to begin by doing one's best impression of others who are highly intelligent. Through much of my twenties, operating as a rather small-time higher journalist, I was chiefly an impressionist, not of the Claude Monet or Camille Pissaro but of the Frank Gorsham and Rich Little variety.

The higher journalism is not only a way—an odd way, perhaps—to gain an education, but it is also a useful training ground for young men and women who wish to write but have not yet come into their literary talent. Unlike in music and art, talent in literature generally matures slowly and shows up late, if at all. After teaching a great many would-be poets, novelists, and essayists over the last few decades, I have come to believe that in writing desire and willpower may be quite as important as talent. All the examples of good, even great writers—Joseph Conrad published his first novel at 38, more recently Penelope Fitzgerald, we learn, began at 60—getting late starts leaves the would-be writer just out of university with a decade or even more on his or her hands. At twenty-five or even older one cannot be sure of the true character of one's talent; like as not, one's point of view (not one's opinions but one's point of view, a very different thing) may not be very well formed. Writing book-reviews, articles, essays in the little magazines may well be—as I think it was for me—an excellent training ground while awaiting the ripening of one's literary quality.

As a reader of the higher journalism, I fairly early began to notice that things I first read in such magazines as *Commentary* or the old *Partisan Review* began to turn up, with only a fairly brief time lag, in *Time, Newsweek,* the *New York Times,* the *Washington Post,* and elsewhere. Susan Sontag, some years ago, wrote an essay published in *Partisan Review* called "Notes on Camp," and, lo!, within a matter of weeks the word "camp"—referring to the homosexual aesthetic of irony applied to taste—began to show up in the national news weeklies and the fashion magazines. Clement Greenberg, writing exclusively in the intellectual magazines, really put abstract expression—the school of Pollock, Rothko, de Kooning—on the map. Jeanne Kirkpatrick, directly after writing an article in *Commentary* on the subject of the distinction between totalitarian and authoritarian regimes, was appointed Ambassador to the United Nations by President Reagan directly because of that article.

Small by the measure of mass journalism though the circulation of the intellectual magazines may be, some people—some key people—out there in what is called the great world were obviously reading them with most careful attention. Irving Kristol has said that, if you wish to communicate with 20 million readers, you ought to write for the *Reader's Digest,* but if you want to influence policy, politics, culture, the way people view the world, you ought to write for *The Public Interest, Commentary, The New York Review of Books, The New Criterion,* and other of the intellectual magazines.

What is the future of these magazines and of higher journalism itself? In our brave new world, are they as outmoded, as dead a form, as verse drama or elegant manners? You've probably heard all the arguments for their being so. I shall rehearse them briefly. Let us begin with the dumbing down of the culture, which works against the higher journalism, which at its heart is about smartening up. Then there is the blurring of high-brow culture, of which the higher journalism was always a part. A *New Yorker* writer named John Seabrook has recently produced a book entitled *Nobrow,* in which he argues that culture and marketing are becoming indivisible, which, if he is correct, spells both the increased dearth and eventually the death of highbrow culture.

But let's move on to the young, of whom we are all Kremlinologists, trying to find out what, precisely, is going on behind those thick walls known as youth culture. The young, everyone knows, spend three quarters of their time on the Internet or at Nintendo games, and the rest at the Cineplex watching *Alien Terminator 96* or strolling the mall, body pierced, tattooed, hair empurpled. The young are, as they say, now visually oriented. They don't care about reading, about the delights of prettily shaped sentences, about the kind of cognition and rumination that are at the heart of cultural acquisition as we have always known it. The young . . . but enough about those swine, the young.

Intellectual curiosity and passion for the life of the mind did not end with people born before 1945, or even before 1980. Although no one can give you anything like even their approximate number in America, readers for the higher journalism and the intellectual magazines are out there: perhaps they are as few as two hundred thousand in a country of more than 300 million. But that is not a negligible number. Besides, people genuinely interested in serious culture and the life of the mind have always and everywhere been a minority.

As long as such people continue to exist, so will the need for little magazines and intellectual marines to fill up their pages. The life of the country would be much poorer without them. They continue to provide an intellectual check and balance, a place to bat down foolish and sometimes pernicious ideas, of a kind today less and less available in universities or elsewhere. They must continue to exist, for the good reason that those audodidacts among us—and I have never met a really educated person who wasn't an audodidact, who didn't finally get his education on his own—cannot hope to live without them.

The American Language

(2018)

> Language, in fact, is very far from logical. Its development is
> determined, not by neat and obvious rules, but by a polyhedron
> of disparate and often sharply conflicting forces—the influence of
> the schoolma'am, imitation (often involving misunderstanding),
> the lazy desire for simplicity and ease, and sheer wantonness and
> imbecility.
>
> H. L. MENCKEN

IN THE PREFACE TO *HAPPY DAYS*, the first of his three autobiographies, H. L. Mencken remarks on his own good fortune, noting that there is nothing in his life, had he to live it over, he would have changed. "I'd choose the same parents, the same birthplace, the same education . . . the same trade, the same jobs, the same income, the same politics, the same metaphysic, the same wife, the same friends, and . . . the same relatives to the last known degree of consanguinity, including those in-law." Henry Louis Mencken was a happy man, a fact that attentive readers will soon enough discover burbling out nearly everywhere in his writing. Walter Lippmann, America's last great newspaper columnist, wrote of Mencken: "When you can explain the heightening effect of a spirited horse, of a swift athlete, of a dancer really in control of his own body, when you can explain why watching them you feel more alive yourself, you can explain the quality of his influence."

Mencken won vast popularity and its accompanying emoluments for doing what he loved to do most: to write vividly about the grand circus that for him was American life. In his essay "On Being an American," Mencken wrote that he liked America "because it amuses me to my taste. I never get tired of the show." Politicians, preachers, prohibitionists, professors, quacks, the South (that "Sahara of the Bozart"), the manifold hypocrisies of the "booboisie" ("*Homo boobiens*"), and much else kept him more than busy.

During the period after World War I and before the onset of the 1930s, Mencken's fame reached its zenith. His iconoclasm, expressed in a style at once elegant and comical, everywhere found a ready audience in the young. "So many young men get their likes and dislikes from Mencken," Ernest Hemingway wrote in *The Sun Also Rises*. In *Black Boy,* his autobiography, Richard Wright tells of discovering a book of Mencken's in the Memphis public library. The then-young Wright, beginning to read it, "was jarred and shocked by the style, the clear, clean, sweeping sentences." Until discovering Mencken, Wright claimed not to know one could use words as weapons.

Mencken was no mere iconoclast. He attacked the genteel tradition in literature, true enough, but he also championed the fiction of Joseph Conrad, Theodore Dreiser, Sinclair Lewis, and Willa Cather. Nor was Mencken's fame on the intellectual-magazine scale merely; it was national. He published a column in the *Baltimore Sun*, which, as an impressive self-promoter, he arranged to have syndicated round the country. In 1924, with the drama critic George Jean Nathan, he began the *American Mercury* magazine. His reporting of the 1925 Scopes Trial on evolution in Drayton, Tennessee, helped elevate it into one of the great trials of the 20th century.

In good part Mencken's fame was owed to his humor. "Mirth," he wrote, "is necessary to wisdom, to comfort, above all, to happiness." Elsewhere he noted that "one good horselaugh is worth 10,000 syllogisms." Although he may be best remembered for his savage yet always delightful mockery, he was a serious thinker whose thought was informed by a deep, life-long skepticism. What he was skeptical about above all was our hope of ever achieving even rudimentary understanding of our place in an uncaring universe. In one of the essays in his books of *Prejudices* he wrote:

No one knows Who created the visible universe, and it is infinitely improbable that anything properly describable as evidence on the point will ever be discovered. No one knows what motives or intentions, if any, lie behind what we call natural laws. No one knows why man has his present form. No one knows why sin and suffering were sent into this world— that is, why the fashioning of man was so badly botched.

And, he might have added, anyone who tells you he does know these things is a fool if not a liar, and richly deserving of Mencken's contumely.

H.L. Mencken was one of that small but superior club of laughing pessimists that among Americans included George Santayana and Justice Oliver Wendell Holmes. Holmes, writing to Harold Laski, remarked on Mencken's "sense of reality," adding "and most of his prejudices I share."

The 1930s were nowhere near so generous to Mencken as the '20s had been. Much of the youthful audience captivated by his writing—Mike Gold, editor of the *New Masses,* accused Mencken of "killing social idealism in young America"—now went over to socialism and some among it to revolutionary Marxism. Because of the exaggerated hatred in the United States of all things German once America entered World War I—Beethoven and other great German composers were often barred from major symphony programs; sauerkraut was rechristened "liberty cabbage"—Mencken, who was himself of German ancestry, became distrustful of anti-German sentiment.

This congeries of opinions, views, and prejudices caused Mencken's journalism to be banned from most magazines and newspapers, including the *Baltimore Sun,* for which he had written since his youth and on whose board he sat. He could scarcely have known it at the time, but this was a blessing in disguise. Being largely excluded from journalism freed him from the ephemera of contemporary politics and caused him to fall back on the writing of books. A number of the books he wrote during this time—his *Happy Days, Newspaper Days, Heathen Days,* and *The American Language* with its two thick *Supplement* volumes—are H. L. Mencken's true literary heritage and his best claim to lasting fame as an important American writer.

In its survey of the 100 greatest non-fiction works in English, the English *Guardian* included—along with Hobbes's *Leviathan*, Boswell's *The Life of Samuel Johnson*, Hume's *A Treatise of Human Nature*, Gibbon's *The History of the Decline and Fall of the Roman Empire*, and Webster's *An American Dictionary of the English Language*—Mencken's *The American Language*. The book in its first edition was published in 1919, but Mencken set to work polishing and enlarging it until its fourth and final edition in 1936, and then added two hefty *Supplement* volumes during the 1940s, finishing the second in 1948, just before the devastating stroke that rendered him bereft of speech and the ability to write, though he lived on, in this sad condition of incapacitation, until 1956.

Mencken claimed to be a bit of a fraud when *The American Language* became a commercial publishing success, for he had no formal training either as a philologist or in linguistic science. In fact, he never went to college. As he wrote in the preface to *Newspaper Days:* "At a time when the respectable bourgeois youngsters of my generation were college freshman, oppressed by simian sophomores and affronted with balderdash daily by chalky pedagogues, I was at large in a wicked seaport of half a million people, with a front seat at every public show, as free of the night as of the day, and getting earfuls and eyefuls of instruction in a hundred giddy arcana, none of them taught in schools."

That a man unarmored by any degrees or other insignia of formal learning wrote this great theoretical lexiographical work of more than 2,300 pages, called *The American Language*, with (at my estimate) no fewer than 10,000 footnotes was, and remains, an astounding intellectual feat. Apart from the knowledge entailed, the work tested Mencken's organizational powers. "An extraordinarily maddening manuscript" he called it. Elsewhere he referred to it as "that damned American language book," which, in a depressed moment, he likened to "a heavy, indigestible piece of cottage cheese"—and this was early in the project when a smaller book was planned. The immensity of the reading, the lavishness of the material, the amplitude of the correspondence required, the mere logistics of the filing—all, taken together, were enough to sink any intellectual enterprise. But Mencken kept at it to its completion, though coming near the conclusion of his second *Supplement* volume (his excellent biographer Marion Elizabeth Rodgers reports in *Mencken: The American Iconoclast* [2005]) he had come to feel something close to hostility at the thought of the language of his countrymen.

Readers of *The American Language* will feel nothing of the kind. Quite the reverse, they are more likely to feel wonder at the endless invention, comedy (conscious and unconscious), and richness of American English as set out by Mencken. The work is organized into twelve chapters: The Two Streams of English, The Materials of the Inquiry, The Beginnings of American, The Period of Growth, The Language Today, American and English, The Pronunciation of American, American Spelling, The Common Speech, Proper Names in America, American Slang, and The Future of the Language. The first *Supplement* volume added to the material in the first six of these chapters; the second *Supplement* volume to five of the final chapters. The *Supplements* provided more up-to-date matter—much of it supplied to Mencken by correspondents, both professional linguists and amateurs among them—corrected his errors in the original volume, and added the findings of his own voluminous reading. Various appendices and elaborate indices are included. English and American honorific titles are also taken up as are "the flowery fields of euphemism" used "to engaud lowly vocations" ("janitor" into "custodian," etc.), elevate products ("used" to "previously owned" cars), and perhaps death ("passing" and worse) above all. On the subject of death and euphemism, one imagines Mencken would have appreciated the joke about the McCormick Company going to court to sue against death being called the Grim Reaper; asked what he would prefer death be called, the company's attorney answered, "The International Harvester."

The distinction between the language spoken and written in America and England is one observed throughout Mencken's immense work. At the outset, English correctness reinforced by snobbery and further backed up by what Mencken calls "Anglomaniacs" prevailed over American latitudinarian inventiveness. In fact, as he points out, "Emerson and Poe wrote English English; so, too, Hawthorne, Thoreau, Longfellow and Holmes." Mencken nevertheless predicted, accurately, that American English would in time predominate over the language spoken and written in England. He made this prediction based on his view that the English of Americans "is much more honestly English in any sense that Shakespeare would have understood," and more so than the so-called Standard English of England, and this on the "very plausible grounds, that American is better on all counts—clearer, more rational, and above all, more charming." Logan Pearsall Smith, the American-born English essayist, brother-in-law to Bertrand Russell, had it right when he wrote that "it is chiefly in America—let us frankly recognize the fact—that the evolution of our language will now proceed . . . for in language it is the *fait accompli* that counts, and in the capacity for putting new words over, the Americans, if only because they have twice the population, are bound to win every time."

The roster of English writers who looked askance at American English is impressive. A number of them, I regret to have to report, are figures from my own pantheon of literary gods, among them Samuel Johnson ("the finicky and always anti-American Samuel Johnson" Mencken calls him), Charles Dickens, Mrs. Frances Trollope, Sydney Smith, John Ruskin, George Bernard Shaw, and H. W. Fowler, who held that "Americanisms are foreign words, and should be so treated." The pro-American side among the English, with Robert Bridges, Wyndham Lewis, and Virginia Woolf, is less impressive.

In the United States, the lineup against American English notably featured Henry James (who wasn't quite an American, but, as T. S. Eliot called him, "a European but of no known country") and Ambrose Bierce. On the pro-American side were James Fenimore Cooper, Walt Whitman, Mark Twain, and Sinclair Lewis. William Dean Howells found the difference between the English written and spoken by Americans and Englishmen, far from deplorable, highly desirable, and added that one has only to depart one's studies or editorial offices "to go into the stores and fields to find a rebirth of 'the spacious times of great Elizabeth' again."

An Americanism, wrote John S. Farmer, a linguist quoted by Mencken, "may be defined as a word or phrase, old or new, employed by general or respectable usage in America in a way not sanctioned by the best standards of the English language." Mencken's own criteria for Americanism are "first, its general uniformity throughout the country . . . secondly, its impatient disregard of rule and precedent, and hence its large capacity . . . for taking in new words and phrases and for manufacturing new locutions out of its own materials."

Throughout the pages of *The American Language* Mencken reminds us of American inventions, some formed by clipping off longer words, back-shortening, or back-formation. He provides the several instances of words formed from the American "-ize," "-ate," "-ify," "-acy," "-ous," and "-ment" endings; also words with an "-ery," "-ette," "-dom," "-ster," and other suffixes. Then there are the countless words formed out of pure imagination: "rough-house," "has-been," "bust," "duck" (not the animal), "scary," "classy," "tasty," "gumshoe," "nothin' doin'," "for keeps," and "billboard." Toss in the trade names that became generic words: "vaseline," "listerine," "kotex," "kleenex," "coke," and more. The terms from the domain of booze, from "hooch" to "bootlegger," from "chaser" to "bartender," including the word "booze" itself, are American inventions. Add in the borrowing from Spanish, Yiddish, German, Scandanavian, Chinese, and other immigrant groups. One could go on and on, and Mencken does, compiling lists of words numbering in the thousands, through the pages of his three volumes, remarking along the way on those characteristics that set the American off from the Englishman: "his bold and somewhat grotesque imagination, his contempt for dignified authority, his lack of aesthetic sensitiveness, his extravagant humor."

Many pages and footnotes in *The American Language* are devoted to etymology. No one is certain, for example, of the origin of that most internationally popular of all Americanisms, "O.K." Mencken provides a lengthy footnote on "hot dog," which is thought to derive from a vendor at the old New York Polo Grounds who was the first to heat the rolls for what until he came along were more popularly known as "weenies" or "frankfurters." The word "phony" is another Americanism without clear origin. Other words without known provenance include "hokum," "sundae," and "jazz," though the last is often taken to have been a synonym for sexual intercourse.

Which brings us to words that, in Mencken's phrase, "suggest blushful ideas." The most obvious is the room in which the toilet is installed.

Many are the synonyms for it, among them "john," "jakes," "donniker," "the plumbing," "necessary room," and "loo" (deriving from Waterloo). My own favorite, "the House of Commons," does not show up in Mencken's pages. Although no prude, Mencken largely takes a pass on the rich trove of words describing sex and the veritable thesaurus of words for the genitals, male and female. Only toward the close of his second *Supplement*, does he bring up the grand f-word, never spelling it out but noting that during World War II "it became an almost universal verb, and with *–ing* added, a universal adjective; another, beginning with *s,* ran a close second to it." Neither word, fair to say, has lost its vast popularity, and cable television has given them even wider currency.

Mencken expends many pages on proper names (also on American place-names). He lists the most common first and last names of his day in America. He takes up ethnic names, first and last. He notes that, during the strong wave of anti-German feeling during World War I, people who had the suffix "stein" in their last names changed the pronunciation to "steen" in the hope of not falling foul of this feeling. Front, or first, names are of course greatly subject to the winds of fashion. Two that have nearly disappeared since Mencken's day are "Bob," the short version for Robert, and "Dick," that for Richard. Today overwhelmingly Roberts are Robs or Robbys, Richards are Ricks or Richs. The Jewish boys' names of my own generation, Irving, Seymour, Norman, Arnold, Harvey, Ronald, Marvin, Melvin, Marshall—names, I have always thought, more fit for English hotels than human beings—have given way to Tyler, Tucker, Taylor, Madison, Belmont, and Scott. Even now there may well be an F. Scott Feldman applying to Princeton. On the distaff side, there are all those Brittanys, Tiffanys, Brandys, and Ashleys. The only thing I can recall from Nora Ephron's novel *Heartburn* is that the heroine's unfaithful husband claims to have dated "the first Jewish Kimberly." Who can say, a Kelly Rabinowitz may even now be walking the streets.

Interesting distinctions and definitions are in play throughout the pages of *The American Language*. Mencken sets out the distinctions among "imbeciles," "idiots," and "morons," among "hobos," "tramps," and "bums," and among "slang," "argot," and "cant." He gives several definitions his own spin. "To go Hollywood," for example, is "to abandon the habits and ideas

of civilization and embrace the Levantine life of the richer movie folks."
One of the definitions of "professor," at least as used in the United States
of Mencken's day, and one as a university teacher I myself always favored, is
the man who plays piano in a bordello.

A few heroic figures emerge from the pages of *The American Language*. Mark Twain is frequently cited for his excellent ear for Americanism; so, too, Ring Lardner. A linguist named Louise Pound is relied upon
as an authority. The work of Otto Jespersen in this realm is uniformly
praised. Walter Winchell, one of what Mencken calls "America's keyhole
columnists," who along with *Time* and *Variety* specialize in "low aesthetic
visibility," is nonetheless credited with many inventions: "infanticipating" (for expecting a child), "debutramp," "Reno-vated" (for contemplating a divorce), the "Hardened Artery" (for Broadway), and many more.
John Galsworthy, Arnold Bennett, and Arthur Conan Doyle are cited
for misusing Americanisms in their fiction.

Among the lengthy lists comparing English and American words
and expressions, setting out the special language of various trades from
soda jerks to steelworkers, recording the infiltration of the everyday language of England by Americanism, noting the manifold oddities and
idiosyncrasies of a language always on the move, what keeps the pages
of *The American Language* humming, the work's occasional longueurs
tolerable, are its many Menckenisms. Mencken was death on pretension, and especially on people with shaky pretensions to learning. He
refers to political science as "the lugubrious discipline." Freudianism
gets the back of his hand, mentioned in a footnote, to the effect that
"the popular craze . . . struck the United States in 1912 or thereabout,
in succession to Coueism, the Emmanuel Movement, and paper-bag
cookery." As for the American Ph.D., in England "it is seldom if ever
given to persons trained in the congeries of quackeries which passes,
in the American universities, under the name of 'education.'" He cites
a book put out by the Modern Language Association as providing "a
sufficiently depressing proof of the stupidity of the learned." He writes
that in American colleges and high schools "there is no faculty so weak
as the English faculty," which is "the common catch-all for aspirants to
the birch who are too lazy or too feeble in intelligence to acquire any

sort of exact knowledge, and the professional incompetence of its typical ornament is matched only by his hollow cocksureness." In a passing reference to Emory University he mentions "the students there incarcerated."

Mencken never comes out directly to announce his own views about language, but these are easily enough surmised. He himself never wrote other than clear, clean English, highlighted at times by a baroque vocabulary and always informed by a comic vision. (Who else but Mencken could refer to the work of funeral parlors as "human taxidermy," to drinkers as the "bibuli," to cussing as "sulphurous language," to the practice of medicine as "leechcraft.") He describes himself at one point as a "purist," but he was a purist who appreciated inventive language, useful neologisms, tangy slang, new words required for medical and scientific discoveries. Above all he understood, as he put it in his second *Supplement*, that "language does not follow a rigid pattern but is extraordinarily flexible and changeable," and any attempt at "fixing a language in a groove is cherished by pedants." In the end he viewed our language as the music accompanying the grand American show.

Some years ago a man with theatrical interests and a heavy wallet approached me with the idea of my writing a one-man show called *Mencken Alive!* "People are always wondering," he said, "what Mencken if he were alive would think or say about nutty things going on today." Nice to think there may still be some people around still wondering, but, whether there are or not, I believe one can sense how Mencken might view most of the changes in American language since his death in 1956.

Mencken is not likely to have been impressed by the slang of the 1960s—"not my bag," "just doing my thing," and the rest—which died early in the 1970s. The dreary drug scene has left only the single word "high." The language bestowed by digital culture—"reset," "default position," "google it"—are unlikely to have wowed him. That the phrase "no problem" has largely replaced "you're welcome" he is unlikely to have viewed as an advance in refinement, while the replacement of "problem" by the word "issue" (as in "I have a knee issue"), causing the loss of the useful word "issue" as an idea or subject in the flux of controversy, would not have come as heartening news to him.

Nor would the word "fun" as an adjective—as in "fun time," "fun place," "fun couple"—have struck Mencken as a happy advance in the language. If someone were to offer him the all-too-commonplace, always perfectly perfunctory salutation "Have a nice day," he figures to have replied, "Thank you but I have other plans." As for contemporary slang, he might have approved "kick back" and "chill out," but be less than enamored of "rock on" and far from awed by "awesome." The use of "community"—as in "artistic community," "Hispanic community," "intelligence community"—would probably have struck him as overdone; and the designation of a "homeless community" as no less than a sick joke.

Political correctness would surely have appalled him. As early as the late 1940s he was on the attack against "saviors of the downtrodden" who forbade Jewish and Negro (as the respectable word then was) jokes. He doesn't figure to have gone any easier on those who wish to save the sensibilities of all women, every minority, and people whose sexual interests he described as "non-Euclidian." He would not have been amused by all the *he and she*-ing, *him or her*-ing ruining the rhythm of academic sentences, which usually don't have all that much rhythm to begin with, though he might be amused in a contemptuous way at the increasingly popular I'm-all-right-Jack sentences that put the feminine pronoun where the masculine is usually found: "Every long-distance truck driver knows that *she* figures to be up against tough winter weather." His reaction to such lilting phrases as "gender norms" would have been the very reverse of delighted. He would shake his head at the rise of the word "guys" to address men and women, owing to waiters and waitresses (I mean "servers," of course) and others being fearful of saying "ladies." That he himself might be described as an "icon" or "iconic figure" he would have viewed as an insult to his standing as a famous agnostic.

What Mencken figures to have found most objectionable is the soft language of psycho-babble that has resulted in all that "reaching out," and "thanks for sharing," and the use of "journey" as a metaphor (so that cancer, depression, or whatever else you happen to have round the house is a *journey*.) A "caring person" does not figure to be someone in whose company he would be caught dead. As for "caregiver," he would have preferred the English word "minder" to describe the costly help hired to tend to the ill or elderly. The heavy overuse of "input," "feedback," and "focus" (in place of "concentrate") would not have been his idea of charming additions to the language. I could go on—and on, and on. . . .

Ah, me, Henry Louis Mencken, perhaps it's best thou shouldn'st be alive at this hour.

University of Chicago Days

(2017)

"Everyone was neurotic, weird, bizarre—it was paradise."

Mike Nichols

THE FORTUITOUS—happening by accident or chance and not by design, never to be confused with the fortunate—plays a larger role in most people's lives than they might think. Certainly, it has in my own.

When I was in the army, stationed at Fort Hood, Texas, I learned that there were openings for typists at recruiting stations in Little Rock, Arkansas, and Shreveport, Louisiana. I applied, and one morning soon after was told that I had been selected for one of these jobs. I met with a Southern staff sergeant, a man I judged to be not long on patience, who said, "Take your choice, Shreveport or Little Rock." I had a nanosecond to weigh my options. Shreveport: Louisiana, good food, Catholic, possibly interesting illicit goings-on; Little Rock: Governor Faubus in power, politically volatile, closer to Chicago. "Little Rock, Sergeant," I said. Subsequently, in Little Rock, I met and married and had two children with my first wife. What, I have often wondered since, if I had said, "Shreveport, Sergeant?"

I had more time to think about going to the University of Chicago, but my thoughts about the place were scarcely more informed than my thoughts about Little Rock and Shreveport. Even though I lived in Chicago all my life, I had never seen the place, with its fake but nonetheless grand gray Gothic buildings. In Chicago one lived in one's neighborhood as if in a village, and my village—West Rogers Park, in the far north of the city—was as far from the University of Chicago yet still in Chicago as it was possible to be. The University of Chicago was reputed to be radical, some said "pinko," meaning vaguely Communist. This reputation derived, I learned much later, from the school's president, Robert Hutchins, making it clear that he wasn't going to be pushed around by Senator Joseph McCarthy and his crude anti-Communism. Hutchins had also eliminated the school's Big Ten football team and installed a program, known jokingly as Hutchins's Children's Crusade, that allowed students as young as 15 to matriculate at the university. The word "nerdy" had not yet come into existence; people who went to Chicago were in those days thought "brainy."

Brainy was the last thing I would ever have been called. A thoroughly uninterested high school student—I graduated 169 in a class of 211—my high-school years were spent playing basketball and tennis, pursuing girls, and establishing myself as a good guy, which is to say, as a genial screw-off. In those days, the University of Illinois in Champaign-Urbana, had, in effect, open enrollment, at least if you were a resident of the state. You could have three felonies and graduate last in your class and the school still had to take you—on probation, to be sure—but take you they did. So, without anything resembling study habits; having read no book of greater complexity than *The Amboy Dukes*; without a single intellectual interest; with no goal in mind but, hope against hope, to avoid flunking out; in 1955 I mounted the train at Chicago's 12th Street station for Champaign-Urbana.

I had never heard the term "liberal arts" until I arrived at the University of Illinois. And then I heard of it as a way out of majoring in business, which most of the boys I hung around with did, no doubt to establish their seriousness, both to their families and to themselves. I did know enough about myself to realize that the dreariness of accounting courses and the rest of it would have paralyzed me with boredom. ("Lloydie," the successful immigrant father of a friend of mine is supposed to have said to his son, who evinced an interest in accounting, "don't be a *schmuck*. You don't study accounting. You hire an accountant.")

My first-year courses at the University of Illinois included Biology, French, Rhetoric (really freshman composition), physical education, and

ROTC, the latter two being requirements at a land-grant college. Biology in those pre-DNA days meant little more than distinguishing among and memorizing the phyla. French meant memorizing, too—irregular verbs and the rest. I made it through Rhetoric by steering clear of anything tricky; and tricky at that time meant using a semicolon or dash or attempting a sentence longer than twelve words. I got mostly Bs.

Bs were good enough to get me into the University of Chicago. This was in part because my generation—those of us born late in the Depression—was a small population cohort, so small that the universities actually wanted us. Then, too, Chicago, for reasons I've mentioned, was not a particularly popular place for undergraduates. When I was there I believe there were fewer than 2,000 undergraduates alongside more than 6,000 graduate and professional students.

I began that summer (1956) at the University of Chicago taking what was called the Math Course. The course itself, I should say, was most impressive. The first two thirds were pure logic in which no numbers were mentioned ("if p, then not q equals?"). The last third was analytical geometry, and, based on what one learned in the first two thirds, seemed easy.

The College at the University of Chicago comprised 14 year-long core courses, in each of which one took a single comprehensive examination, known as "comps," at the end of the year. (By the time I arrived at Chicago, one also had to declare a major outside the College.) Some kids were so well prepared and good at taking examinations that, during placement exams on entering the school, they "placed out," or got credit for, fully two years' worth of courses. No attendance was ever taken in any of the College courses. Essays might be assigned, but grades on them counted only to show students how they were doing. I recall no quizzes. Most mystifying of all, one's teachers, like tutors at Oxford and Cambridge, did not grade students. Something called the College's Examiner's Office did. This simultaneously removed the whole matter of playing up—sucking up—to teachers, and it gave one's grade a more objective feel.

At the University of Illinois, I had been a member of a fraternity, Phi Epsilon Pi, the leading Jewish fraternity on campus. Fraternities and sororities in those days at most schools were strictly segregated by religion, an arrangement about which no one complained. The University of Chicago had nine fraternities and no sororities whatsoever. I moved into the Phi Kappa Psi house, not as a member but as a boarder, because an acquaintance of mine who was a member told me the fraternity had plenty of extra rooms, which it rented out for $35 a month. (Tuition at the University of Chicago in those days was $690 a year; at the University of Illinois it was $90 a semester.)

Phi Psi was a shambles, less a fraternity than a hot-sheet joint. People moved in and out. A fellow in medical school lived there with a beautiful biracial girlfriend with the wonderful name of Arizona Williams, who audited the occasional course at the university and was said to dance at a black-and-tan club (where blacks and whites could mingle) on the edge of the Loop. Another graduate student, working on a Ph.D. in biochemistry, lived with his fiancée and a German Shepherd. A few fellows at Phi Kappa Psi were in their mid-twenties and had dropped out of school but didn't want to leave the university's Hyde Park neighborhood, an enclave, an island, of culture in philistine Chicago. Years later, I had a call from a man named Robert Lucas, a Nobel Prize-winner in Economics, asking me for a donation for our class gift. "What do you mean 'class?'" I said. "There were no 'classes' at the University of Chicago. You entered at 15 and left at 27, often without a degree."

A scruffy bohemianism obtained among University of Chicago students in those days. On campus an even moderately well-dressed person would have looked strikingly out of place. A militant unkemptness ruled, as if to divagate from the pursuit of truth and beauty for the mere niceties of respectable grooming would demonstrate one's peurility. The university, I used to say, had a single quota: among undergraduates only four attractive young women were allowed in at any time. A joke of the day had it that a panty raid on Foster Hall (the women's dormitory) yielded only a field jacket and a pair of combat boots.

In later life I met a number of my teachers at the University of Chicago—a few sent me manuscripts for *The American Scholar* when I was the editor there—and none recognized me as a former student. No reason they should have. My classroom strategy was to hide out. Not coming from a bookish home, I did my best to conceal my ignorance, which was substantial, and looked above all to avoid embarrassing myself. The possibilities for embarrassment were manifold. Had you not seen nor heard them before, how would you have pronounced the names Thales, Proust, Wagner? No doubt wrongly.

Most of my classmates seemed confident in their views, aggressive in their opinions. Many of them were New Yorkers, and, it later occurred to me, were probably reading the *Nation* and the *New Republic* from about the age of 13. Their parents and friends argued about Leon Trotsky, Mikhail Bakunin, Max Shachtman, the Moscow Trials, the Nazi-Soviet Pact. In my family politics wasn't a serious subject; all politicians were crooks until proven innocent, which, in Chicago, few were. Many of them had doubtless been in psychotherapy. Many among them also had a fair amount of musical culture, whereas musical comedy was as high as musical culture reached in West Rogers Park.

By my second year at the University of Chicago, I had acquired a modest cultural literacy. I remember sitting in a modern poetry class taught by Elder Olson, and his mentioning Baudelaire. By then I knew that Charles Baudelaire was a French poet, nineteenth century, dark in subject matter, author of *Les Fleurs du Mal*—and that exhausted my knowledge of Baudelaire. Olson began to chant, *"Hypocrite lecteur!—mon frere, mon semblable ... "* when he was joined in his chant by Martha Silverman, the girl sitting next to me. Which meant Miss Silverman not only knew Baudelaire's poetry, but had it by memory and in French. At that moment I felt the sharp stab of hopelessness, and wondered whether they might be taking job applications at a nearby Shell station.

Among students at the University of Chicago brilliance not solidity seemed to be the goal. George Steiner, Allan Bloom, Robert Silvers, and Susan Sontag might stand in as representative Chicago graduates: each brilliant, all crucially flawed. I never tried for brilliance myself, and wouldn't have come close to achieving it if I had. My body may have been in the classroom, but my mind frequently deserted it. I remember concentrating a fair amount of time on the perilously long ash of Elder Olson's cigarettes. Another teacher might remark on the way one's eye follows a certain sweep in a painting, though my eye never did. A teacher might set out eight reasons for the Renaissance, and I wondered what possessed him to buy that hopeless necktie. For grades I received chiefly

Cs with a light scattering of Bs, and, best as memory serves, not a single A. I have since come to take a perhaps unseemly delight in great figures in literature and philosophy who were less than stellar students, some indeed dropouts: a roster that includes Blaise Pascal, Leo Tolstoy, Henry James, Paul Valéry, F. Scott Fitzgerald, and others. Mike Nichols, from whom I take my epigraph, entered the University of Chicago in 1950 as a pre-med student, and dropped out in 1953 without a degree.

I did better outside the classroom with the bookish offerings at the university. One of the best things about the College was that no textbooks were used. So one didn't read that "Freud said . . . ," "Plato held . . . ," "Marx stipulated . . . ," "J.S. Mill believed . . . ." Instead one read Freud, Plato, Marx, and Mill. Heady stuff, for a 19-year with only *A Stone for Danny Fisher, The Hoods,* and *Knock on Any Door* under his belt. I remember the deep aura of gloom I felt while reading Freud's *Civilization and Its Discontents* and the excitement of noting the dazzling connections made by Max Weber in *The Protestant Ethic and the Spirit of Capitalism.*

Everywhere through the undergraduate curriculum at Chicago in those days one everywhere ran into Aristotle and Plato: the *Poetics*, the *Rhetoric*, the *Ethics*, the *Politics*, the *Phaedrus*, the *Symposium*, the *Crito*, the *Apology*. When it came time to declare a major, I decided on English, only to learn that the university's English Department in those years was heavily Aristotelian in its approach to literature.

Harvard, it was said, was tougher to get into than the University of Chicago, but Chicago was tougher to get out of. (Another saying had it that the University of Chicago was where fun went to die.) No soft spots anywhere for an undergraduate in those years. In the English Department, which might have been thought such a soft spot, undergraduate students, along with their regular course work, were examined at the end of their junior and senior years on two extracurricular reading lists that contained perhaps 75 items each. The items on the lists were precisely those that any young person should prefer, if at all possible, to avoid reading: Hobbes's *Leviathan*, Milton's *Paradise Regained*, Spenser's *The Faerie Queen*, Richardson's *Pamela*, Locke's *Second Treatise on Civil Government*. A better organized student than I might have read them over the regular academic quarters;

I needed to forfeit my summer vacations to do so. In fact, I only finished my second, or senior, reading list while in the army, and took the examination on it on a pool table at Headquarters Company at Fort Hood, proctored by an ROTC second lieutenant from Alabama, the passing of which allowed me to graduate, A.B. *in absentia*, from the university in 1959.

What the University of Chicago taught, even to a student with little preparedness and a wandering mind, was a standard of seriousness. This standard continued long after my departure from the school. In my early thirties I became a close friend of Edward Shils—I would not have been prepared for him any earlier—for decades one of the great figures at the university. I recall him saying, "You know, Joseph, I fear that my colleagues on the Committee on Social Thought labor under the misapprehension that Richard Rorty is an intelligent man." (This at a time when every university in the country was seeking Rorty's services.) On another occasion, Edward said, apropos Hannah Arendt, "No great *chachemess* [wise woman], our Hannah." Toward the end of his career Edward brought Arnaldo Momigliano, the great historiographer of the ancient world, to teach at the University of Chicago. After the loss of a gifted graduate student to Princeton, Arnaldo, himself Jewish, noted: "A Jewish boy. The Ivy League beckons. He is gone." Teachers such as Arnaldo, Christian Mackauer, Enrico Fermi, Louis Gottschalk, Leo Strauss—all of them Europeans—gave the University of Chicago a cosmopolitan tone and serious feeling unavailable anywhere else.

No trivial books were taught at the university during my time there. The only books by living writers I encountered were in a course on the modern novel by Morton Dauwen Zabel: *Howards End* by E.M. Forster, *Brighton Rock* by Graham Greene, and *A Handful of Dust* by Evelyn Waugh. This was of course long before multiculturalism, feminist studies, political correctness, and the rest kicked in, and so there was no need to teach, or for students to read, secondary writers in order to show they were on the side of the progressive political angels.

The University of Chicago in those years favored, in Max Weber's distinction, "soul-saving" over "skill-acquiring" education. If there were then undergraduates majoring in economics, I never met them. The university I knew in those days seemed outside the orbit of capitalism itself (though it would go on to produce a dozen Nobel Prize-winners in economics). A graduate business school was then housed in the main campus quadrangle, but in the era before the MBA became the golden key to open corporate doors, it seemed anomalous, beside the point. The knock on the University of Chicago Law School then was that it was "too theoretical," which really meant too philosophical; if one's aim was to get a job with a Chicago law firm, it was said one did better to go to Northwestern.

Job-getting wasn't what the University of Chicago was about. Only careers in the arts, scientific research, politics practiced at the highest level, with, at second remove, the teaching of artists, scientists, and statesmen also being acceptable, were thought worthy of serious people. A conventional success ethos, such as George Santayana discovered early in the last century while visiting at Yale, was never in force at Chicago. To be lashed to money-making, even if it resulted in becoming immensely wealthy, made a person little more than one of Aristotle's natural slaves, a peasant raking gravel in the sun. No surprise, then, that great economic success has not been notable among the school's graduates. Not without reason has the University of Chicago, compared with other major universities, had a comparatively small endowment.

In the mid-1960s, while working at *Encyclopaedia Britannica*, I would occasionally meet Robert Hutchins, under whose youthful presidency (begun in 1929 when he was 30 years old), the radical institution that was the University of Chicago College had been set in motion, and found him an immensely handsome but weary and sad man. Hutchins had earlier ardently wished to become a Supreme Court Justice, a job Franklin Delano Roosevelt dangled before him but cruelly withdrew. He had instead since 1959 been running the Ford-Foundation-Fund-for-the-Republic-sponsored think tank in Santa Barbara, California, called The Center for the Study of Democratic Institutions—also known derisively as The Leisure of the Theory Class—which wasted its time on such hopeless projects as devising a constitution for a world government. At lunch one day at the Tavern Club in Chicago, Hutchins, knowing I had gone to the University of Chicago, asked me if I knew whether they had restored football there, a remark reflecting his sense of defeat and disappointment and suggesting that his one great accomplishment, founding the College with its Great Books-centered learning, had also come to nothing. I believe they have restored football, though on a modest basis; formerly the university was in the Big Ten.

I should have, but neglected, to assure him that, as far as I was concerned, it had come to a great deal, at least for me. Under the influence of Hutchins's College at the University of Chicago, I set out on a life of high culture, which I may never have attained yet never regretted. Because of the values fostered at Chicago, I determined to become a writer with a confidence in the rightness of my decision that I was unlikely to find anywhere else. Looked upon now, I realize I owe the University of Chicago more than I can hope ever to repay.

Frittering Prizes

(1997)

I F WRITERS CAN BE SAID to have a leading hobby, that hobby is the collecting of grievances. How nicely they pile up, like a child's collection of Beanie Babies, one atop the other, a writer's grievances against his publisher(s), his editors, his agent, of course his reviewers and critics, his fellow writers, all nice and personal. But then there are the impersonal grievances, and leading this category is the batch of grievances writers feel for not having won the prizes they felt they richly deserved, especially considering the swine who have won them.

The prizes writers feel they deserve is a whole comedy unto itself. How great a comedy I first began to realize when some years ago I read, in Burton Bernstein's biography of James Thurber, that Thurber, this most minor of writers, late in his career, was disappointed afresh each year upon discovering that he had not won the Nobel Prize.

But even winning it probably isn't good enough. The number of prizes given for writing is plentiful, even extravagant. The standard prizes—the Nobel, the Pulitzer, the Bollingen, the Lilly, the Lannan, the Tanning and the International, the National Book Award, the National Book Critics Circle, the National Medal of Arts, the American Academy of Arts and Letters Awards, the PEN prizes, the Booker and Whitbread in England, the Prix Goncourt in France—are only, as in the old joke about the anti-Semite, the tip of the greenberg.

I often read the "News Notes" at the back of *Poetry* magazine to discover prizes given to poets, and it turns out there are scores of them, some bringing fairly heavy bread, such as the $50,000 Kingsley Tufts Poetry Award. Many prizes are impressively specialized. Only a few weeks ago I discovered the Fortabat Foundation Prize for the best first novel by an Argentine. In *Publishers Weekly*, I learned about the Rea Award for the short story: $30,000. The *New York Times* recently carried small ads from publishers congratulating three different authors for winning the PEN/Ralph Manheim Medal for Translation, the PEN/Martha Albrand Award for First Non-fiction, and something called the Robert E. Kennedy Book Award, now in its seventeenth year, given, I take it, for nonfiction. So many are the prizes floating around that contemporary literature sometimes begins to seem like one of those progressive schools in which everyone gets a prize, even the child who fouls himself in the most pleasing pattern.

Prizes of course catch writers in that ample soft place between their greed and their vanity. As a sad case in point, I offer Exhibit A: myself. I returned home late one afternoon to find a woman's voice on my answering machine, conveying the following sweet message: "Mr. Epstein, I am calling to inform you that your book of stories, *The Goldin Boys*, has won the Edward Lewis Wallant Prize. Congratulations. We are all delighted and hope you will be, too. I shall call back tomorrow with details. Thank you."

Well, thought I, here is a dandy way to end a day. I knew of Edward Lewis Wallant as the author of *The Pawnbroker*, a powerful Holocaust novel made into a dark and painful movie starring Rod Steiger. That Hollywood was connected to Wallant's name set fire to my own rather easily inflamed financial imagination. Wondering how much the Edward Lewis Wallant Prize was worth, I began estimating it at $5,000, and by bedtime, gathering the covers around me, I had it up to a pleasantly warming $25,000. Twenty-five grand would be a help, yes, no doubt about it.

The next morning when I spoke to the woman who had called, I learned that the jury who awarded my book the prize had two members of whom I had never heard and one whom I heartily disliked. I also learned that the prize itself was to be given at a luncheon in Hartford, Connecticut. The woman said that they were "very excited" about my excellent book having won the Wallant Prize. "I am, too," I said, adding, in what I hoped was a sufficiently casual tone of voice, "Oh, by the way, what is the amount of the prize?" A slight clearing of my respondent's throat prefaced her announcing, "$250." Shit, I thought, blithely.

To make a short story mildly excruciating, I later learned that, in connection with receiving the Edward Lewis Wallant Prize, a speech was expected of me; that I could not get a plane in and out of Hartford in the same day, and so would have to stay the weekend; and that my host and hostess, who gave the luncheon in connection with the prize, expected me to be at their call in a way that made me feel rather less a distinguished prize-winner than hired help.

In the end, I chose to forgo the Edward Lewis Wallant Prize. I said I couldn't give up the weekend, not to mention the time it would take for me to compose an intelligible acceptance speech. So instead of winning the Edward Lewis Wallant Prize, I won the lifelong enmity of the donors of the prize, who soon thereafter wrote in to cancel their subscription to *The American Scholar*, the magazine I then edited, saying that they had rarely met a more miserable human being than yours truly. Another day, I always say, another dolor.

I managed to keep my only other literary prize. In 1989, I won something called the Heartland Prize, for non-fiction, for a book of my literary essays, given by the *Chicago Tribune*, which brought with it a small glass statue of a book and $5,000. As it happened, my mother, then still alive, called just after I learned about it, and so I told her that I had just won $5,000 from the *Trib*. "Oh," she said, "we get that stuff in the mail all the time. I just throw it out."

Some wise person once said that, if someone tells you that you are the best at what you do, ask him whom he thinks is second best, which is guaranteed to restore your humility straightaway. Something similar goes for literary prizes. The questions to ask here are: Who were on the jury, and Who have won the prize before? The answers will generally return you to normal hat size instanter. Far too many hacks serve on prize juries and no American literary prize now exists that hasn't been sullied by having been given to at least mediocrity, out of either a lapse in taste or a desire to seem politically correct.

I have served on a few literary juries. The one that pleased me most was that for the Joseph Bennett Award, given by the *Hudson Review* in the name of one of its former editors. The year I was on the jury the prize went to Andrei Sinyavsky, who wrote under the name Abram Tertz and who had survived the hardest of hard time in the Soviet Gulag. I have been a member of the jury for the Ingersoll Prizes, given by the Rockford Institute, which I was able to win for Jacques Barzun, who, for his own reasons, decided to turn it and its $15,000 check down. One year, too, I was appointed, at a fee of $1,000, a nominator for the MacArthur Fellows—the Big Macs, or so-called genius grants. I don't recall how many people I nominated, but none won.

Please note that none of the above juries involved any real work. Real work here means lots of reading. Being on a literary jury often entails giving up one's regular reading life in order to read the work of the writers up for prizes. I was once asked to be a member of a Pulitzer Prize jury for fiction. I said no without hesitation, for three reasons: because the Pulitzer Prizes in fiction have been very ragged, not to say wretched; because of the amount of reading involved; and because Pulitzer juries can be vetoed by the Pulitzer Prize Advisory Board, which has frequently done just that, vetoing prizes for, among others, Sinclair Lewis's *Main Street* in 1921, Thomas Pynchon's *Gravity's Rainbow* in 1974, and Norman Maclean's *A River Runs Through It* in 1977.

Perhaps the best thing a Pulitzer juryman can do is keep one of the usual suspects from getting the prize. Gertrude Himmelfarb, a friend of mine who was on the Pulitzer jury for biography some years ago recounted to me walking into the jury's first meeting and announcing, "Look here, boys, we aren't going to do the obvious thing and give this prize to Ronald Steel, are we?" Steel had written a much-fawned-over biography of Walter Lippmann that was the obvious favorite for that year, but with my friend's remark, Steel's boat was immediately dead in the water. The Pulitzer for biography that year went elsewhere.

More recently, I was asked to be on the jury for the National Book Awards. A small fee was offered—the exact sum, I believe, of the Edward Lewis Wallant Prize—for which one was expected to read, or at least intelligently skim, more than 200 novels and short-story collections. The prospect of all those jiffy bags coming into my apartment seemed depressing in the extreme. Thank you, I said, but no thank you.

I wonder, though, if I have not been too selfish in declining such jobs. Good work can be done in serving on such juries. In 1967, Hilton Kramer served on a National Book Awards jury and was able to win the prize for criticism for William Troy, a critic of the highest seriousness who had died long before and whose book was published by the rather obscure Rutgers University Press.

Learning that the prize was to go to William Troy, one of the officials for the National Book Awards came in to inform the jury that the prize could not be given posthumously and asked that they provide another book and (living) author. The Kramer jury refused, saying that if the winner weren't William Troy then there would be no winner that year in their category. The official backed down, and the prize went to the late (though still splendid) Troy. I remember thinking at the time that this was a victory for high culture, for the good guys, for artistic integrity generally.

The reason I thought this is that, at the time, who won the National Book Awards seemed very important. By 1967, the prize had gone only to good writers; no mediocre or fake books had yet won it. It was a record worth preserving. If a book, especially a novel, won the National Book Award, it meant it was a work of substance. Winning it could make a writer's reputation. *The Moviegoer*, Walker Percy's first and best novel, had been a commercial and even a critical flop, but it redeemed itself and its author by winning the National Book Award for 1962. National Book Awards were worth having because they were given with real care. It all mattered, greatly.

Now take out a sheet of paper. Quick quiz. What book won the National Book Award last year? Who won the Pulitzer for fiction? Name the last three winners of the Nobel Prize for Literature? Go to your room, you idiot. I'll join you there in a moment, for I don't have the complete answers to these questions either. Cultivated chaps and chapesses though we are, why are we all so ignorant about this?

The reason is that none of these prizes, as the Victorians used to say, signify. Somehow there is a feeling that the giving of prizes in literature is, if not quite rigged, something damn close to it. It all seems a bit irrelevant, pointless, peripheral, the intellectual equivalent of the Special Olympics. The handing out of literary prizes seems, as F. R. Leavis once said of the Sitwells, to have more to do with the history of publicity than with the history of literature.

Some of these prizes have been vastly overrated to begin with. The novelist and critic William Gass gets nicely worked up at the Pulitzer Prize for fiction, arguing that it "takes dead aim at mediocrity and almost never misses." There is an element of hit and miss in many awards in the arts, Gass claims, "yet the Pulitzer Prize in fiction is almost pure miss. The award is not batting a fine .300 or an acceptable .250. It is nearly zero for the season." Only rarely is it given when it might do a writer some good; it usually passes by any original work, and when it is given to important artists, it is usually for their weaker books and long after it might be of any use to them. During their lifetimes, the Pulitzer bypassed Theodore Dreiser, John Dos Passos, F. Scott Fitzgerald, Sherwood Anderson, Thomas Wolfe, Nathaniel West, and Flannery O'Connor.

When a literary prize bungles things so often, it loses its cachet, as the Pulitzer for fiction long ago did. The one exception here may be the Nobel for Literature. This prize itself began on a great bungle by not going, in 1901, its first year, to Leo Tolstoy. Tolstoy was beyond any question the world's greatest living writer and the perfect candidate, especially given the phrase in Alfred Nobel's will about the prize going to writers of "idealistic tendency." Apparently, everyone on the committee that year assumed that everyone else would vote for Tolstoy, and so they decided not to waste their votes on the obvious. As a result, the winner was the redoubtable Sully Prudhomme, the French poet best known today as the man who won the Nobel Prize meant for Leo Tolstoy.

The Nobel was also not given to Henry James, James Joyce, Marcel Proust, Ezra Pound, and Virginia Woolf. Closer to our own day, the Nobel Prize committee passed up Jorge Luis Borges, Vladimir Nabokov, and Graham Greene. Only one writer, Jean-Paul Sartre, ever turned the Nobel down. W. H. Auden is thought knowingly to have blown it by making some objectionable remarks about Dag Hammarskjold in an introduction to the latter's book, *Markings*. Auden's biographer, Humphrey Carpenter, recounts that not winning the Nobel Prize later became an obsession with Auden. "Toward the end of his life, Auden began to be preoccupied with not having won it, declaring that he would have liked it not for the honor but for the money—he said he would have used it to buy a new organ for the Kirchstetten church" near his final home in Austria.

The Nobel Prize must be the world's most remunerative prize—it is now worth well over a million dollars—but it also has the odd effect of making its recipients a little posthumous. Having won it, they find all other prizes come by way of an anticlimax. With the exception of Alexander Solzhenitsyn, very few of its recipients have produced better work after receiving it.

Other prizes also seem to have had the effect of freezing writers. Consider the MacArthur Fellowships, which in recent years seem to have gone less and less to conventional writers and more and more to multicultural exotics: a Thai chef who juggles flaming garlic on Native American reservations, that sort of thing. But earlier, when the fellowships did go to more writers than they do today, it seemed to cause its winners to write less, if not to cease writing altogether. Not a bad thing, really, especially since most MacArthur fellows weren't quite first-class, and most were too prolific to begin with.

Still, the only serious question about the MacArthur Fellowships, which can pay a recipient more than $625,000 over five years, is, Where's mine? A friend once told me that, in his role as a nominator, he had put me up for a Big Mac; and another friend sent me a copy of his four-page recommendation of me, in which he portrayed me as the natural successor to H. L. Mencken and Edmund Wilson but more wide-ranging and deeper than either. It was heavy-handed puffery, but—who knew—maybe the MacArthur Foundation might believe it.

In those days, the head of the Fellowship Program was a nice man well-named Kenneth Hope. I received several messages from him that year; you cannot know what it is like to return home and discover a message on your answering machine from Ken Hope of the MacArthur Foundation. "Ah, Hope," I would say to myself. "This is it. My fellowship is ready, my ship has come in, I can at long last get rid of this cardboard belt." But it never happened.

By now there are a number of people who make more than a nice living out of the literary-prize racket and its attendant scares. The mind is a great wanderer, and in weak moments my own often imagines the mail of the late Toni Morrison, filled with requests for $ 25,000 talks, still more prizes (to go with her Pulitzer, Nobel, and the rest), honorary degrees, and God knows what other little bijoux. The poet Rita Dove is another harvester of prizes. "Rita Dove, the former poet laureate of the United States," a recent *New York Times* story began, "thought there could be no surprises left for her after her appointment to that august post in 1993." Well, you will I know be shocked to learn, she was wrong, for in 1996 she won something called a Heinz Award for $250,000, given to "people who make a difference in their chosen fields." What this difference was went unmentioned in the *Times* story.

Part of all this is, of course, affirmative action. Prize-giving was complicated enough before politics obtruded into it so heavily as it now has. The Nobel has often been awarded geopolitically, or multiculturally on the global level; it goes to a Third World writer one year, to an Eastern European writer the next, and only then to some usually predictable Western writer the year after.

Panels and juries for most literary prizes currently have to be made up of sufficient percentages of minorities, as they are called, and prizes, too, it is understood, must be parceled out the same way. "The only qualification a judge ought to have had is unimpeachable good taste," writes William Gass, "which immediately renders irrelevant such puerile concerns as skin color, sex, and origin." Alas, if Gass thinks this is any longer a serious possibility, I'd like to show him some real estate, perhaps something deep in the Everglades.

Gass says that some writers have been penalized by the Pulitzers for being "known to have the wrong politics." I don't think there can be any doubt about this. Conservatives, with a few notable exceptions, really need not apply for prizes given by PEN, or the American Academy of Arts and Letters, and many other institutions besides. An accomplished novelist such as Mark Helprin probably ended his own chances for any literary prizes by having written a few speeches for Bob Dole.

"I like to believe I could have voted a poetry prize to Marianne Moore," Gass writes, "even though I know she once wore a Nixon button." This has not always been the way things worked. Fifty years ago, a mainly left-liberal group of poets approved the Bollingen Poetry Prize for Ezra Pound, after his having given clearly anti-Semitic radio broadcasts for Mussolini during World War II that left him susceptible to charges of treason, which he was able to elude only through, in effect, a plea of insanity.

At the time of the Bollingen award to Pound, there was still a small body of men and women who constituted what was somewhat pretentiously known as the Republic of Letters. Its members were those who were genuinely devoted to literature, who recognized the real thing when they saw it, lived for it, and could themselves produce it. Their connection to literature was the main thing about them, surmounting their social class, race, sex, and certainly their politics. How else explain that the reactionary politics of so many of the chief figures of literary modernism did not deprive them of immense admiration!

No special pleading made membership in this Republic of Letters possible. One was either a true writer, major or minor, or one wasn't. Prizes were awarded, not so lavishly as now, but they were never the mark of a writer's true stature. What gave a writer his stature was the opinion of his contemporaries—that small number of men and women who also knew the real thing when they saw it.

Today, no matter how wretched a writer, he can usually point to his having won a prize or fellowship or award of some sort. The breakdown in standards across the board in intellectual life is represented in good part by the vast number of available prizes that don't really find worthy recipients and yet—what the hell—are given out anyhow.

Too many prizes are given in the United States generally, of course. We have Emmy Awards for best soap opera acting. There are Rona Jaffe Foundation Writers' Awards for younger writers, Cable Ace Awards for the best programs on cable television, Grammys and scores of other prizes for music. We live in a country, let it not be forgotten, with a Rock 'n' Roll Hall of Fame.

In the best of all worlds, literary prizes would help set standards for excellent work, reward genuine achievement, and publicize originality. As now constituted, literary prizes seem to do none of these things.

Their real point is commerce, the stroking of writers, and the boosting of morale within the publishing business.

As for the stroking of writers, the need for this is endless, and how better than through prizes? Writing to Gore Vidal in 1965, the novelist Louis Auchincloss mentioned the chances of winning the Pulitzer Prize for his novel *The Rector of Justin*: "Do I care? Of course, I care. I have reached the age when I want prizes, any prizes. I want silver cups with gold lining such as I never won at potato races in children's parties; I want gold stars; I want ribbons." The Pulitzer that year went to Shirley Ann Grau.

For writers, prizes represent official praise. But for good writers, even the greatest prizes can't finally do the job. Thomas Mann, a Nobel laureate, used to refer to praise as "Vitamin P," which, as his diaries make plain, he preferred to take in large quantities. Mann knew a thing or two about praise, but the most important thing he knew is that, for the good writer, "praise will never subdue skepticism." Take it from an almost Edward Lewis Wallant Prize winner: true, all too sadly true.

The Tzaddick of the Intellectuals

(2017)

MY FIRST CONTACT with Leon Wieseltier was by letter. The year was 1977. Written on Balliol College, Oxford, letter-head stationery, the letter informed me that I was a force for superior culture in America, one of the few contemporary intellectuals worthy of respect, and through my writing the all but single-handed savior of *Commentary* magazine. The author of the letter, he went on to report, was 25, had gone to Columbia, thence on a fellowship to Oxford, and would be spending the next few years as a member of the Society of Fellows at Harvard. He ended by wondering if, were he to shore up one day in Chicago, we might meet for lunch.

As a scribbler for small-circulation magazines, my threshold for praise may be a touch or two higher than most people's, but even I did not believe the extravagant praise in young Leon Wieseltier's letter. Still, as one grows older, and I was then 40, one is pleased to have the praise of the young. Such praise leads to the doubtless delusionary hope that one's own work will live on after one has departed the planet. I wrote to Leon Wieseltier, thanking him for his generous words and telling him that, yes, sure, should he ever find himself in Chicago, he was to let me know, so that we might meet.

Six or so months later, I received another letter from Wieseltier informing me that he planned to be in Chicago in six days and wondered if we might have that lunch. The letterhead was now that of the Harvard Society of Fellows. I wrote back to say yes, of course, and gave him the address of a Chinese restaurant where I thought we might meet. When he entered the restaurant, he turned out to be tall, slender, with close-cropped dark hair. Conversation flowed easily enough. He told me that, like me, he wished to write for the intellectual magazines. He filled me in on his own background. His parents were immigrants, survivors of the Holocaust. His early education was at the Flatbush Yeshiva, where Talmud study had made all subsequent classroom learning seem a pushover. We told each other Jewish jokes. We searched for the French word for "a light," as in to light a cigarette (*allumer*). I was editing a magazine myself in those days, and he said he would like, if I didn't mind, to send me an essay he was thinking of writing about his Oxford days.

Toward the close of the meal, he took out a scrap of paper and read out an address on Sheridan Road in Chicago and asked how far it was from the hotel in the Loop where he was staying.

"It's roughly a 20-dollar cab ride," I told him. "Who lives on Sheridan Road?"

"Oh," he said, "Saul Bellow. I'm having dinner tonight with him and his wife."

Just then I wondered how many letters of the kind he had written to me, with appropriate variations, he had written to others. I also thought, this kid is doing intellectual tourism, and I am merely Sienna.

Three or so months later, he sent me his essay, which was passable but no great shakes. Still, wanting to encourage the young, I agreed to publish it, which, with a bit of editing, I did. Meanwhile, I noticed his name beginning to turn up over reviews in the *Times Literary Supplement* and the *New York Review of Books*. These reviews were of books on serious subjects—I remember a Gershom Scholem book at the center of one—and were not especially notable, not for distinction of style or for penetrating ideas, but good imitations of the kind of reviews that appeared in both places. His essay on Oxford that I published attracted no comment but for a letter from a reader pointing out that its author had made a factual mistake. I wrote to tell him, Leon, all that was required was his acknowledging his error and apologizing for it. He replied by asking if it were possible that I could attribute the mistake to "a printer's error." I replied absolutely not and printed the letter without a response. This was the second time in my brief acquaintance with him that I sensed Leon Wieseltier was a young man worth watching. And so I did, and continued to do. I never saw him again, but I found myself following his career with fascination and much amusement. Quite a career, close to fabled you might say, it turned out to be.

AROUND THIS TIME, while in New York, I had a meeting with the literary critic Irving Howe. He had been generous to me, running some of my early writing in his magazine *Dissent* and going out of his way to get me, a man with no advanced degrees, a job teaching in the English department in nearby (to me) Northwestern University. We met in Irving's office. He sat behind his desk, upon which sat an ample manuscript. He told me it was for his book to be called *World of Our Fathers* and that its publisher thought it had a chance for a large sale.

"Must be nice to hear," I said.

"I suppose so," Irving answered, "but you know such accomplishments as I've recorded have always been dampened for me by a remark of Elizabeth Hardwick some years ago that got back to me."

"What was it?"

"'Irving Howe,'" she said, "'another Jew-boy in a hurry.'"

I thought, of course, of Leon Wieseltier.

After his years at Harvard, a school useful above all for making connections, Leon had acquired a job at the *New Republic*, a liberal weekly that had not long before been bought by a man named Martin Peretz, a wealthy, part-time instructor at Harvard. During his early days on the magazine, Leon published a longish piece there on, of all things, nuclear war. Nothing very distinguished about it, either, the thought of taking him seriously on such a large subject was in fact slightly gigglesome, but it suggested to me that young Leon, with all the possibilities open to him, the good student with superior *tuchus*-lecking skills, was considering that of becoming our next Henry Kissinger. I subsequently learned he was aiming higher.

Before long Leon was given control over back of the book, the literary and cultural sections of the *New Republic*. His byline would appear mostly over something like a column, not every week but fairly often, on the last page of the magazine. These columns increasingly became moral diatribes. Whatever the subject, one thing they all had in common was that he, Leon Wieseltier, not only had a clearer vision of the world and what was important in it than anyone he was writing about, but also a deeper moral imagination. Along the way, he had developed a style which entailed short-sentences that suggested the aphorism. This style worked nicely to elevate himself while dismissing anyone who happened to disagree as a moral idiot, scum really, who if he understood how wretched he was would go instanter into the intellectual equivalent of a witness protection program.

In this new style, on his single page containing 800 or so words, Leon took on the role of moral conscience of the intellectuals, the Jews, the nation at large. His self-emplacement as spokesmen for the Jews especially caused me to wince and shiver. Still a fairly young man, Leon Wieseltier was setting up shop as one of the leading moralists of our day, and with absolutely no legitimate claims to it that I could see, and a few, from personal experience, that I knew disqualified him. Yes, his was a career worth watching.

M EANWHILE, the name Leon Wieseltier, sometimes accompanied by photographs, began to turn up in places like the *New York Observer* and those small photographs in the party pages at the front of *Vanity Fair*. His hair had turned prematurely white, he had put on weight, his complexion become pinker than I had remembered. Someone told me that on trips to Hollywood he had become not merely acquainted but friendly with those two queens of ditz, Barbra Streisand and Shirley MacLaine. In Washington, where the *New Republic* was located, he was often seen in the company of Al and Tipper Gore. He somehow managed to wangle a small part—two lines at a Jewish wedding—in an episode of *The Sopranos*.

He began turning up on television. I recall him pontificating about the Middle East and fate of Israel on Charlie Rose. Charlie (if I may) asked him to explain the complexities of Middle Eastern politics; Leon obliged. Appearing on the occasional cable station panels, he could have been, if he so desired, among the punditi, but his intellectual allusions elevated at least two stages higher. Leon was one of America's leading experts in—in whatever you've got.

On television I noted that he put on weight, his hairline greatly receded, his skin grew pinker and he, somehow, grosser. (If Orwell was correct when he said that at 50 one has the face one deserves, then Leon was going to need cosmetic surgery at 60.) When I searched him out on YouTube, which I began to do in recent years, he wore a standard outfit, trousers, jacket, T-shirt, outershirt, long *tallith*-like scarf worn indoors, cowboy boots, all of them black; he was a kind of rumpled reversal of Tom Wolfe in his white suits. An Internet photo has him wearing a cowboy hat above his jowly face. His dominant feature, though, was his hair, two great white tufts of it, growing out of both sides of his head, framing his coarsening features and causing Gore Vidal to remark of him that he had "important hair," with the clear if unspoken implication of "and nothing else."

In 1995 an article appeared in *Vanity Fair* written by a man named Lloyd Grove commenting on Leon's social-climbing skills, his unbreakable connection with Martin Peretz and the power it gave him at the *New Republic*, his all-but-self-confessed cheating on his first wife (the Pakistani daughter of a man described in the article as a "merchant prince"). The article also remarked on how these various activities apparently got in the way of Leon, despite his rather extravagant intellectual pretensions, getting any serious intellectual work done: no books, few articles beyond those back-page moral diatribes. He was, he told Grove, contemplating a book on sighing, a fine Leon touch, in the realm of intellectual pretension. The unspoken charge was laziness.

Toward the close of the article what one might have thought a more serious matter arose: that of Leon's reputed cocaine habit, which caused him to load up his Honda with the review copies of books sent by publishers to the magazine and sell them to support his expensive drug habit. I looked at future issues of *Vanity Fair* to see if Leon had written in, in his best moralizing tone, refuting such a story, but no letter appeared.

One might have thought this last item—drugging and petty thieving—might have taken the highfalutinness out of Leon's moral tone, but, near as I could make out, not in the least. The heavy moralizing, the portentousness, the pomposity, all continued, business pretty much as usual. Evidently, he beat his cocaine habit.

Leon grew older, balder, fatter, his white locks longer (the Benjamin Franklin *de nos jours* someone called him). His speaking engagements, at shuls, universities, in Israel, if anything seemed to increase. The role and responsibility of the intellectual became one of his signature topics. But he had many. Watching him on YouTube being interviewed by earnest young rabbis, professors, editors, on one occasion appearing with the female president of Harvard, I sensed that, on the basis of no concrete intellectual achievements, Leon Wieseltier had taken upon himself the role of a tzaddik, for the hasidim one of the world's righteous and all-wise leaders. He was a tzaddik, of course, without followers or even a belief in God, a freelance tzaddik, you might say, working for what I assume were substantial speaking fees.

On these various interviews, it was as if his interlocutors, looking over at him in his black get-up, slouching in his chair, thick fingers on his expansive pot belly, one cowboy-booted leg crossed over the other, were appealing, "Oh, tzaddik, give unto us your wisdom, what do you think of the Holocaust, the future of the university, the role of the humanities, the Netanyahu government, mobile phones, the role of technology in contemporary life . . . ." With neither flinch nor stammer, Leon told them, prattled away, gave them crumbs from the great tzaddik's plate, and they seemed to slurp it all up. Did he believe all, or even any, of his moral pronunciamentos? Who knows? Even Leon may not have known. No one seemed to call him on them, or on his authority generally. He had a tight act.

I noted that in recent years Leon had added to his repertoire the notion that he was, as he put it, "the intellectual son" of distinguished men: of Lionel Trilling, Isaiah Berlin, Saul Bellow, and others. "I have many intellectual fathers," I heard him say in more than one of his interviews. Since all these men were dead, I thought, what a pity they couldn't, as all would doubtless have wished, deny paternity.

Still, Leon Wieseltier seemed to go from strength to strength. He turned setbacks into victories. When a young Internet millionaire, who had bought the *New Republic* two years earlier, announced plans in 2014 to transform the magazine for which he had worked for decades into a "digital media company," Leon resigned in his by now well-practiced high moral dudgeon, accompanied by much favorable publicity, claiming the owner knew nothing of the higher purposes of intellectual journalism.

Upon his quitting the *New Republic*, a famous think tank quickly took Leon on as its Isaiah Berlin Fellow (Daddy would have been proud) and *The Atlantic* appointed him a contributing editor. The wealthy widow of Steve Jobs stepped up to fund a new magazine he planned to edit to be called *Idea*. In a well-known anecdote, the conductor Herbert von Karajan is said to have got into a cab, and when the driver asked him where he wished to go, von Karajan replied, "It doesn't matter. They want me everywhere." Leon Wielseltier seemed to be in the same condition.

A ND THEN—POW! CRASH! CRUNCH!—the roof fell in. Amid a clump of sexual harassment scandals, featuring movie moguls, right-wing television commentators and executives, big-money journalists, Leon Wieseltier's name turned up. For nearly his entire tenure at the *New Republic*, the unrefuted accusation was, he was a regular offender, kissing young women full on the mouth against their wishes, describing their bodies to them, recounting his own sexual exploits, sputtering obscenities, bringing tears and shame to females under his power. Everyone on the *New Republic* apparently knew about it, but, owing to his close connection to the magazine's owner, no one on the staff, man or woman, had the courage to call him out on the awfulness of his behavior.

Leon's modest fame was just ample enough for a lengthy story about his atrocious behavior to appear in the *New York Times*. His villainous behavior was suddenly all over the Internet. Leon made his apology, thereby owning up to the truth of the accusations against him, but the apology, though it seemed little more than perfunctory, did include the nice Leonic moral touch in its last sentence, where he assured everyone that he "will not waste this reckoning." At least he had the decency not to claim that he was going into therapy.

What made it all so rich, of course, was the Tartuffian quality of its perpetrator, Leon Wieseltier, the earnest young man who wrote to me from Oxford some 40 years ago. The great humanist turned out to be inhumane, the tzaddik wore no tzitzit but all these years was mentally undressing and offending his female co-workers. Untopable, such a story, as Molière recognized nearly four centuries ago.

Soon after the story of Leon Wieseltier's years of sexual harassing broke, the wealthy widow canceled his new magazine, the Brookings Institution stripped him of his fellowship, *The Atlantic* dropped him from its masthead, other journals on whose boards he sat found him, to put it gently, an embarrassment.

I, for one, shall miss Leon in, as he might say, the public square, or rather I shall miss his act, which over the years has been a source of high amusement for me, who viewed it as a one-man intellectual sitcom at the spectacle of which I may have been the only one laughing. In his middle sixties, now that he has been publicly shamed and self-confessed as a creep, the Leon Wieseltier Show would seem to be over. No comeback for its star, surely, is possible, or so one might think. But I wouldn't bet on it.

The Menace of
Political Correctness

(2019)

THE FIRST TIME I heard the name "Ralph Northam" was when he proposed what seemed a radically dangerous abortion scheme for the state of Virginia, of which he is governor. When I heard what he proposed, I merely thought, in the way of the political dilettante that I am, how likely this was to stir up the country's pro-life forces, adding to the nation's already high GDP, or Gross Divisiveness Product.

But, then, later, when a putative photograph of Ralph Northam either in blackface or wearing a Ku Klux Klan hood taken from his medical-school graduation yearbook showed up, I began to feel sympathy for him. My sympathy increased as, on the news, I heard various people, many but not all of them African-Americans, say that now that this photograph has been revealed Northam surely can no longer govern and must step down from his office as governor. Ralph Northam graduated from medical school in 1984, and so the photograph was taken fully 35 years earlier. The incident reminded me that political correctness, for which Ralph Northam was the latest victim, knows no statute of limitations.

What may now be thought of as "the yearbook ploy" surfaced later in the egregious Brett Kavanaugh hearings, where scribblings in Justice Kavanaugh's high-school yearbook were used against him. The Kavanaugh hearings of course were not generally about Kavanaugh's legal fitness for the Supreme Court but about his political correctness or incorrectness. (About whether, in high school, he was a sexual predator or not.) Why, I wondered when the opposition brought out a few obscure scribblings from his high-school yearbook, stop at high school? What about the grammar-school playground, where one might have an eyewitness for a fifth-grade student pulling a girl's pigtails (an early act of sexism), or another witness might have heard a political candidate when in the third-grade say the "Eeney-meeny-miny-moe" poem (purest racism)? Or in preschool, the same candidate laughing after having fouled himself?

Many tend to find political correctness amusing in its absurdity. Notable in this line is the politically correct person who objected to the vagina caps worn by women in a recent feminist protest march on the grounds that not all vaginas, like the caps, are pink and, besides, she (or was it "he") added that not all women have vaginas. A friend in Evanston, the progressive community in which I live, recently told me that in a local CVS she remarked on the beauty of an infant to its mother, and asked whether the child was male or female. "Oh," said the young mother, "we haven't gendered it yet."

I have myself found mild amusement watching academics, nervous about that relentless division of political correctness known as the pronoun police, write sentences that demonstrate that their hearts—if not their minds—are in the right place. "Every student knows that she needs to be careful about student loans." Or better: "The contemporary professional basketball player is aware of the perils facing her over the long season." I first encountered this pronoun nervousness more than 25 years ago when the head of a Ph.D. orals committee I sat in on had signed off on the graduate student's performance as "Chair." "Be brave," I said, "put down 'Chairman.'" He turned away. No bloody chance.

On another occasion, a graduate student I had become friendly with happened to mention that a friend of his girlfriend was taking my course on Joseph Conrad. "I hope she's not disappointed in it," I said, no doubt fishing for a compliment. "Well, if you must know," he said, "she thinks you're sexist." When I ask on what grounds, he answered that she notices that in class I call on more male than female students. "Tell her, please, that if I thought it had something interesting to say, I would call on a hermaphroditic armadillo." But I couldn't get out of my mind the notion of that young woman sitting there counting out the number of male or female students I called on each day in class.

Something not merely humorless but mentally dull there is about the mindset of political correctness. Subtlety under political correctness is out. So, too, complexity of character. To be politically correct one must also firmly believe that people do not change: If they were the least racist, sexist, homophobic forty years ago, they must still be so now. The mental map of the politically correct consists of a minuscule pale, with much of what is genuinely interesting or amusing in life beyond that pale. For the politically correct, what someone says, as distinguished from what he does, is crucial. This precludes of course the many men and women who have harsh, even objectionable opinions but lead generous, entirely honorable lives. H. L. Mencken was such a man. In many of his essays Mencken referred to African-Americans as "blackamoors," yet in his professional life he praised and promoted black writers whenever he came upon them. Much more common are people with perfect sets of opinions—race, check; the environment, check; LGBT, check;...—and whose actions are selfish, insensitive, even cruel.

The politically correct tend to be unremitting, unforgiving. One comment they find objectionable is enough to sink otherwise splendid careers. Saul Bellow is supposed to have said, apropos of the drift toward multiculturalism in academic life in his later years: "Who is the Tolstoy of the Zulus? The Proust of the Papuans? I'd be happy to read them." This was sufficient to stand, in Bellow's words, as "a proof that I was at best insensitive and at worst an elitist, a chauvinist, a reactionary and a racist—in a word, a monster." The righteousness of rage, Bellow wrote, was much the fashion of the day. "We can't open our mouths without being denounced as racists, misogynists, supremacists, or fascists," he wrote, adding: "As for the media, they stand ready to trash anyone so designated."

One doesn't even have to say anything thought to be egregious under the reign of political correctness to be put out of business. At the *New York Review of Books*, Ian Buruma, the journal's relatively new editor and previously a longtime contributor to the paper, was fired for printing an article by a Canadian radio broadcaster attempting to clear his name from charges of sexual assault of which Canadian courts had found him not guilty. Whether he was guilty or not, one might think he at least deserved a hearing, which could subsequently be attacked by his accusers. Not, in actual practice, so. Instead Mr. Buruma, who agreed to run the essay, was fired straightaway for doing so—and will no doubt henceforth be marked permanently *non grata* in all the right places. The politically correct are merciless not merely in their judgments but in their actions. And why not, they might argue: They have right on their side; to be politically incorrect is for them a euphemism for regressive, toxic, evil.

Humor is not a specialty among the politically correct. Political correctness is in many ways the death of humor. Under its regime no ethnic jokes are allowed, no nationality, no mother-in-law, no battle-of-the-sexes jokes. So don't, please, ask me what is the difference between a Romanian and a Hungarian—at least don't ask me in a public place or be surprised if I check before telling you to make sure you're not wearing a wire.

The only humor in a politically correct world is the unconscious humor occasioned by the full-court humorlessness of the politically correct themselves. This past winter, for example, they discovered that "Rudolf the Red-Nosed Reindeer" was politically incorrect; it's a song, you see, about bullying ("All of the other reindeers, laughed and called him names"). "Baby, It's Cold Outside" turns out to be about potential sexual assault, so best not to be caught humming it, either. The reign of political correctness may be thanked for the paucity of current-day comedians. The only new name in comedy to make her mark has been Sarah Silverman, who has done it chiefly, it turns out, by making jokes about political correctness itself.

The American university is the place where political correctness flourishes more than any other. Diversity is currently one of the leading goals of the contemporary university, except in the realm of opinion and point of view. Speakers with heterodox views, should these views even faintly smell of the politically incorrect, are there shouted down by students confident they have right on their side, and are rarely censured by their professors for doing so. In the university anything outside the realm of the politically correct is held to be dangerous, unsafe, and the First Amendment exists in theory only. The university in its homogeneity of outlook has become the utopia dreamt of by political correctness made flesh.

Political correctness itself originated in the generation of student revolutionaries of the mid-1960s. Thinking themselves victims, they honored the victim above all and made victimhood a form of secular sainthood. The chief victims were African-Americans, Hispanics, gays and lesbians—later, Islamics. Among other minorities, Asian-Americans and Jews, not so much.

Many of these '60s students remained in the university as professors, and by the 1980s and '90s were in positions of power there. The contemporary university is where bad ideas find a second life—a second and, thanks to tenure, lengthy life. Where else but in English and History departments in American universities will one still find Marxists? Where but there are so many subjects politicized? Fortunately, no way has been found to teach feminist physics or Hispanic chemistry or gay engineering, or the university would be an entirely worthless enterprise.

In going along with the program of political correctness, the university has greatly helped spread its doctrines beyond its politically correct confines. I recently complained to a friend still teaching at Northwestern University, where I taught for thirty years, about the waste entailed in hiring an associate provost for diversity, at a salary I take to be around $200,000 a year. My friend, more knowledgeable than I about these matters, replied that without an associate provost for diversity on the staff the university might not qualify for federal funds for science projects. One wonders where would the federal politicians would get such ideas, but then remembers that they, too, attended university. Thus, do the tentacles of political correctness reach out beyond the university itself.

Rare is the university professor of the current day who is ready to speak out against political correctness. My own experience of this conformity bred of want of courage was when, in the middle 1990s, I was fired owing to political correctness from the job of editor of Phi Beta Kappa's quarterly magazine *The American Scholar*. With the exception of the historian

Eugen Weber, the vote to fire me among the all-academic senator of Phi Beta Kappa was, I am told, unanimous. As for the reason for my being fired, it had nothing to do with politics, since I made it a point to clear the journal's pages of all contemporary political content, but to do with my not running any articles in the journal on the subjects of feminism or African-American Studies—with in another words, political correctness. I didn't do so because I received no articles on these subjects that seemed of any genuine interest. I sought such articles from a few members of the Phi Beta Kappa Senate itself, with the proviso that I wasn't interested in the clichés on the subject and hoped for work that went beyond standard victimology. None were forthcoming. I was, then, replaced as editor, given, in the best slow-motion academic fashion, two years to clean out my desk.

Political correctness rears up everywhere in the business of the university. To find a commencement ceremony of a major university that does not provide honorary degrees for a few women and African-Americans would not be an easy task. The grandson of a friend of mine, a brilliant student who has mastered Chinese, showed up for a Rhodes Scholarship interview to discover that a dozen women were also being interviewed for the same scholarship and knew his goose was cooked.

The aroma of goose-cooking brings us back to Ralph Northam. The gang up against him has been nothing if not impressive. After the original yearbook photograph was revealed, he claimed that he did not appear in it as either the man in blackface or the figure in KKK hood and gown. He did allow that, for a dance contest, in 1984, he dressed himself as Michael Jackson and used blackface as part of his get-up. It also somehow leaked out that his nickname in those days was "Coonman," origin of the nickname in his case unknown. "Those days," recall, were thirty-five years ago. That he has apparently been a strongly liberal governor cuts no ice with the political correctors.

The Democratic National Committee has asked for Ralph Northam's resignation from the governorship of Virginia. The state's two senators have done likewise. The Republican Party of Virginia insisted that, with the yearbook revelations out in the world, he can no longer govern and must go. "The Republican Party of Virginia is committed to removing Ralph Northam NOW!," it announced, joining the herd of independent minds. Black politicians across the country have stepped forth to mutter the usual phrases about "the pain he has caused," that only his resignation will "help us heal," nothing less than his removal from public life will "stop the pain." Only Barack Obama, who campaigned for Northam, has remained silent.

Ralph Northam refused to resign, and, though I suspect I share few of his political ideas, I, for one, am glad he remained in office. What is really at stake here has almost nothing to do with pain, healing, or racism, and everything to do with political correctness. Northam was the object of the bullying of the self-righteous, providing them, by dressing up as a young man more than three decades ago as Michael Jackson, an opportunity to demonstrate their grand virtue under the klieg lights of television publicity. A young man dressing up and doing an impression of Michael Jackson dancing—not, one would think, a big deal. Nor is it, really, except in the world of the politically correct, where human nature is judged incapable of change, humor is not allowed, any sense of proportion is precluded, and virtue invariably resides with the accuser.

Hail, Mommsen

(2018)

THEODOR MOMMSEN'S FAME during his lifetime was such that it earned the awe of even so skeptical an observer as Mark Twain. In one of his newsletters to America, Twain, while in Berlin, describes attending a student dinner when Mommsen arrived in the hall. Twain writes:

> Then there was an excited whisper at our table—"Mommsen!"— and the whole house rose. Rose and shouted and stamped and clapped, and banged the beer mugs . . . . Here he was, clothed in a Titanic deceptive modesty which made him look like other men. Here he was, carrying the Roman world and all the Caesars in his hospitable skull, and doing it as easily as that other luminous vault, the skull of the universe, carries the Milky Way and the constellations.

After earning a doctorate in Roman law, Theodor Mommsen (1817–1903) became a professor of law and of Roman history, serving for a time in the Prussian and German parliaments. His most significant work of pure scholarship was his editing of the *Corpus Inscriptionum Latinarum*, a multi-volume collection of all the Roman inscriptions found on material objects, an editorial enterprise that was the foundation of modern epigraphy (the study and interpretation of ancient inscriptions). But Mommsen's fingerprints are all over the study of Roman history, from Roman law to the Church Fathers, and more. His bibliography runs to more than a thousand items. In a too brief biographical article the *Encyclopaedia Britannica* calls Mommsen "one of the greatest of the nineteenth century German classical historians," cites his uniting in his work on "jurisprudence and history, philology and archeology," and ends by noting that "he achieved an unequaled grasp of the totality of history." In what must have been his highly limited leisure, Mommsen also fathered 16 children.

Mommsen's great general work was his three-volume *History of Rome*, running from the putative beginning of Rome in 753 BCE to the victory of Julius Caesar over his adversaries in 48 BCE. A planned fourth volume on the Roman emperors was never completed. Some say Mommsen failed to complete it because he feared he could never rival Edward Gibbon, whom he much admired and who set his indelible stamp on this portion of Roman history; others because Mommsen felt himself depressed, in his words, by the "leaden dreariness" and "empty desert" of the Roman emperors after the grandeur of the Roman Republic. Mommsen also claimed that, at this stage in his life, he preferred research to writing. He did, nevertheless, publish a fifth volume, *The Provinces of the Roman Empire from Caesar to Diocletian*. Another volume, *The Roman Emperors*, composed out of student notes from his lectures on the subject, was published in English in 1992.

Mommsen won the Nobel Prize in 1902, not for History, in which no prize is awarded, but for Literature. Despite the nearly scientific scrupulosity with which he wrote history, Mommsen could not have been in the least disappointed to have his work honored for its literary value. Early in *The Provinces of the Roman Empire*, he wrote that imagination "is the author of all history as of all poetry." By aligning the two, history and poetry, he surely meant that documents, inscriptions, accurate chronology alone are never sufficient in themselves to explain the past. Imagination is required to connect the dots, fill in the background, limn the characters of key actors, discover and reveal complex motivation, grasp larger movements.

All these things Mommsen did consummately, always with certain knowledge that a complete picture was never fully available to the historian. He would have subscribed to Lewis Namier's aphorism that "we study history so that we can learn how things didn't happen." Mommsen's work is studded with disclaimers: "cannot be determined"; "we cannot tell"; "conjectures that wear an aspect of probability"; "the information that has come to us gives no satisfactory answer"; "like a distant evening twilight in which outlines disappear"; "our information regarding it comes to us like the sound of bells from a town that has been sunk into the sea."

Mommsen was among that small but select line of historians, including David Hume, Edward Gibbon, and Thomas Babbington Macaulay, known, in Gibbon's phrase, as philosophic. These historians are philosophic in the sense of being interested in human nature as it plays itself out on the ample fields of political and military affairs, of culture and economics; for them history is centered as much in character as in event. Owing to this interest in human nature and the character of great men (mostly) and women, they themselves have found a prominent and well-deserved place not merely in historiography but in literature.

Ambitious, even risky, generalization attracted them all. Thus Mommsen describes Roman religion—with "the peculiar character at once of shallowness and of fervor," its augurs and Vestal Virgins, yet in which "oracles and prophecy never acquired the importance in Italy which they obtained in Greece"—as a religion better "fitted rather to stifle than to foster artistic and speculative views." But this same religion, he recognizes, lent its imprimatur to the moral nature of Roman law. "At the very core of the Latin religion there lay that profound moral impulse which leads men to bring earthly guilt and earthly punishment into relation with the world of the gods, and to view the former as a crime against the gods, and the latter as its expiation."

After comparing Roman and Greek religion, he writes:

> It is time therefore to desist from that childish view of history which believes that it can commend the Greeks only at the expense of the Romans, or the Romans only at the expense of the Greeks; and, as we allow the oak to hold its own beside the rose, so we should abstain from praising or censuring the two noblest organizations which antiquity has produced, and commend the truth that their

distinctive excellences have a connection with their re-
spective defects.

Of course, it is against the Greeks that the Romans, in Mommsen and
elsewhere, are inevitably compared. "Hellas is the prototype of purely
human," he notes in his first volume, "Latium is not less for all time the
prototype of national development." Only the Latin Romans attained
national unity and ultimately empire, which they commanded for centuries, while the Greeks, endlessly quarrelsome among themselves, could
not adhere as a nation apart from such times of national peril as the Persian Wars. "In Latium," Mommsen writes, "no other influences were
powerful in public and private life but prudence, riches, and strength; it
was reserved for the Hellenes to feel the blissful ascendancy of beauty."

Inward art, Mommsen held, was not available to the Romans. For the
Romans art was always of subordinate importance, the artist himself scarcely
above the artisan in status. Science—physics and mathematics—were little
studied in Rome. "For centuries," Mommsen reports, "there were none but
Greek physicians in Rome," and the most sought-after teachers tended to
be Greeks. He writes: "The Italian is deficient in the passion of the heart,
and in the longing to idealize what is human and to give life to things of the
inanimate world, which form the very essence of poetic art." In the realm of
art, Romans seemed to respond best to irony, comedy, and farce, and consequently did without their own Homer, Euripides, or Phidias.

Yet it was Rome that, as Mommsen wrote, "pursued her purpose with
undeviating steadfastness, and displayed her energetic far-reaching policy—more even than on the battlefield—in securing the territory which
she gained by enveloping it, politically and militarily, in a net whose
meshes could not be broken." The old saying had it that "If Rome conquered Greece, the Greeks vanquished her rude conqueror by art." Yet,
as Mommsen wrote toward the close of his second volume, "Rome was,
what Greece was not, a state," and it was because the community, the
state, was always primary in Rome, the individual secondary.

As for that state, Mommsen writes:

> [T]he imperial period marks a climax of good government,
> very modest in itself, but never withal attained before or

since; and, if an angel of the Lord were to strike the balance whether the domain ruled by Severus Antoninus was governed with the greater intelligence and the greater humanity at that time or in the present day, whether civilisation and national prosperity generally have since that time advanced or retrograded, it is very doubtful whether the decision would prove in favour of the present.

Mommsen's talent for arresting aphorism plays throughout his *History*. A sampler: "To continue an injustice is to commit injustice." "The world, however, belongs not to reason but to passion." "In ancient times it was necessary to be either anvil or hammer." "*History* has a Nemesis for every sin—for an impotent craving after freedom, as well as for an injudicious generosity." "Political orthodoxy knows nothing of compromise and conciliation." This talent is all the more extraordinary for Mommsen's having written his History as a young man (by today's standard); his third volume was published in 1856 before he was 40.

Mommsen the brilliant historical portraitist doesn't fully emerge until his pages on the Punic Wars in the 3rd century BCE First, though, he fills in the background by noting that "the policy of the Romans was always more remarkable for tenacity, cunning, and consistency than for grandeur of conception or power of organization." In Rome, as elsewhere, grandeur of conception, the plans of "wiser, more resolute, and more devoted men . . . always find themselves hampered by the indolent and cowardly mass of the money-worshippers, of the aged and feeble, and of the thoughtless who are minded merely to gain time, to live and die in peace, and to postpone at any price the final struggle."

Wiser, more resolute, more devoted men do from time to time arise, and in the Punic Wars notable among them were the two great generals, Hannibal and Publius Cornelius Scipio (later Africanus). Both men are rendered in *The History of Rome* with an admirable artistic distance and detachment. Of Hannibal, Mommsen writes that "every page of the history of the period attests his genius as a general," and "the power which he wielded over men is shown by his incomparable control over an army of various nations and many tongues—an army which never in the worst times mutinied against him. He was a great man; wherever he went, he riveted the eyes of all."

The modern military historian B. H. Liddell Hart awarded the highest possible marks to Scipio Africanus, placing him, as a strategist and tactician, above Alexander, Julius Caesar, Napoleon, and all other military commanders, and staking out the additional claim that he was a man of the highest personal character. Mommsen is less charitably disposed: "But Publius Scipio also, although setting the fashion to the nobility in arrogance, title-hunting, and client-making, sought support for his personal and almost dynastic policy of opposition to the senate in the multitude, which he not only charmed by the dazzling effect of his personal qualities, but also bribed by his largesse of grain ... [and] only the dreamy mysticism, on which the charm as well as the weakness of that remarkable man so largely depended ... allowed him to awake" others to his belief that among all Romans he was the *primus inter pares*, and this by a long stretch.

The fates, as Mommsen understood, are not cowed by greatness, real or assumed. Hannibal was "constrained at last to remain a mere spectator while Rome overpowered the East as the tempest overpowers the ship that has no one at the helm, and to feel that he alone was the pilot that could have weathered the storm." When Hannibal died in 183 BCE "there was left to him no further hope to be disappointed." Scipio Africanus' final act was scarcely more rewarding. Earlier Mommsen writes that the senate (the "somewhat boorish fathers of the city") was put off by "his Greek refinement and his modern culture and tone of thought." Even after his impressive military victories, "he too spent his last years in bitter vexation, and died when little more than fifty years of age in voluntary banishment, leaving orders to his relatives not to bury his remains in the city for which he had lived and in which his ancestors reposed." Hannibal and Scipio were two exemplars of Solon's admonition never to say you have had a fortunate life until you have breathed your last.

Some of the liveliest pages in Mommsen are those that end each of his volumes on the manners and arts of the Romans at different stages in their history. Played against these are those devoted to Roman violence and cruelty. The latter may have set in with the advent of what Mommsen calls "the detestable amusement of gladiatorial combats—the gangrene of the later Rome and of the last epoch of antiquity generally." He recounts the sale at one go, from the seven townships in the Epirus, of no fewer than 150,000 slaves, the largest slave sale in recorded history. The Greeks, he reminds us, treated their slaves as servants, the Romans as property, with all that implies of the savagery implicit in the Latin word *dominus*. Mommsen writes that "it is very possible that, compared with the sufferings of the Roman slaves, the sum of all Negro suffering is but a drop."

Under the rule of Sulla (81 BCE), Mommsen notes that "the times of mercy were past." The hands of entire male populations of captured towns were sometimes chopped off, women and children sold into slavery. Before Sulla the city of Corinth was captured, its male population put to death, all its women and children sold into slavery, the city itself burned, an act Mommsen describes as "a dark stain on the annals of Rome." Corruption was ubiquitous. More imagination was spent on torture than on the arts, and not in Rome alone. When Mithradates captured the Roman general Aquillius in 88 BCE "molten gold was poured down his throat— in order to satiate his avarice," an act, Mommsen writes, that "alone suffices to erase the name of its author from the roll of true nobility."

The cavalcade of major players in the drama of Rome march past in Mommsen's pages: the Brothers Graachi (Tiberius and Gaius), Marius, Sulla, Marcus Livius Drusus, and lesser figures, the acts of each assessed, their strengths and weaknesses recounted. The endless struggle between senate and people, the optimates (aristocrats) and the populares (populists), plays out. Honorable patriotism struggles against short-sighted selfishness, with the former nearly always going down in defeat. Great careers are no longer founded on action in battle but in the Roman equivalent of backroom dealings, or "the ante-chambers of influential men." Soon the Roman army itself will change from a citizen to a professional army. Extravagance—in dining, concubinage, displays of vulgar opulence—is rampant. Mommsen records the story of the Roman aristocrat "who cried over the death of his favorite fish but not over the death of three wives."

Of the ancient historians, Mommsen is high on Plutarch (CE 46–120), "one of the most charming, most fully informed, and withal most effective writers of antiquity." Others may have greater depth or stronger talent, "but hardly any second author has known in so happy a measure how to reconcile himself serenely to necessity, and how to impress upon his writings the stamp of his tranquility of spirit and his blessedness of life." Of Tacitus, Mommsen says little, referring to him chiefly in footnotes, where, among other comments, he is critical of his account of the Roman war in Britain. ("A worse narrative than that of Tacitus concerning the war, Ann. XIV. 31–39, is hardly to be found even in this most unmilitary of all authors.") Later he remarks that Tacitus' "pen was frequently driven by hatred." Livy gets scant mention.

Polybius (200–118 BCE), like Plutarch a Greek, is the historian who gets the highest marks. Present at the destruction of Corinth and Carthage, he seemed educated, Mommsen writes, "by destiny to comprehend the historical position of Rome more clearly than the Romans of that day could themselves." Mommsen is not without criticisms of Polybius: his treatment of questions "in which right, honor, religion are involved, is not merely shallow, but radically false." His narrative is "correct and clear, but flat and languid, digressing with undue frequency into polemical discussions or into biographical, not seldom very self-sufficient, description of his own experiences." Yet Mommsen closes his pages on Polybius on this high note:

> Polybius is not an attractive author; but as truth and truthfulness are of more value than all the ornament and elegance, no other author of antiquity perhaps can be named to whom we are indebted for so much real instruction. His books are like the sun in the field of Roman history; at the point where they begin the veil of mist which still envelops the Samnite and Pyrrhic wars is raised, and at the point where they end a new and, if possible, still more vexatious twilight begins.

Marcus Tullius Cicero (106–43 BCE), the first known intellectual in politics, is thoroughly trashed in *The History of Rome*. He is characterized by Mommsen as "notoriously a political trimmer," "a dabbler," without "conviction and passion," and later a coward. "As a statesman without insight, opinion, or purpose, he figured successively as democrat, as aristocrat, and as a tool of the monarchs, and was never more than a short-sighted egotist." Cicero the writer is shown even less sympathy: "In the character of an author, on the other hand, he stands quite as low as in that of a statesman." Mommsen writes that Cicero's correspondence "mirrors most faithfully his character," which is to say that, "where the writer is thrown back on his own resources . . . it is stale and empty as was ever the soul of a feuilletonist banished from his familiar circles." His dialogues "are no great works of art, but undoubtedly they are the works in which the excellences of the author are most, and his faults least, conspicuous." As for Cicero the great orator, "if there is anything wonderful in the case, it is in truth not the orations, but the admiration which they excited." That admiration was extinguished by the generation that followed, who "found Cicero's language deficient in precision and chasteness, his jests deficient in liveliness, his arrangement deficient in clearness and articulate division, and above all his whole eloquence wanting in the fire which makes the orator." So damaging was Mommsen's attack on Cicero's reputation that, according to Anthony Grafton, it did not fully recover until the twentieth century.

Mommsen can kill a historical figure with a single sentence. Marcus Aemilius Lepidus he calls "an insignificant and indiscreet personage, who did not deserve to become a leader either in council or in the field." The counsel Servius Sulpicius Rufus, was "a very timid man who desired nothing but a quiet death in his bed." Marcus Cato he calls "the Don Quixote of the aristocrats." Gnaeus Pompeius, known to his contemporaries as Pompey the Great, was, in Mommsen's view, far from great: "neither a bad nor an incapable man, but a man thoroughly ordinary, created by nature to be a good sergeant, called by circumstances to be a general and a statesman."

Given Mommsen's hyper-critical views of the pretensions of Roman leaders, one is brought up by his—it is not going too far to say—adoration of Julius Caesar. This is the Caesar whose masterly command of his army transferred to it "his own elasticity," but in whom "the officer was thoroughly subordinate to the statesman." This Caesar "was monarch; but he never played the king," a man "who finished whatever he took in hand." He was "the sole creative genius produced by Rome, and the last produced by the ancient world, which accordingly moved on in the track that he had set out for it until its sun had set." His was "a nature so harmoniously organized [that if] there is any one trait to be singled out as characteristic it is this—that he stood apart from all ideology and everything fanciful. As a matter of course Caesar was a man of passion, for without passion there is no genius; but his passion was never stronger than he could control." He was no less than "a master of the world."

The oddity of this is that, as Mommsen acknowledges, Julius Caesar put paid to the end of the Roman Republic, which at its best the historian much admired. But Mommsen thought the era of the Republic had ended, and that the future belonged to the empire of Caesar. When queried about whether the American Founders had given the people a monarchy or a republic, Benjamin Franklin famously replied, "A republic, if you can keep it." The Romans couldn't keep theirs, though it had a good run, lasting more than 500 years throughout Italy and in the countries on the Mediterranean. Through Mommsen's magisterial prose, we see "it brought to ruin in politics and morals, religion and literature, not through outward violence, but through inward decay, thereby making room for the new monarchy of Caesar." Rome under the monarchy lived on another 300 or so years, until finally eroded and undermined by the departure of the Emperor Constantine to Byzantium and the subsequent spread of Christianity.

"It is true," Mommsen wrote, "that the history of past centuries ought to be the instructress of the present; but . . . it is instructive only so far as the earlier forms of culture reveals the organic conditions of civilization generally—the fundamental forces everywhere alike, and the manner of their combination everywhere different—and leads and encourages men, not to unreflecting imitation, but to independent reproduction." In his *History of Rome* Theodor Mommsen brings the past strikingly to life. If its lessons for the present may be limited, through its author's vivid eye we, his readers, nevertheless achieve glints of freshened understanding of the intricate relation between event and character, and a renewed sense of how richly fascinating the world is and always has been.

Big Julie

(2019)

JAMES BOSWELL, who knew a thing or two about hero worship, called Julius Caesar "the greatest man of any age." Alexander Hamilton told Thomas Jefferson that Caesar was "the greatest man who ever lived." Theodor Mommsen, in his *History of Rome*, called Caesar "the sole creative genius produced by Rome, and the last produced by the ancient world." Jacob Burckhardt called Caesar "the greatest of mortals."

That word "greatest," superlative of all superlatives, has been much overused in our day. Some of us may have first heard it in connection with the Ringling Bros. Circus, "The Greatest Show on Earth." Tom Brokaw contributed "The Greatest Generation" for those Americans who fought in World War II. Then there was Muhammad Ali who, with characteristic modesty, called himself "The Greatest." But in our era of easily assigned superlatives, one can't help but feel how apposite, how comfortably, the word "greatest" sidles up to the name of Julius Caesar—to call him "the greatest" might even be an understatement.

Julius Caesar is generally, and rightly, regarded as one of the six most successful military commanders of all time, alongside Alexander the Great, Hannibal, Scipio Africanus, Frederick the Great, and Napoleon. Plutarch wrote that Caesar "above all men was gifted with the faculty of making the right use of everything in war, and most especially of seizing the right moment" to attack. Statesman as well as warrior, more than anyone else in history he embodied Carl von Clausewitz's maxim that "war is the continuation of politics by other means." He is a perennial favorite of empire builders who prize bold action and recognize that power politics requires genuine power. Napoleon took Caesar as a model and wrote a long commentary on his wartime adventures while exiled (and carefully guarded) on St. Helena.

In our time of distrust, if not utter contempt, for imperialism and for great-man theories in politics, Julius Caesar's is not a name everywhere honored. Too many putatively great men of the past century—Lenin, Stalin, Hitler, Mao—turned out to be merchants of mass death, villainous to the highest power. Yet Caesar's career is of a different kind. Even now, two millennia after his dramatic assassination, the verdict on him is less than clear, the meaning of his extraordinary life not yet fully fathomed. Perhaps it never can be, but even thinking about him somehow enlarges one's sense of the scope and grandeur of human ambition.

CAESAR'S *THE GALLIC WAR* is widely known as a Latin school text— *Gallia est omnis divisa partis tris*. It has been assigned for generations because it combines simplicity of expression with perfection of style. "I certainly read Caesar with rather more reverence and awe than is usual for the works of men," Montaigne wrote, "at times considering the man himself and the miracle of his greatness, at others the purity and inimitable polish of his language which not only surpassed that of all other historians, as Cicero said, but perhaps that of Cicero himself." Of Caesar the author, Mommsen notes "the self-possessed ease with which he arranged his periods as well as projected his campaigns," adding that "while Alexander could not sleep for thinking of the Homeric Achilles, Caesar in his sleepless hours mused on the inflections of the Latin nouns and verbs." Caesar wrote both *The Gallic War* and his *The Civil War* while fighting those wars. As a test of his powers of concentration, Caesar was said, according to Christian Meier's biography, to have been able to "dictate four important letters to his scribes simultaneously, and as many as seven unimportant ones." He apparently could also compose on horseback.

Caesar's mastery of language extended to the spoken word. Although none of his speeches have survived fully intact, Cicero, himself a master of oratory, remarked on the "chaste, pellucid, and grand, not to say noble" quality of Caesar's eloquence as a speaker. "Do you know any man who, even if he has concentrated on the art of oratory to the exclusion of all else, can speak better than Caesar?" Cicero wrote to Cornelius Nepos. "Or anyone who makes so many witty remarks? Or whose vocabulary is so varied and yet so exact?" Caesar demonstrated this skill not just in the senate and earlier in Roman law courts, but in brief inspirational speeches delivered to his troops before battle, speeches so effective that these men came to feel themselves fighting less for Rome than for their commander.

Not that Caesar was without his flaws—major flaws. The military historian Theodore Ayrault Dodge, in his otherwise admiring biography of Caesar, catalogues some of these with impressive concision. So concentrated was Caesar on ends, means were of negligible interest to him. At war he was capable, as Dodge wrote, of "holocausts before which the devastations of Alexander shrink to naught." He might lop off the hands of the men of an entire town that had shown him resistance, while selling its women and children into slavery. Dodge reckons that "the sum of his massacres in Gaul overruns a million souls, paying no heed to those who perished by a worse fate than the edge of the sword." Caesar brooked no resistance even from men who otherwise supported him. He had no compunction in sending one of his own loyal soldiers, who complained that none of the booty of war should be shared with civilians, off to be executed, or about doing the same to a baker whose bread disappointed him.

A FTER THE DEFEAT OF POMPEY at Pharsalus in Thessaly, Caesar cultivated and acquired a reputation for clemency, forgiving many enemies, foreign and Roman—including, unfortunately for him, Marcus Brutus, who earlier had aligned himself with Pompey against Caesar. Caesar may not have been naturally vindictive, but Roman clemency needs to be highly qualified. When, as a young man, Caesar was kidnapped by pirates and released only after arranging for his own ransom, he pledged revenge by crucifixion. Later, after having captured these same pirates, before crucifying them as promised, he is said to have shown clemency because, as Suetonius writes, "he first mercifully cut their throats." Such was mercy in antiquity, an age of proscriptions, poisonings, beheadings, and crucifixions, not to speak of decimations, the act of killing one in ten of one's own troops for dereliction of duty. One recalls, too, when Marcus Crassus quelled the slave revolt led by Spartacus in 73 BCE, he had the 6,000 or so slaves he captured crucified at intervals of forty yards over a one hundred and twenty-mile stretch of the Appian Way—human billboards advertising his victory.

"Caesar's much-vaunted clemency," writes Peter Green, "can be dated, with some confidence, to 51 BCE, no earlier"—or, in other words, beginning after his successes in the Gallic Wars. "His record of mercy in the Civil War [against Pompey]," Green holds, "was simply a proof of his far-sightedness. It was more convenient for his purposes to make friends than enemies, especially if those friends could be of use to him." Besides, clemency is, as Ronald Syme writes in his book on Sallust, "the virtue of a despot, not of a citizen and an aristocrat," for it "is the mercifulness of someone who can put you to death. That is to say a god, a tyrant, a master of slaves." Resentment at Caesar's lofty clemency may well have been among the motives of his assassins.

A man of many appetites, Caesar's sexual escapades are best chronicled by Suetonius, who was a connoisseur of the salacious. Suetonius writes that Caesar's "affairs with women are commonly described as numerous and extravagant," and then goes on to catalogue the wives of Roman patricians he seduced, including Servilia, the mother of Brutus. (Some, Caesar perhaps among them, believed Brutus was his child.) His most famous love affair was of course with Cleopatra, who gave him his only son, Caesarion, later murdered at the command of Caesar's adopted son and heir Octavian, who is said not to have wanted any more Caesars around other than himself. Suetonius also devotes a few paragraphs to rumors of Caesar's supposed youthful liaison as the catamite of Nicomedes, King of Bithynia. Montaigne, cribbing from Suetonius, repeats the stories of Caesar's sex life but makes plain, rightly, "the inequality" of Caesar's appetite for sex and for power, the latter, not being merely vastly stronger than the former, but unlike it, "not being susceptible to satiety."

What makes Julius Caesar's military career all the more extraordinary is that it did not begin until he was forty, and lasted less than fifteen years until his death at fifty-five. Plutarch has Caesar in Spain, at the age of thirty-one, bemoaning the limitations of his scope of action. "Do you think," he reports Caesar saying, "I have not just cause to weep, when I consider that Alexander at my age had conquered so many nations, and I have all this time done nothing that is memorable?" There is some doubt that he ever said any such thing, for Alexander was a king and a tyrant, both terms of the highest abuse in first-century BCE Rome, and thus scarcely likely to serve as a model.

If anyone was on an Alexander program, it may have been Gnaeus Pompeius, whose early military victories in Spain and Africa earned him the sobriquet Magnus, so that he became—for some the title was used ironically—Pompey the Great. By twenty-five, Pompey had already had his first triumph, the ceremonial parading of victorious commanders in Rome, their victims and booty displayed in tow. Superior military organizer though he was, Pompey was plagued by a tic of hesitation that proved his ultimate undoing in battle against Caesar. Yet Pompey sought applause and fame rather than power and influence, whereas Caesar, the more ambitious man, sought and eventually gained all four.

BORN OF THE PATRICIAN FAMILY OF THE JULII, nobility of fading repute, a family claiming a relation to the goddess Venus, Julius Caesar (born in 100 BCE) came of age during the civil war between Sulla and Marius. A favorite aunt of his, Julia, married Marius. Caesar's first marriage was to the daughter of Cornelius Cinna, who joined Marius on the losing side against Sulla and was eventually put to death for it. Sulla wanted Caesar to divorce his wife, but Caesar, demonstrating his early intransigence against authority, refused. (Caesar would eventually marry three times: In republican Rome, marriage, like war, could also be politics by other means.) Much of Caesar's early career was spent in opposition to the Sullan faction in the Roman Senate, attempting to secure the supreme place he felt was his by right of birth and even more by right of talent. On paper—make that on parchment—he sought the support of the populares (the people) and was opposed to the optimates (the senatorial oligarchy), but ultimately Julius Caesar appears always to have been in business for himself.

Accounts of Caesar's youth are a touch blurry. His father died when he was fifteen; his mother was the important figure in his early life. His was the traditional training of the Roman aristocrat: athletics, horsemanship, off to Greece for training in oratory. Along with high birth, skill at oratory and a history of military victory were the path to Roman *dignitas*, or the highest political and social standing. Theodore Ayrault Dodge describes Caesar as a boy erect of carriage, with a "manner open and kindly," and with "countenance singularly engaging and expressive, if not handsome." Suetonius reports that he "was of imposing stature—white-skinned, slim-limbed, rather too full in the face, and with dark lively eyes."

The Alcibiadean exhibitionist in Caesar emerged early. Plutarch refers to his riding at full gallop "with dropped reins and his hands joined behind his back." His vanity about his looks was notable, from his rather louche dress—a belt hanging loosely round his toga—to his careful shaves and manicures. He was a sedulous spendthrift, early and often in heavy debt. His baldness pained him, and his was the first prominent comb-over— more precisely in his case, comb-down—in history. His epilepsy, which Plutarch describes as "his distempers," and Shakespeare as "the falling sick-ness," did not slow him in any significant way.

CAESAR'S CLIMB UP THE ROMAN POLE, or *cursus honorum*, began early but was far from smooth. From quaestor to aedile to praetor to consul—technically administrative posts all, but necessary steps on the run to Roman power—up he climbed, ending, briefly before being assassi-nated, as Dictator for Life. Caesar's too obvious ambition turned off other insiders who preferred to keep him outside. Sulla was the first to sense the danger to the senatorial oligarchy that the young Caesar represented.

"Beware of that boy with the loose clothes," he warned his fellow oli-garchs, prophetically telling a follower that he would "one day prove the ruin of the party which you and I have so long defended." Cicero, from early in Caesar's career, was wary of his unbounded ambition.

At stake in that career was the future of the republic. The Roman senators, led by Marcus Porcius Cato, viewed themselves first as the preservers, then as the on-the-run defenders of the Roman *res publica*. The entrenched Roman oligarchy had known threats before: from the brothers Gracchi, from Marius, and from Sulla himself, whose personal power and cruel proscriptions threatened the republic even while ostensibly fighting for it. After Pompey's defeat at Pharsalus and subsequent death in Egypt, Metellus Scipio's defeat at Thapsus, and Cato's suicide, Julius Caesar was now without rivals, and posed the greatest threat of all.

Even before Caesar's rise, evidence was beginning to accumulate that the Roman Empire was becoming too vast and unwieldy to continue in business under traditional republican political arrangements. One such arrangement was the republic's seemingly admirable term limits of one year for each of its two consuls, with a ten-year gap required between holding a second consulship. At the end of their terms, the two consuls went off under the title proconsul to govern one of the ever-increasing number of Roman provinces, often enriching themselves there by plunder. Elections to the various magistracies, including that of consul, were becoming corrupted by bribery and unredeemable promises. The Roman citizen-soldier, the finest in the ancient world, perhaps the finest ever, was more and more being replaced in the Roman army by foreign auxiliaries and mercenaries fighting under the Roman eagle. Empires, as Montesquieu held, seem at their most stable when they are expanding; they apparently cannot bear too lengthy periods of peace. Peace, somehow, in Rome was an encouragement to civil war.

JULIUS CAESAR, a true freelance, was the wrong man at the wrong time—wrong, that is, if saving the republic was the name of one's desire. No party or faction in Rome was strong enough to resist him. *Alea iacta est*, the die is cast, Caesar is supposed to have said when he crossed the Rubicon and brought his legions into Rome. Caesar was an inveterate gambler, tossing the dice on many occasions, a gambler upon whom fortune seemed never to frown. But he had more than fortune alone going for him. He had an indomitable army, the support of the sprawling Roman population, and an apparently unslakable appetite for power. After the crushing effect of lengthy civil war, one-man rule must have been viewed by most Romans as a relief. The only thing in question was whether he, Caesar, wished to rise to the abominable title of king—though many felt he was already that without the title.

Given the roll of honors lavished on Julius Caesar after his victories in Gaul and his crushing defeat of the shaky partnership of Pompey, Cato, and Metellus Scipio, the title of king might have seemed a downgrade. These honors included a life-dictatorship; the title imperator before his name, *pater patriae* after it; a statue of him set among former kings; a ceremonial chariot to carry his statue in religious processions round the circus; a golden throne in the senate; divine status (*divus Iulius*), with all its accoutrements; and other honors that, as Suetonius writes, "as a mere mortal he should certainly have refused." Far from refusing these honors, Caesar not only accepted them all but sometimes in doing so showed his contempt for them.

In *The Roman Revolution*, Ronald Syme declares Caesar "stands out as a realist and an opportunist," lacking "fear or scruple," and refers to him as "a Sulla but for clementia, a Gracchus but lacking a revolution-ary programme." Caesar's military victories—first over the Gauls, then over Pompey & Co.—combined with his political savvy meant, as Syme writes, "the lasting domination of one man instead of the rule of the law, the constitution and the senate; it announced the triumph soon or late of new forces and new ideas, the elevation of the army and the provinces, the depression of the traditional governing class." Caesar did not champion one class above another, and once established as dictator, was himself above party. Whether or not he intended it, he paved the way for the generations of emperors that followed him. "About Caesar's ultimate designs there can be opinion," Syme contends, "but no certainty." He adds: "The question of ultimate intentions becomes irrelevant. Caesar was slain for what he was, not for what he might become." Maximum Leader is what he was.

ALONGSIDE THE IMMENSE SIGNIFICANCE of Julius Caesar's military and political career is the richness of the surrounding cast of characters in play during the time of his rise. Anyone with a lit-erary eye cannot but be swept up by the possibilities they suggest. The morally dithering Brutus (*The Noble Conspirator*, as a recent biography of him by Kathryn Tempest is titled); the rigidly virtuous Cato ("the Don Quixote of the aristocracy," Mommsen calls him); the crucially hesitant Pompey (whose "ancient habit of procrastination," as Theodore Ayrault Dodge describes it, eventually did him in); the contriving Marcus Crassus (in whom the desires for money and for power fought to a standstill); the dissolute Antony (given, in Plutarch's phrase, to "gross amours" and "impudent luxury"); the ultimate trimmer Cicero—what boldly outlined and cogent types they all seem.

Joseph Addison wrote *Cato*, a play said to have greatly influenced the thinking of the American founding fathers. Shakespeare of course got two plays out of the subject. Cicero stands out as, among other things, the first intellectual in politics—and perhaps a salutary warning that intellectuals generally do well to stay out of politics. (Mark Antony, it will be recalled, had Cicero killed, his head and right hand—the one that wrote the attacks upon him—nailed to the speaker's place in the forum.) Brutus died at Philippi at the end of his own sword. Antony, overestimating himself and underestimating everyone else, expired in Egypt with, so to say, his pants down.

THE ONLY CHARACTER that doesn't emerge with crystalline clarity in this splendid cast is Caesar himself. If one wishes to understand the mind and motives, the heart and soul, of Julius Caesar, perhaps the last place to go, the biggest disappointment of all, is Shakespeare's eponymous but ultimately mistitled play. The true title of the play should have been not Julius Caesar, for Caesar has scarcely more than a cameo role in the proceedings, but Marcus Brutus, for the central conflict, the truly tragic figure in the play is Brutus. Caesar is of course assassinated, but Brutus, in the play and in life, comes to understand the logical end of his actions to be his own suicide. Worse: The assassination of Julius Caesar turned out to be a highly dramatic but ultimately pointless act, leading not, as Brutus and his co-conspirators hoped, to a return to republican values, but to the Julio-Claudian dynasty of chiefly unsatisfactory emperors that followed soon enough, beginning with Octavian (later Augustus), his adopted son, and running through Tiberius, Caligula, Claudius,

Nero, and the rest. But Shakespeare has put his impress on Caesar, not all of it historically accurate. Doubt resides even about the long-famous last words Shakespeare put in Caesar's mouth, "*Et tu*, Brute?" Two rival candidates for Caesar's last words are "You, too, my child" and "See you in hell, punk." I prefer to think he said the latter.

Although several biographies have been written about Julius Caesar and the most brilliant minds—Bacon, Montaigne, Pascal, Montesquieu, and others—have commented on him, no one has fully captured the great man in print. Bacon allowed that "he was, no doubt, of a very noble mind; but yet as aimed more at his particular advancement than at any merits for the common good." Montesquieu called Caesar "a man with many great qualities, with no defects—although many vices . . ." and went on to contemn him as the man who, in forming his triumvirate with Pompey and Crassus, ultimately brought about the destruction of the republic. On the credit side of the Caesarian ledger, Goethe thought Caesar "a great fellow," planned to write a play about him, and held his assassins in contempt. Nietzsche, perhaps no surprise, hailed Caesar as the very type of the *Ubermensch* and referred to him as "an ornament to the world." Mommsen, everywhere else a critical spirit, quite lost it when writing about Caesar: "A statesman of genius," he called him, "the mighty magician" and "master of the world," a man fit "to contend with nature herself."

Peter Green makes the point that there is a different Caesar for different ages. Over the centuries, Julius Caesar has gone back and forth in reputation from bloodthirsty monster to magnanimous genius. Ages of monarchy revered him—the very words "czar" and "kaiser" of course derive from the name Caesar—republican eras not so much. The grand Winston Churchill and the preposterous Benito Mussolini both admired him. After World War II, with Hitler now in the books and Mao and Stalin still afield, one-man rule was anathema, and Caesar (and Caesarism) not in good odor.

Hㅤow is Caesar accurately measured, his worth properly weighed? He hasn't made the task easy by having, in effect, written his own history in *The Gallic War* and *The Civil War*. In those works, he portrays himself in the third person. In the words of Keith Fairbank, Caesar crafts his own self-image as "this cool, collected leader who moves quickly and deliberately, deals decisively with political and military challenges, is concerned for and close to his troops, and has things firmly under control." Fairbank adds that the self-described Caesar is "a man of action, well informed, sharp in his assessments and decisions, ready to seize control of the situation, caring for his men and admired by them, and always bringing his plans firmly but justly to the desired end."

Ronald Syme thought that one could write a biography of Cicero, "but probably not of Caesar." He doesn't specify why, but it may well be that the legend of Caesar gets in the way. His success seems almost fabled, the good fortune he counted upon never letting him down until, of course, that day in the middle of March when it did. He was, as Christian Meier notes, "able to realize almost everything that lay with him." He was also a man without close friends. Others might do his bidding on the battle-field and in the senate, but in Meier's words, "He ultimately owed every-thing he accomplished to himself, to his art as a commander, a leader of men, and a diplomat, to his untiring energy—and to his good fortune."

Julius Caesar was one of those rarest of rare human beings whose talent was up to his ambition, and in his case that ambition was towering. Ron-ald Syme writes that by the year 44 BCE, when Caesar was fifty-five years old, he "had no competitors left. And he had wrecked the playground." His vast success—all his foes routed, little world left to conquer—had put an end to the high-stakes game that had given his life meaning. There was talk around this time of his going off on a mission to defeat the per-petually troublesome Parthians, but another military victory at this stage would have added little to his renown. "My life has been long enough, when you reckon it in years or in glory," he said. He is also supposed to have declared, at a dinner party at the home of Marcus Lepidus on the evening of March 14, that "the best death is the quickest." The following day, in the theater built by his now dead rival Pompey where the sen-ate was about to convene, Julius Caesar, the *divus Iulius*, discovered that, thanks to his assassins, that wish, too, had come true.

Our Gladiators

(2018)

ETWEEN THE NATIONAL FOOTBALL LEAGUE'S motto "Football Is Family" or the National Basketball Association's assertion "The NBA Cares," which has the lower truth quotient? Without the finest calibrated of instruments, it is, I suspect, impossible to measure. Major League Baseball thus far makes no similar claims to caring, sharing, or dispensing herring, which is just as well. But why the need for this sad public-relations effort on behalf of football and basketball and of professional sports generally?

Part of the answer is that there is something askew about the entire enterprise, at least in its contemporary phase. How else consider a situation in which (mostly) men in their twenties and early thirties are able to earn millions of dollars hitting or throwing or kicking balls or banging pucks or one another around before audiences willing to pay exorbitant sums to watch them do so?

As salaries and ticket prices soar, so do the size of the athletes themselves: The 300-pound NFL lineman is now commonplace, so, too, the seven-foot NBA basketball center; the majority of current-day major-league pitchers appear to be around 6'4", and the New York Yankees have only one pitcher under six foot and five over 6'7." Of the top ten ranked male tennis players, five are over 6'5"; six-foot-tall women tennis players are not uncommon. Just about everything about professional sports these days is outsized, out of proportion, swollen.

Two of the three major American professional sports, football and basketball, have a preponderance of African-American players. For football, the percentage is 64 percent, for basketball it is 75 percent. (Of NBA games a friend of mine noted that they are over not when the fat lady sings but instead when the white guys go in.) Meanwhile the number of black players in Major League Baseball has slipped to 7.7 percent, with the Hispanic players in the game now at a high of 29.8 percent and Asian players coming up slowly on the outside. Baseball, the national pastime, is getting less and less national every day.

Every boy with an interest and prowess in sports harbored—and many as older men may well still harbor—the fantasy of playing his favorite sport for a living, with all the rewards that would flow therefrom in the coin of fame, glory, and now heavy coin itself. Yet the sports fantasy is wearing thin. Football, for example, with its strong possibility of lasting head injuries, is no longer the uncomplicated field of speed, brawn, and physical courage it once seemed. Head injuries resulting in Chronic Traumatic Encephalopathy (CTE), causing early dementia and sometimes death, has clouded both the present and future of football. Some years ago, Doug Planck, an old Chicago Bears safety, said, more prophetically than he knew, that the first thing one must give up if one is to play in the NFL is one's sense of self-preservation.

Another thing one may have to give up to play sports in college is any hope of obtaining even a simulacrum of an education. The son of a friend of mine, who had a baseball scholarship to Northwestern, dropped off the team when it was made clear to him that, along with the official NCAA sanctioned four hours for practice, he would do well to put in still extra hours in the weight room. One of the sad joke phrases of our time is "scholar-athlete" to describe college jocks; even "student-athlete" has come to have a bitter, unreal ring. The proof of this is in those pre-and post-game, barely literate interviews with professional athletes. Years ago, it was said of a certain NBA all-star that he led the league in "you knows."

Yet the pool of admiration for athletes in America never quite empties. While politicians come and go, actors increasingly make dodos of themselves through their politics or going into confession mode on talk shows, a select number of athletes—Sandy Koufax, Derek Jeter, Bill Russell, Joe

Montana—remain enshrined in their countrymen's good graces. The special honor in which athletes have been held is of long standing. Thucydides tells how the people of Scione, after having been rescued by the Spartan general Brasidas, "would come up to him and deck him with garlands, as though he were a famous athlete."

From a fairly early age, gifted athletes often live in a privileged status. Today, kids with professional athletic ability are spotted as early as 13 or 14 and cultivated by high school coaches and sometimes college coaches. At 17, LeBron James's high school basketball games were shown on national television. For a brief spell, some of the best players in the NBA took a pass altogether on college, and many others took up the option known as "one-and-done," by which is meant that after a single year at college, which gave the pros a chance to scout them, they departed with a hefty contract for the NBA and all the associated rewards that go with it.

The effects of such early adulation on personality aren't easily reckoned. A number of years ago, the Chicago Bulls basketball team had a player named Scottie Pippen, whose sobriquet around town was "No Tippin' Pippen," owing to his being known for never leaving a tip at restaurants. But then how could he have known about tipping, when all his lifelong he probably never had to pick up a check?

The real toll on superior athletes may be in the narrowing of perspective, and thereby personality, that great athletic prowess often brings in its train. To become a great athlete calls for endless practice, to the exclusion of much else in life. The rewards for the truly promising are palpable. Imagine you are 20 years old, in top physical shape, playing in the NBA or NFL or MLB and earning, say, $8 million a year, with the promise, barring serious injury, of lots more to come.

How would any of us non-athletes, at that age with that kind of money available to us, have come through? Could we handle it, keep it all in perspective? In 2009, *Sports Illustrated* published a study that showed that two years after retirement, 78 percent of NFL players were either broke or struggling financially, and after five years of retirement 60 percent of NBA players were broke. Sad though this is, it doesn't seem in the least shocking.

I watch an unseemly number of baseball, basketball, football, hockey games, tennis matches, prize fights (in an earlier day), track meets, and more on television, but reading 400-page biographies of athletes is far from my idea of a good time. Especially biographies of golfers. A condominium on a golf course is the notion of Valhalla for many of the boys, now retired men, I grew up with. But I, in one of the sounder decisions of my youth, sedulously steered clear of playing golf, a sport that has been described as a good walk ruined. (Golf on television, for me, has long been a fine nap encouraged.) I mention all this because I have recently read a 485-page biography of Tiger Woods, and found it unexpectedly fascinating, not least on the subject of the perils of the life of the highly successful professional athlete.

BEFORE RECOUNTING THE LIFE OF TIGER WOODS as set out in Jeffrey Benedict and Armen Keteyian's full-court-press and iconoclastic biography, it needs to be emphasized that not all professional athletes are selfish, unintelligent, blinkered by their own fame or wealth. The Chicago Cubs' current first-baseman, Anthony Rizzo, himself the survivor of cancer, spends a fair amount of time visiting child cancer victims at the Ann & Robert H. Lurie Little Children's Hospital in Chicago, and has committed $3.5 million from his personal foundation to the hospital. Tim Anderson, the White Sox shortstop, at the opening of the current school year, bought a hundred ghetto kids haircuts and backpacks filled with school supplies. Other athletes have set up charitable foundations. Not a few retired NFL players have devoted funds to research into the effects of CTE. Some former athletes, baseball players especially, working as announcers, are sharp, amusing, subtle.

Perhaps the essential sadness at the heart of the professional athletic life is that such lives are essentially over by the age of 40, when everyone else is beginning to attain mastery over his or her own work. If they have managed to save their money, other possibilities are of course open to the former professional athlete. Or, if they prefer, they can hit golf balls for the remainder of their days as they watch their fame slowly diminish. Several years ago, at the Standard Club in Chicago, I was introduced to Marshall Goldberg, once an All-American at Pitt and then an All-Pro running back for the Chicago Cardinals, and his pleasure in my recognizing him was nearly boundless, for there are not many people left who do.

Tiger Woods, who is now 42 and still on the PGA Tour, need not soon worry about his own fame diminishing. He falls in that select inner circle of first-name fame, along with Oprah, Michael (Jordan and Jackson), Frank (Sinatra), Serena (Williams), and a few rarified others. "Tiger Woods was the kind of transcendent star that comes around about as often as Halley's Comet," write Benedict and Keteyian. "He was something no one had ever seen or will ever see again." Here since 1996, his first year as a professional golfer, is a partial account of what he has accomplished:

- He won 79 PGA tournaments, including 14 so-called Majors, and more than 100 tournaments worldwide.

- Player of the Year eleven times, he has earned more than $110 million in tournament prize money.

- When he appeared in a tournament, attendance records shot up, as did television ratings; when he played on a Sunday, the PGA usually beat the ratings of the NFL and the NBA.

- His popularity allowed the amount of tour prize money awarded to players to jump from $67 million in 1996 to $363 million today, thereby making millionaires of more than 400 PGA tour golfers.

In the words of Benedict and Keteyian, Tiger Woods "changed the face of golf—athletically, socially [as a bi-racial golfer in a formerly country-club sport not known for its generous integration policies], culturally, and financially."

Even in our day, when the word "millionaire" has lost much of its punch, Woods's earnings are impressive. His agent at the International Management Group brought in roughly $120 million in endorsements for him: from Nike, American Express, Disney, Gillette, General Motors, Rolex, Accenture, Gatorade, General Mills, and the video-game company called EA Sports. He was paid $1 million merely to appear in a golf tournament in Germany, $3 million to appear in another in Australia. His instructional book *How I Play Golf* sold a million copies in hardcover. By 2010, he is said to have earned more than $1 billion through golf and investment deals. His caddy, for God's sakes earned $12 million dollars over eleven seasons with him. Woods had enough money to be able to pay one of his fourteen mistresses $10 million in hush money (making our president's alleged payment of $130,000 to Stormy Daniels seem chump change) in the hope of keeping his marriage intact.

As his biographers note, "one of the perks of being a celebrated athlete is that tact and personality are not prerequisites for securing female companionship." Woods took sufficient advantage of this perk so that for the better part of four years The *National Enquirer*, the scandal-sheet, had him under nearly full-time surveillance. The *Enquirer* did eventually run a story about his extramarital affairs, but everything really fell apart when Elin, his wife and mother of his two young children, discovered texts on his phone from one of his mistresses.

Things get a bit blurry here. What is known is that at 2:00 a.m. on November 27, 2009, Woods rushed from his house, got into his Cadillac Esplanade SUV, lost control peeling out of his own driveway, ran over a fire hydrant, and wound up crashing into a tree in his neighbor's yard. His biographers write: "When the police arrived after responding to a 911 call from Tiger's neighbor, they found that both sides of the back seat of his vehicle had been smashed out with a golf club that had been swung by Elin."

This provided a splendid feast for the gutter press, and a lengthy Schadenfreudeian holiday for the media generally. From the *New York Times* to *Us Weekly*, everyone had a shot at Tiger, golf great and cheating husband. His biographers report that he appeared on the front page of the *New York Post* 21 days in a row, "surpassing the previous record of twenty consecutive covers devoted to the 9/11 terrorist attacks. "God, the media is pounding me," Tiger said to a friend, a former golf instructor named Hank Haney. "They're such vultures."

Tiger Woods claimed not simple abysmal irresponsibility for his errant sexual rompings but the latest psychological excuse, sex addiction (W. H. Auden claimed that the motto of psychology ought to be "Have you heard this one?") and, not long after he crashed his car, went into a facility for sex addiction in Hattiesburg, Mississippi. Although he publicly apologized for his adulteries, his wife divorced him. Perhaps more important, his golf game went into a deep schlunk. He failed to win a tournament for a full five-year stretch; his PGA ranking dropped from his perennial first to thirteenth.

Tyger, tyger, burning bright, / In the Forst of the Night; / What immortal hand or eye, / Could frame thy fearful symmetry?" William Blake's question, in regard to the Tiger of our time, is easily enough answered—two sets of hands, both mortal, each belonging to his parents. They decided from the outset that Eldrick (Tiger's name at birth) would be among the favorites of the gods, would himself be a god. His father, Earl, an African-American and retired U. S. Army lieutenant colonel, referred to his son as "the Chosen One," and, early in Tiger's professional career claimed that, because of his son's half-black, half-Thai ethnicity, "he'll have the power to impact nations. Not people. Nations." Earl Woods also believed that, as he told a journalist, "the first black man who is a really good golfer is going to make a hell of a lot of money." (He got that right.) Tiger's mother, Kultida, an immigrant from Thailand, was both his protector and cheering section, instructing him that only victory mattered and victory was meant exclusively for him.

Tiger was raised one stage beyond pampered. His biographers tell us that as a boy he was never asked to do household chores, never held a job, mowed lawns, delivered newspapers, or did anything else. Golf was his only job. Beginning at age two, the baby Tiger practiced swinging a golf club two hours a day. As he grew older, his sole mission was mastering control over a small hard white ball, smashing it vast distances off the tee, down the fairway, out of the rough or sand trips, onto the green, and in a putt or two, plonk, into the hole. On a normal day he would hit at least 600 practice balls. He later came to view his golf swing as his most precious gift. Golf was all he did, pretty much all he knew, his life.

This narrowing of Tiger Woods's interests produced a less than impressive, one might even say a less than full, human being. As a boy, apart from golf (and his father did not permit him to play other sports, lest he injure himself) he spent long hours at video games. He had few friends. Gratitude seems not to have been in his quiver of emotions. Later in life, once his fame had set in, according to his biographers, "for Tiger even the most basic of civilities—a simple hello or thank you—went missing from his vocabulary." A Vegas night-club owner said, "he got mean." A sports journalist named Jimmy Roberts remarked that "there's more 'f--- you' in Tiger Woods than in any athlete I've ever seen." Perhaps all major athletes have to be self-centered, but, as his biographers write, "the secret to Tiger's dominance [in golf] was that he was the most one-dimensional human being on the PGA Tour."

Tiger Woods is doubtless in many ways an exceptional case—more protected by his family and agents, more famous, more narrow in his interests, more stunted in his general development. But aren't most professional athletes almost of necessity self-centered, one-dimensional, stunted, because of the nature of their work? They are adulated from boyhood on, later lavishly rewarded, catered to in every way. I think here of Joe DiMaggio, one of the greatest of all baseball players, who played before the big money kicked in. During his years on the New York Yankees, when he came in each half-inning from his position in centerfield, he found on the edge of the dugout a hot cup of coffee and a lit cigarette awaiting him. I think of the Los Angeles Lakers' Kobe Bryant, who in 2003 was charged with rape by a hotel employee in Colorado. The charges were eventually dropped, though sexual intercourse was admitted, but my guess is that Bryant, who had probably not before then ever been said no to, must have been confounded when what he construed merely as *droits du seigneur* was taken for rape.

The morning Michael Jordan announced his retirement from professional basketball at a heavily attended press conference in Chicago, I watched on television his stepping up to the microphone in what looked to be an $8,000 suit and his noting that a policemen had been shot the night before and the press that was here for him should really be covering that much more important event. If for a moment you believe he really meant it, there are some O. J. Simpson souvenirs I should like to sell you.

As a young man, Tiger Woods claimed he wanted to be "the Michael Jordan of golf." He later became close to Jordan, thought of himself as his younger brother, the same Michael Jordan of whom Benedict and Keteyian claim one "didn't have to travel far to find stories of [his] barely tipping, or stiffing caddies, locker-room attendants, card dealers, bartenders, or of his driving his tricked-out North Carolina blue golf cart down the middle of a fairway . . . music blaring as he blew by one foursome or another while yelling, 'Hurry the f--- up. You guys are slow as f---' . . ."

IN OUR PROFESSIONAL ATHLETES we have created a gladiator class. Not, to be sure, an enslaved class, like the gladiators in Rome, but a highly paid and privileged one. Yet gladiators in their function our contemporary athletes remain, a function much the same as their Roman precursors: to provide circuses (hold the bread) for a large portion of the male citizenry of the American republic.

This gladiatorial status is true across the spectrum of professional sports. Even tennis, once a vaguely aristocratic game, has felt the deadening hand of professionalization through the infusion of huge sums of money. (First-prize money, for men and women, in the US Open this past year was $3.8 million.) When tennis players win tournaments, they now customarily thank their "team." By team they mean coach or coaches, trainers, physicians, and psychologists. As for graceful play on the court, turn on a tennis match, close your eyes, and from the grunting, often on the part of both players, men as well as women, you are more likely to think it coming from a Masters & Johnson laboratory than from, say, the green courts of Wimbledon. Watching Rafael Nadal in his muscle shirt, twitching, groaning, and grunting away, feels more like watching a wrestling than a tennis match. In tennis, elegance, even sportsmanship, is out. Winning is all.

Please understand, I make these strictures with no moral authority whatsoever, since I have watched, and continue to watch, my share of professional sports on television. Would I, I have sometimes asked myself, have been one of those besheeted and benighted Romans seated in the Coliseum 2,000 years ago, turning my thumbs down and screaming for the death of defeated gladiators? In fact, I have begun to feel a touch queasy about watching college and professional football now that I know that the men who participate in it are risking their health and mental balance for their profit and my entertainment. I may need to see a sport-spectator therapist, but, apart from baseball, which continues to seem a game of great subtlety, with only a minimum of barbarity, basketball, tennis, hockey, and other sports are beginning to bore me.

Think of it: We have been paying a select group of overly trained men, and a few women, grand sums, at the expense of their not leading normal lives, to perfect and perform for our pleasure what are in effect games devised for children. Then there is the obvious yet still disturbing fact that we fans of many of these games are more loyal to the teams we follow than are the men who play for these teams. (I still run into the occasional older man who has never forgiven the Dodgers for moving from Brooklyn to Los Angeles.) In an earlier day, great professional athletes—DiMaggio, Stan Musial, Bob Cousy, Johnny Unitas, Gordie Howe—stayed their entire careers with the same teams in the same cities. Now, with free agency, arbitration, sports agents, a player is offered more money, and it's yo, dude, catch you later.

The contradictions inherent in professional sports—in playing them, watching them, paying for them—are too glaring to overlook. Yet most of those among us who spend a disproportionate amount of our time engaged with them overlook these contradictions easily enough. Has the time come to cease to do so? I suspect it has. If you feel as I do, and wish to discuss this further, don't hesitate to be in touch, but, please, don't call before the playoffs and World Series are over. Sundays after that, I shall be busy watching Chicago Bears games. In October, the NBA season begins; so, too, that of the NHL. The first of the tennis majors is played in Australia in January. April the new baseball season gets underway, with a promising young Chicago Cubs team. On second thought, if you wish to be in touch, maybe you would do best to make an appointment.

Diamonds are Forever

(2016)

A S THE MAJOR LEAGUE PLAYOFFS continue on into the World Series, there is lots of talk—complaining, really—about the lengthening time it takes to play, and therefore watch, a baseball game. The average time of a baseball game is now three hours and five minutes. I don't know if the average time of a baseball game was even tracked in the good/bad old days of my youth, but I remembered games with fast-working pitchers on the mound—Bob Gibson, Fergie Jenkins—that were completed at just under two hours, roughly the length of a movie. The young today seem especially put off by the slowness of baseball; the average age of the baseball television audience is 57, with only 7 percent of its viewers under the age of 18.

Worrisome, all this, especially if one owns a baseball franchise or even if one has an emotional investment in baseball such that one wishes it not to lose its place as the national pastime and dwindle into a game enjoyed chiefly by codgers. Former baseball commissioner Bud Selig was sufficiently worried to have formed a committee composed of baseball owners and executives, general managers and field managers to come up with ways to speed up the game without, the hope is, changing its essential character. The new commissioner, Rob Manfred, is even more intent on shortening the game. Thus far the only change put into effect is that teams no longer have to go through the paces of an intentional walk by purposely throwing four bad pitches; the intentional walk can now quickly be executed by the manager's simply signaling for it from the dugout, though the time saved by this reform is minimal, less than a minute, I'd guess. Talk is also being bruited about reducing the number of pitching changes allowed in a game, about shortening the time permitted a pitcher between pitches (it is now 12 seconds, although the rule is notoriously unenforced), about the number of trips a catcher can make to the mound to confer with his pitcher, about limiting the times a batter is allowed to step out of the batter's box between pitches and, who can say, about not permitting an outfielder, in his lonely isolation, to adjust his crotch.

Boredom is the great enemy here. Too many people now find baseball, because of its slowness, tedious in the extreme. Why aren't I—a man easily bored by unstylishly written books, dull lectures, misfired TV sitcoms, most theater, much of the news, and all politicians—also bored by baseball? Far from being bored by the sport, the older I get the more I have come to appreciate the genius inherent in the game. As a man who has had the sports disease from the age of 6, I now find baseball easily the most intricate, the most pleasing, the best of all sports.

In what other sport can a last-place team beat a first-place team three or four games in a row and sweep a series? (In basketball or football, where superior skill if not brute force wins every time out, this is unlikely to happen even once.) In what other sport is tension so extended as in baseball, where in a playoff or World Series or even mid-season game a pitcher, in late innings in a tied game or with a one-run lead with the bases loaded and no one out, is in a fix—a fix that could take him as long as 20 or more tense minutes to work out of or that could prove his team's undoing? In what other sport is what not Yogi Berra but Aristotle called *peripeteia*, or reversal of fortune, so frequent as in baseball, where a single error or an unexpected injury can close down a team's hopes for a season or the acquisition of a new player in a trade completely revive its prospects? In what other sport is there a season of similar length—162 games—which over this longish haul allows for impressive comebacks after poor beginnings and which requires an almost philosophical perspective to accept rises and falls on the part of players and fans alike, while providing, for roughly seven months, nearly everyday entertainment for its devotees?

No other sport is so intricate in its maneuverings as baseball. The former manager Tony La Russa, in George Will's excellent 1990 book *Men at Work: The Craft of Baseball*, posited eight different strategies available to a manager with men on first and third and one out. To grasp the richness of baseball's complications, its language, its arcana, one needs to have grown up with it, to have played it as a kid. At a Cubs-Dodgers game, I once attempted to explain baseball to Bonnie Nims, the wife of the poet John Frederick Nims, and at the end of my six-inning-long instruction, I asked if everything was becoming clear to her. "I think so," she said. "I believe I understand just about everything you've said except for this concept of 'the out.'"

Baseball may also be the last major American sport in which one doesn't have to be freakishly large—a 300-pound lineman or 250-pound running back in football, a 6' 10" power forward or 6' 5" guard in basketball—to succeed. Tony Gwynn, the greatest hitter in the game over the past 40 years, was a pudge who probably couldn't have qualified as the mascot for any major college athletic program.

For the sports-minded, as for the politically minded, there is a spectrum ranging from conservative to radical, and it is not uncommon for a radical in politics to be arch-conservative in the realm of sports, and sometimes vice versa. Sports radicals do not in the least mind changes in their sport— ranging from designated hitters in baseball, to shot clocks in basketball, to coaches' red-flag challenges of referees' calls in football. Sports conservatives would like everything in the games they love to stay forever the same. Sports conservatives, for example, loathe the American League designated hitter rule in baseball to this day, even though it has been in practice since 1973, a full 44 years. Sports radicals think improvement through change always possible and usually desirable. I'm surprised no one among them has yet proposed solving the problem of the lengthening of baseball games in a single stroke by reducing all games to five innings, thereby allowing everyone to return home early to his video games and Reddit.

Change there has of course been in baseball, undeniable and irrecoverable. As was argued in the *Wall Street Journal* by Brian Costa and Jared Diamond, baseball has become ever more analytic in recent decades, in ways that invariably extend the length of the game. By analytic, they mean driven and controlled by sabermetrics, the study of stats that measure in-game action. The whole business probably began when someone discovered that, statistically at least, left-handed pitchers do better against right-handed hitters, and right-handed pitchers do better against left-handed hitters. This paved the way for more pitching changes and differing batting orders to face either right- or left-handed pitchers. In the 1920s there were pitchers who pitched both games of a doubleheader. As recently as the 1940s, relief pitchers were a rarity. In our day, if a pitcher can get through six innings, he is thought to have had a successful outing. So specialized has the game become that pitchers make a living—often a handsome one—as one-inning (the seventh, the eighth) specialists.

As with pitching, so with other aspects of baseball: Change and complication has made for longer games. More and more teams have devised defensive shifts for opposing batters, which in turn causes the batters to disdain hitting ground balls and instead to swing for the fences. In recent years there were record numbers of home runs and strikeouts, both making for a longer time at bat. Costa and Diamond note that on average the ball is put into play only every 3 minutes 48 seconds. A batter who fouls off six or seven pitches can be in the batter's box for five full minutes and more.

Then, of course, there is the matter of the influence of money in lengthening games. When a journalist approached the late television sports producer Don Ohlmeyer saying he had a question for him, Ohlmeyer replied: "If the question is about sports, the answer is money." Striking out, once a matter of disgrace in baseball, is now of negligible concern—negligible, that is, if a player can hit 30 or more home runs during a season. The big money goes for the dingers. A Chicago Cubs outfielder named Kyle Schwarber in a recent season in 422 times at bat struck out 150 times, but he hit 30 home runs. Yankees rookie Aaron Judge was at bat 542 times and 208 of those times he struck out, but over the season hit 52 homers. No one is going to remember those strikeouts. His agent will lead with that 52 homers statistic when negotiating a vastly enriched renewal of Judge's contract, which he is sure to acquire.

Staying with the subject of the influence of money, a sports Marxist might argue that the most efficient way to reduce the time it takes to play major league baseball is to cut down on, if not eliminate, commercials. I have recently timed the commercials between half-innings at baseball games, and they run to three minutes each. This means that given 17 such breaks over nine innings, television commercials alone account for 51 minutes; add in another 18 minutes for the commercials aired during six pitching changes, and you have 1 hour and 9 minutes of a ball-game given over to commercials. A sports Marxist might be inclined here to argue, on the model of socialized medicine, for socialized (or commercial-free) baseball, though none has thus far come forth to do so.

The slowness of baseball doesn't seem such a problem if one goes to the park to watch a game. The punishment of the commercials, with their dreary repetition, makes it so. (Speaking of punishment, on my recent trips to Wrigley Field to watch the Cubs, I note that management, on the mistaken assumption that it is enhancing the entertainment value of the outing, has decided to play thunderous rock music between innings, making conversation about the game and about anything else impossible.)

But the solution of the between-inning and pitching-change commercial breaks that lengthen the time of baseball games is really quite simple. Give me a drum roll here: It's called reading. Keep a magazine or lightish book on your lap during these breaks, as I invariably do, and revert to it during them. You can usually get in a page of reading during commercial breaks, and sometimes even get in a brief paragraph between foul balls during a lengthy, or what these days is called a quality, at bat.

Baseball, like 19th-century novels, has always contained its *longueurs*, or dullish, if sometimes necessary, stretches: the foul balls, the trips by managers and pitching coaches to the mound, and now the camera reviews of challenged umpire calls. It's part of the deal and for most of us not too much to have to put up with in exchange for witnessing a game of great difficulty—as has often been remarked, if a batter gets a hit one of three times at bat, he's thought immensely successful—and impressive subtlety played with astonishing skill. If the game is too slow for you, best perhaps to walk away and to turn instead to wrestling or mixed martial arts or perhaps choose a becalming participatory sport: checkers or tiddlywinks. You won't, I'm fairly sure, be missed.

What's the Story?

(2017)

I

F I WERE A REPUBLICAN STRATEGIST, which I'm pleased to say I'm not, I would pay especial attention to a Shelby Steele op-ed "Why the Left Can't Let Go of Racism" in the *Wall Street Journal*. Toward the close of his article, Mr. Steele writes that "the great problem for conservatives is that they lack the moral glibness to compete with liberalism's 'innocence'"—innocence, in this case, from the evil of racism and social injustice generally. Mr. Steele then goes on briefly to suggest that "reality" should be the "informing vision" of conservatism. By "reality" I take him to mean more than arguments countering the unreality of the empty utopianism of much liberalism.

What Shelby Steele holds in his op-ed is that liberals have a story and conservatives do not. The liberal story is an old one, in many ways a false one, but it works for them, and, as he points out, they are adamantly sticking to it. Their story—nowadays the approved word is "narrative"—is one of impressive simplicity: They hate social injustice in any form, despise capitalism for its selfishness and blame it for the despoiling of the environment and the planet generally, and cannot find an ethnic or sexual minority they don't wish to help. Through this program, they have, or at least feel they have, cornered the market on virtue. To put the liberal story in two words: They care. This has left conservatives in the unattractive position of not caring.

Like most simple stories about the motorforce of human behavior—the class struggle, the Oedipus complex—the side-effects of the liberal story, which go unmentioned, are sometimes as pernicious as the disease. Liberals, in recent years, have a lot for which to apologize. Thus, owing to the successful attempts at implementing an essentially liberal program of diversity and giving way to every possible strain of multiculturalism, the contemporary university controlled by liberal ideas has been so badly watered down in its humanities and social sciences divisions as to dilute the quality of higher education itself, with political correctness, trigger-warnings, and microaggressions putting on the finishing touches. Thus, in their relentlessly reassuring African-Americans of their continuing victim status—ignoring the more deadly tragedy of black-on-black gang murders in the inner city—the liberal program on race has ensured bad feeling all round and brought on the worst in black leadership. As Shelby Steele himself remarked some years ago, if racial progress in the country is ever admitted, Jesse Jackson and Al Sharpton would be out of business.

A liberal in good standing through my late twenties, the liberal story lost credence for me when I began to teach at a middlewestern university. There I discovered young professors, good liberals all, sleeping with their students, older professors backing down before radicals who openly proclaimed they had no use for free speech—never have I witnessed such cowardliness when there was so little to fear—and behavior so grasping (and for such very low stakes) that it made the Robber Barons look like an order of Dominicans. Liberals, as is well known, are much better at proclaiming than living up to their ideals.

If liberals frequently turn out disappointing, conservatives are uninspiring. Conservatives don't have a story, or at least an impressive one. They are left only with their insistence on the unreality of contemporary liberalism, which when proclaimed is usually turned against them by charges of racism, blindness to the beauty of idealism and the larger project of the good of eminently improvable humankind, and insensitivity generally. Conservatives need a story of their own. But what might it be?

Economics has long been at the heart of the conservative story. Friedrich Hayek correctly held that the loss of economic liberty soon results in the loss of other, more essential liberties. The prime example here is the

Soviet Union, whose leaders, having captured the means of production, for 75 brutal years promptly closed down the means of decent life itself.

Unarguably true though it is, the conservative insistence upon the importance of free markets is not necessarily useful as an arguing point for winning the good opinion of independents. The emphasis on free markets in current-day conservatism is more likely to convince them, and reconfirm liberals in their fixed belief, that conservatives merely wish to preserve the status quo—preserve, in other words, the wealth of the One Percent and all that. The conservative story ought somehow to show that conservatism itself is not identical with, is richer and more complex than, business interests. The business of America, they need to emphasize, contra Calvin Coolidge, is greater than mere business.

My friend Edward Shils once remarked to me apropos of Milton Friedman, George Stigler, Gary Becker, and their colleagues in the University of Chicago Economics Department that they were decent men, honorable and obviously highly intelligent, but "insufficiently impressed by the mysteries of life." Those mysteries need to be part of the conservative story. While endorsing free markets as the most efficient arrangement known under successful capitalism, the conservative story must not allow a belief in the importance of economics to block out the more significant elements in life. In defense of his own Communist politics, Bertolt Brecht said, "first grub, then ethics." Through an undue emphasis on economics, conservatives convey essentially the same skewed message.

As Chesterton is supposed to have said, "when a man chooses not to believe in God, he does not choose to believe in nothing, he believes in anything." In the realm of economics, confirmation of Chesterton's aphorism is available at Exhibit A: the invisible hand of the market.

On the subject of God, liberals and conservatives are divided. Those liberals who profess religious belief feel that their belief impels them to join the fight for social justice. Among religious institutions given over to politics, the Episcopal church, once the citadel of the East Coast social establishment, appears to have been captured by liberalism. Unitarianism has for decades seemed an appendage of liberalism. Reform Judaism, it has been said, is little more than the Democratic party platform, with holidays added. True, evangelical Christians have supported the Republican party in recent years, but they have done so chiefly because they felt their faith under attack by the social arrangements promoted by secular liberalism.

In this melee of religious passion, conservatives do well to present themselves as defenders not of the Faith, but of faith itself. (I have, in this connection, a conservative friend who calls himself a "pious agnostic.") By this I mean conservatives ought, insofar as possible, to defend all respectable religious worship while stressing that religion is above mere politics and as such does best wherever possible to steer clear of direct involvement in political activism.

The attack on Big Government has long been another part of the conservative story. However high its truth factor, this, too, has a commensurately low persuasion quotient. The closer it gets to impinging on personal life—in the realms of health, setting and reinforcing social norms, and the rest—the more inept, not to say interfering, Big Government does indeed seem. Yet to be against all Big Government is to chew much more than one should bite off. The need for FEMA, the FDA, ICE, and the other of the lettered federal agencies that comprise the alphabet soup of Big Government has if anything grown greater in recent years. The conservative argument ought not to be against Big Government *per se*, but on the underlying assumption that government is the greatest force available for bringing about human welfare and happiness.

THE INSISTENCE ON FREE MARKETS and the attack on Big Government and the retreat into tradition that takes the form of disparagement of advanced guard social behavior (gay marriage, abortion, and the rest) come to little more than a melancholy and defeatist creed, when what is missing and much needed in the conservative story is an affirmative philosophy.

At the heart of the liberal-conservative argument is a dispute about human nature. Liberals find human nature infinitely malleable—"A path out of poverty and poor health" runs the happy headline to a story about a recent study conducted by psychologists and developmental scientists— conservatives view it as hardily resistant to change. Liberals see humanity as on a relentless march of progress, conservatives see civilization itself as inherently fragile, a beautiful but thin construct always in danger of tearing.

In his one strongly political novel, *The Princess Casamassima*, Henry James has a character, Madame Grandoni, the companion of the radically chic princess, remark in a manner to which most conservatives would, I think, readily subscribe: "I take no interest in the people; I don't understand them and I know nothing about them. An honorable nature of any class, I always respect it, but I will not pretend to a passion for the ignorant masses." Conservatives are not, like liberals, under any obligation to take up the cause of supposed victim groups en masse, but only that of individuals of honorable character. Hyacinth Robinson, James's hero in the novel, a boy born poor, orphaned, and raised in the London slums, undergoes an inner revolution and gives up the outer revolution to which he had been committed, abandoning his political resentment and anger and falling in love with "the beauty of the world." Later in the novel James remarks about the limits of politics, a limit conservatives need to make part of their story: "The figures on the chessboard were still the passions and jealousies and superstitions and stupidities of man, and their position with regard to each other, at any given moment, could be of interest only to the grim, invisible fates who played the game—who sat, through the ages, bow-backed over the table." Such thoughts do not make for simple political messaging, but, conservative at their core, they can supply the philosophy behind a persuasive conservative story.

THE CONSERVATIVE ENGLISH NOVELIST EVELYN WAUGH once jokingly remarked that he was never again going to vote for the Tories as they had been in power for eight years and hadn't turned the clock back one minute. Neither should American conservatives expect their political representatives to have any better luck with turning back the clock. Arthur M. Schlesinger Sr. held a cyclical view of American history, with liberal changes sweeping the board for a time, at which point, having exhausted itself, liberalism is replaced by conservatism. Thus, do Democrats and Republicans shuffle in and out of power, though with the changes made during the liberal years generally accepted and becoming part of the status quo.

But the most recent liberal changes seem unacceptable, and not to conservatives alone. The identity politics that, along with an inept campaign,

cost Hillary Clinton the presidency have also gone a long way to destroying the universities, made race relations more jagged than ever, and left
American foreign policy in a great muddle of indecision. So demoralized
had the nation become by liberalism that in Donald J. Trump it elected a
man richly unprepared for the job whose only attraction was his promise
that he could put a stop to the business-as-usual of liberal identity politics and foreign policy dithering and, you should pardon the expression,
Make America Great Again.

With a good conservative story in place, the Trump presidency, with
all its unnerving volatility, might have been avoided. But none of the candidates who opposed Donald Trump in the Republican primaries was in
possession of that story or any other moderately convincing story, leaving them all seeming little more than men and one woman in business
for themselves.

I myself do not have that much-needed conservative story, but I do
have a strong sense of what its general lineaments ought to be. The conservative story ought to be respectful of business but not dominated by
its values. It ought to be sympathetic to those who have fallen or are otherwise unfit to compete in a competitive society and relieve their misery
wherever possible. It ought to recognize the centrality of immigration in
our history and do all in its power to turn recent immigrants into true
Americans, not merely people who have come here seeking work and the
enjoyment of superior consumer goods. Connected with this it needs to
recognize that the United States is no longer a dominantly white country, which statistically it isn't, and to give up any false notions of our having an aristocratic class ("Ah," said the Italian to the Englishman who
was bragging about his lineage, "when your people were still painting
their behinds purple and baying at the moon, in my family already we
had homosexuals"). Finally, in a hard world, conservatives ought to be
good-humored. As for that world, permit me to allow Henry James, in a
passage from his 1878 collection *French Poets and Novelists*, to have the
last word:

> Evil is insolent and strong; beauty enchanting but rare; good-
> ness very apt to be weak; folly very apt to be defiant; wicked-
> ness to carry the day; imbeciles to be in great places, people

of sense in small, and mankind generally unhappy. But the world as it stands is no illusion, no phantasm, no evil dream of a night; we wake up to it again for ever and ever; we can neither forget it nor deny it nor dispense with it.

Nothing cheerful about that, to be sure, but it seems impressively realistic in the way that Shelby Steele called for "reality" to be "the informing vision" of conservatism and to help furnish conservatives with a powerfully persuasive story of their own.

University Presidents

(2019)

Q UICK QUIZ: Name the current presidents of Harvard, Yale, and Princeton universities.

Not to worry if you can't, for neither can I, though I do recall that the president of Harvard is a woman, or was a woman until recently. Sixty years ago, when I was an undergraduate, I could have told you that Robert Goheen was president of Princeton, Whitney Griswold was president of Yale, and Nathan Pusey, following upon the more famous James Conant, was president of Harvard. I could have done so because these men, and a number of other university presidents of the time, were educational leaders. An educational leader, in that distant day, was someone who had firm ideas about the principles required to run a university and the ultimate rewards of higher education. They weighed in on these ideas when called upon to do so, and sometimes without waiting to be called upon. The reason you are unlikely to know the names of the presidents of Harvard, Yale, and Princeton is that the university president as an educational leader is today as quaint as the set-shot, the hoola-hoop, or the intrauterine device. You can't find one anywhere.

I have not myself studied or worked in a university run by a great president, though, as an undergraduate at the University of Chicago, I was the recipient of the intellectual endowment of such a figure. Robert Hutchins had left the presidency of the University of Chicago in 1950, six years before I arrived there, but so strong was his impress on its under-graduate education that my classmates and I were among its beneficiaries. What Hutchins had done, without so far as I know asking the permission of anyone else, was revamp the undergraduate curriculum in favor of great books over text books, protect the academic freedom of his faculty during a time when it was endangered by congressional committees and witch-hunting right-wingers, internationalize the tone of the school by bringing in foreign scholars (Enrico Fermi, Leo Strauss, and others) on the run from European fascism, invent interdisciplinary study through forming the Committee on Social Thought, and remove the university from Big Ten football competition. "Football has the same relation to education," Hutchins said, "that bullfighting has to agriculture."

Unlike the majority of current-day university presidents, Robert Hutchins had little interest in public relations. He said what he thought, and what he thought generally went flush up against the educational platitudes of the time. Although a successful fundraiser, he never fawned over the wealthy, or even took them altogether seriously. What the rich had in common, he once claimed, was a short attention span. He kept in his desk a sign, brought out only in the presence of trusted colleagues, that read, "Dirty Money Laundered Here." Robert Hutchins had wit, integrity of a kind that could not be trifled with, and more than a touch of grandeur.

Historically, Charles W. Eliot of Harvard, Nicholas Murray Butler of Columbia, Daniel Coit Gilman of Johns Hopkins, were men who represented the university president as educational innovator, guardian of the mission of higher education, standard bearer, and they became famous as such. Today a university president is more likely to become known—never famous—for finding the money to build vast athletic facilities, having a highly ranked (by the fourth-rate *US News & World Report*) MBA program, or bringing diversity to and protecting political correctness within his institution. How did this come about? How did the role of university president become so diminished in our time?

Through means many and various, but in my view by two chiefly: by democratization where democracy really has no place; and, the second connected to the first, by a radically altered vision of the nature of the institution of the university itself.

When I say that democracy has no place in the university, I mean that the university is, or at any rate was and ought still to be, a hierarchical institution, as befits an elite enterprise. The hierarchy is based upon scholarly and scientific accomplishment. The accomplishment makes for authority. The implied assumption was that intellectual achievement would give one an understanding of the true mission of the university that no amount of administrative skill or experience could hope to replace. That mission, with which current-day university presidents have no connection, is the pursuit and promulgation of truth. The limerick about Benjamin Jowett, Master of Balliol College, Oxford, from 1872 through 1880, captures the point:

> My name is Benjamin Jowett.
> There's no knowledge but I know it.
> I am Master of this College,
> What I don't know isn't knowledge.

The hierarchical character of the modern university based on scholarly achievement broke down, as did much else in university life, during the years of the student protest movement. During those years establishments of all kinds were under attack. Many caved in, but the educational establishment caved in most completely. As a result, students henceforth were asked to evaluate their teachers and in some cases were called in to serve on committees to hire university administrators, including university presidents. At the departmental level, where formerly a department chairman was the most distinguished man or woman in the department, now the chairmanship became a rotating position, given with the new goal of diversity more than intellectual distinction in mind and time off or a reduced course load as a reward for those agreeing to serve in the post.

The effect of all this was the breakdown in authority in universities. Without authority, standards quickly fell. Imagine a young English department assistant professor coming to his department chairman to announce he planned to teach a course in novels about the Vietnam War. That chairman, if he or she were anything like the chairmen of old, would likely tell the young professor that, sorry, but the subject fell beneath the department standard. Students passionate about Vietnam could surely read those novels on their own, he is likely to have said, and, besides, we have these students for a severely limited period of time, and so perhaps the young professor would do best to return to teaching his course on John Milton. In that earlier time, the young professor would, no doubt sulkily, have left the chairman's office and returned to his own office to dust off his Milton. Today, more likely, he would claim a breach of his academic freedom and insist the decision be made by the entire department, where he would probably win out. How could he not, when his colleagues in the department were teaching courses (as they will be next quarter at the English Department at Northwestern University) with such titles as: "Queer Modernisms," "Asian-American Fiction as Counter-Archive," "Confederate Monuments and Union Memory," and "Postcolonial Postmodernism?" Would a Charles Eliot, a Nicholas Murray Butler, a Daniel Coit Gilmore, a Robert Hutchins have allowed such obviously tendentious, parochial, blatantly political courses in universities under their leadership? The question, I believe, answers itself.

Yet if a contemporary university president were to attempt to quash such courses, a major scandal would surely result. The furies of protest would be aroused. Howls of dire infringement of academic freedom would rend the air, and, just possibly, be taken up by the media. Forget that academic freedom, in its origin, was meant to free academics from the pressures of outside forces, so that a professor could not be fired owing to a trustee or politician not agreeing with his views, say, on labor unions. Today academic freedom is generally interpreted to mean that a teacher may teach just about anything he or she damn well pleases, and anyone who says otherwise is a tyrant, a fascist, you fill in any other opprobrious words that come to mind.

In any case, the disgruntled young professor in my previous paragraph is unlikely to have called in the president of his university. Increasingly nowadays the understanding is that education, what goes on in classrooms and laboratories, is well outside a contemporary university president's jurisdiction, interest, ken. The university provost, the deans of the various colleges and professional schools, run all that secondary stuff. A university president can, to be sure, help boost endowment, enrollment, and his school's reputation in the dependably myopic eyes of the outside world. But about education itself, he is largely without influence or even interest.

The president is the public face of the university, which is to say, staying with anatomical metaphors, its public relations arm. His job is to be photographed in sweaters and neckties in university colors surrounded by racially and ethnically diverse students, to recount great advances made under the school's roofs in medical and technological research, to blab away about the happy victories the university has scored in the realms of diversity, inclusivity, and widened tolerance generally, to show up at football and basketball games with wealthy alumni in tow.

The traditional purpose of the university has in recent decades been dealt a near deathblow by the incursions of political correctness. In recent years large contemporary universities have increasingly taken on, at what one assumes to be serious salaries, associate provosts or deans in charge of diversity, generally appointing a black man or woman to the job. Might they do this because of a strong need, or because the federal government requires them to do so? If they are to continue to receive federal grants for their scientific and other programs, have they any choice? In any case, the contemporary university president is likely to be the last person to object.

A similar pressure, to do not the right but the necessary-because-expected thing, occurs in the choices universities make for their commencement speakers and honorary degree recipients. Here, too, political correctness stretches out its long, dirty finger-nailed hand. Commencement speakers were once scientists, scholars, artists, men and women of intellectual accomplishment. No honorary degrees were bestowed upon billionaires, politicians, television anchormen, famous jocks. Currently, though, no commencement ceremony could be complete without honorary degrees given to African-Americans and women, preferably both. If, along with being politically O.K., a commencement speaker is also amusing, all the better. Bill Cosby, black and amusing (at least in an earlier day), and the holder of some 60 university honorary degrees, killed a good thing when he bought all those Quaaludes.

Today many universities now go to speakers' bureaus or even talent agencies to find politically correct speakers. The majority of commencement speakers this past year (2018) were—no surprise here—women. Rutgers landed Queen Latifah; the University of Connecticut, Anita Hill; Yale, Hillary Clinton; MIT, Sheryl Sandberg; and Northwestern, which last year had Billie Jean King, this year had Renée Fleming. The fees paid to such people are not, one assumes, negligible. But for universities they are worth every dollar, for a disappointing—which is to say unamusing or God forfend politically incorrect—commencement speaker might send the customers (the students and their parents who are now paying $50,000 a year and more for undergraduate education at private schools) away unhappy.

Here we come to the changed view of the university as an institution. Where once its leaders were content to view the university as existing in splendid isolation, nicely distanced from the noise of the world, devoted to the tradition of the liberal arts and to pure scientific research, leaders of the contemporary university more and more view their students and their families as customers, and the schools that house them for four years as something like a hotel. These customers, the hope is, will spread the word about how they enjoyed their stay, and, who can say, some among them may be good for a million or two in future fundraising endeavors.

The money is likely to be spent on new buildings. The contemporary university president has increasingly become more realtor than educator. His main heritage will be in the buildings erected on campus during his time in office. With great good luck, such a building, or an entire school within the university will be named after him. Whether the buildings are needed or not is quite beside the point. These often-otiose edifices suggest progress, and progress, for university presidents as for once upon a time General Electric, is their most important product.

The highest paid public employee in every state, it was recently revealed, was the state university football coach, who earned a great deal more than the state's university president. The same is largely true of private universities with Division I teams. As of 2016, the salary of Duke's basketball coach was $8.89 million; its president's salary, or total compensation package, was $1.3 million. In the early 1960s, when I lived in Little Rock, Arkansas, the football coach's salary was $25,000, the president's salary, if only in those days to save face, was pushed up to $26,000. Of course, the coaches of winning football and basketball teams—or "programs," as these money-making and fundraising outfits are called—are worth more, often vastly more, than mere university presidents. The chef (or football coach), to stay with my notion of the contemporary university as a hotel, deserves to be paid more than the maitre d' (or university president).

Different universities are controlled by different sources of power. At some universities, the center of power is the administration; at some it is the trustees; at state schools it is often the state legislatures; at some rare schools, it is the faculty. At most private universities the president's chief job, the ultimate measure of his success under the current dispensation, is raising funds, both among alumni and trustees. Hanging with the wealthy in a position of unspoken but obvious subservience cannot be much fun. But, then, that is why university presidents are paid what they are, and why they are allowed to live—in mansions, with servants, plush pensions to follow—as if they are themselves rich.

The average tenure of a contemporary university president seems to be eight or ten years. Afterwards some go back into teaching; others go off to head or work in foundations; some sit, for impressive emoluments, on corporation boards. In my thirty years teaching at Northwestern, no university president has left any notable impress on the quality of the school's education, or at least none that I have been able to notice. What has been true of Northwestern has, I suspect, been so almost everywhere else. Each university president has merely kept the pot boiling without noticing what wretched fare was cooking inside it. None has prevented or even slowed any of the continuing rot of the humanities and social sciences within their institution, nor even thought to do so.

A strange job, that of president of a contemporary American university, one filled with ambiguities and ironies. In our time every university president is in his day a minor-league Ozymandias, within the small compass of his realm a king of kings—and yet a king without any real power to change things that matter. How many, when it is time to depart, have had the introspection to look upon his own works and despaired? Too few, I fear.

Immaturity on Campus

(2020)

I HAVE NO WISH TO BRAG—well, perhaps a small wish—but the timing of my retirement in 2002 after thirty years of university teaching was exquisite. Smartphones had not yet become universal. Political correctness was still in its incipient, not yet in its tyrannous, stage. I did not have to undergo sex sensitivity training, which I could not have done with a straight face. In the classroom professors, not yet students, were still in control.

Signs that change was in the offing were evident when I began teaching in 1973. Not all male teachers wore ties and jackets nor female teachers skirts to class. Teachers had begun to address students by their first names. (I cannot recall having been so addressed once through my undergraduate years at the University of Chicago.) Students moreover were now sometimes invited to address teachers by their first names.

I recall a young female student, on the edge of tears, during an office hour, asking why I had marked up her papers, as she thought, so severely. "Jerry [an associate professor in the same department]" she said, "is never so hard on my writing." Hmm, "Jerry?" I concluded there was a good chance that "Jerry" had been, to use the Victorian phrase, "intimate with her." Lots of that, I soon discovered, was going on, at least between younger male faculty and undergraduates. Not a good sign.

The first formal opening to the change in professor-student relations may have come with the advent of teacher evaluations by students. Such evaluations might be useful in reporting genuine pedagogical delinquencies—"He is always late to class, alcohol on his breath"; "She returns our papers weeks after we've handed them in, unmarked and uncommented upon"—but most, or so I found, of those I received, were trivial: "He knows his stuff." "I like his bowties." "What does he have against contemporary poets?" But, then, who ever said that students were in a position properly to judge the true quality of teaching? The only memorable evaluation I received in all my years read: "I did well in this course, but then I would have been ashamed not to have done." Reading it I wondered what exactly I had done to induce that shame, so that I might do it again and again and again.

Student evaluations of their teachers may well have stimulated grade inflation, which seems to have emerged roughly around the same time. A teacher who was a "tough grader" figured not to get pleasing student evaluations; he might even find himself with low student enrollments for his courses. In any case, where once Cs were common and As rare, somehow the grade of C jumped up to B and As were more common than not. At the school where I taught a proudly left-wing teacher was said to give black students automatic As as an act of reparation. One quarter I would arrive for the 10:30 a.m. class I taught to find large, empty Dunkin' Donuts boxes on the table. The teacher who preceeded me in the classroom, I learned, passed out donuts to his 9:00 a.m. class, a sad instance, I thought at the time, of a teacher sucking up to his student. I hope the donuts received a strong evaluation.

I once had a call from the mother of a student asking how it was her daughter Kimberley received only a B in my course. "Kimmy always gets As. What's the story, Professor?" she wanted to know. The story, I told her, was that in my courses B was not a dishonorable grade. I didn't bother to add that in my own undergraduate days I had myself received a pathetic paucity of As.

Perhaps the real significance of student evaluations of their teachers was to allow an entering wedge for students to criticize and thereby seem in some rough sense the equal of their teachers. (For those who taught without tenure, poor evaluations could also be a deadly weapon used against them to block permanent appointments.) From complaining on paper, it wasn't all that long before students, now supported by political correctness, began to complain about their teachers in person and in public: accusing them of sexism, racism, Eurocentrism, and whatever else they happen to have around the joint. Students demanding the right to in effect edit assigned readings—the comically called "trigger warnings"—passages in works or whole works that might offend their sensibilities (betcha didn't know they had any) followed naturally enough. Let us not speak about the generalized demand that everything should be done to ensure that the university is a "safe place," when once upon a time the complaint about the university was that it was altogether too safe, too much an "ivory tower," which was to say too distanced from the so-called real world.

Student evaluations of their teachers came about as a result of the student protests in universities during the latter half of the 1960s. The general student protest movement, which now slides in under the rubric of "The Sixties," above all enshrined youth. "Don't trust anyone over thirty" was one of its chief shibboleths. The effect of that decade on those who lived through it when young has, I suspect, been even stronger than the Depression of the 1930s was on those who came into maturity during it. The general aura of protest, of the righteousness students of the day felt about their attacks on what they called the establishment, of their unshakeable belief in the inherent wisdom of the young, never really left most of those who felt themselves part of The Sixties. Many of those same people went on to become university professors, administrators, presidents. Their sixties background, and the strong ideological and psychological residue it left, has made it all but impossible for them to come out against even the most egregious demands of current-day students. Not for them to insist that these demands are foolish, coarse, stupid, some (such as barring speakers with whom they disagree) opposed to the very idea of education itself—not for them to say knock it off.

All the new nuttiness on the part of current-day students did not come about exclusively within the precincts of the university alone. Something radical in the realm of child-rearing in the culture at large had prepared the way for an entire generation of university students to behave well below what once would have been thought appropriate conduct at their age. "Act your age" in fact was a standard invocation of an earlier day, one that was called into use perhaps at the beginning of grammar school and remained in use long thereafter. Another, alternate version of act your age was "Grow up!" always with an exclamation mark at its close.

But all this changed with the advent in American life of the "Kindergarchy," or rule by children, ushered in by new, more intensive methods of child rearing. At the heart of these methods is the reigning notion of the utter preciousness and precariousness of the child, who must never be harmed—not physically, of course, but more seriously never psychologically. The Kindergarchy came in with what Philip Rieff has called "the triumph of the therapeutic," in his book of that title. That triumph has, among its other conquests, replaced the emphasis on the development of character with an emphasis, in Rieff's words, on "the richness of living." Under the therapeutic culture, self-esteem has become the first order of business and, as Rieff wrote, "a sense of well-being has become an end, rather than a by-product of striving after a communal end." The therapuetic culture is, in other words, self-centered, one in which all are devoted foremost to pleasing themselves.

Nowhere has this been felt more keenly than in the raising of children. No other generation has been so mentally curried and worried about. Under the therapeutic culture one's children were understood to be delicate creatures, so easily injured psychologically, even permanently maimed. Kid gloves in one's dealings with them needed to be worn round the clock. The hovering parent, applying a full-court press on his children, became a standard figure of the day. Children were also now thought an investment of sorts, one that, one hoped, might pay off in social prestige. How grand to be able to say that one had a daughter at Yale, a son working for Goldman Sachs! How splendidly such things reflected on oneself, as a good parent, a grand person, an altogether successful man or woman!

The children under the therapeutic regime had to have sensed their own importance—an importance quite possibly new in history. Kids were coddled well beyond the ages they once were. This was evident in various ways, large and small. Fran Leibowitz noted the rising ages of children being conveyed in strollers, and remarked that the person who comes up with the first shaving mirror for a stroller was likely to make a fortune. One of the results of the extended coddling of their upbringing has been to make recent genenerations greatly impressed with their own significance. I can recall grading student compositions that radiated with a false and unearned self-confidence, the result doubtless of their relentless succour by therapeutic-minded parents, on which I had to restrain myself from awarding a D and adding, "Too much love in the home."

My own generation—those people born between 1930 and 1945—was brought up along distinctly non-therapeutic lines. So many of my contemporaries, I have noticed, have brothers or sisters, roughly five years older or younger than themselves. The reason for this, I have concluded, is that mothers then decided to have a second child only after the first had begun school. This was done at the convenience of the parent, not for the psychological benefit of the children.

Mine were excellent parents, honorable, good-humored, without the least meanness, nor in any way neurotic (or, as we should have said in the non-therapuetic age, nutty), but I always sensed that they had a life well apart from their interest in their two sons. (I have a brother who is, you will have guessed it, five-years-younger than I.) When my brother and I were quite young, our parents would sometime go off on vacations without us, leaving us in the care of a paid sitter who lived in the neighborhood (the redoubtable Miss Charlotte Smucker) or with a childless aunt.

I have no recollection of my parents ever telling me they loved me. I have no memories, either, of being hugged by either of my parents. But, then, I needed neither the declarations nor the hugs, for I was supremely confident of my parents' love. In exchange for full-time attention, my parents allowed my brother and me immense freedom: to form our own friendships, go our own way, make most of our own decisions, including where we would go to college. So long as we did not get in trouble, our lives were pretty much our own. Freedom in place of intense attention still strikes me as a damn fine deal, and a hand I continue to feel I was lucky to have been dealt.

My parents and most of their contemporaries were pre-psychological. If I had ever told my father I was feeling insecure about a task, a job, a relationship,' he would have replied, "Face up to the problem. Don't be a coward." Insecure didn't exist as a category for him. As a small boy shaking my father's hand, I recall his saying, "You call that a handshake? That's a limp fish. A man shakes hands firmly." To be a man was from an early age the name of my, and also of most of my boyfriends', desire.

Drivers licenses then being awarded in Chicago at fifteen, we soon had the run of the city. By sixteen most of us were smoking. By seventeen, thanks to the sex-service stations (also known as cat-houses) in Kankakee and Braidwood, Illinois, few of us were virgins. We bet football parley cards; played poker and gin rummy (Hollywood-Oklahoma, spades double) for what then seemed serious stakes; drove out to the harness races at night; a few among us had bookies. This was very much in the then approved Chicago style, but the intention behind it all was to be a man, a grown-up, and as early as possible. Girls, apart from the gambling and whoring accessible to us boys, comported themselves as young women, adults.

We had no wish to be children any longer than necessary. We wanted all the freedom that adulthood implied. The poet Philip Larkin, whose parents had a less than happy marriage, reports that he couldn't wait to grow up. "I never left the house," he wrote, "without the sense of walking into a cooler, cleaner, saner, and pleasanter atmosphere, and if I hadn't made friends outside, life would have been scarcely tolerable." Larkin claimed he gave up on Christianity when he learned that the Christian heaven promised a return to childhood. He wanted no part of that return. He yearned for adulthood and its accountrements: liquor, long-play records, beautiful women, keys.

One senses that recent generations of Americans can wait to grow up—wish, in fact, to delay growing up as long as possible. One sees all sorts of dismaying statistics about the young living at home into their thirties and beyond, marrying late if at all, producing fewer if any children of their own. Some day-glo color their outlandish hairdos, pierce their faces, tattoo their bodies, as if to announce they aren't ready for adulthood yet, and may well never be.

Alongside the self-obsession they display and the victimhood they claim, current-day students often shout down speakers whose views they don't approve, everywhere issue demands for different food, free birth control, elimination of student debt, greater diversity in professorial appointments; they claim sexual harassment, confront teachers they think insufficiently sympathetic to their causes; and generally carry on like nothing so much as children, badly spoiled children at that.

What is the response of the putative adults in the room—of the college presidents, administrators, professors—to such behavior? Best one can determine it is by and large to collapse, to cave into the demands of the bratish students. They nod and call for more "dialogue"; express the wish to continue the "convsersation"; organize endless panels; claim, in the recent words of the president of Sarah Lawrence confronted by a group calling itself the Sarah Lawrence Diaspora Coalition, to be "grateful for the willingness of our students to share their concerns with me and the campus community." One can imagine the students' reaction to such piffle: "Yeah, right, sure, Grandma!"

Panels meet, dialogue ensues, the conversation rambles on, while one awaits the next set of student demands. New deans and associate provosts are hired and put in chage of diversity, inclusivity, safety, soon no doubt of sexual satisfaction, transgender bathroom maintenance, and who knows what else. The beat, as the old disc jockeys had it, goes on, and is likely to continue until an impressively authoritative figure arises to cry out to these kids: "Enough! Cut the nonsense! Act your age! Grow up!

Heinrich Heine

(2018)

Friendship, Love, the Philosopher's Stone,
These three things are ranked alone;
These I sought from sun to sun,
And I found—not even one.

HEINRICH HEINE

HEINRICH HEINE was one of those writers, rare at any time, welcome always, who found it impossible to be dull. In everything he wrote, he captivated, sometimes infuriated, often dazzled. Heine, who was born in 1797 and died in 1856, wrote poetry, plays, criticism, essays, fiction, travel books, and journalism. All of it was marked by passion and wit, not a standard combination. "I hate ambiguous words," he noted, "hypocritical flowers, cowardly fig-leaves, from the depth of my soul." He thought himself, not incorrectly, in the line of Aristophanes, Cervantes, Moliere. Matthew Arnold called Heine "the most important German successor and continuator of Goethe in Goethe's most important line of activity . . . as 'a soldier in the war of liberation of humanity.'"

George Eliot, that other great Victorian, wrote of Heinrich Heine that he was one of the most remarkable men of this age:

> no echo but a real voice . . . a surpassing poet, who has uttered
> our feelings for us in delicious song; a humorist, who touches
> leaden folly with the magic wand of the fine gold of art—
> who sheds his sunny smile on human tears, and makes them

a beauteous rainbow on the cloudy background of life; a wit, who holds in his mighty hand the most scorching of lightnings of satire; an artist in prose literature, who has shown even more completely than Goethe the possibilities of German prose; and—in spite of all the charges against him, true as well as false—a lover of freedom who has spoken wise and brave words on behalf of his fellow men.

H EINE SUFFERED THE CHINESE CURSE of having lived in interesting times. He was born while Napoleon, whom he much admired as a young man and once saw riding through the streets of Dusseldorf, was setting out to acquire his empire. He twice met Goethe. He knew Karl Marx, who admired his poetry more than Heine, in the end, admired Marx's politics. He was a friend to Balzac, and probably a lover of George Sand. He lived through two revolutions, those of July 1830 and of February 1848. He was the victim of censorship under Metternich— a warrant for his arrest in Prussia was issued in 1835—the beneficiary of French freedom of expression, and a writer one of whose sidelines was informing each of those two always rivalrous nations about the other.

No nation ultimately met Heine's mark. He found the English self-satisfied, uninspired, and England itself made dull by the mercantile spirit. He held that the secret of the English superiority in politics "consists in the fact that they do not possess imagination." His native Germany was for him "the land of bigots," where patriotism consisted of "hatred of the French, hatred of civilization, and hatred of liberalism," and where "servility was in the German soul." The French, true enough, could be "not only the wittiest of nations, but also the most compassionate," yet French verse was for him "lukewarm rhymed gruel" and "Marseilles is French for Hamburg—a thing I cannot stand even in the best translation." America, which he never visited, he called "that monstrous prison of freedom . . . where the most repulsive of tyrants, the populace, holds vulgar sway" and "all men are equal—equal dolts . . . with the exception, naturally, of a few millions, who have a black or brown skin, and are treated like dogs."

In May 1848, Heine took to his bed in his Paris apartment, the bed he subsequently called his "mattress grave," from which he never arose. There he would spend the last eight years of his life with a wretched illness caused by degeneration of the spine, which left him paralyzed from the chest down and blinded in one of his eyes. He could avail himself of the other eye if it were raised open by a finger. He suffered cramps and throbbing headaches and a wracking cough that only opium and morphine could relieve. Add in the tortures of 19th-century medicine. Through this wretched illness, Heine's passion for writing never subsided, and his best volume of verse, *Romanzero*, and much else was written from his mattress-grave.

As a thinker, Heine was neither deep nor strikingly original. He did not so much contribute to as dabble in philosophical and theological debates. He did nothing directly to change the politics of his time. In prose his talent lay in satire and polemic. He did not mind making enemies, and, more difficult still, he found ways to keep them. His verse could be lyrical and lilting but also coarse and profane. Yet even after one has said the worst about Heine, things that might destroy the reputation of any other writer, he cannot be diminished or otherwise disqualified. His spirit, which shone through all he wrote, was indomitable.

Remarking on Heine's book-length essay *On the History of Religion and Philosophy in Germany,* the scholar J. P. Stern begins by writing that "Heine had neither the scholarly equipment nor the detachment to write anything that a respectable historian would wish to put his name to." But Stern goes on to add that "so much of it is true, that so much of the book consists of brilliant, apparently casual and quite unexpected insights—that more truth and good sense is said here about certain important aspects of German history and culture, about the German mind, than any other single book I know—said implicitly and by innuendoes, but also explicitly, also in a grand rhetorical style." As for Heine's essays, Stern held that "only Nietzsche's have a comparable vigor." Nietzsche himself thought Heine Germany's greatest lyric poet.

HARRY HEINE, as he was known before his fame, grew up as the oldest of four children in a petit-bourgeois Jewish family in Dusseldorf. The family was more sentimentally than religiously Jewish. Heine's father, Samson Heine, an amiable flop, was in the textile business, at which he ultimately failed. His Uncle Salomon, a Hamburg banker, is said to have been one of the wealthiest men in Germany—and Heine spent a fair amount of time calculating through his life in an only partially successful attempt to have this uncle underwrite his freelance career. His best biographer, Jeffrey L. Sammons, reports that Heine "held a paying position for only six months of his life."

The great force in Heine's early life was his mother. She had many plans for her oldest son, none of which came to fruition. She first thought he might find his calling as a diplomat, then as a banker. His Uncle Salomon set him up in a textile business of his own. "A poet always cheats his boss," a Russian proverb has it, only half true in this case since Heine did not cheat but, out of a want of interest, failed his uncle. He had neither the taste nor the least talent for commerce. Law school was the next option. Heine took up the study of the history of Roman law and German jurisprudence at the universities of Bonn, Berlin, and Göttingen, which left him bored blue. "If the Romans had been obliged to learn Latin," he later remarked about the complexities of mastering the language, "they would never have conquered the world." Heine never practiced law either.

In 1825, Heine put himself through a conversion to Protestantism, for in the Prussia of that time Jews were not permitted to practice law or take up academic positions and were excluded from much else. He called his baptism as a Protestant "the ticket of admission to European culture," though he would later remark that "if the Protestant church didn't have an organ, it would be no religion at all," and he expressed regret at having allowed himself to be baptized, however perfunctorily.

In Bonn, Heine encountered August Wilhelm Schlegel, one of the great German literary critics of his day, who instructed him in Romantic theory and taught him a good deal about German prosody while editing some of his youthful poems. At the University of Berlin, he attended the lectures of Hegel, whom he recalled lecturing on God and the gods and "looking around anxiously, as if in fear that he might be understood." He later called Hegel "the circumnavigator of the intellectual world, who has fearlessly advanced to the North Pole of thought, where one's brain freezes in abstract ice." Only after subsequent reflection did Heine feel he came to true understanding of Hegelian thought, at which point he rejected it. Among his store of anecdotes, he liked to report that on his deathbed Hegel was supposed to have said, "Only one person has understood me," then quickly added, "and he didn't understand me either."

Despite his failures at conventional occupations, Heine's confidence in his poetic genius never flagged. His early fame came from his first collection, *Book of Songs*, the poetry from which is today best known from having been set to music by, among others, Robert Schumann, Franz Schubert, and Felix Mendelssohn. (By one estimate, Heine's early poems provided the lyrics to no fewer than 2,750 pieces of music.) Early in his career Heine called poetry "a beautiful irrelevancy," and soon turned to prose, though through most of his life he produced both simultaneously. As in the very different case of T. S. Eliot, Heine's fame as a poet lent his prose additional authority.

J. P. Stern describes that prose as "a unique compound of the eternal *raconteur's* fun and the precise intellectual wit of the guest at the ideal High Table." Stern wrote that his "lightness of touch, the effortless responsiveness of the medium, the quickness of the insights and the melodramatic sharp edges of Heine's expressiveness . . . all these are quite unprecedented in the annals of German prose." Stern was particularly struck by "that ambiguity, that ironical illumination of the truth, which are his most successful stylistic device." Karl Kraus, the 20th-century Viennese journalist and wit, attacked Heine's prose for its newfound informality, writing that "he loosened the bodice of the German language to the point where any clerk can today fondle her breasts." Ernst Pawel, author of *The Dying Poet*, a brilliant little book on Heine's last years, wrote, correctly, that for Heine "the poetry brought fame, the prose notoriety."

DESCRIBING IN HIS *MEMOIRS* a youthful kiss with the daughter of a professional executioner, Heine notes that "at that moment there flared up in me the first flames of two passions to which my subsequent life was to be devoted: the love of beautiful women and the love of the French Revolution." For Heine women were objects both of longing and contempt, and he by turns elevated and debased them, sometimes both at once. Two of the witticisms on women that Louis Untermeyer quotes in his introduction to his translation of Heine's poems: 1) "I will not say that women have no character; rather, they have a new one every day"; and 2) "Women have just one way of making us happy, but thirty thousand ways of making us miserable."

The misery of unrequited love is the central theme of Heine's early poetry. "Madame," he once said, "anyone who wants to be loved by me has to treat me like dirt." For a long while his chief unrequiting lover was supposed to be his cousin Amelie, the older of his wealthy Uncle Salomon's two daughters. In his biographical study, *The Elusive Poet*, Jeffrey Sammons convincingly dispels this story. Heine may have been interested in Amelie and later in her younger sister Therese, but if he had been it was perhaps as much for their father's money as for their beauty or largeness of soul. Salomon Heine supplied his nephew Harry with an allowance all his days; after his death, the allowance—never sufficient in Heine's complaining opinion—was continued by Salomon's son Carl.

As for the requited loves in Heine's life, not all that much is known. He was a handsome man. In most drawings and paintings of him, many done in three-quarters profile, he resembles, if one can imagine it, a Jewish Lord Byron, with a slightly more emphatic nose and minus the clubfoot. When young, Heine took Byron for a model, both in his poetry and revolutionary fervor. In the Berlin salons of his youth he was regarded as a German Byron.

Many of Heine's poems not devoted to the subject of unrequited love take up the subject of past lovers ultimately found inadequate. A characteristic quatrain on the theme runs:

> The joy that kissed me yesterday
> Today looks pale and sickly,
> And every time I've known true love
> It's faded just as quickly.

Yet, as Ernst Pawel writes, "Heine's actual love life appears to have been considerably less extravagant than, with an ostentatious show of discretion, he would have liked his public to believe."

Heine's best poems have a satiric edge, taking up such subjects as how far Germany is from the Rome of Brutus. Others are prophetic, in one case of Hitler: "Where men burn books," he wrote in his play *Almansor*, "They will burn people in the end." As S. S. Prawer writes: "He was able to detect tendencies in his time whose full unfolding would not come until well over a full century later."

Some of Heine's poetry could be erotic, some bordering on the obscene. Here is a two-quatrain sample from his "Song of Songs":

> A pair of polished epigrams—
> The rosebuds of the breast;
> A fair caesura lies between—
> It adds a certain zest.
> The heavenly sculptor shaped the thigh—
> A parallel he drew.
> The figleaf-veiled parenthesis
> Has quite an interest too.

He wasn't bad at bawdy, either, as in the poem called "Castratis":

> The castratis all started out tut-tutting
> As soon as I'd sung the first bar:
> They complained (and were really quite cutting!)
> That my tone was too ballsy by far.

At 37, Heine contracted a marriage that, unlike his putative love affair with George Sand, is perhaps best described as improbable. This was with a 19-year-old shop girl named Crescence Eugénie Mirat. She was French and barely literate. In a letter to his mother, Heine wrote: "If she were smarter, I'd worry less about her future. Which again goes to show that stupidity is a gift of the gods, because it forces others to take care of you." Mathilde, as he called her, never read anything he wrote, was scarcely aware that he was a writer of considerable fame, didn't know he was Jewish. Heine's efforts, a la Henry Higgins, to remake his wife, to educate and polish her, were apparently unavailing. He worried about her fidelity while he lived, and about her well-being after his death. She stayed with him through all his mattress-grave years, and there they were, the oddest of odd couples.

THE PROBLEM WITH HEINE," wrote Ernst Pawel, "is that no statement of his can ever be taken at face value." Nor is anything about
him straightforward, uncomplicated, simple. This is partly owing to his
rarely telling the truth about himself. "Heine," Robert C. Holub, editor
of *A Companion to the Works of Heinrich Heine,* writes, "is an unreliable
reporter about Heine.' Théophile Gautier, Sainte-Beuve, Gérard de Ner-
val, all picked up on the contradictory nature of Heine. Here is Louis
Untermeyer on the subject:

> A German who dreamed of a greater Germany, he was an expa-
> triate from his homeland and spent most of his life in France.
> A proudly race-conscious Jew, he became a Protestant and, af-
> ter a liaison of seven years, married his Catholic mistress. . . .
> The most dulcet of poets, he was also one of the bitterest and
> bawdiest; a born Romantic, he exposed the spectral hollow-
> ness of Romanticism. A cynical wit, he was a political idealist;
> a journalistic hack, a pot-boiling newspaper correspondent,
> he was at the same time an impassioned fighter for humanity.

Heine's contradictory spirit shows up in heightened form in his regard
for his own Jewishness, which has been the subject of endless scholarly
essays and a splendid 1986 book, S. S. Prawer's *Heine's Jewish Comedy.*
Heine's conversion may have been without true religious conviction or
significance, but for him it was, in retrospect, not a negligible act. The
need for it, implying the inferior standing of the Jews in Prussia, angered
him. Heine was German and Jewish both, but his true religion was that
which promised human freedom. (In later years he showed anger at the
conversion of Felix Mendelssohn: "Had I the good fortune to be the
grandson of Moses Mendelssohn, I would not use my talents to set to
music the Lamb's urine.") Yet if he, Heine, never engaged Judaism, neither did he ever quite give up on his Jewishness.

Throughout his life Heine struggled with religion. As a young man in
Germany he was a member of a group that called itself the Society for the
Culture and Science of the Jews (*Verein fur Kulture und Wissenschafter
der Juden*), which sought to preserve the Jewish heritage while joining it
to modern science and enlightenment values. He was less a champion of

Judaism than a strong advocate for Jewish civil rights. Above all he hated anti-Semitism, which he described as that hatred of the Jews "on the part of the lower and higher rabble." The subject, if not the theme, of many of his middle and late period poems, is the world's ignorant anti-Semitism.

Heine despised the pressures of assimilation that Jews underwent to find acceptance in Germany. For all their backwardness, he found more to admire in the *shtetl* Jews of Poland than in the sadly assimilated but self-divided Jews of Germany, wearing the fashions of the day and quoting second-class writers, neither fully German nor fully Jewish. What Heine admired about the Polish Jews, and admired about Judaism generally, was that, unlike Greeks and Romans who clung to their soil and other peoples whose fealty was to their princes, the Jews "always clung to the Law, to the abstract idea . . . [to] the law as the highest principle," the Bible their "portable fatherland." Yet, whatever his sympathies for his people, he could not give himself over entirely to Judaism: "It would be distasteful and mean if, as people say of me, I had ever been ashamed of being a Jew, but it would be equally ridiculous if I ever claimed to be one."

As the enemy of all positive, of all organized, religions, Heine felt he could "never champion that religion which first introduced fault-finding with human beings that now causes us such pain; and if I nevertheless do it after a fashion, there are special reasons: tender emotions, obstinacy, and care to maintain an antidote." In his *Confessions* he wrote that for years he failed to show his fellow Jews sufficient respect, blinded as he was by his partiality to Hellenic aestheticism: "I see now that the Greeks were only beautiful youths, but the Jews were always men, powerful, uncompromising men, not just in the days of old but right up to the present, despite 18 centuries of persecution and misery."

In Heine's search for the true religion, he rejected Christianity because, in its organized form, it "killed more joyous gods," and was "too sublime, too pure, too good for this earth." Besides, as he said, "no Jew can believe in the divinity of another Jew." He believed that religions are "magnificent and admirable only when they have to compete with one another, and are persecuted rather than persecuting," and that "a system of religion is as harmful to religion as to trade; [religions] remain alive only through free competition, and they will only return to their original splendor when political equality of worship is introduced—free trade in gods, as it were."

Yet, as he wrote, "from my earliest years I saw how religion and doubt can live side by side without giving rise to hypocrisy." Heine never claimed to be an atheist, and referred, mockingly, to "the monks of atheism," by which he meant those for whom atheism was a fanatical religion of its own. Late in life, laid low by his illness, he claimed to have found God, though he did so without the aid of organized religion. "The religious revolution that has taken place within me," he wrote to his publisher Julius Campe, "is a purely intellectual one—more the product of thought than of beatific sentimentality, and my illness has a small share in it, I am sure." As for the pain accompanying that illness, he wrote to his younger friend Hans Laube that "though I believe in God, I sometimes do not believe in a good God. The hand of this great animal baiter sometimes lies heavy on me." He added still later that he would "bring charges with the SPCA against God for treating me so horribly."

Moses, the lawgiver, is in Heine's pantheon of heroes. So, too, is Martin Luther, that most German of Germans, "at once a dreamy mystic and a practical man of action" whose "thoughts had not merely wings but also hands; he spoke and acted." Add another Moses, this one with the surname Mendelssohn, to the pantheon, who "overthrew the authority of Talmudism and founded pure Mosaism." Then there was Goethe, who, as an artist, "holds the mirror up to nature, or, better, he is the mirror."

These choices of heroes are dictated by Heine's larger view of mankind. "I believe in progress," he wrote in his *History of Religion and Philosophy in Germany*, "I believe that mankind is destined to be happy, and thus I think more highly of divinity than pious people who think mankind was created only to suffer. Here on earth, by the blessings of free political and industrial institutions, I should like to establish that bliss which, in the opinion of the pious, will come only in heaven, on the day of judgment." This belief was perhaps more Jewish than Heine could have known. Heinz Graetz, the 19th-century historian of Judaism, wrote: "Judaism is not a religion of the present but of the future"—a future that "looks forward to the ideal age . . . when the knowledge of God and the reign of justice and contentments shall have united all men in the bonds of brotherhood."

IN HIS EARLY YEARS, Heine himself saw the world in a battle between the senses and the spirit, and himself on the side of the senses. He was a free spirit, in the sense he himself defined it: a man "duty bound to engage seriously in the battle against evil that struts about so blatantly, and against the commonplace that swaggers insufferably." As Pawel puts it, Heine "had always been rebel rather than revolutionary, nay-sayer rather than would-be prophet, [who] never for a moment shed his skepticism."

Heine called himself, alternately, a monarchical republican, or, on alternate days, a republican monarchist. He believed in the freedom and potential for happiness for all people. Yet he distrusted most of those people, the masses, who were all philistines and whose utopia left no room for poets or poetry. Imagining a Communist society to come, he noted that "some grocer will use even the pages of my *Book of Songs* to wrap coffee and snuff for the old women of the future." Always more precise about what he loathed than about what he loved; incapable of leading or of following any party; exile, poet, Jew, Heinrich Heine was the ultimate outsider.

Of literary works, Heine much admired *Don Quixote*. He recounts first reading Cervantes's great novel as a young boy, unarmed in his reading by any awareness of the great Spanish writer's irony, utterly saddened by the defeat after defeat suffered by the knight of the woeful countenance. Later, after he came to appreciate the irony, his love for the Don was undiminished and he came to view himself as a Don Quixote of his own day—but acting, as he put it, "from diametrically opposed points of view." Heine writes:

> My colleague mistook windmills for giants; I, on the contrary, see in our giants of today only windmills; he mistook leather wineskins for mighty wizards; I see in our modern wizards only leather wineskins; he mistook every beggars inn for a castle—every donkey driver for a knight, every stable wench for a lady of the court—I, on the other hand, look upon our castles as disreputable inns, on our cavaliers as donkey drivers, on our court-ladies as common stable wenches. Just as he took a puppet play to be a noble affair of state, I hold our affairs of state

to be wretched puppet plays. But as doughtily as the doughty Knight of LaMancha I fall upon the wooden company.

Heine called Quixotism generally "the most precious thing in life." A world filled only with Sanchos Panza, after all, would be one of unrelieved drabness, philistine, sensible but ultimately dull and dreary—whereas, in Heine's words, "Quixotism lends wings to the whole world and to all in it who philosophize, make music, plough, and yawn." They do not come along all that often, but when they do authentic Quixotes reveal life's larger possibilities and thereby enliven its quality and enlarge its scope. On February 17, 1856, Heinrich Heine was removed from his mattress grave to a dirt one at Montmartre Cemetery in Paris. Asked as he was dying if he wished to have a clergyman in attendance, he replied that none was required: "*Dieu me pardonnera. C'est son metier.*" He will always be among the small but indispensable band of Quixotes. Let the last words be in his own verse:

I am a German poet,
In German lands I shine;
And where great names are mentioned
They're bound to mention mine.

Joseph Roth

(2018)

I N *OSTEND,* his book about the German and Austrian émigré literary group that gathered in the Belgian resort town after Hitler came
to power, Volker Weidermann describes Joseph Roth, the most talented of these writers, looking "like a mournful seal that has wandered
accidentally onto dry land." Roth was small, thin yet potbellied, slightly
hunched over, with a chosen nose, a bad liver, and missing lots of teeth.
He began most mornings, like the serious alcoholic that he was, vomit-
ing. Always in flight, one of the world's permanent transients, Roth was
a one-man diaspora: "Why do you people roam around so much in the
world?" asks a Galician peasant in one of his novels. "The devil sends you
from one place to another."

Joseph Roth happens also to have been a marvelous writer, and he might
have gone on to be a great one had he not died in 1939, in his 45th year. (He
is of that uncharmed circle of writers—Chekhov, Orwell, F. Scott Fitzgerald—who died before they reached 50.) Not the least of Roth's marvels was
his astonishing productivity. In his short career between 1923 and 1939, he
published, in German, no fewer than 15 novels, a batch of short stories,
and, by his own reckoning in 1933, something on the order of 3,500 newspaper articles, most of them of the genre known as feuilleton, those short,
literary, free-form, usually non-political essays that were once a staple in

French and German newspapers. None of his writing that I have read, even the most ephemeral journalism, is without its felicitous touches, its arresting observations, its striking evidence of a first-class literary mind at work.

Roth's work is bedizened with metaphor, laced with simile. In the short story "Strawberries" one finds: "The sun came out, as though back from holiday." "Later they planted pansies on the lawn, beautiful big pansies with soft, clever faces." Crows "were at hand like bad news, they were remote like gloomy premonitions." In *The Emperor's Tomb* (1938) there falls "a rough sleet, failed snow and wretched brother to hail." In the same novel a landlady appears "as broad in the beam as a tugboat." In *The Radetzky March* expensive "wine flowed from the bottle with a tender purr."

A strong taste for aphorism and risky generalization runs through all Roth's work. In his early novel *Hotel Savoy* (1924) one finds: "All educated words are shameful. In ordinary speech you couldn't say anything so unpleasant." "Industry is God's severest punishment." "Women make their mistakes not out of carelessness or frivolity, but because they are very unhappy." In *The Emperor's Tomb* we learn that "honor is an anesthetic, and what it anaesthetized in us was death and foreboding" and "to conceal and deny frailty can only be heroic." Joseph Roth was a writer, as was once said of Henry James, "assailed by the perceptions."

At the same time, Roth's eye for detail is unerring. In a story called "The Place I Want to Tell You About," a character, setting out for Vienna, remembers "the umbrella with the ivory handle" before leaving. That ivory handle puts one in the room. A minor character in *The Radetzky March* is "the father of three children and the husband of a disappointed wife." Another minor character in the same novel reveals "a powerful set of teeth, broad and yellow, a stout protective grill that filtered his speech." A woman in the story "The Triumph of Beauty" has "a long but unexciting chin"; a man in the same story has a large square torso that makes him look like "a wardrobe wearing a blazer."

Travelling in steerage to America the family at the center of his novel *Job: The Story of a Simple Man* sleeps along with 20 or so others, "and from the movements each made on the hard beds, the beams trembled and the little yellow electric bulbs swung softly." In his preface to *The Nigger of the Narcissus* and "The Secret Sharer," Joseph Conrad wrote:

"My task which I am trying to achieve is, by the power of the written word, to make you hear, to make you feel, it is, before all, to make you see. That and no more—and it is everything." Roth understood.

A second marvel is that Joseph Roth was able to get as much done as he did under the strained conditions in which he worked. The strain was financial. Roth was a money writer, less by temperament than by necessity. A spendthrift always hovering on personal pauperdom, he had the additional heavy expense of a wife who fairly early in his marriage had to be placed in various sanatoria for schizophrenia. (In 1940, Friederike Roth was removed from a Viennese hospital and murdered under the Nazis' euthanasia program.) Much in Roth's letters—published recently in English as *Joseph Roth: A Life in Letters*—is given over to pressing publishers and newspaper editors for the payment of advances or for raising his fees, complaints about his barely scraping by, and the expressions of guilt because of his need to borrow from friends, chief among them the commercially much more successful Stefan Zweig, who was his dearest friend and practically his patron.

MANY OF JOSEPH ROTH'S NOVELS are of modest length, some barely beyond that of the standard novella. (His final work, *The Legend of the Holy Drinker,* published in 1939, runs to 49 pages.) The four of these novels I find most accomplished are *Right and Left* (1929), *Job: The Story of a Simple Man* (1930), *The Emperor's Tomb* (1938), and, the lengthiest and most fully realized, *The Radetzky March* (1932). An account of life under and a tribute to the Dual Monarchy, as the Austro-Habsburg dynasty was also known, *The Radetzky March* is one of those extraordinary works of fiction that, like Lampedusa's *The Leopard,* cannot be anticipated by what has gone before in its author's oeuvre. (Michael Hofmann, Roth's ablest translator and most penetrating critic, writes of "the accelerated development otherwise known as genius.") The novel's title derives from Johann Strauss's famous march and is one of those books that when two people meet who discover they have both read it sends a pleasing shock of recognition between them, followed by the bond of mutual admiration for an extraordinary work of literary art.

The range and variety of Roth's fiction are impressive. That fellow in Eliot's great poem might have done the police in different voices, but Roth in his fiction could do poor *shtetl* Jews and the Emperor Franz Joseph, Polish nobles and Ruthenian peasants, down-and-outs and successful entrepreneurs, Romanians, Czechs, Poles, Germans, Cossacks—in short, the entire Austro-Habsburg Empire, and all in perfect pitch.

Moses Joseph Roth was born in 1894 in Brody, a Galician town of roughly 18,000 people, two-thirds of whom were Jewish, on the border between Poland and Ukraine, 54 miles northeast of Lemberg (now called Lviv). He never knew his father, who died in a mental asylum. In 1913 he earned a scholarship to the University of Lemberg, and after a year there went on to the University of Vienna, where he dropped the Moses from his name and claimed his father was (variously) a Polish count, an Austrian railway official, an army officer, and a munitions manufacturer; at one point he took briefly to wearing a monocle; later he would claim to have been an officer, not the enlisted man that he was in the First World War. All this in the attempt to shed the identity of the *Ostjude*, then held in much contempt in Vienna. This outsider, outlander even, became the great chronicler, and eventually the prime mourner, for the Dual Monarchy, later in life declaring himself a monarchist. On his gravestone in a cemetery outside Paris the words "*Écrivain Autrichien*" are engraved.

Of the cards dealt at birth, not the least significant is that of the time into which one was born. Here Roth drew a poor card. He came into his majority with the onset of the Russian Revolution and the First World War—"world," as a character in *The Emperor's Tomb* says, "because of it, we lost a whole world"—and left it as Hitler was gearing up the machinery for his Final Solution. (Communism, he noted in a letter to Zweig, "spawned Fascism and Nazism and hatred for intellectual freedom.") Meanwhile, the First World War, the Russian Revolution, and the Treaty of Versailles finished off the Dual Monarchy, reducing what was once a sprawling empire to a shriveled Austrian Republic. The multitudinous fatherland Roth knew as a young man evaporated in the fog of nationalism. In his splendid story "The Bust of the Emperor," Roth quotes the Austrian playwright Grillparzer on the fate of the Dual Monarchy: "From humanity via nationality to bestiality."

What Roth valued in the Austro-Habsburg Empire was the fluidity it allowed its subjects, who could travel from country to country without the aid of passports or papers, and its discouragement of nationalism, which worked against the nation-less Jewish people. "I love Austria," he wrote in 1933. "I view it as cowardice not to use this moment to say the Habsburgs must return." In 1935 he wrote to assure Stefsn Zweig that "the Hapsburgs will return. . . . Austria will be a monarchy." Before the approaching Anschluss of 1938 he even attempted, through the offices of Kurt Schuschnigg, the chancellor of the Federal State of Austria, to restore the monarchy by installing Otto von Habsburg, heir of the Emperor Franz Joseph, on the empty throne.

Not that there wasn't anti-Semitism, that endemic disease, under the Dual Monarchy. Nor was it absent in France, where, after Hitler came to power in Germany in 1933, Roth lived out his last years, but, as he wrote in a strange little book called *The Wandering Jews* (1927), there "it is not one hundred proof. Eastern Jews, accustomed to a far stronger, cruder, more brutal anti-Semitism, are perfectly happy with the French version of it." Never other than unpredictable, Roth, that most cosmopolitan of Jews, valued the *shtetl* Jews of Eastern Europe above all. He valued their Jewish authenticity and felt that those Jews who had taken up the assimilated life in Germany and elsewhere and pretended to a patriotism that ultimately wasn't returned to them, "those rich Jews," as he wrote in *Right and Left,* "the ones who want more than anything else to be native Berliners" and who "go on celebrating their holiest festivals in a kind of shamefaced secrecy, but Christmas publicly, and for all to see," these were the Jews most deceived and hence most to be pitied.

The real subject at the heart of *The Wandering Jews* is the distinctiveness of Jews. "Of all the world's poor, the poor Jew," Roth writes, "is surely the most conservative . . . he *refuses* to be a proletarian." The difference between the Russian and the Jewish peasant is that "the Russian is a peasant first and a Russian second; the Jew is Jew first and then peasant." Roth underscores the intellectual cast of the Jews. "They are a people that has had no illiterates for nearly two thousand years now." Not wishing to fight other people's wars, "the Eastern Jews were the most heroic of pacifists. They were martyrs for pacifism. They chose crippledom"—a reference, this, to the

Jews who inflicted self-mutilations to avoid fighting in the army of the tsar, especially since only in Russia was anti-Semitism, more than the usual free-floating version, "a pillar of government."

Zionism was the best answer to the Jewish question for Roth, "for it is surely better to be a nation than to be mistreated by one." The Jews "are forced to be a 'nation' by the nationalism of the others," and "if one must be patriotic, then at least let it be for a country of one's own." Even though "the American cousin is the last hope of every Eastern Jewish family," it is only the presence of blacks that "insure[s] the Jews won't have the lowest status in America." Whether Roth would have made *aliyah* had he lived longer cannot be known—toward the end of his life he called himself a Catholic—but there is little doubt that he yearned for an end to "the flight out of Egypt, which has been in progress now for thousands of years."

INTENSELY JEWISH THOUGH HE WAS, apart from *Job: The Story of a Simple Man*, his novel with a *shtetl* setting, Jews tend to figure only peripherally in Roth's fiction. Until the small commercial success of *Job*, Roth was in fact better known for his journalism. His early fiction is always brilliant but emotionally spare. Roth wrote against the grain of the ascending modernism of his day. He thought little of James Joyce. "No Gide! No Proust! Nor anything of the sort," he wrote to a journalist and novelist named Hans Natonek. He criticized Natonek's penchant for abstraction. "A novel is not the place for *abstractions.* Leave that to Thomas Mann." In his novel *Right and Left*, the criterion he sets for a wealthy character's buying art is "that a picture should repel his senses and intelligence. Only then could he be sure of having bought a valuable modern work."

In *Right and Left*, Roth lays out the fictional program under which he worked, holding foremost that "passions and beliefs are tangled in the hearts and minds of men, and there is no such thing as psychological consistency." Change interested him more than consistency. We are, he held, chameleons all, changing character with the opportunities life provides us: "The more opportunities life gave us, the more beings it revealed in us. A man might die because he hadn't experienced anything, and had been just one person all his life." Roth the novelist believed that in the drive through life none of us is really at the wheel.

"No interest in day-to-day politics," Roth wrote to Natonek. "They distort. They distort the human." Elsewhere he referred to "the hollow pathos of revolutionaries." In a brilliant passage in "The Bust of the Emperor," he writes that "the inclinations and disinclinations of the people are grounded in reality." Reality is quotidian life. "After they have read the newspapers, listened to the speeches, elected the representatives, and discussed the news with their friends, the good peasants, craftsmen, and traders—and in the cities the workers—go back to their homes and workshops. And their misery or happiness is what awaits them there: sick or healthy children, quarrelsome or agreeable wives, prompt or dilatory customers, pressing or easygoing creditors, a good or bad supper, a clean or squalid bed."

The characters in Roth's own fiction may be sentient but are rarely sapient. Never heroic, they are more acted upon than acting. Consider the opening paragraph of *Job: The Story of a Simple Man:*

> Many years ago there lived in Zuchnow a man named Mendel Singer. He was pious, God-fearing and ordinary, an entirely everyday Jew. He practiced the modest profession of a teacher. In his house, which consisted of only a roomy kitchen, he imparted to children knowledge of the Bible. He taught with genuine enthusiasm but not notable success. Hundreds of thousands before him had lived and taught as he did.

Like the Biblical Job, Mendel Singer's essential decency is repaid with relentless sorrow. His two sons are unruly, and one goes off eagerly to join the tsar's army; he has a daughter who is arranging trysts with Cossacks and who will later, when the family emigrates to America, descend into insanity; a wife whose regard for him is dwindling and who will die an early death; and, worst of all, a last-born son, Menuchim, deformed in figure and barely able to speak. Mendel Singer did nothing to deserve any of this, but must somehow cope with all of it. "All these years I have loved God," Mendel thinks, "and He has hated me."

The only flaw in Roth's *Job* is the uplifting reversal of fortune on which the novel ends. In the realm of plot, the art of fiction consists in making the unpredictable plausible. In this one novel of Roth's, alas, the predictable seems implausible. Forgive my blasphemy, but I have never been much convinced by the ending of the Biblical version of Job either. Yet, as with the Biblical story, so with Roth's novel, the (relatively) happy ending merely soils but does not spoil the story.

ROTH'S NEXT BOOK, *The Radetzky March*, embodies his central ideas about the human condition: that we are at the whim of happenstance, our fate despite what more romantic novelists might hold not finally in our own hands, with ours not to reason why but to live out our days with what dignity we might manage and then die.

What is surprising is the drama that such dark notions of character can evoke in Joseph Roth's skillful hands. *The Radetzky March* is a family chronicle, recording three generations of a Slovenian peasant family, the Trottas, whose rise begins with a son, serving in the Austro-Hungarian army, who one day, almost as much by accident as through bravery, takes a bullet intended for the emperor. He is immediately raised in rank, known in the textbooks as "the Hero of Solferino," and his family, henceforth allowed to call itself the von Trottas, ennobled. The novel centers on the lives of the son and grandson of the Hero of Solferino.

The son, though wishing for a military career like his father, instead, at his father's order, becomes a midlevel bureaucrat, serving out his life as a district commissioner in Moravia. Dutiful, punctilious, a man with no vices apart from the want of imagination, District Commissioner von Trotta not only thinks of himself as the son of the Hero of Solferino, but raises his son in that tradition. "You are the grandson of the Hero of Solferino," he tells him. "So long as you bear that in mind nothing will go wrong." But everything does.The boy, Carl Joseph, is unfit for the cavalry, for the military, for life generally. He dies a useless death in the First World War fighting for a lost cause that will mark the end of the very world in which he was brought up to believe.

One of the signs of mastery in a novelist is his skill at making his subsidiary characters quite as rich and fascinating as his main characters. In *The Radetzky March*, the Jewish Army surgeon Max Demant and Count Chojnicki are two such characters. Count Chojnicki is "forty years old but of no discernible age." Nor is he of a discernible country, for, as Roth writes in another place, "he was a man beyond nationality and therefore an aristocrat in the true sense." Everything Chojnicki says in the novel is of interest, and it is he, the count, who predicts the fall of the Austro-Habsburg Empire well in advance of the actual event: "This empire's had it. As soon as the emperor says good night, we'll break up into a hundred pieces."

The emperor, Franz Joseph himself, shows up in the pages of *The Radetzky March*, once to inspect Carl Joseph's battalion, late in the novel to meet with Carl Joseph's father, the district commissioner. The emperor is also given a chapter to himself, a brilliant chapter, in which he gauges his own position as a leader thought near to a god even as his mental powers are slipping. Roth assigns the emperor, while inspecting the troops, "a crystalline drop that appeared at the end of his nose" that "finally fell into the thick silver mustache, and there disappeared from view," thus in a simple detail rendering him human. (Roth's portrait of Franz Joseph is reminiscent of Tolstoy's of Napoleon in *War and Peace* and Solzhenitsyn's of Stalin in *The First Circle*.) Herr von Trotta and the emperor die on the same day, and "the vultures were already circling above the Habsburg double eagle, its fraternal foes."

In Michael Hofmann's translator's introduction, he refers, percipiently, to *The Radetzky March* as a work that "seems to have been done in oils." What gives the novel that done-in-oil aspect is its weight, its seriousness, ultimately its gravity. No better introduction, for the student of literature or of history, is available for an understanding of the Austro-Habsburg Empire than this splendid novel, written by a small Galician Jew, who came of age in its shadow, grieved over its demise, and owes to it his permanent place in the august, millennia-long enterprise known with a capital L as Literature.

Stefan Zweig

(2019)

IN *THE STRUGGLE WITH THE DAEMON*—one of his three studies in the typology of writers—Stefan Zweig describes three writers, Hölderlin, Kleist, and Nietzsche, each possessed by his daemon, or inner spirit. Not one of the three, along with their congeners Michelangelo and Beethoven, married or had children, or had a regular income or possessions. "Their friendships were transitory," Zweig writes, "their appointments fugitive, their work unremunerative; they stood ever in vacant space and created in the void." Zweig is here describing the reverse of his own career and life—that is, until 1942. On February 23 of that year, in a mountain town outside Rio de Janeiro called Petrópolis, at the age of sixty, along with his second wife Lotte, who was twenty-seven years younger than he, Stefan Zweig took his own life.

Stefan Zweig was an internationally bestselling author of both fiction and biography. Born in Austria, brought up in Vienna, he was a true cosmopolitan, at home in France, Italy, England, and the United States, able to give formal lectures in French, Italian, and English. ("I was sure in my heart from the first of my identity as a citizen of the world," he wrote in his autobiography, *The World of Yesterday*.) His splendid biography of Marie Antoinette was made into an MGM movie starring Norma Shearer and Tyrone Power. Twenty-four hundred people attended a lecture he gave in Carnegie Hall in 1938. He wrote libretti for Richard Strauss. At one point he was said to be the most translated writer in the world. Rilke, Rodin, Freud, Paul Valéry, Benedetto Croce, Maxim Gorky, and Romain Rolland were among his friends and acquaintances.

At fifty, Zweig felt that he had been

> given far, far more than I had hoped or expected. My wish to develop and express myself through writing works of some literary merit had been granted beyond my wildest child-hood dreams. . . . My existence had had immeasurable in-fluence beyond the confines of my life. I had made friends with many of the finest people of our time; I had seen and enjoyed wonderful artistic performances, immortal cities and pictures, and the most beautiful landscapes in the world. I had remained free, independent of any official position or career, my work was a pleasure to me, and even better it had given pleasure to others! What could go wrong?

What went wrong was, in a word, Hitler. The political victory of Adolf Hitler in 1933 meant the personal defeat of Stefan Zweig. With fascism in the saddle, Zweig's books were banned in Germany and Austria and often burned by fascist youth; he lost his house in Salzburg and with it much of his collection of rare literary and musical manuscripts and artifacts (he owned, among other notable items, Beethoven's desk and Goethe's pen); and his first marriage collapsed. Zweig was an internationalist by instinct and political philosophy—that is, a believer in the compatibil-ity of all nations—but Hitler's Germany put paid to that dream. On the attack throughout Europe, Germany, a nation to which, Zweig said, "good order had always seemed more important than liberty and justice," had turned Stefan Zweig from a contented cosmopolitan into a woeful exile. "It is over," Zweig wrote in his diary, "Europe finished. Our world destroyed. Now we are truly homeless."

IN 1934 ZWEIG PUBLISHED HIS BIOGRAPHY OF ERASMUS, the great scholar and perhaps the first, certainly the primary, humanist of medi-eval Europe. Zweig called Erasmus "my revered master of an earlier cen-tury" and classed his own book about him as among his "most personal, most intimate work." His *Erasmus of Rotterdam*, he wrote, "presented my own views in veiled form through the person of Erasmus" and was "a thinly veiled self-portrait."

Zweig's Erasmus is a man, like Zweig himself, dedicated, in politics as in life, to "a supranational and panhuman ideal." Like Zweig again, Erasmus was condemned to live through "a time of storm and stress," the religious revolution led by Martin Luther. At a period of heightened contention, Erasmus felt it the duty of the artist and the intellectual "to act as sympathetic mediator between the politicians and the leaders and misleaders of a one-sided passion; he was to be the man of moderation who worked towards the golden mean." Like Zweig, too, Erasmus was an international bestseller: His book of aphorisms and observations, *Adagia*, went through twelve editions in his lifetime; his *In Praise of Folly* (*Laus stultitiae*) was a book popular in its day, still readable in ours, and singled out by Zweig as "in reality a bomb whose explosion opened the road to the German Reformation."

Zweig-like yet again, Erasmus's life, owing to the tumult of his times, ended in exile. He was "forced to leave Louvain because it was too Catholic; he was forced to leave Basle because it was too Protestant." Zweig writes: "He who had so implicitly believed in the possibility of a resurrection and renovation of man and his world by the workings of the spirit and the mind grew bitterer, more mocking, and more ironical in his attitude to the world without." Yet Erasmus, his integrity intact, died peacefully, chatting in Latin with friends gathered round his bed. Stefan Zweig died by his own hand, preferring death to a world that looked to be permanently darkened by Hitler.

ALL PARADISES, Proust held, are lost paradises. By his own account, Stefan Zweig was born in 1881 into one such paradise—the Austro-Hungarian Empire toward the end of the nineteenth century. Vienna at that time, as he writes in *The World of Yesterday*, offered "the noble delusion [of security, progress, and moral advancement] that our fathers served." Zweig's father, whose family's origins were in Moravia, was a successful manufacturer of textiles. His mother's family, which had greater social and cultural pretensions, was in banking. They were among those middle- and upper-middle-class secular Jews who "made significant contributions to Viennese culture, only to be exterminated root and branch by way of thanks." But this was to come later, and Zweig claimed to have known no anti-Semitism while growing up in Vienna.

What he did know was the passionate interest in culture that pervaded the Viennese. "You were not truly Viennese," he writes of the days of his youth, "without a love for culture, a bent for both enjoying and assessing the prodigality of life as something sacred." This made for a world that, as he wrote, "offered itself to me like a fruit, beautiful and rich with promise." The city's culture was "a synthesis of all Western cultures," and the Jewish bourgeoisie was preeminent in its intellectual life. "In fact, it must be said in all honesty," Zweig wrote, "that a good part, if not the greater part, of all that is admired today in Europe and America as the expression of a newly revived Austrian culture in music, literature, the theater, the art trade, was the work of the Jews of Vienna, whose intellectual drive, dating back for thousands of years, brought them to a peak of achievement." In Vienna, too, Zweig "learnt early to love the idea of community as the highest ideal of my heart." This ideal, apolitical at its core, did not serve him well with the advent of fascism in Europe.

As do so many artists and scientists, the youthful Zweig found school a great bore. In the classroom he found only compulsion and dreary rote learning, "a place where you had to absorb knowledge of subjects that did not seem worth knowing, sliced into neat portions." What Zweig did acquire in school, along with working knowledge of several languages, was "a passion for freedom . . . and with it a hatred for all that is authoritarian, all dictums issued from on high, and it has accompanied me all my life."

The action, for Zweig and his coterie of closer school friends, was outside the classroom. They went to the theater, the philharmonic, the opera; read Rilke, Nietzsche, Strindberg. Viennese coffeehouses provided newspapers and copies of the reviews of the day, including the *Mercure de France* and the *Burlington Magazine,* which carried short stories and feuilletons and cultural news around the continent. "We were particularly keen to know all about what was not generally acknowledged, and was difficult to get hold of, extravagant, new and radical," Zweig wrote. "Nothing was so abstruse and remote that our collective and avidly competitive curiosity did not want to entice it out of hiding." Zweig closes the portion of his autobiography about his education by remarking that of all his fellow *gymnasium* students, "I am the only one in whom the creative passion has lasted, has become the meaning and core of my whole life."

ZWEIG HELD THAT "the true desire of a Jew, his inbuilt ideal, is to rise to a higher social plane by becoming an intellectual." This, certainly, was the name of Zweig's desire. He began to establish his own intellectual bona fides when he first emerged into print at the age of nineteen with a book of less than immortal poems. His breakthrough came with his publication in the *Neue Freie Presse*, edited by Theodor Herzl, the founder of modern Zionism. He attempted to write for the stage, but without much success. He next turned to translation, working on the poems of the Belgian poet Émile Verhaeren. He began to write and publish stories. He lived for a spell in Berlin, then moved on to Paris, which offered "wise instruction in how to be both creative and free." In Paris he acquired the lesson of artistic concentration from Rodin. The lives of artists, the motives and methods of their creation, would become one of his great subjects.

Stefan Zweig's most famous book may be *The World of Yesterday,* begun in 1934 and mailed off to his publisher a day before his and his wife's deaths in 1942. *The World of Yesterday* is at once an homage to Austro-Hungary and a threnody over its passing. The book is not deeply introspective, but then Zweig felt that true introspection was rarely available in autobiography. In his introduction to *Adepts in Self-Portraiture*, his book about Casanova, Stendhal, and Tolstoy, he remarks that "autobiography is the hardest of all forms of literary art" and observes how difficult it is "to discern the innermost happenings of the soul; few even of the accomplished artists that have attempted autobiography have been successful in the performance of this difficult and responsible task."

Shame is the stop sign in nearly all introspective autobiography. Too great frankness in autobiography is to be suspected. Zweig notes that Tolstoy had no difficulty in revealing his whoremongering and much else in the line of youthful roistering and irresponsibility, but couldn't bring himself to reveal his consistently ungenerous treatment of Dostoevsky, which makes him seem small, pathetic, mean-spirited. As Zweig notes elsewhere, "naked truth demands from the artist an act of peculiar heroism; for the autobiographer must play the traitor to himself."

Confession, in any case, was not Stefan Zweig's preferred mode. He was more interested in the revelations he could wring from the characters in his fiction, and the men and women who were the subjects of his biographical portraits, than in setting out his own flaws, weaknesses, and sins. Modesty and self-doubt are keynotes in Zweig. "I never considered myself important enough to feel tempted to tell others the story of my life," he writes early in *The World of Yesterday*. He goes on to report that he has always been "doubtful of myself." He wasn't counting on immortality for his works—"my own rather ephemeral books," he calls them. In a letter to his first wife, he wrote that he knew "how relative all literature is, don't have any faith in mankind . . . expect nothing from the future."

Zweig wrote essays, journalism, brilliant portraits of Montaigne, Casanova, Stendhal, Tolstoy, Nietzsche, Balzac, and others, and innumerable bits and fragments, or *Schnipsel*, as the Germans call them. He published many stories, and a number of novellas—"the blest *nouvelle*," Henry James called the form, midway between novel and short story—but, with the exception of *Beware of Pity*, not one of his stronger works, he never, for reasons that will become clear, wrote a successful novel. No wonder that by forty-six he had begun to feel "as if the screws are coming loose in the machine: the best thing would be to switch it off completely in its fiftieth year and make another attempt to experience the world again instead of describing it."

N OT THE LEAST NOTABLE THING about Stefan Zweig's writing is how varied the reactions to it have been. Among contemporaries, Thomas Mann thought Zweig a mediocrity. Robert Musil, Bertolt Brecht, Hermann Hesse, and Hugo von Hofmannsthal did not think much better of him. When told that Zweig had conquered all the languages of the world, Karl Kraus responded by saying, "Except one." (Zweig called Kraus, rightly, a "master of venomous ridicule.") But, then, these German and Austrian writers were quite possibly envious of Zweig's commercial success.

In our own day, a distrust of Zweig's quality remains, even among those ostensibly writing on his behalf in introductions to his recently reprinted

books. André Aciman notes "the Old-World charm and velvety composure of Zweig's narratives." Joan Acocella remarks on a certain "uphol-
stered" quality to Zweig's fiction. Peter Gay upbraids Zweig for a want
of candor: "Before the all-too-final act of suicide, Zweig, writing *Chess
Story,* might have included his readers more frankly, more openly, about
the desperate struggles within him." Michael Hofmann, in a 2010 demolition job in the *London Review of Books,* writes: "Stefan Zweig just tastes
fake. He's the Pepsi of Austrian writing." Hofmann claims that "every
page he writes is formulaic, thin, swollen, platitudinous," and compares
Zweig to "someone walking up a down escalator, his eyes anxiously fixed
on Parnassus—all those people and friends whose manuscripts he collected—toiling away and not coming close."

On the other side of the ledger, Zweig has never lacked for admirers,
critics ready to compare his stories to those of Turgenev, Maupassant,
Chekhov, his biographical interpretations like unto those of Montaigne,
and to cite Zweig himself as "the incarnation of humanism." Critics have
admired his "concision and subtlety"; others his "passion and dedication." But his most impressive contemporary defender is the critic Clive
James, who devotes the final chapter of his *Cultural Amnesia* to the works
of Stefan Zweig, thus suggesting that it is precisely our neglect of writers
such as Zweig—cultivated and learned, a man who lived for art—that is
likely to bring on cultural amnesia in our time.

Clive James is keener on Stefan Zweig as a biographical portraitist than
as a storyteller. James notes that Zweig "always wrote wonderfully about
Montaigne, with whom he shared the gift of summarizing and assessing the
actions of historical figures." He goes on to suggest what I believe is true,
that behind Zweig's skill as a biographer was a powerful admiration for
those he wrote about. "Zweig was the sum total of his appreciations," James
writes, "to which his style gave the spiritual unity that they never had in life."

A S FOR STEFAN ZWEIG THE STORYTELLER, here his reputation
seems to suffer from his stories and novellas being too well-made, if
that can really stand as a criticism. They are all truly stories; in them moral
crises are encountered and resolved, people learn about themselves, lives are
changed. The endings do not disappoint. Zweig claimed to be entranced by

"the tragedy of losers," noting: "I am always most attracted to the character who is struck down by fate in my novellas, and in my biographies it is those who are morally right but never achieve success who appeal to me." Several of the characters in his fictions are obsessives—mono maniacs, chess fanatics, passionate bibliophiles, dog-lovers among them. He is also attracted to the sadder emotions: confusion, pity, fear. But in all his fiction the people come alive, one wants to read on, and the unpredictable never seems implausible—three tests for excellent fiction, which Zweig never fails to pass.

Then there are the touches, little and large, that show the hand of a master. Aperçus and aphorisms abound: In "Downfall of the Heart," we learn that "to know yourself is to defend yourself, but it is usually in vain." In *Beware of Pity*, we find that "only those with whom life had dealt hardly, the wretched, the slighted, the uncertain, the unlovely, the humiliated, could really be helped by love. . . . They alone knew how to love and be loved as one should love and be loved—gratefully and humbly."

In *Confusion,* a story about a student's infatuation with a teacher, Zweig accounts for the infatuation by presenting snippets of a brilliant lecture on the Elizabethan playwrights and poets, so that the reader himself becomes infatuated. Early in *Chess Story*—which tells of a shipboard chess match between an idiot-savant champion and a man who learned his chess from a book on famous chess-master matches while being brutally interrogated by the Nazis—Zweig offers a description of chess, "the royal game," that is as good as any I know:

> But is it not already an insult to call chess anything so narrow as a game? Is it not also a science, an art, hovering between these categories like Muhammad's coffin between heaven and earth, a unique yoking of opposites, ancient and yet eternally new, mechanically constituted and yet an activity of the imagination alone, limited to a fixed geometric area but unlimited in its permutations, constantly evolving and yet sterile, a cogitation producing nothing, a mathematics calculating nothing, an art without an artwork, an architecture without substance and yet demonstrably more durable in its essence and actual form than all books and works, the only game that belongs to all peoples and all eras, while

no one knows what god put it on earth to deaden boredom, sharpen the mind, and fortify the spirit? Where does it begin, where does it end? Any child can learn its basic rules, any amateur can try his hand at it; and yet, within the inalterable confines of a chessboard, masters unlike any others evolve, people with a talent for chess and chess alone, special geniuses whose gifts of imagination, patience and skill are just as precisely apportioned as those of mathematicians, poets, and musicians, but differently arranged and combined.

Perhaps Stefan Zweig's current low reputation as a storyteller is owing to his not having written a single great work of fiction of novel length, unlike his friend Joseph Roth (whom Zweig financially supported for nearly a decade) with *The Radetzky March*, or Ivan Goncharov with *Oblomov*, or Boris Pasternak with (his one novel) *Dr. Zhivago*. In *The World of Yesterday*, Zweig provides a clue to why he never wrote a great novel, and it lies in his method of composition. One of the many divisions among writers is that between those who endlessly add to their manuscripts (Balzac and Proust spring to mind) and those who cut them down. Zweig was one of the latter. Calling himself an impatient reader, suffering keenly from tedium—"anything long-winded, high-flown, or gushing irritates me, so does everything that is vague and indistinct"—he readily took the cleaver to his own writing. (Though not everywhere: His excellent biographies of Marie Antoinette and of Balzac both come in at around four hundred pages.) "If I have mastered any kind of art," Zweig wrote, "it is the art of leaving things out. . . . So if anything at least partly accounts for the success of my books, it is my strict discipline in preferring to confine myself to short works of literature, concentrating on the heart of the matter." But the concision that made for popular success in his day may have hurt his reputation in ours.

Zweig's art of concision works to maximum effect in his biographical portraits. Consider those of Casanova and Nietzsche, two men who would have found little to say to each other, but both of whom spoke to the imagination of Stefan Zweig.

Casanova, Zweig begins, is "a chance intruder in world literature, above all because this famous charlatan has as little right in the pantheon of creative geniuses as the name of Pontius Pilate has in the Creed." Casanova was not only a fraud, but a man for whom "fraud is not merely a fine art, but a supreme moral duty." Zweig reports that "he lacked will, resolution, patience," cared only to be free, and had the unremitting courage to insure his freedom. "Courage," Zweig writes, "that is the keynote of Casanova's art of life, that is his gift of gifts." Here, as set out by Zweig, is Casanova's philosophy:

> Live for this world, unconcernedly and spontaneously; do not allow yourself to be cheated by regard for another world (which may indeed exist, but whose existence is extremely doubtful), or by regard for posterity. Do not let finespun theories divert your attention from things close at hand; do not direct your endeavors towards a distant goal; follow the promptings of the moment. Foresight will cripple your activities here and now. Do not trouble your head with prudential considerations. Some strange deity has set us down in our seat at this gaming table of a world. If we wish to amuse ourselves there, we must accept the rules of the game, taking them as they are, without troubling to inquire whether they are good rules or bad.

As befits the professional seducer, the paneroticist, Casanova eschewed anything resembling ethics. Boredom was his greatest enemy, induced tension among his chief desiderata. When not in the boudoirs of women—in love, as Zweig notes, "he is nothing more than an episodist"—Casanova sought out the gambling tables, where he found "the titillation of anxiety" played nicely off the "shuddering expectation" of victorious profit. Zweig, with his instinct for all that will interest his readers, takes a moment to describe Casanova's physique: "This *bel uomo* is no ephebe; nothing of the sort! He is a stallion of a man, with the shoulders of the Farnese Hercules, the muscles of a Roman wrestler, the bronzed beauty of a gypsy lad, the impudence and audacity of a condottiere, and the sexual ardour of a satyr."

Sword wounds, venereal disease, prison terms, poisonings—"none of these things," Zweig writes, "abate his phallic energy by a jot." He describes

Casanova's memoirs, written in old age when this energy was depleted, as "an occidental *Kama-sutra,* an *Odyssey* of the wanderings of the flesh, an *Iliad* of the eternal masculine rut for the eternal Helen." Casanova wrote them out of boredom while serving as librarian to Count Waldstein in Bohemia, feeling none of the normal constraints of autobiography since he knew no shame and must have felt he was writing less about his own life than about the history of a campaign.

F RIEDRICH NIETZSCHE WROTE NO AUTOBIOGRAPHY. Nor is it possible to imagine him on a night on the town—any night, any town—with Giacomo Casanova. The chief point of Stefan Zweig's dazzling portrait of Nietzsche is his utter loneliness. Zweig's object, he proclaims, "is to portray Nietzsche's life, not as a biography but as a tragedy of the spirit, as a work of dramatic art, for me his true work began when the artist in the man was released and became conscious of enfranchisement." The release came when Nietzsche left his academic post at the Basel and went off on his own in search of truth. "Now, what renders this life unique and tragical," Zweig writes, "is precisely the absence of repose in Nietzsche's searchings, his incessant urge to think, his compulsory advance."

What Nietzsche sought was style, or, in Nietzsche's own words, "morality in the grand style." According to Zweig, "he did not want to be happy but to be true. Nine-tenths of philosophers seek rest. Not so Nietzsche." Zweig traces the relentlessness of this quest, and the dangerousness of it. As a hero of thought, Nietzsche "loved life precisely because it was dangerous and annihilated his personal existence." Nietzsche wrote: "I know my fate. On a day to come my name will be associated with something quite out of the ordinary, with a crisis such as the world has never heretofore experienced, with the profoundest clashes in the conscience, with a decision entered upon in defiance of all that has so far been held sacred and as an article of faith."

Zweig compares the intellectual career of Nietzsche with that of Goethe, whose life was orderly, carefully paced: "After going through a revolutionary period he [Goethe] turned conservative, after a phase of lyricism he became a man of science, after being prodigal of himself he learned how to be reserved." Nietzsche went in the opposite direction, from professor to the ultimate freelance, cultivating intellectual passion, shedding religion and conventional morality, courting disintegration. "This led him in the end," Zweig writes, "to an excitability of mind which bordered on madness and had fatal results."

The influence of music in Nietzsche went well beyond his tangled relationship with Wagner. Zweig discovers it in his prose, and in a brilliant passage he writes:

> The *andante maestoso* of his earlier works changed into a sinuous and flexible movement possessing the qualities of a genuinely musical idiom. The delicacies of touch we expect from a master of the art are there for the seeking: the crisp *staccati* of the aphorisms, the *mezza* voce of the hymns, the *pizzicati* of his mockery, the daring harmonization of his prose and his maxims. Even his punctuation—unspoken speech—his dashes, his italics, could find equivalents in the terminology of the elements of music.

Zweig does not so much elucidate Nietzsche's ideas as limn the nature of his extraordinary quest. He describes Nietzsche's collapse as "a sort of carbonization in his own flames" brought on by the intensity of his own feelings. The reward of the man who follows his daemon unstintingly turns out, in Nietzsche's case, to be oblivion. "One who has gazed so intently into the eyes of the daemon," Zweig writes, "is henceforth blinded"—in Nietzsche's case, by madness.

NIETZSCHE IS A HERO for Stefan Zweig not least because "he alone recognized how frightful a hurricane was about to disturb our civilization." Nietzsche was for Zweig "the spearhead of a revolt against the triviality of habitual thought and the monotonousness of conventional morality," but it was his prophetic powers that attracted Zweig most of all. "No one felt so strongly as he that the old order was decayed and done with, and that, amid death-dealing crises, a new and mighty order was about to begin. Now at length we know it, as he knew it decades ago." This was the order—or rather, disorder—of disputatious nations, wars, fascism, communism, and mass murder on a scale unknown through all earlier barbarous ages.

Zweig had fame, wealth, the love of a younger woman, but all of it was not enough to brace him to go on living in a world blanketed by what he felt was unrelieved darkness, with only worse to come. So on the morning of February 23, 1942, Stefan Zweig was found, fully dressed, on his back, in an iron bed, holding hands with his wife, both dead from an overdose of Veronal.

Vasily Grossman

(2011)

"Well, comrade Mostovskoy," said Sofya, "so much for your twentieth century. So much for its humanity and culture. . . . All I see is unprecedented atrocities."

Stalingrad

IN A CONVERSATION sometime in the mid-1970s, Saul Bellow remarked to me on the crucial difference between European and American writers of his generation. Writers in Europe have looked the devil in the eye, he said, while in America writers have to make do with irony, comedy, and anything else that comes to hand. The devil, of course, was totalitarianism, in particular fascism and Communism, which promised its adherents heaven and brought them unmitigated hell.

The European writers Bellow had in mind were Arthur Koestler, George Orwell, Albert Camus, Aleksandr Solzhenitsyn, Stefan Zweig, Andre Malraux, Boris Pasternak, and others. Vasily Grossman (1905–1964), a writer Bellow surely did not know about at the time we spoke, perhaps stared that devil in the face with greater intensity than anyone else, and came away the most impressive of all literary witnesses of the malevolence of totalitarianism. Judged by the centrality, the significance, of his subject and his aesthetic grasp of it in powerful novels and penetrating essays, Grossman may have been the most important writer of the past century.

Vasily Grossman had the misfortune of being born in Russia, a country that, under the Czars as under the commissars, has traditionally treated its people as if they were a conquered nation. "There was only one thing Russia hadn't seen during these thousand years," thinks a character in Grossman's novel *Everything Flows*—"freedom." Another character in the same novel remarks: "Happiness doesn't seem to be our fate in this world." In 2014, the actor Leonid Bronevoy, whose father had been sent off to the Gulag, described the Soviet experiment as "an absurd horror film stretching over 70 years." Government-organized famine, hideous show trials, brutal gulags, mass murder, life in the Soviet Union made the plagues that fell upon Egypt seem a week in the Catskills.

Grossman was also a Jew, who under the Czars were for the most part kept segregated in the Pale of Settlement and victimized by pogroms. (There were more than 1,200 pogroms in the Ukraine alone.) Under Stalin, Jews were systematically hunted down after the false Doctors Plot of 1952–1953, in which Russians were told that a group of mostly Jewish doctors supposedly plotted to assassinate the dictator. Grossman somehow evaded the fate of death by execution that befell those two other immensely talented Jewish writers, Isaac Babel and Osip Mandelstam. But his mother was murdered by the Nazis in Berdichev in 1941 in Ukraine, where some 62,000 Jews were massacred.

Like Aleksandr Solzhenitsyn, Vasily Grossman was trained as an engineer, in his case a chemical engineer. During World War II, owing to near-sightedness and poor health, he failed to qualify for the military but served primarily as a journalist covering all the major battles of the war for *Red Star* and other Soviet publications. Grossman arrived with the Soviet troops at Treblinka, the death camp, and was among the first, in a devasting essay called "The Hell of Treblinka" (1944), to reveal the deadly mechanics of Hitler's Final Solution. As a journalist he was also at Stalingrad, the great battle that marked the beginning of the end for the Nazis.

Grossman is best known for his two connected and hefty novels—together, in their *New York Review* editions, they weigh in at a combined 1,830 pages. These are *Stalingrad* and *Life and Fate*. His unfinished novel *Everything Flows* (1961), written toward the end of his life, is a root-and-branch attack on Soviet Communism as told through the lucubrations of a man, one Ivan Grigoryevich, who had spent nearly 30 years in the Gulag.

The story of the publication of Grossman's books under Soviet Communism could be the source of an impressively complex novel of its own.

Grossman wrote his *Stalingrad* while Stalin was still alive, and thus under the artistically crushing restraints of Socialist Realism, which Maxim Gorky defined as "the ability to see the present in terms of the future" and which Grossman later said was as "convention-ridden as the bucolic romances of the 18th century." What Socialist Realism actually meant was that no art was allowed that did not support, defend, extol the Soviet Union, which of course meant no art of any independence, complexity, ultimate worth was permitted publication.

In his introduction to *Life and Fate* and his Afterword to *Stalingrad*, the translator Robert Chandler offers an admittedly partial account of the fiery hoops through which Grossman had to jump to get his work published. The editors of the Soviet journal *Novy Mir* made so many radical editorial suggestions to render *Stalingrad* "safe"—including cutting some characters, adding others, altering the occupations of still others—that the original manuscript underwent six heavy revisions and was set in type no fewer than three times before finally being run in serialization in a much altered version. About the no less complicated editorial maze through which Grossman's *Life and Fate* was put, it is more than enough to say that its author failed to live long enough to see it in print. He died in 1964.

Grossman's book was arrested instead of its author; Grossman spoke of *Life and Fate* as being "imprisoned." The novel in fact wasn't published in the Soviet Union until the late 1980s, and even today Grossman is apparently not all that well known in his native land. Imagine the utter frustration, leading to the deep depression that Grossman suffered, of having written a masterpiece of world literature and never getting to see it in print!

In *Vasily Grossman and the Soviet Century*, Alexandra Popoff, a Russian journalist who has written books about Countess Tolstoy and about Tolstoy's disciple Vladimir Chertkov, has turned out an excellent biography of Grossman. Hers is a biography that offers no striking psychological portrait of its subject or radical reading of his works. Instead it is what I think of as a *Dragnet*, or Jack Webb, biography—"Just the facts, Ma'am"—the accretion of which is no small accomplishment about a life lived almost entirely in the murky and heavily censored atmosphere of the Soviet Union.

GROSSMAN, Alexandra Popoff recounts, was "descended from well-to-do merchants," a fact that needs to be qualified, as she also notes, by the fact that Jews, however well-to-do, were "first among non-equals in the Russian Empire." His parents were divorced soon after his birth in 1905, though they remained friendly. His mother was a cultivated woman, educated in Europe and fluent in French, a subject she taught. She took her son to live in Switzerland between the ages of five and seven, where, as Ms. Popoff writes, he was "introduced to Western values, including the respect for individual rights and freedoms he later believed essential." Grossman himself read the French writers, the classics, Kipling and Conan Doyle, was a great admirer of Tolstoy and Chekhov. "Although Grossman lived all his adult life in a totalitarian Soviet state," Popoff writes, "he had the mentality of a man from the free world." Friends early noticed the qualities in him of attentiveness and detachment, a combination suggesting a future novelist.

Grossman set out in life to be a scientist, but fairly early sensed that he could not do first-class work in science. Social questions began to absorb him, and by the age of twenty-three he decided that his true vocation was for literature. How literary talent comes to fruition remains one of the mysteries of the arts. Musical talent and skill at visual art tend to show up early, and appear to be, as they doubtless are, gifts from God. But literary talent is an acquisition that often comes only later in life—Joseph Conrad published his first novel, *Almayer's Folly,* at thirty-nine—if it isn't earlier set adrift by discouragement. In the Soviet Union, with its strict censorship, the decision to become a writer, always a risky venture, had the further disadvantage of being fraught with danger. Only in the Soviet Union, it used to be said, do they truly take writers seriously; only there did they take them seriously enough to kill them.

Writing against the grain of Socialist Realism was not yet a problem for the young Vasily Grossman. If he was never an ideologue, he nonetheless respected the idealism of the early Communists. (His father was a Menshevik.) In a 1934 story, "In the Town of Berdichev," he wrote of a female commissar who finds herself pregnant, and during her lying-in lives with a poor Jewish family, the Magazaniks, until the birth of her child. Once born the child awakens deep, previously unexpected maternal feelings in her. But when the Poles attack the town of Berdichev, she leaves her child behind—permanently, we are given to believe—to go off and fight with her old regiment. Great sympathy is shown for the Jewish family, and the details in the story are nicely done, yet the moral of the story is clear: The state comes first, yes, even over motherhood. One likes to think that the older Vasily Grossman would have despised this story.

"In the Town of Berdichev" marked Grossman's arrival as a Soviet writer. It paved the way for him to publish two rather negligible early novels. He was given a much-desired apartment in Moscow. Never a member of the Party, he was a member in good standing of the Soviet Writers Union. Grossman in those days was not cynically playing the system—he claimed at the time that he owed everything to the Soviet government—but neither was he fighting it.

One of the low points in his career came in 1953 with his agreeing, along with fifty-six other prominent Soviet Jews, to sign a document that denounced the Jewish physicians who supposedly led the Doctors Plot. Grossman later came greatly to regret it, and in *Life and Fate* he assigns the character Viktor Shtrum, who signs a similar document, "a feeling of irreparable guilt and impurity" for his having done so. Grossman's upbringing was secular; Jewishness did not loom large in his early life. Popoff remarks that he had nevertheless read the Bible and "was deeply influenced by the Jewish belief in the need for compassion, in the need to love life and resist death to the last minute, in the need and obligation to remember the past and honor the dead, and in the need to bear witness."

Many of these qualities are at the heart of *Stalingrad*. The book is chiefly about the effects of the German invasion on the citizens at all levels of Soviet life, and of the attack on Stalingrad—"a battle," as Grossman writes, "more grinding, more relentless than Thermopylae or even the siege of Troy . . . the city on the Volga where the world's fate was being decided." In *Life and Fate*, Grossman wrote that "every epoch has its own capitol city, a city that embodies its will and soul. For several months during the Second World War this city was Stalingrad."

Stalingrad qualifies nicely as one of Henry James's "loose and baggy monsters," those novels without the aesthetic form that for James was essential. The novel has no fewer than 151 characters, not counting those who appear only once. These run from Soviet scientists to German generals to Russian peasants to Stalin and Hitler, who put in appearances, the former in a full-length portrait. ("It was indeed during these hours of ugly, troubled sleep that Hitler was closest to being human.") New characters are introduced as late as page 868. Domestic scenes are played out, characters intricately described (General Yeromenko "was massive yet stooping; his build did not make it easy for tailors."), and observations on human nature offered: "Love has meaning only when it inspires people to sacrifice—otherwise it is just base passion." Grossman's account of the battle of Stalingrad, its confusions, its arbitrary destruction, its deadliness—some 400,000 Germans and between 650,000 and 850,000 Russians were killed or captured there—is no less compelling than Tolstoy's account of the battle of Borodino in *War and Peace*.

"Human suffering," Grossman writes. "Will it be remembered in centuries to come? The stones of buildings endure and the glory of generals endures, but human suffering does not. Tears and whispers, a cry of pain and despair, the last sighs and groans of the dying—all this disappears along with the smoke and dust blown across the steppe by the wind." In *Stalingrad* Grossman set himself to record the human suffering brought on by Hitler's war. Apart from that visited upon the Jews, no people endured more suffering during World War II than the Russians. Through the build-up of detail—of depredations, devastation, death—Grossman succeeds in his self-appointed task of enshrining suffering and its brutally high cost for ordinary people.

It is a splendid, an important book, possibly a great book, but not, alas, a great novel. *Stalingrad* is too diffuse to have the special power, the concentration and intensification, that only fiction carries. At its end, too many loose ends have not been raveled, significant characters go unaccounted for, themes are set out but left inadequately unexplored. Much of this may well be owing to the endless editing and relentless revisions that beset the book by its Soviet editor-censors. One is nonetheless pleased to have read *Stalingrad,* not alone for its bringing one of the great battles of history down to personal cases, but for its testimony on behalf of the brave dead.

A QUESTION THAT ARISES is whether *Stalingrad* is meant to stand as the first half of a diology, with *Life and Fate* its second half. The books' translator Robert Chandler is moderately confident that Grossman intended the two books as a single work. Certainly, *Life and Fate* can be read on its own, and before reading *Stalingrad*, which is the order in which I read them. Yet the latter volume enhances the former by providing what in film scripts is called back story to a novel that already has something akin to classic status among its coterie of devoted readers, among whom I have long been one.

Tzevtan Todorov, the Bulgarian critic, wrote of the Vasily Grossman of the 1950s, the author of *Life and Fate* and *Everthing Flows*, that he "is the only example, or at least the most significant, of an established and leading Soviet writer changing his spots completely. The slave in him died, and a free man arose." This is an over-simplification, but it is true that the Grossman of the 1950s was a different writer from the Grossman of the 1930s and '40s. Nitika Khrushchev's famous "Secret Speech" of 1956, setting out some of the sins of Stalin and suggesting a "thaw" in the realm of Soviet culture, was doubtless partially responsible for the change in Grossman. But one wonders if his own Jewishness didn't even more influence the change, however gradual.

In covering the war as a journalist, Grossman also learned about the slaughter of Jews in the Ukraine. Along with his article on the inhuman ghastliness at Treblinka, which was put in evidence at the Nuremberg Trials, Grossman saw Babi Yar, the ravine in Kiev where nearly 100,000 Jews were executed and dumped into mass graves in 1941. He knew that many Ukrainians had been complicit in the slaughter of Jews during the Shoah. Add to this his mother's murder at Berdichev. During these years Grossman worked in collaboration with Ilya Ehenberg on a volume called *The Complete Black Book of Russian Jewry*, a book that was not allowed publication in Stalin's Soviet Union. Stalin, himself an anti-Semite, had famously declared "Do not divide the dead," by which he meant that emphasizing the mass murder of Jews was prohibited.

Grossman had come a long way and the evidence of what he learned along that way is plain in the advanced artistry and political candor of *Life and Fate*. Among the most stirring pages in *Life and Fate* are those about a non-Jewish Soviet physician, Sofya Osipovna Levinton, who chooses not to save her own life so that she can comfort a child, David, a small Jewish boy, in the gas chambers of Treblinka and feels herself thereby his mother in the moments before her own death—an episode that might be taken as the very reversal, and thereby a repudiation, of "In the Town of Berdichev."

The miseries of Stalinism and the grave mistakes of Stalin himself in his direction of the war, which are generally given a pass in *Stalingrad*, are not ignored in *Life and Fate*. The novel opens on a number of brief chapters in which an old Bolshevik, Mikhail Sidorovich Mostoyskoy, begins to lose his faith in "the cause of Lenin." A figure of wisdom and much looked up to in *Stalingrad*, Mostoyskoy, now in a German prisoner camp, "was unable to recover his former sense of clarity and completeness . . . 'I must be getting old,' he said to himself." In *Life and Fate*, true believers often have their belief shaken.

Life and Fate offers several brilliant pages on anti-Semitism, Soviet and worldwide. "Anti-Semitism," Grossman writes, "is also an expression of a lack of talent, an inability to win a contest on equal terms—in science, in commerce, in craftsmanship or in painting. States look to the imaginary intrigues of World Jewry for explanations of their own failure." He sets out the different levels of anti-Semitism, and notes that "historical epochs, unsuccessful and reactionary governments, and individuals hoping to better their lot all turn to anti-Semitism as a last resort, in an attempt to escape an inevitable doom." In this novel, too, Grossman offers a brilliant portrait of Adolf Eichmann, which one wishes Hannah Arendt had read, as it might have prevented her from writing her wretched book portraying Eichmann as a mere banal bureaucrat.

Told from the point of view of several different characters, with several plots and subplots, *Life and Fate* is not readily summarized. Life under the two totalitarianisms—communist and fascist—is set out as is the connection between the two, their commonality, as enemies of humanity. What holds the novel together is the material about the family of Alexandra Vladimorovna Shaposhnikova, a laboratory chemist, her three daughters, their husbands, and their children. One of the husbands, Viktor Pavlovich Shtrum, is a theoretical physicist whose views in many respects resemble those of Grossman. Shtrum not only signs the document blaming colleagues that he much regrets; he holds a grudge against his wife, Lyudmila, whose demands prevented him from saving his mother from the Holocaust. "Good men and bad men alike are capable of weakness," Grossman writes. "The difference is simply that a bad man will be proud all his life of one good deed—while an honest man is hardly aware of his good acts, but remembers a single bad act for years on end."

Many of the characters who appear in *Stalingrad* are more fully developed, richer, somehow more memorable in *Life and Fate*. If in its form *Life and Fate* tends to imitate *War and Peace*—the only book Grossman claimed to have read during the battle of Stalingrad—the tone of the novel is closer to that of Chekhov, and many of its chapters, as Robert Chandler suggests, read as if they were Chekhovian short stories. *Life and Fate* is a novel that fully engages its readers with the lives of its characters while revealing the life of an entire society—the kind of work otherwise known as a masterpiece.

No one would call *Everything Flows*, Grossman's final novel, a masterpiece, but, more than anything he had written earlier, it fully reveals his views about the Soviet Union. In this unfinished work, Grossman wrote, perhaps aware he was dying of stomach cancer, without filter. Stalin, so central a figure in the life of all Russians of Grossman's generation, is revealed as what he was, "a European Marxist and an Asian Despot." At Stalin's death, "the death day of the earthly Russian god, the pockmarked cobbler's son from the town of Gori," many villagers "breathed a sigh of relief," in the camps he had created many millions rejoiced. "Stalin Had Died," Grossman writes. "In this death lay an element of sudden and spontaneous freedom that was infinitely alien to the nature of the Stalinist State."

Vladimir Ilyich Ulyanov, the sacrosanct Lenin, fares little better in the pages of *Everything Flows*. The notion that the purity of Lenin's revolution having been distorted by the monstrosities of Stalin is roundly rejected. "The murder of millions of innocent and loyal people masqueraded as cast-iron logic" all had its origin in Lenin. "The destruction of Russian life carried out by Lenin was on a vast scale,"

Grossman writes. "Lenin destroyed the way of life of the landowners, Lenin destroyed factory owners and merchants." Stalin stepped in and with his brutal collectivization finished off the peasants. But it was "Lenin's obsession with revolution, his fanatical faith in the truth of Marxism and absolute intolerance of anyone who disagreed with him, [that] led him to further hugely the development of the Russia he hated with all his fanatical soul."

Lenin and Stalin are for Grossman among history's great enemies of freedom, and it was his belief that "there is no end in the world for the sake of which it is permissible to sacrifice human freedom." The only progress Grossman recognized was in the realm of freedom. He even implicitly criticizes Tolstoy and Dostoevsky when he writes that "the mystique of the Russian soul is simply the result of a thousand years of slavery." Grossman asks toward the end of *Everything Flows*: "When will we see the day of a free, human, Russian soul? When will this day dawn? Or will it never dawn?"

Grossman did not entirely despair, for he felt that not even Stalin— who presided over a state that was the enemy of freedom, that overcame freedom in every sphere of life—was able, in spite of all the millions he killed, to do away with freedom entirely. Or with human kindness.

In *Life and Fate* the old Bolshevik Mikhail Mostovskoy is interrogated by a Gestapo agent who explains to him all that the Nazis learned from the Lenin and Stalin and the similarity of the two regimes. Mostovskoy is disgusted at the thought, but back in his cell he reads the pages of a fellow prisoner, a strange, half-saintly figure named Ikonnikov, thought to be slightly unhinged, who has written about the role of kindness in the human condition.

"This kindness, this stupid kindness, is what is most truly human in a human being," writes Ikonnikov. "It is what sets man apart, the highest achievement of his soul. No, it says, life is not evil." Ikonnikov goes on to note that "kindness is powerful only while it is powerless"—the point here being that religions, when in power, lose their goodness in attempting to maintain and protect that power. For Ikonnikov, "the powerlessness of kindness, of senseless kindness, is the secret of [human] immortality. It can never be conquered." Ikonnikov concludes:

Human history is not the battle of good struggling to over-
come evil. It is the battle fought by a great evil struggling to
crush a small kernel of human kindness. But if what is human in human beings has not been destroyed even now, then
evil will never conquer.

Mostovskoy, the life-long committed Bolshevik, thinks these the observations of a mad man. Yet they leave him confused and depressed. They
have quite the reverse effect on Grossman's readers. We think of the act
of Sofya Osipovna Levinton in comforting the child in the gas chambers.
We think of the six-year-old girl who comforts an eighty-two-year-old man
on his way to the firing squad in Grossman's story "The Old Teacher," and
of scores of other acts of kindness that play through the pages of Grossman's fiction. Only a certain kind of writer can bring such truth home to
his readers through the vividly persuasive examples enacted by his characters—only a great writer, which is what Vasily Grossman was.

Evelyn Waugh

(2017)

W HEN THE FINAL REVIEWS—that is, the obituaries— came in, Evelyn Waugh's were mixed. His literary accomplishments were noted, so too his Catholic apologetics, but heavy emphasis was put upon his reactionary views and his snobbery. Waugh's son Auberon, responding to these notices, countered that they were wrong about his father's snobbery (he scarcely cared about pedigree) and his politics ("politics bored him"), and missed the main point about him: "[I]t is simply that he was the funniest man of his generation."

Quite so, though it needs to be added that in the case of Evelyn Waugh funny was not always the same as amusing. Amusing suggests light, whimsical, charming. P. G. Wodehouse is amusing. Waugh's humor tended to the dark, and, given his often-gratuitous pugnacity, usually had a victim, or at least an edge. When the favorite of his seven children, his daughter Margaret, wished to live on her own, he told her "you are no more ready for independence than the Congo." After Randolph Churchill had what turned out to be a benign tumor removed through surgery, Waugh remarked that it was the only thing about Randolph that wasn't malignant and they removed it. When someone called his attention to a typographical error in one of his books, he replied that one cannot get any decent proofreading now "that they no longer defrock priests for sodomy." Waugh's humor was also strong in the line of mischief. While serving in the British army in Yugoslavia during World War II, he spread the rumor that Marshal Tito was a woman—and a lesbian into the bargain. Of his teaching at a boys' school in Wales he claimed to take "a certain perverse pleasure in making all I teach as dreary to the boys as it is to myself." When his friend and fellow convert Ronald Knox asked him if he, Knox, seemed to nod off while giving a lecture, Waugh replied that indeed he did, but only for "twenty minutes." He described travel to Mexico as "like sitting in a cinema, seeing the travel film of a country one has no intention of visiting." Of the reception in America of his novel *Brideshead Revisited* (1945), he wrote: "My book has been a great success in the United States which is upsetting because I thought it in good taste before and now I know it can't be."

Waugh soon enough acquired a reputation for social ruthlessness, a ruthlessness nicely abetted by his heavy drinking. "Even his close friends were not spared," Nancy Mitford wrote, "he criticized everyone fiercely and was a terrible tease, but he set about it in such a wildly comic way that his teasing was easily forgiven." Not by everyone. Martha Gellhorn, a friend of Waugh's friend Diana Cooper, called him "a small and very ugly turd." Duff Cooper, Diana's husband, reacting to a malicious comment Waugh made about Lord Mountbatten at a dinner party, lashed out: "How dare a common little man like you, who happens to have written one or two moderately amusing novels, criticize that great patriot and gentleman. Leave my house at once!" On his own social combativeness, Waugh has Gilbert Pinfold, his autobiographically based, eponymous character in *The Ordeal of Gilbert Pinfold* (1957) ask, "Why does everyone except me find it so easy to be nice?"

PHILIP EADE'S NEW BIOGRAPHY OF WAUGH goes a fair way to answering that question. Eade's book is subtitled, with some precision, *A Life Revisited*, for it is Evelyn Waugh's life and only glancingly his work to which Eade devotes his attention. His is a chronicle of Waugh's recent ancestry and early childhood, his education, two marriages, and career on to his death in 1966 at the age of 62. Waugh's books and their reception are mentioned in due course, but it is his career and the formation of his character that hold chief interest.

Rightly so, I should say, for Evelyn Waugh's novels, travel writings, and biographies (of the painter and poet Dante Rossetti, the Jesuit martyr Edmund Campion, and Monsignor Knox) do not really require elaborate critical exploration. All his writing requires is attentive readers, alive to his elegant prose, his craftsmanship at plotting, and the manifold comical touches that fill his pages. "Germans," a character in *Brideshead Revisited* remarks, "sometimes seem to discover a sense of decency when they get to a classical country." In *A Handful of Dust* (1934) a secondary character, Mrs. Rattery, reveals that she has children, two sons:

> I don't see them often. They're at school somewhere. I took them to the cinema last summer. They're getting quite big. One's going to be good-looking, I think. His father is.

Rather a different angle on parenting, this, one might say.

Eade recounts Waugh's life in an admirably economic, straightforward manner, with a nice sense of measure and in a prose style free of jargon and cliché. He neither Freudianizes Waugh nor condemns his lapses into social savagery. Without a trace of tendentiousness, free of all doctrine, the biographer seeks to understand the strange behavior of his subject through telling the story of his life without commenting censoriously on it. The task is far from a simple one. Waugh's friend Freddy Smith, the second Earl of Birkenhead, in a memoir of his war days with him, wrote:

> Evelyn, like Max Beerbohm, but probably for different reasons, had decided to drop an iron visor over all his intimate feelings and serious beliefs and by doing so excluded one from any understanding of his true character. . . . This deep reticence detracted in a sense from his conversation, which was of the highest order, because however brilliant and witty, one always felt that he was playing some elaborate charade which demanded from him constant vigilance and wariness.

Early in the pages of *The Ordeal of Gilbert Pinfold*, a novel recounting the nervous breakdown of its hero, Waugh stages an interview for Pinfold with a journalist from the BBC. (Waugh himself underwent such a break-down owing to his overdosing on bromide and chloral combined with his heavy alcohol intake, a potion he hoped would help him attain sleep.) Of this interview Pinfold notes that the interviewer "seemed to believe that anyone sufficiently eminent to be interviewed by him must have something to hide, must be an impostor whom it was his business to trap and expose, and to direct his questions from some basic, previous knowledge of some-thing discreditable." When during an actual interview by John Freeman of the BBC, Waugh was asked why he lived in the country, he answered that it was not because of a love of sport or rural life, but "to get away from people like you." From behind the screen of Pinfold, Waugh describes his own menacing social profile with a nice exactitude. The novel's narra-tor observes that "his habits of life were self-indulgent and his utterances lacked prudence." As for his tastes, the strongest of them were negative. "[H]e looked at the world *sub species aeternitatis* and he found it flat as a map; except when, rather often, personal annoyance intruded." The part he decided to play "was a combination of eccentric don and testy colonel . . . it came to dominate his whole outward personality" as "he offered the world a front of pomposity mitigated by indiscretion that was as hard, bright and antiquated as a cuirass."

SOON AFTER HE CAME TO CONSCIOUSNESS Evelyn Waugh was made aware that he was not his father's favorite child. His older brother, Alec—later a popular, now a largely forgotten, novelist—was. A five-year difference in age separated the two brothers, just the right dis-tance to prevent closeness and make intimacy difficult. Evelyn did not so much hate his father as hold him in contempt. His father was a reviewer (of more than 6,000 books), essayist, publisher (with the firm of Chapman & Hall). Evelyn would later say that he "did everything at deleterious speed." He also early noted his father's pomposity, which, combined with his gross sentimentality, precluded all possibility for admiration on the part of his younger son. The older he grew the more dismissive, not to say derisive, of his father he became. Waugh found succor as a child with his mother and his nanny. He would always find intimacy easier with women—Diana Cooper, Nancy Mitford, Ann Fleming, among them—than with men.

"Golden Boy" is the title that Alexander Waugh, grandson of Evelyn and son of Aubernon, in *Fathers and Sons* (2007), his family history, gives to the chapter on Alec Waugh. Golden he may have seemed to his father but rather a zinc dud he must have seemed to his younger brother. While at Sherbourne, the public school of choice for the men in the Waugh family, Alec was caught in a homosexual scandal that made it impossible for Evelyn to attend the same school, and so he had to attend Lancing, a public school a step down on the status ladder.

The young Waugh was also less than enamored of his first name, with its sexual ambiguity. His first book, *Rossetti: His Life and Works*, published in 1928 when he was 25, was reviewed in the *Times Literary Supplement* under the assumption that its author was female, the reviewer referring throughout to its author as Miss Waugh. This was another annoyance in a life that seemed to be filled with annoyances. He was early and perennially a victim of boredom; in his uncompleted novel, *Work Suspended*, he speaks of "ruthless boredom." His friend Douglas Woodruff noted: "He was constantly suffering from *ennui*, which ought to be recognized as a major affliction more wearing and painful than most physical disabilities." One ready-to-hand weapon in the combat against boredom, according to Woodruff, was to be found in his readiness "to say the disconcerting thing in the hopes of making something happen or getting a rise, or in some other way breaking the monotony of all too easily predictable social exchanges." In Yugoslavia, for a notable example, Waugh put it about that Birkenhead was having a homosexual affair with an Istrian intellectual and had also become a drug addict through the use of morphia. And, one must understand, he rather liked Birkenhead. Such free-floating malice evidently helped him get through the day.

AS EARLY AS HIS SCHOOL DAYS, Waugh's terror of boredom and taste for the ridiculous combined to made him a figure of subversion. Max Mallowan, later an archeologist and husband to Agatha Christie, remembered him at Lancing as "popular among the boys for he was amusing and always ready to lead us into mischief, but had a way of getting others into trouble and himself invariably escaping." Mallowan adds that "[h]e was courageous and witty and clever but was also an exhibitionist with a cruel nature that cared nothing about humiliating his companions as long as he could expose them to ridicule." Eade tells of a fellow student who made the mistake of using the word "preternatural," for which he paid the price of being known forever after as "Preters." Cecil Beaton, who first encountered Waugh when they both attended Heath Mount School in Hampstead, remained terrified of him all his life.

Waugh won a scholarship to Hertford College, Oxford, where he continued his high jinks, with heavy drinking and homosexuality now added. He spoke of the "aesthetic pleasure of being drunk," by which one gathers he meant the glow of giving way without hesitation to his social effrontery and inherent outrageousness. As for homosexuality, "everyone was queer at Oxford in those days," the poet John Betjeman remarked. Waugh's great homosexual flame was a young man named Alastair Graham, one of the figures upon whom he partially modelled his *Brideshead Revisited* character Sebastian Flyte, and through whom he gained his first entrée into the upper-class English world he later portrayed in that novel. Harold Acton, who read T.S. Eliot's *The Waste Land* (1922) out of a megaphone from the window of his rooms at Oxford, was another university connection. Never at all serious about study, Waugh finished Oxford with a disappointing third-class degree.

H IS FIRST AMBITION was to become a draughtsman, and so after Oxford he went off to the Heatherley School of Fine Art in London. He also briefly tried his hand at cabinet making, until he realized, as he put it, "that there was nothing for it but to write books; an occupation which I regarded as exacting but in which I felt fairly confident of my skill." In the meantime he spent his nights drinking and bonking about town among the Bright Young Things—the decadent London society between the wars that was his social milieu of choice—gathering material, though he may not have known it at the time, for *Vile Bodies* (1930), his novel about the young dissolutes of the day.

Having shed his homosexuality in the way public-school Englishman of the era seemed to do, Waugh played a wide field of women, and, when it came to marriage, chose Evelyn Gardner, perhaps the ditziest of them all, who had been previously engaged no fewer than nine times; sometimes, it was said, to more than one man simultaneously. They were both twenty-four, and in the spirit of the times he proposed marriage by saying, "Let's get married and see how it goes."

"I saw a young man," Gardner noted of her first impression of Waugh, "short, sturdy, good-looking, given to little gestures, the shrugging of a hand which held a drink, the tossing of a head as he made some witty, somewhat malicious remark. He was easy to talk to and amusing." Diana Cooper described Gardner as "though very pretty wasn't much else." A friend of Evelyn Gardner—now called "Shevelyn" to distinguish her from her husband—noted that "I don't think she is wildly in love with E. W., but I doubt if she is capable of sustained passion." The friend was correct. The marriage lasted less than two years, broken off when Shevelyn began an affair with a man of negligible significance named John Heygate, whom she later claimed never to have loved. At the break-up of his marriage Waugh was twenty-six. His own comment on the marriage was that "fortune is the least capricious of deities, and arranges things on the just and rigid system that no one shall be very happy for very long."

NOT LONG AFTER HIS MARRIAGE ENDED, Waugh underwent what his father called his "perversion to Rome." Much evidence exists that the breakup of his marriage was not the sole cause of his religious conversion, though it must have weighed in heavily on the decision. In his autobiographical volume, *A Little Learning* (1964), Waugh notes that he had much earlier attempted suicide by drowning, and was only stopped from completing the job by the incessant biting of jellyfish. In *Vile Bodies*, a novel he felt he had botched, Waugh more than suggests the emptiness of life among the higher bohemia of Bright Young Things. Modernity itself became an affront to him and Catholicism was the spar he chose to grasp against its choppy seas.

The Jesuit Father Martin D'Arcy, who oversaw Waugh's religious instruction, remarked that he came to Catholicism through his revulsion with the modern world and its faithlessness, hoping, as D'Arcy wrote, that through it he could regain "a recrudescence of hope and even gaiety." Eliot claimed in *The Waste Land* to show "fear in a handful of dust." Evelyn

Waugh, before his conversion, already knew that fear. *A Handful of Dust* is of course the title of what many find to be Waugh's most perfect novel.

On September 29, 1930, Waugh was received into the Catholic Church. Why Catholicism? Because he felt it was the oldest, and hence most fundamental, version of Christianity. Eade quotes Waugh as saying that "Catholicism was Christianity, that all other forms of Christianity were only good insofar as they chipped little bits off the main block." In an essay titled "Conversion to Rome," Waugh wrote that he saw the world as essentially a struggle "between Christianity and Chaos," and Christianity represented order. Did his conversion alter his behavior? Not, apparently, outwardly. Hilaire Belloc told Mary Herbert, the mother of Waugh's second wife, Laura, that "he has the devil in him." Waugh himself told John Betjeman's wife, Penelope, that he was "by nature a bully and a scold." After witnessing his rudeness to a French intellectual to whom she introduced him, Nancy Mitford asked him if it weren't a contradiction that he was so rude a man and yet he claimed to be a practicing Catholic. "You have no idea," he replied, "how much nastier I would be if I was not a Catholic. Without supernatural aid I would hardly be a human being." He might have added, as he wrote in his essay on his conversion, that "[t]he Protestant attitude seems often to be, 'I am good; therefore I go to church'; while the Catholic's is, 'I am very far from good; therefore I go to church.'"

W AUGH DIDN'T LIKE BEING LABELLED a Catholic writer, in the way that Graham Greene, François Mauriac, and J.F. Powers were. Saul Bellow and Philip Roth similarly chafed at being called Jewish writers. Such labels do not make a writer seem minor so much as parochial. Yet Waugh led a very Catholic life. His closest friends—Greene, Ronald Knox, Christopher Sykes—were Catholics, and he was himself mass-going, confession-giving, orthodox on theological matters, observing of all ritual, deeply disappointed by the loosening of Church doctrine and practice that followed the Second Vatican Council in the mid-1960s. Catholicism ultimately changed the kind of novelist he was, taking him beyond comedy while never really abandoning it.

Comical all Waugh's novels indubitably are, often riotously so. He may be the only modern novelist in whom one remembers secondary characters and comic bits as vividly as anything else in his books. Who can forget the vicar in *A Handful of Dust* who continues to give sermons originally written during his time in India, citing tropical conditions and colonial distance, to his congregation gathered in wintry England? Or in the same novel the bit in which the friends of Tony Last's adulterous wife search out a mistress for Tony to divert his attention from his wife's betrayal, and one suggests "Souki de Foucauld-Esterhazy," to which another responds: "He [Tony] isn't his best with Americans." Or the prostitute with her out-of-wedlock child who, despite her lowly station, is not above a touch of anti-Semitism. Or in *Brideshead Revisited*, Charles Ryder's quite balmy father; or Anthony Blanche, "ageless as a lizard, as foreign as a Martian"; or the voice of a London hotel receptionist that sounded the note of "hermaphroditic gaiety." Or Captain Apthorpe in the *Sword of Honour* trilogy (1952–1961) who never travels without his own portable water closet; or, in *Scoop*, the definition of "the news" as "what a chap who doesn't care much about anything wants to read. And it's only news until he's read it. After that it's dead."

WAUGH'S WAS THE COMEDY OF DETACHMENT, both in his fiction and in his life. His grandson Alexander claimed this detachment came as Evelyn's reaction to his father's sentimentality. Who else but he could write of his firstborn child, his daughter Teresa: "I foresee that she will be a problem—too noisy for a nun, too plain for a wife? Well, standards of beauty may change in the next 18 years." In Yugoslavia, his reaction to a German bombing raid was to compare it to German opera—"too loud and too long." He did deadpan in prose, no easy literary maneuver. He could nab a character in a single sentence, or phrase, such as the younger sister, Cordelia, in *Brideshead Revisited,* who moved "in the manner of one who has no interest in pleasing."

In a *Paris Review* interview three years before his death, Waugh remarked: "I regard writing not as investigation of character, but as an exercise in the use of language, and with this I am obsessed. I have no technical psychological interest. It is drama, speech, and events that interest me." Precise, pellucid, flawless in usage and deployment of syntax, confidently cadenced, Waugh's was perhaps the purest English prose written in the past century.

Evelyn Waugh has been viewed as chiefly a comic writer. V.S. Pritchett noted that Waugh was always comic for serious reasons, and Prichett distinguished his earlier from his later books by claiming that the former "spring from the liberating notion that human beings are mad," while his later ones, especially his war triology *Sword of Honour*, "draws on the meatier notion that the horrible thing about human beings is that they are sane." Even these earlier books, though, spoke to a yearning for a steadier, more stable world.

AFTER HIS CONVERSION TO CATHOLICISM, Evelyn Waugh found a theme: the emptiness of life without faith. For some this theme diminished him and deprived his writing of interest. Of *Brideshead Revisited*, Waugh's most unremittingly Catholic novel, Isaiah Berlin noted that it "seems to start so well and peter out in such vulgarity," and referred to Waugh as "a kind of [Charles] Maurras—a fanatical, angry, neurotic, violent writer, thoroughly un-English in most ways." In his diary Noel Coward lamented the infusion into Waugh's novel *Unconditional Surrender* (1961) of "long tracts of well-written boredom. The whole book is shadowed by a dark cloud of Catholicism, which suffocates humor and interferes with the story." Edmund Wilson, who in 1944 considered Waugh "the only first-rate comic genius that has appeared in English since [George] Bernard Shaw," two years later, on the occasion of the American publication of *Brideshead Revisited*, found himself "cruelly disappointed," the novel "more or less disastrous," the work a failure of taste, "mere romantic fantasy," its author's snobbery "shameless and rampant," with Waugh's hitherto laudable style gone "to seed." Wilson would later sketchily review Waugh's *The Loved One* (1948), his satire on American funerary rites, and exclaim that "to the nonreligious reader, however, the patrons and proprietors of Whispering Glades (the posh California cemetery mocked in the novel) seem more sensible and less absurd than the priest-guided Evelyn Waugh."

Wilson, always a bit of a village atheist, a man readier to believe in revolution than in God, suffered a want of sympathy for writers—Joseph Conrad and Franz Kafka among them—given to spirituality. Myself a bit of a village agnostic, though a pious agnostic, I find Waugh's delving into questions of faith elevated his fiction. One doesn't have to be Catholic, or consider conversion to Catholicism, to be interested in the theme of faith—understanding it, finding it, retaining it under difficult conditions. The drama of faith, Waugh's ultimate subject, went directly against the grain of a secular age, but in taking it up in his novels Evelyn Waugh, the brilliant humorist, became a major writer.

P. G. Wodehouse

(2018)

66 **T**HE OBJECT OF ALL GOOD LITERATURE," thinks Sue Brown, a chorus girl and a character in P. G. Wode-house's novel *Summer Lightning,* "is to purge the soul of its petty troubles." Something to it, quite a bit actually, though Céline, Samuel Beckett, Edward Albee, and a number of other modern writers who pass for serious would strenuously have disagreed. The writing of P. G. Wodehouse—the author of some 95 books of fiction and three of memoir, recently republished in a handsome hardbound collection by Everyman's Library in London and The Overlook Press in New York—was not merely unserious but positively anti-serious, and therein lay much of its considerable charm.

As for that anti-seriousness, who other than Wodehouse would describe a figure in one of his novels by saying that "if he had been a character in a Russian novel, he would have gone and hanged himself in a barn?" Who but Wodehouse could mock the moral tradition of the English novel in a single phrase by writing in a novel of his own of "one of those unfortu-nate misunderstandings that are so apt to sunder hearts, the sort of thing that Thomas Hardy used to write about?" Who but he, through the cre-ation in his novel *Leave it to Psmith* of a poet named Ralston McTodd, would find humor in the hopeless obscurity of much modern poetry? Only Wodehouse would have the always-to-be trusted Jeeves instruct Bertie Wooster about Nietzsche: "He is fundamentally unsound, sir." Or have Bertie disqualify a young woman because after 16 sets of tennis and a round of golf she expected one in the evening "to take an intelligent interest in Freud." Who but Wodehouse would say about a character whom he clearly doesn't admire that he "was an earnest young man with political ambitions given, when not slamming [tennis balls] over the net, to reading white papers and studying social conditions"—thus flicking off politics as a time-wasting, if not altogether fatuous, preoccupation. At a lower level of anti-seriousness, Wodehouse amusingly mocked crime fiction, crossword puzzles, and antique collecting.

Pelham Grenville Wodehouse (1881–1975) was, like Kipling, Saki, Orwell, and Somerset Maugham, a child of the empire, which meant that growing up in England he saw very little of his parents, who were off across the seas tending to the British colonies. The third of four sons, Wodehouse grew up in Hong Kong, where his father served as an imperial magistrate. Between the ages of three and fifteen, his biographer Robert McCrum conjectures in *Wodehouse: A Life* (2004), he saw his parents little more than a total of six months. Owing to such circumstances, Wodehouse was naturally never close to his family, and was especially distanced from his mother, a woman said to be cold, imperious, and forbidding. If he was cut off from normal family feeling, Wodehouse seems to have made up for it by an ingrained optimism, a sunny disposition, a love of sport, and a powerful imagination for fantasy. From his earliest days, he wanted to be a writer. In his fiction, he created a world that never quite existed but is so amusing as to make one feel it a pity that it didn't.

Wodehouse's public-school days, at a place called Dulwich—C.S. Forester went there, as did Raymond Chandler—were perhaps his happiest. McCrum notes that on the status scale Dulwich was neither Eton nor Winchester, but "it offered an excellent education for the sons of the imperial servant." The young Wodehouse was an exuberant sportsman, and excelled at both rugby and cricket, sports that he followed avidly his life long. As a boy he was an ardent reader of Dickens, Kipling, J.M. Barrie, and Arthur Conan Doyle, and also adored Gilbert and Sullivan. At Dulwich he studied on the classics side, and his own novels and stories are dotted with references to Queen Boudica, the Midians, Thucydides, Marius among the ruins of Carthage, the Gracchi, and others.

When Wodehouse was 19, his father announced that there weren't sufficient funds to send him to Oxford, where his older brothers had gone. He
seems to have taken it in stride. He went instead to work at The Hongkong
and Shanghai Bank in London, interning in the Bob Cratchit-like role
of lowly clerk. In the evenings he wrote stories and articles and supplied
comic bits for newspapers and magazines, and in fairly short order wrote
his way out of the bank and into an economically independent freelance
life. Writers divide between those who may write well but don't need to do
it and those who find life without meaning if they aren't writing. Wodehouse was clearly of the latter camp. Over a long career (he died at ninety-
three) along with his novels and stories he wrote plays, musicals (collabo-
rating on occasion with Jerome Kern), supplied lyrics for other people's
shows (he wrote the song "Bill" for *Showboat* and worked with Cole Porter
on *Anything Goes)*, and did his stint in Hollywood. He appears always to
have thought himself a professional writer rather than a literary artist, with
a wide following more important to him than the praise of critics.

For a writer who never aspired to be other than popular, in later life
Wodehouse acquired accolades from many writers who easily cleared the
high-brow bar, including T.S. Eliot, W.H. Auden, Evelyn Waugh, Dorothy Parker, Kingsley Amis, Eudora Welty, Lionel Trilling, Bertrand Russell, and Ludwig Wittgenstein. Hillaire Belloc called him "the best writer
of English now alive," a handsome tribute seconded by H.L. Mencken.
"Temperate admirers of his work," wrote the English drama critic James
Agate, "are non-existent."

Wodehouse wrote no faulty sentences, and countless ones that, for
people who care about the pleasing ordering of words, give unrivalled
delight. In his biography McCrum offers the following splendid example, one of hundreds, perhaps thousands, that could be adduced:

> In the face of the young man who sat on the terrace of the
> Hotel Magnifique at Cannes there crept a look of furtive
> shame, the shifty, hangdog look which announces that an
> Englishman is about to talk French.

The comic touches that light up Wodehouse's prose are one of its chief
delights. A drunken character is described as "brilliantly illuminated."

An overweight baronet "looks forward to a meal that sticks to the ribs and brings beads of perspiration to the forehead." A woman supposed to marry that same stout gentleman has the uneasy feeling that, so large is he, she might be "committing bigamy." A minor character "has a small and revolting mustache," another "is so crooked he sliced bread with a corkscrew." Wodehouse spun jokes out of clichés. His similes are notably striking. A man known to be unable to keep secrets is likened to "a human colander." Another character is "as broke as the Ten Commandments." The brains of the press departments of the movie studios resemble "soup at a cheap restaurant. It is wiser not to stir them." These similes often arise when least expected: "The drowsy stillness of the afternoon was shattered by what sounded to his strained senses like G. K. Chesterton falling on a sheet of tin." There is a passing reference to "a politician's trained verbosity," a phrase I find handy whenever watching a contemporary politician interviewed on television. Like Jimmy Durante with jokes, so P. G. Wodehouse with arrestingly amusing phrases—he had a million of 'em.

"I believe there are two ways of writing novels," Wodehouse wrote. "One is mine, making a sort of musical comedy without music and ignoring real life altogether; the other is going right down deep into life, and not giving a damn." No one would accuse P. G. Wodehouse of ever flirting with realism. His fiction is uniformly preposterous. "I don't really know anything about writing except farcical comedy," he wrote to his friend the novelist William Townsend. "A real person in my fiction would stick out like a sore thumb."

Nobody dies in Wodehouse novels or stories. In his fiction there are no wars, economic depression, sex below the neck, little *Sturm* and even less *Drang,* with only satisfyingly happy endings awaiting at the close. English country-house scenes were his favorite milieu. These are populated with aimless young men in spats with names like Stilton Cheesewright, Bingo Little, Tuppy Glossop, and Pongo Twistleton; troublesome young women, terrifying aunts, and eccentric servants; notable props include two-seater roadsters, cigarette holders, monocles, and lots of cocktails.

"Romps" seem to me perhaps the best single word to describe Wodehouse's novels and stories, yet artfully organized romps. The first task of the writer of fiction is to make the unpredictable plausible. Wodehouse's own method, going a step further, was to think of something very bizarre and then make it plausible. But given his outlandish characters, the impossible confusions they encounter, the unlikely coincidence that everywhere arise, plausibility never really comes into play; more accurate to say that he made the improbable delectably palatable.

Wodehouse allowed that he wrote his novels as if they were plays. "In writing a novel I always imagine I'm writing for a cast of actors," he wrote to Townsend in one of the letters printed in *Author, Author!* (1962), their collected correspondence. "One of the best tips for writing a play, Guy [Bolton, his chief theatrical collaborator] tells me, is 'Never let them sit down.'" Wodehouse kept his characters in action, and felt the earlier the introduction of dialogue the better, the more, given his dazzling touch for it, the jollier. "But how about my flesh and blood, my Aunt Julia, you ask," says his character Stanley Ukridge. "No, I don't," says the story's narrator. "I'm in the soup," says Gussie Fink-Nottle. "Up to the thorax," replies Bertie Wooster.

Ronald Eustace Psmith is a former Etonian, monocled, appallingly fluent, a master of comic hauteur. Clarence, the ninth Earl of Emsworth, lord of Blandings Castle, is interested only in gardening and in pigs and is two stages beyond absent-minded, described in *Leave It to Psmith* as "that amiable and boneheaded peer . . . a fluffy-minded man" who has "a tiring day trying to keep his top hat balanced on his head." Aunt Agatha is female tyranny to the highest power, pure menace, a woman "who eats broken bottles and wears barbed-wire close to the skin." Along with his valet Jeeves, Bertie Wooster—the best known of Wodehouse's characters and a man self-described as having "half the amount of brain a normal bloke ought to possess"—is a classic instance of the Edwardian knut, those upper-class idlers, often second and third sons, with nothing more pressing on their agendas than choosing their dandaical outfit for the day, meeting Algy for lunch at the club, and avoiding those tradesmen foolish enough to have extended them credit.

As for Jeeves, he, undoubtedly, is Wodehouse's greatest creation, a man who does not so much enter as flow into rooms, omniscient in his learning, formally correct in his syntax, infallible in his good sense, ingenious at getting his master Bertie Wooster and Bertie's friends out of misbegotten marriage alliances, entanglements with aunts threatening their inheritances, creating along the way innumerable plots thicker and stickier than carnival taffy. "In the matter of brain and resource," thinks Bertie of Jeeves, "I don't believe I have ever met a chappie so supremely like mother made." Jeeves, who recognizes that his master is "of negligible intelligence," notes that "in an employer brains are not desirable." Not for comedy they certainly aren't.

Wodehouse's fiction does not abound in sympathetic female characters. He was himself not so much misogynistic, McCrum rightly points out, as gynophobic. Whether bluestockings or ditzy airheads, women in Wodehouse tend to be objects of terror, interfering, dangerous in their potential to undermine the knut way of life. Madeline Bassett— with whom the prospect of a marital connection sends Bertie into shivers—is one of these women who, though of attractive exterior, is on the "point of talking baby talk . . . the sort of girl who puts her hands over a husband's eyes, as he is crawling in to breakfast with a morning head, and says: 'Guess who?'" Aunts—there are no mothers I have encountered in Wodehouse—are "all alike. Sooner or later out comes the cloven hoof." When Bertie remarks that he had "no idea that small girls were such demons," Jeeves laconically replies: "More deadly than the male, sir." Galahad Threepwood notes that "the one thing a man with a cold in his head must avoid is a woman's touch." Stanley Ukridge notes that "women have their merits, of course, but if you are to live the good life, you don't want them around the house." None of Wodehouse's heroes is married.

Wodehouse himself married, at thirty-three, to Ethel Wayman, an actress twice-widowed with a ten-year-old daughter. The marriage appears to have been an untroubled one, owing chiefly to each of its partners allowing the other to go off on his or her own. In Ethel Wodehouse's case, this seems to have been chiefly to go off shopping, mild forms of social lion-hunting, and acquiring expensive places for her family to live. In Wodehouse's, it meant being left alone to write, with time off for lengthy walks with one or another of the couple's many Pekingese. They had no children together, but Wodehouse came to love his stepdaughter, Leonora, to whom he dedicated one of his books: "To Leonora without whose never-failing sympathy and encouragement this book would have been finished in half the time." She was the closest he came to having a true confidant and her death at forty was a great loss to him.

Life generally, though, was good. Wodehouse's high productivity paid off amply in what Bertie Wooster would call doubloons or pieces of eight. In London he and Ethel lived in Mayfair. They had a butler, cook, maids, footmen, two secretaries, and a chauffeur-driven Rolls-Royce. He had become, in Robert McCrum's phrase, "seriously rich." Praise for his writing, meanwhile, flowed in, with only occasional demurrers. In 1939 Oxford, the university he wasn't allowed to attend for want of funds, presented him with an honorary degree. Pelham Grenville Wodehouse was on what looked like a life-long roll.

And then the roof, walls, and floor along with it, caved in. The onset of World War II found Wodehouse and his family living in Le Tourquet, in northern France near the English Channel, and when the Nazis marched in, Wodehouse, who didn't flee in time, found himself interned. At first the internment turned out to be more an inconvenience than anything else, and during it he was even able to complete a novel. Soon, though, the Nazis learned of his fame and, gauging the propaganda value of their prisoner, encouraged him through subtle suasion to recount the relative mildness of his detainment in a series of five radio talks, which he gave in the summer of 1941.

The talks were innocuous enough, though it was a grave mistake for the politically naïve Wodehouse to have made them. Doing so over Nazi radio put him in company with such genuine traitors as William Joyce, known as Lord Haw-Haw and hanged by the English for treason after the war. He also published in the *Saturday Evening Post* an article, under the title "My War with Germany," in which, in his extreme naïveté, he remarked that he was unable to work up any hostility toward the enemy: "Just when I'm about to feel belligerent about some country I meet a decent sort of chap" from that country, he wrote, causing him to lose "any fighting feelings or thoughts." Wodehouse, in other words, used the occasion of the most murderous events in modern history for light laughs.

The reaction was swift and crushing. Anthony Eden, in Parliament, accused Wodehouse of lending "his services to the German war propaganda machine." Duff Cooper, Churchill's minister of information, held

Wodehouse's behavior to be traitorous. A general piling on was not long in coming. Harold Nicolson refused to believe in Wodehouse's innocence being the cause for his betrayal. A *Daily Mirror* columnist named Cassandra, whose real name was William O'Connor, gave a talk over the BBC that began: "I have come to tell you tonight of the story of a rich man [Wodehouse] trying to make his last and greatest sale—that of his own country," and went on to compare him to Judas. The playwright Seán O'Casey called Wodehouse "English Literature's performing flea." Oxford was said to be considering reclaiming his honorary degree. Deep readers began finding evidence of fascism in his books, which were banned from some provincial libraries and in a few places even burned. Songs to which he had written the lyrics were not allowed over the BBC. There was talk about Wodehouse being hanged as a traitor.

Wodehouse called his own conduct "a loony thing to do"; later he would say it was "insane." Yet it is far from clear that he truly grasped the gravity of his mistake. Malcolm Muggeridge, who later became his friend, thought Wodehouse had a "temperament that unfits him to be a good citizen in the ideological mid-twentieth century." The best defense of Wodehouse, made by George Orwell in 1945, just after the war was over, was that he was not only a political naïf, but gave his talks for the Nazis at precisely the wrong time: the summer of 1941, as Orwell wrote, "at just that moment when the war reached its desperate phase." Orwell ends his defense of Wodehouse by writing "in the desperate circumstances of the time it was excusable to be angry at what Wodehouse did, but to go on denouncing him three or four years later—and more, to let an impression remain that he acted with conscious treachery—is not excusable."

Yet decades passed before Wodehouse was finally forgiven this mistake. In 1947 he moved, permanently, to America, and in 1955 took up American citizenship. His friend the humorist Frank Sullivan said his doing so made up "for our loss of T. S. Eliot and Henry James combined," an amusing touch of hyperbole. His wartime broadcasts continued to haunt him, though he claimed to be without self-pity. "I made an ass of myself," he wrote to William Townsend, "and must pay the penalty." Still, he was as productive as ever, producing a book a year. At his 80th birthday, in a newspaper ad for one of his books, a literary all-star cast that included W.H. Auden, Ivy Compton-Burnett, Graham Greene, Rebecca West, and others signed on to pay tribute to him as "an inimitable international institution and a master humorist." Wodehouse wrote to his old friend Guy Bolton: "I seem to have become the Grand Old Man of English Literature." In 1975 he was knighted by Queen Elizabeth, who was among his most ardent readers, which formally closed the book on his wartime fiasco.

For the better part of the past two months I have been reading P.G. Wodehouse early mornings, with tea and toast and unslaked pleasure. Although I haven't made a serious dent in his 95-book oeuvre, before long, I tell myself, I must cease and desist from this happy indulgence, this sweet disease which one of his readers called "P. G.-osis." "You can," says a character in an Isaac Bashevis Singer story, "have too much even of *kreplach.*" (Something of a literary puritan, I feel I ought to add that during these past months I have followed up each morning's reading of Wodehouse with four or five pages of Aristotle's *Rhetoric* and his *Nicomachean Ethics*—an intellectual antidote, a breath mint of seriousness, you might say.) In a 1961 talk on Wodehouse over the BBC, Evelyn Waugh ended by saying: "Mr. Wodehouse's world can never stale. He will continue to release future generations from captivity that may be more irksome than our own. He has made a world for us to live in and delight in."

The work of humorists is not usually long-lived. Among Americans, two very different examples, James Thurber and S. J. Perelman, seem to have bitten the dust, at least they have for me. Yet Wodehouse remains readable and immensely enjoyable. Perhaps this is owing to his having written about a world that never really existed, so that his work, unlike Thurber and Perelman's, isn't finally time-bound. "I'm all for strewing a little happiness as I go by," Wodehouse wrote to William Townsend, and he did so in ample measure. He would have been pleased to learn that for his readers the gift of that happiness has yet to stop giving.

Tom Wolfe

(2018)

*America is a wonderful country! I mean it! No honest writer
would challenge that statement! The human comedy never
runs out of material! It never lets you down!*

TOM WOLFE, "Sorry, But Your Soul Just Died"

TOM WOLFE, who had a genius for garnering publicity, would
not have been disappointed by that accompanying his death on
May 14 at the age of eighty-eight: praising op-eds in both the
Wall Street Journal and the *New York Times*, a page on his stylishness in
the latter and a full page, with four photographs, recounting his life in
the former. There were two further articles in the *Wall Street Journal*,
two in the *Washington Post*, and pieces in *Time, Forbes*, the *New Yorker*,
and just about every other general-interest publication, print and online
both. The words "great" and "greatness" were much bandied about.

All mentioned Wolfe's clothes, the dandiacal get-ups, chiefly in white,
with foppish accoutrements—high-collared shirts and homburgs and co-
respondent shoes—without which, so far as anyone knows, he never left
his apartment. One obituarist, Graeme Wood in *The American Scholar*,
wrote that Wolfe "leaves behind a widow, two children, and (one assumes)
a grieving Upper East Side dry cleaner." Mark Twain, in his day, was known
as the "Man in White." Whether Tom Wolfe in selecting his wardrobe set
out to be the Twain of our own day is not known—he left no *Adventures
of Huckleberry Finn* certainly—but the white duds seem to have worked in
gaining attention for both men.

To go along with gaudy threads, the young Tom Wolfe devised an even gaudier prose style, which went well beyond the legal limit for ellipses, capital letters, exclamation marks, and ornate vocabulary. Nearly every sentence he wrote seemed a verbal extravaganza. One of Wolfe's first successes was a 1963 article for *Esquire* written in garishly Technicolor prose—"shotgun baroque edging over into machine-gun rococo" is how I described it in the *New Republic* as long ago as 1965. The legend behind this article, titled "There Goes (Varoom! Varoom!) That Kandy-Kolored (Thphhhhhh!) Tangerine-Flake Streamline Baby (Rah-ghhh!) Around the Bend (Brummmmmmmmmmmmmmmmm) . . . . . ," is that Wolfe had scribbled 49 pages of notes that he couldn't pull together into a coherent article. With deadline pressing, Byron Dobell, *Esquire's* managing editor, told him to bring in the notes, which Dobell then published without change. The story is one of the foundational myths of what came to be called the New Journalism.

Perhaps the quickest way for a school of thought, political program, or other phenomena to reach obsolescence is to term itself New. Hence the New Deal, the New Criticism, the New Frontier, and, inevitably, the New Journalism. In its heyday, the New Journalism, whose home fields were *Esquire* and *New York* under the editorships, respectively, of Harold T. P. Hayes and Clay Felker, featured nonfiction using the techniques and devices of fiction: shifting point of view, present-tense description, foreshadowing, stream of consciousness. It also permitted its practitioners to insert themselves into their work, which in an earlier time would have outraged traditional journalism's goal of objectivity. Under this reign of subjectivity, the author himself or herself—Joan Didion comes prominently to mind here—was not infrequently the subject.

Tom Wolfe was one of the leading lights of the New Journalism, along with Didion, Gay Talese, Hunter S. Thompson, Nora Ephron, and David Halberstam. Two famous novelists, Truman Capote and Norman Mailer, soon stepped out onto the New Journalism dance floor: Capote with *In Cold Blood* (1966), Mailer with *Armies of the Night* (1968), both of which works their authors termed "nonfiction novels." How much of the New Journalism remains readable in our day cannot of course be known, but high estimates would doubtless be a mistake.

What Wolfe had was a dead eye for the telling detail especially where it touched on the status life. He would become statistician-in-chief of American life. In "The Secret Vice" (1966), an essay on custom haberdashery, Wolfe wrote of a New York lawyer who divides the world between men "with suits whose buttons are just sewn onto the sleeve, just some kind of cheapie decoration, or—yes!—men who can unbutton the sleeve at the wrist because they have real buttonholes and the sleeve really buttons up." In "Putting Daddy On" (1964), he described an advertising executive who calls his hat, a "sort of homburg with a flanged brim," a "Madison Avenue crash helmet and then wears one."

At the beginning of his career Wolfe wrote about the American sideshow: racecar drivers, Ken Kesey and his acid-dropping (not very) Merry Pranksters, Las Vegas, rich divorcées in Manhattan, the Rolling Stones, whom he designated like the Beatles, "only more lower-class deformed." Good copy all, but still very much in the realm of journalism, however New the presentation. Wolfe's subjects were people who had, in the cant phrase of the day, lifestyles, but not really lives, in the sense that they didn't seem to live very deep down. He caught the sheen of their surface with great skill.

An admirer of Max Weber and of Thorstein Veblen, Wolfe established himself as a sociologist without license, a social scientist who took no surveys but operated out of pure instinct and subtle observation. He could tell you that the current teenage word for French kissing was "tonsil hockey" or that the CEOs of Silicon Valley corporations do not carry smartphones (they have vice-presidents to carry their phones around for them) and other *petits faits vrais*. Recounting a moment from a session at Esalen, in his 1976 essay "The 'Me' Decade and the Third Great Awakening," Wolfe, honing in on the feast of self-regard of 1970s psychology, wrote:

> Each soul is concentrated on its own burning item . . . my
> husband! my wife! my homosexuality! my inability to com-
> municate, my self-hatred, self-destruction, craven fears, pul-
> ing weaknesses, primordial horrors, premature ejaculation,
> impotence, frigidity, rigidity, subservience, laziness, alcohol-
> ism, major vices, minor vices, grim habits, twisted psyches,
> tortured souls—and yet each unique item has been raised to
> a cosmic level and united with every other.

FOR ALL THE DAZZLE, Wolfe often seemed just another interesting journalist, a fellow who had developed a wow and whoopee style, little more. Then, in 1970, he wrote his breakout piece, the work that made him a writer to be reckoned with. "Radical Chic" was an account of the most famous case of reverse slumming of its time: the party that Leonard and Felicia Bernstein gave for the Black Panthers. The phrase "radical chic" was a perfect description of the behavior of an upper class with nothing at risk cultivating fashionable progressive opinions to reinforce its own self-esteem and at the same time seeming to demonstrate its large-hearted sensitivity to the condition of the underclass. The point about the phenomenon was that it was risk-free. As Wolfe later noted: "A Radical Chic protester got himself arrested in the late morning or early afternoon, in mild weather. He was booked and released in time to make it to the Electric Circus, that year's New York nightspot of the century, and tell war stories."

The roster of guests gathered at the Bernsteins' Park Avenue penthouse duplex for an evening of fundraising for the Black Panthers was a splendid combination of the well-known and the well-to-do. Included were Jason Robards and Schuyler Chapin, Goddard Lieberson and Mike Nichols, Lillian Hellman and Larry Rivers, Aaron Copland and Richard Avedon, Stephen Sondheim and Jerome Robbins, Adolph and Phyllis Green and Betty Comden. A party for the Panthers had its complications: Black servants had to be replaced by Hispanic ones, for a start. Then there was the question of the Black Panthers' taste in hors d'oeuvres and so much more with which the thoughtful hosts had to contend. The Bernsteins' mistake, of course, was letting Tom Wolfe in the door.

What he set indelibly on display in "Radical Chic" was that people who can afford them can wear their opinions as if they were designer clothes. Some opinions, like some clothes, were more *comme il faut* than others. Expressing support for the Black Panthers, a group that should its members' dreams come true would have everyone in the Bernstein apartment that evening on a tumbril on the way to the guillotine, was the political equivalent of Dior, Herès, or Givenchy.

Just behind the Panthers in progressive social prestige in those days came Cesar Chavez and his National Farm Workers Association. In the same essay, Wolfe gave a brief account of a fundraiser arranged for them by Andrew Stein in Southampton. "From the beginning," Wolfe writes of Stein's fête, "the afternoon was full of the delicious status contradictions that provide much of the electricity for Radical Chic."

The men in their Dunhill blazers and Turnbull & Asser neckerchiefs, the women in their Pucci dresses, Gucci shoes, and Capucci scarves listened to heartrending accounts of grape pickers and their children rising at 3 a.m. for 12-hour days in the blistering hot fields with nothing to eat but a baloney sandwich. How sad, how gripping, how unjust it all was, until, Wolfe interjected, "the wind had come up off the ocean and it was wrecking everybody's hair." Perfecto!

Perfecto, that is, if one wishes to show how feeble, thin, and ultimately fraudulent was the sympathy of the rich and famous for the poor and downtrodden. "Radical Chic" put a serious dent in the radical movement that was then sweeping America and that today chiefly finds a home in the much shabbier surroundings of university humanities and social-science departments. Many thought the essay the work of a right-winger, but they were wrong. The essay was the work of a man who enjoyed the comedy of rich contradictions played out by people prepared to desert their common sense in the hope of boosting their status. And Wolfe didn't in the least flinch when naming names: Jean vanden Heuvel, Jules Feiffer, Carter and Amanda Burden, Sidney and Gail Lumet, and other glittering names all hosted events like that of the Bernsteins. "Who do you call to give a party?" Wolfe quoted the then-high-profile New York art dealer Richard Feigen asking.

Wolfe never minded making enemies. Early in his career he took on William Shawn and the *New Yorker* in an essay called "Tiny Mummies! The True Story of the Ruler of 43rd Street's Land of the Walking Dead!" guaranteeing that he would never appear in that magazine's pages. Later, he wrote of Robert Silvers, the Anglomaniacal editor of the *New York Review of Books*, that "his accent arrived mysteriously one day in a box from London. Intrigued, he slapped it into his mouth like a set of teeth." In those two strokes, he made himself permanently *non grata* with two of the most powerful editors in the land. He was no more tender about the leading intellectual figures of the day. He described Susan Sontag as "just another scribbler who spent her life signing up for protest meetings and lumbering to the podium encumbered by her prose style, which had a handicapped parking sticker valid at *Partisan Review*."

ALONG WITH CONFERRING GREATER FAME on him than he had hitherto known, "Radical Chic" gave Wolfe a strong taste for provocation. Literary and intellectual provocateur was a role he felt comfortable playing. He seemed greatly to enjoy a ruckus of his own devising. After "Radical Chic" came his book *The Painted Word*, a dazzling takedown of the pretensions of the contemporary art world and its star critics, which was excerpted in 1975 in *Harper's*. (Six years later, in *From Bauhaus to Our House*, he would perpetrate a similar massacre of modern architecture.)

Wolfe was a brilliant titlist, and "The Painted Word" conveys the chief idea in the work—namely, that no contemporary painting could have any serious standing without a critical theory certifying and explaining it. Twenty-five years from the time of his essay, he prophesied, there would appear on the walls of the Museum of Modern Art "huge copy blocks, eight and a half by eleven feet each, presenting the protean passages. . . . Beside them will be small reproductions of the work of leading illustrators of the Word from that period such as Johns, Louis, Noland, Stella, and Olitski." The essay is a reminder that in Joseph Roth's novel *Left and Right*, the criterion a wealthy character sets for buying art is "that a picture should repel his sense and intelligence. Only then could he be sure of having bought a valuable modern work."

Wolfe grasped what difficult abstract and minimalist art did for its collectors:

> Today there is a peculiarly modern reward that the avant-garde artist can give his benefactor: namely, the feeling that he, like his mate the artist, is separate from and aloof from the bourgeoisie, the middle classes . . . the feeling that he may be *from* the middle class but he is no longer *in* it . . . the feeling that he is a fellow soldier, or at least an aide-de-camp or an honorary cong guerrilla in the vanguard march through the land of the philistines. This is a peculiarly modern need

and a peculiarly modern kind of salvation (from the sin of Too Much Money) and something quite common among the well-to-do all over the West, in Rome and Milan as well as New York. That is why collecting contemporary art, the leading edge, the latest thing, warm and wet from the Loft, appeals specifically to those who feel most uneasy about their own commercial wealth . . . . Avant-garde art, more than any other, takes the Mammon and the Moloch out of money, puts Levi's, turtlenecks, muttonchops, and other mantles and laurels of bohemian grace upon it.

I have an acquaintance in Chicago, a lawyer, an unembarrassed right-winger in his politics, who has an apparently valuable collection of social protest art from the 1930s, a collection that he obviously feels sets him apart from his confreres. That art collection, in his mind, is the white ass upon which he intends to ride into Jerusalem.

Hilton Kramer, in a powerful essay called "Revenge of the Philistines," praised Wolfe's account of the sociology of the visual art of the time. On the comedy inherent in the subject, he noted, Wolfe "is illuminating and often hilarious." Yet, when it came to the analysis of ideas, Kramer felt, "when it comes down to actual works of art and the thinking they both embody and inspire, Wolfe is hopelessly out of his depth . . . and, no doubt, beyond his true interests." He faulted Wolfe for his inability to understand the historical context of the contemporary situation in art or how we have come to where we are in a way that carries us well beyond "the drawing-room comedy of *The Painted Word*." Kramer concluded: "It is this fundamental incomprehension of the role of criticism in the life of art—this enmity to the function of theory in the creation of culture—that identifies *The Painted Word*, despite its knowingness and its fun, as a philistine utterance, an act of revenge against a quality of mind it cannot begin to encompass and must therefore treat as a preposterous joke."

Tom Wolfe's style, cast of mind, and literary mission were essentially satirical. The satirist is chiefly interested in exposé—in exposing the pretensions, hypocrisies, fraudulence, and even the hidden anxieties of others. In his work, the satirist is allowed—actually, requires—simplification, caricature, and hyperbole. Interested though he is in the truth, he doesn't wish to be derailed, or slowed down even, by the whole truth. So when Hilton Kramer, in reviewing *The Painted Word*, pointed out Wolfe's ignorance of, and indeed probable uninterest in, the history of the work he is mocking, he was correct. But unless that history were inherently comical, to recount it would only have obscured the sharpness of Wolfe's attack, which was worth making and best made without stopping to deal with messy complication. When, in *The Kingdom of Speech*, Wolfe's 2016 book about language and evolution, he remarked that upon learning that Alfred Russel Wallace had arrived at the basic notion of evolution before him, Charles Darwin *"freaked"* and that through the remainder of his life Darwin, because he was able subtly to edge Wallace out of his position of deserved primacy as the discoverer of the theory of evolution, "over and over, until the day he died, . . . sent up flares signaling his guilt," one knows that, far from the way things happened, this is the comic artist, the satirist, at work.

Apart from Jonathan Swift's Houyhnhnms, who aren't quite human, there are not many heroes for satirists. Nor are there, in the works, nonfictional and fictional, of Tom Wolfe. Wolfe approvingly quoted Nietzsche and Marshall McLuhan in various of his works and wrote admiringly about Robert Noyce, the physicist and founder of Intel, and about the test pilots turned astronauts and their wives in his book *The Right Stuff* (1979). But the charivari of comic misbehavior in his time was too loud to leave much room for heroes.

IN THE EARLY 1980S, Tom Wolfe turned to writing fiction, and in 1987 brought out *The Bonfire of the Vanities*, about the high-priced status life in Manhattan. "There it was," the novel's protagonist notes, driving in from the Bronx, "the Rome, the Paris, the London of the twentieth century, the city of ambition, the dense magnetic rock, the destination of all those who insist on being *where things are happening*—" The book was a great success, commercially and critically, and made the kind of stir its author most enjoyed. *The Bonfire of the Vanities* tells of the life of Sherman McCoy, a player in the bond market, one of the self-acclaimed "Masters of the Universe," earning $980,000 a year and, owing to his headlong plunge into the New York status life, not making his nut.

McCoy's life goes bust when his twenty-six-year-old mistress, driving his Mercedes, runs over a thuggish young black man late one night, and they flee the scene. The full nightmare of modern life—a pestiferous media, glory-seeking politicians, corrupt prosecutors, race-activist charlatans looking for a cause to stir up trouble—comes down upon him with full force. The vanities of the novel's various characters compete in a combined effort to promote themselves at the expense of Sherman McCoy.

Yet his plight is not what is most memorable about *Bonfire of the Vanities*. What is memorable is the relentless detail in which Wolfe demonstrates how far from the real McCoy is the life of his novel's hero. Doing the math, setting out the numbers, he shows how a man earning a yearly salary only $20,000 short of a million can fall into debt. He recounts how a night out on the town in little ole Manhattan—what with renting a limo, babysitting fees, hairstylists, and the rest—can run a man $2,000.

The scope of the novel is impressive, even for its 659 pages. Wolfe's characters range from gay lawyers and Jewish cops to alcoholic journalists and lower-middle-class Greek bimbos—the dialogue of this gallimaufry never striking a false note—his scenes from grand Park Avenue apartments to haute-cuisine French restaurants to police lockups. Wolfe was more than merely attentive to all his characters' clothes and accessories. No surprise there. A character in the novel carries his shoes to work in a shopping bag and we learn that they are "not very elegant" Johnston & Murphy shoes. Another wears an English riding mac that was "bought at Knoud on Madison Avenue." Henry James, as far as possible from Tom Wolfe's model in the realm of writing fiction—Wolfe claimed Thackeray and Dickens as his literary forebears—notes of his character Gilbert Osmond, in *The Portrait of a Lady*, that "he was dressed as a man dresses who takes little other trouble about it than to have no vulgar things." How much more economical, and effective, to leave such matters to the imagination of readers.

In 1987, political correctness hadn't fully kicked in, and so Wolfe could produce despicable lawyers who are clearly Jewish (quite as despicable as not a few Jewish lawyers I have known)—though one of the few admirable characters in the novel, a figure of courage and competence, is the obviously Jewish judge Myron Kovitsky. The character Reverend Bacon, who attempts to make great hay over Sherman McCoy's running over a black kid, is a portrait for which our own Reverends Jackson and Sharpton might have sat. McCoy's wife Judy refers to three "V. I. F.'s," which, as she explains to her husband, stands for "Very Important Fags." I mention all this not to indict Wolfe for political incorrectness—the last thing I should want to do—but to show his social accuracy and fearlessness. Wolfe, like every sensible person, judged all groups not by their ethnicity or social status but one man or woman at a time.

Yet rich as it is, something is missing at the heart of *The Bonfire of the Vanities*—as it would be in the three further novels Wolfe went on to write. And this was due to his greater interest in social scene than in character. In his fiction, Wolfe set out to show, to borrow the title of a Trollope novel, the way we live now—or rather, lived then. But the central task of the novel at its finest, recording the twists and turns of the human heart, eluded Tom Wolfe.

What one remembers from his novels are not specific characters, but the details of social scenes and situations. This is owing, I strongly suspect, to Wolfe's view that the motor force of modern life is the struggle to achieve high status, whatever one's line of work or station in life. Wolfe was dedicated, as he put it in his 1989 essay "Stalking the Billion-Footed Beast," to a fiction that "would portray the individual in intimate and inextricable relation to the society around him." Somehow Wolfe, like the good journalist he was, so artfully created the society that the individual got lost.

WHEN TOM WOLFE'S SECOND NOVEL, *A Man in Full* (1998), a book eleven years in the making, was attacked by John Updike, Norman Mailer, and John Irving, Wolfe fired back in an essay called "My Three Stooges." He had already set out his novelistic credo in "Stalking the Billion-Footed Beast," which rightly contemned those academic novelists of the day—John Gardner, John Hawkes, Robert Coover, John Barth— for the aridity of the enclosed worlds of their work and called for a return to realism in fiction. He argued that there is a wealth of material available to the novelist, but to acquire it he needs the reportorial skill of a Zola, a Dreiser, a Dos Passos, a Sinclair Lewis. "Literary genius, in prose," he wrote, "consists of proportions more on the order of 65 percent material and 35 percent talent in the sacred crucible." Wolfe's argument, in short, was that novelists needed to do what journalists do—the necessary legwork to get the story or, better, the story behind the story.

In "My Three Stooges"—Updike, Mailer, Irving being the stooges in question—he took things further and argued that the school of realism is the primary, the best, and really only worthwhile school of fiction. George Costanza-like, he then went too far. If a novel doesn't sell well, Wolfe concluded, it is probably not very good. By falling back on the success of certain novels constructed out of the principles of realism, he suggests that the ultimate judge of great art is neither enlightened criticism nor time but popularity, citing the commercial success of his own second novel, *A Man in Full* (first printing 1.2 million copies with further printings to follow).

"It was not until after the First World War," Wolfe wrote, "that there came into being that sweaty colonial, the American 'intellectual,' who would value a James above a Dreiser, a Dos Passos, or a Sinclair Lewis." Proust, Joyce, and James were figures of contempt for Wolfe, treated as if no one but an intellectual, a person dead to life, could value their work above the pulsing-with-life novels of Zola. Elsewhere Wolfe compared the tedium of graduate school with reading *Mr. Sammler's Planet*, Saul Bellow's least solipsistic novel. When Wolfe named contemporary novelists working in the realism mode that he admired—James Webb, Richard Price, Pat Conroy, Jimmy Breslin, Terry McMillan, Joseph Wambaugh, Po Bronson—the list was disappointing.

Wolfe was opposed to the cerebral in fiction. In his ardor to capture the larger story of the battle for status, the journalist in him set society in the foreground, leaving the individual well in the background. In doing so, he mistook the true mission of the novel, which has always been to study human nature in moral conflict, and the home truth that the greatest novelists—Tolstoy, George Eliot, Henry James, Proust, Thomas Mann, Willa Cather—have been those with the most powerful moral imaginations. Tom Wolfe, percipient about so much, missed this.

Abundant and on the whole admiring though most of the obituaries of Wolfe have been, none attempted to find a pattern in his long career.

Some, mistakenly, used the occasion of his death to score off what they took to be his politics. But he never wrote directly about politics or politicians. Here he doubtless reserved the right to attack figures on both the left and the right. When Michael Jordan was asked why a man of his renown didn't speak out more about politics, he answered, "Republicans buy sneakers, too."

If Wolfe was ultimately conservative, as satirists tend to be, his was a cultural conservatism. And this conservatism extended beyond what we normally think of as culture. Behind his preoccupation with status, and apart from the comedy with which he portrayed it, was an abiding sadness at what fools people were to devote, and thus lose, their lives to the pathetic snobbery that lies behind all such systems. As a cultural conservative, he viewed most contemporary social revolutions as bringing out the worst in people. He thought the so-called sexual revolution, for example, "rather a prim term for the lurid carnival that actually took place."

Wolfe could be death on pretension, and on none more than intellectual pretension. He mocked those intellectuals who always sought out the worst in America and found the country on the edge of incipient fascism. He loved America and knew what tremendous advantages it had provided for all who lived here. In an essay attacking American intellectuals, "In the Land of the Rococo Marxists" (2000), he wrote:

> The country turned into what the utopian socialists of the nineteenth century, the Saint-Simons and Fouriers, had dreamed about: an El Dorado where the average working-man would have the political freedom, the personal freedom, the money, and the free time to fulfill his potential in any way he saw fit. It got to the point where if you couldn't reach your tile mason or pool cleaner, it was because he was off on a Royal Caribbean cruise with his third wife.

In *The Kingdom of Speech*, his last book, Wolfe expressed his disdain for cosmogonists, those thinkers who devise theories that Explain Everything (his capital letters). In this case the chief such thinker he had in mind was Charles Darwin. But the real point of attack in the book is

Noam Chomsky, who, with his theory that owing to evolution humans are born with a universal grammar and his organized arrogance in defending it, represents all that Wolfe disdained. In a single sentence, he tied together Chomsky's politics and, as several devastating pages show, his illegitimate authority as a linguist:

> Chomsky's politics enhanced his reputation as a great linguist, and his reputation as a great linguist enhanced his reputation as a political solon, and his reputation as a political solon inflated his reputation from great linguist to all-around genius, and the genius inflated the solon into a veritable Voltaire, and the Voltaire inflated the genius of all geniuses into a philosophical giant . . . Noam Chomsky."

Although he mentions him only once in his writings, and that far from favorably, Tom Wolfe is a writer in the line of H. L. Mencken. Both devised original, altogether inimitable prose styles. Both were in hot pursuit of the quacks of their time: Mencken of healing and holy-rolling preachers, fatuous professors, and others, Wolfe of many of the sad social climbers and savant-idiots who went under the name of intellectuals. Each man in his work brought a literary sensibility to keen sociological instincts. Each exhibited his greatest energy on the attack: Mencken on such figures as William Jennings Bryan and Warren Harding, Wolfe on Leonard Bernstein and Noam Chomsky. Like Mencken, Tom Wolfe deserves a place in American literature for doing so much to pull the wool off the eyes of his countrymen. May the line of Mencken and Wolfe never run out.

Susan Sontag, Savant-Idiot

(2019)

Serious-minded people have few ideas.
People with ideas are never serious.

PAUL VALÉRY

A N IDIOT-SAVANT, as is well known, is a person with serious learning disabilities but gifted in a peculiar, usually extraordinary way, often mathematically or musically. A savant-idiot, as is not well known, since I have only just now coined the phrase, is a person who is learned, brainy, brilliant even, but gets everything important wrong. Simone Weil, who starved herself for the good of humankind, was a savant-idiot. So was Jean-Paul Sartre, never giving up on revolutionary communism even in the face of the mass murders of Stalin and Mao Tse-tung. Theodore Adorno, who among other things held that the true role of popular music was to keep the populace enslaved to the status quo, qualifies nicely. Hannah Arendt, who wrote a significant book on the crushing oppression of totalitarianism, then turned around to argue that the Jews, faced with the most systematically murderous totalitarian system of all, conspired in their own death, was yet a fourth savant-idiot.

The classic American savant-idiot, surely, was Susan Sontag. This is the Susan Sontag who called white civilization "the cancer of human history"; after a trip to Hanoi during the Vietnam War idealized the North Vietnamese ("they genuinely believe life is simple . . . full of joy . . . they genuinely love and admire their leaders"); claimed that the more than

3,000 innocent people killed on 9/11 in effect had it coming to them, for America, through its imperialist policies, had brought this attack on itself; waited until 1982 to decide that Communism was little more than "fascism with a human face" (what, one wondered at the time, was the least human about it?). Only a savant could be so idiotic.

A savant is a thinker, someone less specialized than a scholar or scientist; he or she is a generalist, an intellectual. The word *savant* is of course French, and while there have been and are English, German, Italian, and American savants, the French have long bred the savant, or intellectual, in its purest type. "To tell about him," wrote the nineteenth-century Russian novelist Nikolai Leskov of one of his characters, "one should be French, because only the people of that nation manage to explain to others things that they don't understand themselves." In her literary and philosophical enthusiasms, Susan Sontag aspired to French intellectuality in all its abstract loftiness, and, fair to say, she often achieved it.

Sontag's life, now documented by two biographies, various memoirs, and the publication of large portions of her own journals, provides the best example of how a savant-idiot is formed. Born Susan Rosenblatt in 1933, Sontag never really knew her father, who travelled extensively in China for his fur business and died when she was five years old. She took up the more rhythmic, the trocheeic name of Susan Sontag from Nathan Sontag, her mother's second husband.

The young Susan Sontag lived with a mother who largely turned her upbringing over to nannies. Starved for affection, she retreated into books. In high school, already a subscriber to *Partisan Review,* she read a copy of Kant behind the *Reader's Digest* the class was assigned to read. At sixteen she attended the University of California at Berkeley, where, with a woman named Harriet Sohmners she explored the gay underground of San Francisco and had her first lesbian experiences. The following year she went off to the University of Chicago. There the critic Kenneth Burke claimed "she was the best student I ever had" and called a paper she had written for him "stunning." At Chicago, after little more than a week-long romance, she accepted the marriage proposal of a twelve-years older-than-she instructor named Philip Rieff. A son, David, was born two years later.

Benjamin Moser, Sontag's most recent and authorized biographer, holds that Susan Sontag's relationship with her mother early settled her character and hence her fate. Her mother, said to be quite beautiful on the model of the actress Joan Crawford, was an alcoholic, not a mean or boisterous alcoholic, but one who retreated to her bedroom there to achieve quiet oblivion by drink. "Our mother never really knew how to be a mother," Susan's three-years-younger sister Judith said. In her journal Susan wrote: "I was (felt) profoundly neglected, ignored, unperceived as a child." Her mother treated her not with cruelty but with indifference, which from a parent may be the greatest cruelty of all.

This same indifference, in Benjamin Moser's reading, left Susan Sontag, perpetually off-key in her behavior, in her understanding of others, in her exaggerated self-regard. His account of her life, though on the whole admiring, is in good part a chronicle of her misperceptions, outlandish behavior, broken relationships, including off and on that with her son and only child. Of her marriage with Philip Rieff, she claimed that "not only was *I* Dorothea [from Geoge Eliot's *Middlemarch*] but that I had married Mr. Causabon." A comic touch in connection with their divorce is that Rieff and Sontag apparently came to blows over who would get to keep the couple's collection of back issues of *Partisan Review*.

Doubtless the most controversial aspect of Benjamin Moser's biography is his assumption that Susan Sontag, in her late teens, wrote *Freud, The Mind of the Moralist*, a work long attributed to Philip Rieff. Sontag herself claimed it was she who wrote the book, and Moser takes it for the truth, and on various places in his biography writes sentences beginning "As she wrote in *The Mind of the Moralist*. . . ." My own guess is that Sontag did what in the trade is known as a heavy edit of Rieff's book, a re-write. Rieff, true enough, was not an easy writer, but he could be a powerfully intelligent one, and his *Triumph of the Therapeutic* (1966) is one of the key books of the past sixty or so years. A nineteen-year-old girl, no matter how precocious, could not have written his *Freud, The Mind of the Moralist*.

In compensation for her mother's indifference, Susan Sontag did her best to arrange her life so that the world would never be indifferent to her. Her weapons in this endeavor were her wide and international reading; her keen sense of the *Zeitgeist*, or spirit of the time; and her highly photogenic good looks. As for those good looks—tall, dark, with lush long hair, and pleasing strong features, every young man's fantasy notion of a bohemian lover—it is not easy to calibrate to what extent they figured in Susan Sontag's fame. Her writing alone, which was often abstruse, without distinctive style, often reading as if a translation from the French ("The thinness of my writing," she noted in her journal, "it's meager, sentence by sentence—too architectural, discursive.") is unlikely to have received the attention it did had been written by a homely, even a plain young woman named Susan Rosenblatt. At her death the *New York Times* printed no fewer than four photographs with her obituary. Sontag was, no doubt about it, intellectual cheesecake.

She was also, as Benjamin Moser writes, "America's last great literary star, a flashback to a time when writers could be, more than simply respected or well-regarded, *famous.*" How her fame came about is perhaps of greater interest than anything Sontag wrote over a career of nearly fifty years. As F. R. Leavis said of the Sitwells in England, Susan Sontag, one often feels, belongs less to the history of literature than to that of publicity.

Susan Sontag's fame began in 1964 with an essay in *Partisan Review* called "Notes on Camp." The essay was a study of sensibility, homosexual sensibility chiefly, one that was "wholly aesthetic." Camp was about "the spirit of extravagance," about "a seriousness that fails." Positing a comic vision of the world, "the whole point of camp is to dethrone the serious." What is most interesting about the essay is Sontag's far-flung connections and examples of camp, perhaps the best of which come from the movies. Camp movie actors in her reading included "the corny flamboyant femaleness of Jayne Mansfield, Gina Lollobridgida, Jane Russell, Virginia Mayo; the exaggerated he-manness of Steve Reeves, Victor Mature. The great stylists of temperament and mannerism, like Bette Davis, Barbara Stanwyck, Tallulah Bankhead, Edwige Feuillere." Other examples in the essay are less telling. What is campy about "much of Mozart," for one; or "the qualities of excruciation in Henry James," for another, beats me.

"Notes on Camp" was published in *Partisan Review*, a magazine that never had more than 5,000 readers. But in that day the editors of the mass-market magazines scoured it and other little magazines for news of the next great thing, and "Notes on Camp," announcing a new sensibility, qualified beautifully. The essay was quickly taken up by *Time* and discussed in the *New York Times Magazine*. Thought among the hippest of the hip and dazzlingly attractive into the bargain, its author became grist for *Vogue*, dined with Jacqueline Kennedy and Leonard Bernstein, became a celebrity herself. She would later be on the cover of *Vanity Fair*; play in Woody Allen's movie *Zelig*; be photographed by Andy Warhol, Joseph Cornell, Richard Avedon, her lover Annie Liebowitz and others; and appear in an Absolut Vodka ad.

With the publication of "Notes on Camp," Sontag also became the enemy of those who held high culture to be sacrosanct. "One cheats oneself, as a human being," Sontag wrote in "Notes on Camp," "if one has *respect* only for the style of high culture, whatever else one may do or feel on the sly." Sontag was proposing more than merely an interest in popular culture. Her essay was in fact an attack on the importance of content in art. Camp, for her, "incarnates a victory of 'style' over 'content,' 'aesthetics' over 'morality,' of irony over tragedy." She offered a mild disclaimer about her own position: "I am strongly drawn to Camp, and almost as strongly offended by it." But it was as the Queen of Camp, its champion and explicator, that she initially achieved prominence.

Benjamin Moser quotes Hilton Kramer against the essay. In vaunting the aesthetic over the moral, Kramer wrote, Sontag made "the very idea of moral discrimination seems stale and distinctly un-chic." On *Partisan Review* itself there was opposition to publishing "Notes on Camp," this coming from Philip Rahv, one of the magazine's two co-editors, who thought Susan Sontag bad news generally and loathed this essay in particular. Sontag, apparently, was undaunted. She ended her other famous essay of the time, "Against Interpretation," by writing: "In place of a hermeneutics we need an erotics of art."

Which brings one to the erotics of Susan Sontag. She was, technically, bisexual, but, like most bisexuals, favored her homosexual side. In instinct and inclination she was lesbian, though she preferred not to have this public knowledge. Until nearly the end of her life, for example, her sister did not know Susan was lesbian. Her relations with male lovers were for the most part casual, transitory; those with women, of longer duration, left her confused, often heart-broken.

Jasper Johns, Joseph Brodsky, Warren Beatty, and Roger Straus, her publisher at Farrar, Straus, Giroux, were among Sontag's male liaisons. One of Benjamin Moser's more interesting revelations is the extent to which Roger Straus in effect supported Susan Sontag, paying most of her bills and later in her career giving her, whose books did not sell well, an $800,000 advance on four books. She slept, apparently once, with Robert Kennedy, and also, in the Kennedy circle, with Richard Goodwin, to whom she paid what I consider perhaps the greatest mixed compliment I have ever come across: "The ugliest person I've ever slept with was the best in bed."

Benjamin Moser, who is himself gay, takes Sontag to task for not coming out and announcing her own homosexuality during the AIDS epidemic. So famous a figure making her homosexuality known in support of the dying could not, he argues, but have had a great effect in helping reduce the stigma then associated with homosexuality generally. "Silence=Death" was a motto of the anti-AIDS campaign of that day. Despite the pleas of friends, Sontag held back. She didn't want to be reduced to being a lesbian, or even merely a woman, writer. Her ambitions were grander than that.

One can tell a good deal about a person, and especially about a writer, by his or her admirations. In Sontag's case two prominent savant-idiots were among them. She much admired Hannah Arendt: "the kind of writer she wanted to be," Moser writes, "a woman but a writer first of all," and took her as a model writer. She also greatly esteemed Jean-Paul Sartre. "I realize how important Sartre has been to me," Sontag wrote in her journal. "He is the model—that abundance, that lucidity, that knowingness. . . ." (If Sartre and Simone de Beauvoir were to have had a daughter, Susan Sontag would have filled the bill nicely.) Walter Benjamin, Moser reports, occupied "pride of place" in her personal pantheon. Her admiration for Paul Goodman, a 1960s guru, was unbounded: "He was our Sartre and our Cocteau." (Did America, one wonders, need either?) She praised the avant-garde composer John Gage. She saw herself in the intellectual line of Kierkegaard, Nietzsche, Wittgenstein, and the Rumanian aphorist E. M. Cioran. She esteemed Antonin Artaud, Samuel Beckett, and Roland Barthes. Not, as a group, a lot of laughs here.

Unlike many of these figures, Susan Sontag was herself very much an establishment figure—established, that is, among the radical left and among what remained of the avant-garde. A regular contributor to the *New York Review of Books*, she was a figure of the 1960's, a member of high standing of elite leftism. Her *Against Interpretation* appeared in 1967, and was, according to Camille Paglia, "among a dozen books that defined the cultural moment and seemed to herald a dawning age of revolutionary achievement, by students of the Sixties as well as Sontag herself."

Sontag may have been radical, she may have been wildly detached from reality, but she was never unfashionable. However *outré* her opinions, however abstruse her writing, the world had nonetheless decided to shower its attentions on her. She claimed to have no interest in fame yet, Jasper Johns reported, "she very early on believed she would win the Nobel Prize," and at the end of her life fell into depression when J. M. Coetzee, and not she, won the Nobel Prize for Literature in 2003.

Much of Sontag's non-fiction—her books *On Photography*, on *Illness as Metaphor*, her essays, and the rest—is an elaborate attempt to grasp reality behind the various screens and masks the world tends to place before it and the metaphors used to describe it. ("Metaphors mislead," she wrote in her essay "On Style.") Yet she was oddly miscast for the task. The photographer Lisette Model wrote of *On Photography* that "this is a book by a woman who knows everything and understands nothing." Many of her friends and others who knew her attested to Susan Sontag's inability to put herself in the place of others. "She was not smart or intuitive emotionally," a friend named Don Levine told Moser. Joan Acocella, interviewing her late in life for a *New Yorker* profile, was astonished at how extraordinarily unaware of herself she was. After spending time in Sarajevo during the Bosnian crisis, she began to think of herself as Joan of Arc, a self-image that did not get in the way of her ordering vast quantities of caviar on her friend Larry McMurtry's tab.

None of these qualities, or rather absence of qualities, made for the accomplished novelist Susan Sontag hoped to become. As Benjamin Moser notes, "she recognized her own inability to write narrative fiction." Janet Malcolm called her novel *The Benefactor* "a very advanced kind of experiment in unreadability." Herbert Marcuse, who for a period lived with Sontag and Philip Rieff, said that "she could make a theory out of a potato peel," but, without a feeling for experience and understanding of other people, she never wrote fiction with characters who came alive. As a young woman she much admired the arid, idea-driven fictions of Nathalie Sarraute and Alain Robbe-Grillet (an admiration she later disavowed). Benjamin Moser, who wishes to put the best face on Sontag's fiction, calls her novels "brave, noble failures—unforgettable." Brave and noble, I am not prepared to say, but I can personally attest that they are eminently forgettable. "Maybe art has to be boring, now," she wrote, and hers—including her fiction, her two films shot in Sweden—all driven solely by ideas, too often was.

The last sentence of Benjamin Moser's *Susan Sontag* reads: "And she warned against the mystifications of photographs and portraits: including those of biographers." In his biography Moser, I believe, came to praise Susan Sontag. Biographer and subject, after all, seem to share the same politics, that of conventional American leftism. He gives her writing the benefit of nearly every doubt. In his summing up final pages, he writes that, though her answers to the questions of the day may not always have been right, she, for nearly fifty years, "more than any other prominent public thinker, had set the terms of the cultural debate in a way no intellectual had done before or has done since."

Yet Susan Sontag did not make it easy, even for an admiring biographer. In Moser's biography it soon enough becomes plain that Susan Sontag, not to put too fine a point on it, was not a nice person. Once fame had arrived, she became a diva, with all the deficiencies of temperament inherent in the role but without the great voice for justification. The record of Sontag's kindly and generous acts is brief; that of her egotism, selfishness, and cruelty copious.

For openers, the Susan Sontag who resented the inattention of her mother was herself a less than attentive mother. She often exclaimed her love for her son to various friends. Yet early in the child's life she abandoned him to spend a year in Oxford. At age four she had him reading *Candide, Gulliver's Travels,* Homer; at eleven she had him reading *War and Peace.* Maria Irene Fornes, a Cuban-American playwright and one her lovers, thought she gave David, in Moser's words, "a bad combination of too much latitude and too little attention, and told her so." Another lover, Eva Kallisch, said "I think she shortchanged him of a lot of love and affection." She often deposited the boy in the care of others, and pretty much left him to raise himself. The writer Jamaica Kincaid wrote that "she really wanted to be a great mother, but it was sort of like wanting to be a great actress, or something... I would say there was [in Susan] no real instinct for caring for another person unless they were in a book."

In Moser's biography several people attest to Sontag's insensitivity, her tactlessness, her humorlessness, her self-grandiosity. "It was not that she wanted to hurt people," said a friend who knew her from University of Chicago days. "It was that she was simply oblivious." Eva Kollisch claimed Sontag "was one of the most immoral people I ever knew." Moser records that she had no compunction in sleeping with her best friend's husband. She saw nothing wrong with regularly humiliating Annie Leibowitz, the photographer and her last and perhaps most faithful lover—a woman that Benjamin Moser estimates spent more than $8 million dollars on her—correcting her grammar and pointing out her ignorance in public.

Sontag was also ignorant of the basic facts of life. On more than one occasion Moser refers to her poor hygiene: "not brushing her teeth or bathing, not knowing that she was going to get her period or that childbirth was painful. . . ." She early went on amphetamines, to stay awake and hasten her writing, and suffered the effects in mood swings, rudeness, loneliness, and fear of abandonment. She was one of those people who needed others to clean up after her, and she found them in paid assistants, editors, friends, sycophants. She couldn't stand to be alone yet treated nearly everyone near her badly.

So how, then, could a woman who was so inadequate a mother, so untrustworthy a friend, so out of touch with the most commonplace realities, have been a penetrating analyst of culture and politics? The short answer is that she wasn't.

In politics, Susan Sontag's views were standard left-wing ones. She couldn't seem to imagine figures of greater evil than Ronald Reagan and George W. Bush. She early revered Fidel Castro. She contemned that by now hoary leftist cliché, the consumer society. All this fitted nicely into her general anti-Americanism. In 1967 she declared that "living in the United States hurts so much. It's like having an ulcer all the time." America was for her a "too-white, death ridden culture." All this culminated in her famous incendiary *New Yorker* statement that on 9/11 America got what it deserved.

Sontag's observations on culture, though pitched on a higher level, were scarcely more subtle. Here her central idea was that, in art, style trumps content. The perfect example of this was her early reverence for the films of Leni Riefenstahl, *The Triumph of the Will* and *The Olympiad*, both produced under the Nazis. "The Nazi propaganda is there," she wrote in her essay "On Style." "But something else is there, too, which we reject at our loss . . . these two films of Riefenstahl (unique among works of Nazi artists) transcend the categories of propaganda or even reportage. . . . Through Riefenstahl's genius as a film-maker, the 'content' has—let us assume even against her intentions—come to play a purely formal role." Sontag later, as we now say, walked back her views of Riefenstahl, but not her view that a central concern with the content of art was to miss its point and was essentially Philistine. What eluded her was that style was the way an artist, any artist, views the world—that style is, in the end, content.

Friends claimed that Susan Sontag was blind to much visual art; others that, though she regularly dragged herself to the opera and concerts, she was not truly responsive to music. Ideas, and ideas alone, lit her fire. Her own ideas in the political realm unfortunately were unoriginal, those in the realm of culture unhelpful. Yet the utter absorption in ideas, which permit no contradiction from experience, no rebuff from reality, is of course the hallmark of the savant-idiot, and what made Susan Sontag the great American savant-idiot she ultimately was.

Lionel Trilling

(2019)

66 "T*HE AGE OF CRITICISM*"—that is what Randall Jarrell called the period between the 1930s and the early 1960s, a time when the power of literary criticism threatened to swamp the power of literature itself. In England, the magisterial T. S. Eliot was at work, as were F. R. Leavis, William Empson, I. A. Richards, and others. In America, Edmund Wilson was at the top of his game, and at our universities, the prestige of the critics who made their living on campuses—R. P. Blackmur, Allan Tate, Cleanth Brooks, and John Crowe Ransom among them—made the philologists and literary historians look like mere pedants.

The name missing from this roster of distinguished academic critics was the most famous of them all, Lionel Trilling. Then and now, Trilling doesn't seem quite to fit in anywhere. He was never entirely comfortable with Columbia University, where he taught for decades—or, for that matter, with thinking himself an academic or even a critic. He was often listed among the group known as the New York Intellectuals, which included Philip Rahv, Irving Howe, Harold Rosenberg, Dwight Macdonald, Alfred Kazin, Delmore Schwartz, Lionel Abel, and others, but he was less political and more intellectually refined than they. He wrote for the same magazines they did—*Partisan Review* and *Commentary* here, *Encounter* in England—but he was never fully in the mix.

What set Trilling apart above all is that he was a critic not alone of literature but of that wider entity, culture. "My war," he wrote to the English writer John Wain, "was always a cultural rather than a political one." Culture, he noted in his essay "The Sense of the Past," should "be studied and judged as life's continuous evaluation of itself. . . ." Cultural criticism, even when grounded in literary criticism, widens the lens, considers the outside forces that produce certain works and reckons the importance of the works themselves to the culture that produced them. Thus Trilling, in a reconsideration of the novelist Sherwood Andeson, writes that Anderson was of "the tradition of the men who maintained a standing quarrel with respectable society and have a bone to pick with the rational intellect." By considering the novel through the lens of culture, Trilling could not merely assert but establish why *The Great Gatsby* seemed to grow better with the passage of time. Money, social class, snobbery, politics, history—all these fell within his purview as a cultural critic.

The Liberal Imagination (1950), Trilling's first collection, includes essays on the liberal imagination in literature, F. Scott Fitzgerald, Freud and Literature, Henry James's *The Princess Casasmassima,* intellectual magazines, *Huckleberry Finn,* Rudyard Kipling, Wordsworth's "Immortality Ode," art and neurosis, and *The Kinsey Report.* This partial table of contents gives some notion of his range. Criticism for Lionel Trilling was part of the history of ideas.

All the essays in this rich intellectual buffet remain readable today, which is remarkable for a work of criticism, a literary form not noted for its lengthy shelf life. If the book may be said to have a theme, it is the literary poverty of liberalism, the inability of writers under liberalism's sway to convey in their writing anything like life's rich complexity. The essay that gives the book its title ends by noting the contradiction that the writers most valued at the time, Yeats and Proust, Eliot and Joyce, D. H. Lawrence and Andre Gide, "are indifferent to, or even hostile to the tradition of liberal democracy as we know it." Yet, Trilling argued, they supply what writers in the liberal tradition do not: "The sense of largeness, of cogency, of the transcendence which largeness and cogency can give, the sense of being reached in our secret and primitive minds—this we virtually never get from writers of the liberal democratic tradition at the present time." Trilling would later write to Bruce Bliven then editor of the *New Republic*, "nothing could be more useful to a liberal political point of view than the fostering of a strong interest in literature."

As the work of poets and novelists have voices, so, too, do those of critics. Trilling's criticism was written in the voice of a highly intelligent companion—sophisticated, urbane, metropolitan—patiently explaining complex matters. As he writes in a letter of 1951 to his former student Norman Podhoretz:

> What I would have said about my own prose is that there is a need for a tone of reasonableness and demonstration, that it was of the greatest importance that we learn to consider that the tone of civil life has its necessity and may even have its heroic quality, that we must have a modification of all that is implied by the fierce posture of modern literature.

At its best Trilling's critical voice had a fine fluency, a measured modesty, and an authoritative persuasiveness. If Matthew Arnold, as he held, was "the first literary intellectual in the English-speaking world," Trilling was the closest America has come to producing a descendent in Arnold's line.

Trilling did not indulge in autobiographical allusions in his criticism. When he was alive one acquired scraps of information about him from people who knew him. His own closest friend at Columbia was Jacques Barzun. Among his better-known students were Melvin Lasky, Norman Podhoretz, Steven Marcus, and Allen Ginsberg. He was a longtime—nearly a lifelong—psychoanalysand, undergoing three separate analyses. His wife Diana, herself a book reviewer for the *Nation* and more political than her husband, was a strong anti-Communist, in temperament a pure diva (without the music), and said to be impressively neurotic: fearful of ants in her food, terrified of heights, a true-believing Freudian. Life with her could not have been easy, though in a memoir, *The Beginning of the Journey*, written after her husband died, Diana Trilling claimed that life with him, his depression and erratic behavior generally, was not a day at the beach either.

Life in Culture: Selected Letters of Lionel Trilling provides the most extended intimate view of Trilling that we have. He was a prodigious correspondent; in one of his missives collected here Trilling estimates that he writes 600 letters a year. Adam Kirsch, now an editor at the *Wall Street Journal*, has produced an admirable selection that touches on Trilling the critic, the teacher, and the Jew, setting out his aspirations, his antipathies, his disappointments.

Trilling had an early Marxist phase, and as a young man served on the Committee to Defend Leon Trotsky. But as early as 1935, during a time "when we were all political," he wrote to Jacques Barzun that he was "essentially a non-political man in point of activity. . . ." He despaired of liberalism, and saw himself as battling against its superficialities from within: "I conceived my role to be that of a critic of the ideology and sensibility of these people, although counting myself one of them." His opposition to liberalism was not to its ideals—tolerance, freedom, etc.—which he shared, but to "the tone in which these ideals are uttered [that] despress[es] me endlessly." To a correspondent named Hyman Juskowitz he wrote that "what I want to make plain is my deep distaste for liberal culture."

Though Trilling was not politically conservative, he was indubitably conservative in temperament and literary tastes. He wrote to John Aldridge that in criticism "I don't think of myself as having a position." But when it came to specific authors and literary movements, a position can nevertheless be deduced. For him "the four transcendently great novelists" were Dostoyevsky, Proust, Cervantes, and Dickens. He also much appreciated Balzac. He called D. H. Lawrence "pretty great," and so would not have agreed with Bertrand Russell's assessment, which is close to my own, that Lawrence was "a writer of a certain descriptive power whose ideas cannot be too soon forgot." He later came immensely to admire Henry James.

Of the magazine *Partisan Review*'s split interest in Marxist and Modernism, Trilling shared fully in neither. To C. P. Snow he wrote, "I don't think of myself as being either *pro* or *con* in relation to modern literature. I have a good deal of resistance to it, the expression of a stubborn humanistic conservatism; at the same time I am implicated in its enterprise." To the poet Allen Ginsberg he wrote: "I am very largely an old-fashioned humanist," and allowed that he had "never been a great welcomer of the new." To the theater critic Eric Bentley he noted "that Brecht, I am sure, will never be my dish." He thought Eugene O'Neill's mind a "dreadful miasma." He disdained J. D. Salinger, James Thurber, and E. B. White "for a covert self-cherishing and self-pity that I find in their work." He wrote to Norman Mailer's about Mailer's "The Time of Her Time," a story about female orgasm, that "I am in favor of a lot of explicitness for ten, maybe twelve years; then everybody shut up." In 1956 he wrote stingingly to Ginsberg about his new collection *Howl* that "I don't like the poems at all. . . . They are not like Whitman—they are all prose, all rhetoric, without any music."

For Trilling, literature, with its emphasis on the rich variety and fortuitousness of life, was the best antidote to too-confident politics. In his earlier days, there was "all the blindness and malign obfuscations of the Stalinoid mind of our time" to contend with. In later years there were the superficialities of liberalism. "To the carrying out of the job of criticizing the liberal imagination, literature has a unique relevance . . . because literature is the human activity that takes the fullest and most precise account of variousness, possibility, complexity, and difficulty." He added: "Unless we insist that politics is imagination and mind, we will learn that imagination and mind are politics, and of a kind we will not like."

Owing to his standing as a critic, Trilling in 1958 was offered and turned down a job at Harvard, yet one of the revelations of *Life in Culture* is that Lionel Trilling preferred not to think of himself as a critic. His doubts about being a critic at all crop up through his letters and miscellaneous writings. This first appears in a letter of 1942 to the critic Newton Arvin, in which he writes of William Empson, Allen Tate, and Cleanth Brooks that "they've done good work and I've learned a great deal from them but I wonder if it is they who make me feel that though I want to write criticism I *don't* want to read it." Six years later, to John Crowe Ransom, he described having "an impatience with myself in the role of critic, which often presents itself as an impatience with literature itself." He added that "I never really think of myself as a critic." To Isaiah Berlin he declared that he had "become impatient with criticism in general and find it harder and harder to read it."

In an introduction to an anthology he edited called *Literary Criticism: An Introductory Reader*, Trilling asks if criticism isn't even inimical to literature. "There are times," he writes, "when criticism seems beyond the point of literature and it is literature beyond the reach of criticism that we want, just as there are times when literature seems beside the point of life and it is life itself beyond the reach of literature we want." He wrote to the French philosopher Etienne Gilson to thank him for noting that "I am not a literary critic."

If Lionel Trilling preferred not to think himself a critic, what in fact did he think himself? In "Some Notes for An Autobiographical Lecture," from 1974, he reports that he had originally envisioned himself as a novelist, and that the writing of criticism was "always secondary, an afterthought: in short, not a vocation, an avocation." When he did write about literature, he tended not to examine it aesthetically but for its moral content. The moral imagination, the "questions raised by the experience of life and by the experience of culture and history," as he put it, were his true subject.

Trilling's sense of his relation to literature was acquired in his undergraduate days at Columbia in the 1920s under the sway of the great books course called General Honors. In that course the study of literature had no pretensions to scholarship. "It did not have in mind [as its aim] a learned man, a scholar," Trilling writes, "but a well-read man, a widely read man, precisely an intelligent man, for there was an intelligence of the emotions and of task." The study of literature and philosophy set out in the General Honors course showed the way of escaping the confines of one's narrow social background by contemplating "great models of thought, feeling, and imagination, and great issues which suggested the close interrelation of the private and the personal life with the public life, with life in society." The critic, then, in Trilling's conception of him, was little more than an intelligent man reporting on the thoughts stirred by his reading.

If Lionel Trilling was less than enamored of the mantle of critic, neither, we learn from his letters, was he enthusiastic about university teaching. First among his problems with it was Columbia, where he seems to have been given his job as much on sufferance as on genuine enthusiasm. "I don't think there are ten men in the university who have the right to pass on us," he told Barzun in 1935. "I don't think this is arrogance. I am sure there are scores who surpass me intellectually and hundreds in knowledge, but I think they are *wrong*—wrong and desiccated and liars and fatheads." He soon discovers he has no appetite for teaching graduate students; when in 1951 he is released from supervising dissertations, he describes it as "pure bliss." To Irving Feldman, a poet and former student, he writes that "even in my quite good situation I find that teaching is an unhappy business, harder and harder to justify. I don't always feel this, but very often, and more and more often." Despite these misgivings, he had the reputation of a popular teacher. In an essay on Jane Austen written yet not completed at the end of his life he recounts teaching a class that he had wished limited to thirty but which ended up with an enrollment of 150 students.

The students themselves began to seem a problem to him. In one of his best-known essays, "On the Teaching of Modern Literature (1961)," he sensed the arrival of what he termed "the adversary culture"—that radical counter-culture that contemned and set out to destroy established culture, and its incipient prominence among students. In teaching the darker modern writers—Nietzsche, Dostoyevsky, Eliot—Trilling felt himself playing into the hands of this adversary culture. In the essay he writes that to teach modern literature is "to engage in the process that we might call the socialization of the anti-social, or the acculturation of the anti-cultural, or the legitimization of the subversive: I asked them to look into the Abyss, and, both dutifully and gladly, they have looked into the Abyss, and the Abyss has greeted them with the grave courtesy of all objects of serious study, saying: 'Interesting, am I not? And *exciting*, if you consider how deep I am and what dread beasts lie at my bottom. Have it well in mind that a knowledge of me contributes materially to your being whole, or well-rounded, men.'"

If Lionel Trilling was unhappy as a teacher and dissatisfied with his reputation as a critic, what, then, did he want? The answer comes through plainly enough in *Life in Culture:* he yearned to be a writer of fiction, a novelist. He had published a handful of stories and in 1947 a novel, *The Middle of the Journey*, about a group of middle-class progressives in the 1930s in a summer town that resembles Westport, Connecticut, who fall out over their relation to Soviet Communism. The novel never quite gets off the ground, and the characters fail to come alive, even though one of them was clearly based on the then very much alive Whitaker Chambers. The subject, which Trilling treats with great moral earnestness, might better have been played for comedy. Re-reading the novel I was reminded that I once mentioned to Saul Bellow that in the letter's pages of the *New York Review of Books* Irving Howe and Philip Rahv were engaged in a controversy over the nature of revolution. "Ah," said Bellow, "two elderly Jews arguing noisily in the back of the synagogue. Approaching closer, one discovers what they are arguing about is Lady Astor's horse."

In the letters in *Life in Culture* Trilling is always about to get back to writing fiction. Soon after completing *The Middle of the Journey*, he hopes to write "a second, third, fourth novel," but never gets around to it. To Richard Chase he wrote that his "new novel has been going badly but I just begin to see it again." In 1965, he told Irving Feldman that "I mean to begin a new novel in a few months . . . it engages me more and more deeply and the prospect makes me happy." Instead he put in two years on *The Experience of Literature*, his anthology of literary criticism. In 1972, only three years before his death from pancreatic cancer, he informed the English publisher Frederic Warburg that he still thinks of writing novels "if I can get myself to have confidence in the possibility of its transcending the 'reasonable' tone of *Middle of the Journey*, of its taking itself out of my hands and going its own way." At his death he left a portion of a novel, roughly a third completed, called *The Journey Abandoned*. It was published in 2008 by Columbia University Press. But it, too, stubbornly refused to reach, or even approximate, his ideal for the grand fiction of the moral imagination that was the name of his desire.

Of all the reviews of *The Middle of the Journey*, Trilling was especially aggrieved by that of Robert Warshow in *Commentary*. Among other deficiencies Warshow noted in the novel was its author's failing to make any of his characters Jewish, when so many radicals in 1930s America had themselves been Jews. Trilling had a Jewish problem. He was nothing so pathetic as a self-hating Jew. Nor was he of that rarified type, the anti-Semitic Jew, or the superior Jew who looked down on other Jews. The problem was that he just didn't see how his own Jewishness in any way influenced or had any connection with or meaning for him. This comes up over and over again in his letters. This first time was in 1945 when he turns down the offer of becoming a member of the board of contributing editors of the newly fledged *Commentary*, responding to the offer by saying, "I do not think I am a man who should—let alone could—have a quasi-official position in Jewish life." He informed the rabbi who was the counselor to Jewish students at Columbia that he cannot accept his invitation to attend services because "I am not a synagogue goer and cannot properly appear as an example of one." To another correspondent he wrote that the culture of Eastern European Jewry "has injured us all dreadfully," adding that "the anti-sexual impulse of Eastern European Jews is extreme." He wrote to Clement Greenberg that "I feared and disliked everything I knew about American Jewish life." If he saw little value in Jewishness, he had little better to say about Judaism, the religion itself. To the English philosopher Alan Montefiore, he wrote that "the nature of my alienation from Judaism is in large part an irritable response to the unsatisfactoriness—the dimness—of its theological utterances." All this can seem, as the English say, a bit of a muchness coming from a man whose middle name was Mordecai.

Lionel Trilling wished not so much to disown or even to deny his Jewish connection as to seem above it or above any parochialism implicit in the connection with religion or ethnicity. He wanted to stake out a position of philosophical detachment, the detachment of true critic of the culture. This he may have achieved, but at high cost to the would-be novelist. In a letter to Saul Bellow's editor at Viking, Pat Covici, he praised Bellow's 1953 breakthrough book *The Adventures of Augie March*, remarking that it "is Saul's gift to see life everywhere" and going on to praise Bellow for forging a new style that "is really wonderful in its vivacity and energy, in its fusion of the colloquial and the intellectual tradition."

Such a style wasn't available to Trilling for his own fiction, owing to his withdrawal from the nub and rub of everyday life, to his very detachment. Aristotle spoke of tragedy as representing men as better than they are, comedy as representing them as worse. But it is the novel at its best that represents them as they really are. Such knowledge wasn't available to Trilling. Wrapped in the cocoon of the university all his adult days, having retreated from the religion of his birth, he never had the experience of quotidian life required by the kind of novels he himself most admired. As with everyone who sets out on a career in art but discovers his talent isn't up to his ambition, Lionel Trilling's was in the end a disappointed life, one in which he had, much to his chagrin, to settle for being America's last important critic.

Proust's Duchesses

(2018)

A T THE CENTER OF *IN SEARCH OF LOST TIME*, Marcel Proust's masterwork, a novel of seven volumes, more than 3,000 pages, roughly 1.5 million words, and 400 or so characters, is the Duchesse de Guermantes. In Proust's portrayal of her, the Duchesse is a woman at the zenith of *belle époque* social life. The *belle époque*, that period in France bounded by the end of the Franco-Prussian War (1871) and the beginning of the First World War (1914), wasn't *belle* for everyone, as Captain Alfred Dreyfus would have been the first to attest, though it did witness the final flowering of French aristocracy, also known as *le monde, le gratin*, the "born."

In one of the novel's crucial scenes, the Duchesse de Guermantes is told by her friend Charles Swann that he has only a few months to live. A moment later her husband, the Duc, points out that she is wearing black shoes with her red dress and insists she return to her room to put on red shoes. Riven between compassion for Swann's impending death and the need to coordinate her outfit for the evening, she chooses to return for the matching shoes, thus revealing a heartless superficiality that anyone who has read the scene does not soon forget.

Caroline Weber, a professor of French and comparative literature at Columbia University, certainly hasn't forgotten it. The cover of her *Proust's*

Duchess has a single high-heeled red slipper under the book's title. A triple biography of three women—Geneviève Halévy Bizet Straus (1849–1926), Laure de Sade, Comtesse Adhéaume de Chevigné (1859–1936), and Élisabeth de Riquet de Caraman Chimay, Vicomtesse (later Comtesse) Greffulhe (1860–1952)—Weber's book recounts the conquest by these women "of a world where projecting an image was the precondition, and the price, of belonging." *Proust's Duchess* also chronicles the salon culture of aristocratic France between the years 1870 and 1890. This was a culture whose ethos is nicely captured in a remark by the Duc de Doudeauville upon his blackballing the writer Paul Bourget from membership in the Jockey Club: "I'd like to think there's still one place in Paris where individual merit doesn't count for anything."

Proust's Duchess is a handsome piece of bookmaking, elegantly printed, with photographs in both color and black-and-white, set out on the pages to which they are most relevant, a book with a substantial look and comfortable feel in the hand. Caroline Weber has supplied her book with more than 100 pages of back-matter—footnotes, bibliography, appendices—making it, as its author hoped it would be, a work both of scholarship and of compelling storytelling. She notes that the completion of her book was slowed by her relentless search for "*le mot juste*," a largely successful search, for her writing is admirably clear, often amusing, and precise in its formulations of matters of considerable subtlety. In her next book, though, I hope she will eliminate those less than *juste* words "gender norms," "feedback," and "mindset" and take a pass, too, on the much overworked "icon," "lifestyle," and "charisma."

T HE THREE WOMEN at the center of Weber's study—the Mesdames Greffulhe, Straus, and Chevigné—all married badly. Élisabeth Greffulhe, easily the most beautiful of the three, married a brute, a wealthy, deeply philistine man thought to have had affairs with no fewer than 300 women while remaining jealous of his wife and who saw no breach in etiquette in bringing some of these mistresses to dine at his wife's table. Geneviève Straus, Jewish, of Sephardic lineage, was born a Halévy; her father was a composer famous in his day; and after her first husband, Georges Bizet, the composer of *Carmen*, died at 36, she married a well-to-do bore, a

Rothschild lawyer named Émile Straus. (Famous for her witticisms, when asked why she married the dullard Straus, she replied, "It was the only way I could get rid of him.") Laure de Chevigné, born a Sade, of the Marquis de Sade Sades, was the least physically attractive of the three women, but hers was the most secure pedigree. Her husband, thought to be homosexual, was among those aristocrats in the retinue gathered around Henri d'Artois, putatively Henry V, last Bourbon pretender to the throne of France, then living in exile in Austria.

These three women operated in a society that Lord Lytton called "brilliantly superficial." It was a society where, in Maupassant's words, "laughter is never genuine," one in which intelligence was not valued, striving was thought vulgar, and the only ignorance that counted was ignorance of dress, pronunciation, and the pecking order. This society in the middle of Paris, as Princesse Marthe Bibesco notes in her novel *Égalité*, "formed a world as distant from ordinary people on the streets as the moon is from the earth."

For people on the outside, mere earthlings, the members of the *monde* radiated a powerful, almost magical attraction. A young Englishwoman named Barbara Lister, mentioned in another of Princesse Bibesco's books, happened to be in a Parisian bookstore when Laure de Chevigné and her mother were in the shop. "When they left the shop," Miss Lister afterwards wrote, "I thought the sun had gone in."

Proust's Duchess describes the world of the *gratin* of the *belle époque* and along the way reveals how thin, how shallow, how nearly bogus it all was. "Life," said Bismarck, "begins at baron," meaning that in 19th-century Europe without a title one was rabble, rubbish, scarcely existent. Theatergoing, boxes at the opera, elaborate costume balls—these were the events in which the *gratin* appeared outside the social fortresses of their homes and salons. Summer months they spent under the roofs of grand mansions in the country; parts of the autumn and winter were given over to shooting foxes and pheasants. A sycophantic press chronicled their comings and goings. The *monde*, in Caroline Weber's phrase, "existed in a time warp."

A woman in this select inner circle, Weber informs us, required as many as seven or eight changes of clothes daily, which of course implied a cadre of servants. "The 'born' Parisienne's golden rule: always look perfect, no matter how shaky one's finances or one's marriage," she writes. The game of keeping up was costly. The dirty little secret among the born was not sex, Weber notes, but finances.

The men in this strange world seemed, most of them, to have little to do other than fill up the salons and kill afternoons in this matriarchal, entirely self-enclosed society. Their numbers included retired military men, superannuated political figures, heirs aspirant. The Prince of Wales, awaiting the long-delayed death of his mother, Queen Victoria, would put in an occasional appearance. Geneviève Straus's salon, the one into which Proust first gained entry, was unusual in having among its denizens painters, writers, and composers, lending it a vaguely bohemian air.

Easily the most exotic among the male salon frequenters of the *belle époque* salons was Robert de Montesquiou, uncle to Mme. de Greffulhe, who would later serve Proust as his model for the Baron de Charlus. Ardent for gossip, Montesquiou was a snob of the first order and said to be the soul of indiscretion. Sarah Bernhardt, the actress of the age, was the only woman Montesquiou claimed ever to have made love to, and he remarked that for fully a week afterward he vomited continuously.

FOR THOSE WHO SEEK LIVING PARALLELS for the characters in Proust's novel, the leading candidate for the Duchesse de Guermantes is probably Élisabeth de Greffulhe. Certainly, she looked most like the Duchesse Proust describes in *In Search of Lost Time*. Tall, blonde, blue-eyed, always strikingly turned out, wealthy through marriage, the Duchesse de Guermantes at Proust's narrator's first sight of her seems "a whole poem of elegant refinement and the loveliest ornament, the rarest flower of the season." On the other hand, perhaps the model for Proust's Duchesse was Mme. de Chevigné—"the woman in whom," wrote Princesse Bibesco, "the genius of Marcel Proust, divining her perfect essence by the light of his worship, found the archetype of his Duchesse de Guermantes." What seems most likely is that, as Caroline Weber suggests, Proust's Duchesse is an amalgam of all three women.

Marcel Proust, the better part of whose own life—born 1871, died 1922— was lived in the *belle époque*, was its great, its unsurpassable chronicler and the Duchesse de Guermantes among his most memorable creations. The character Charles Swann remarks of the Duchesse that "she is one of the noblest souls in Paris, the cream of the most refined, the choicest society." But as the novel plays out, the Duchesse de Guermantes proves simultaneously bewitching and bitchy, clever and shallow, generous and malicious, charming and anti-Semitic, a snob whose chief pretense is that she values talent and intellect over birth and breeding, which in all her actions she clearly does not.

As a young man, Proust knew the three women at the center of Caroline Weber's book, but just as he knew their world generally: from the outside looking in, nose pressed against the glass. Half Jewish, on his mother's side, his only connection with the world described in *Proust's Duchess* was his schoolmate Jacques Bizet, son of Geneviève Halévy Bizet Straus. When older, Proust implored Robert de Montesquiou to help him gain entrance to Mme. de Greffulhe's salon. "Do you not see," Montesquiou told him, "that your presence in her salon would rid it of the very grandeur you hope to find there?" He would eventually come to know Mme. Greffulhe quite well. As for her, when much older she recalled Proust as "a displeasing little man who was forever skulking about in doorways."

Groucho Marx famously said that he wouldn't care to join any club that would have him as a member. Poor Proust was never able to test the Groucho rule, for he was never extended a full invitation to the club to which as a young man he so yearned to belong. The earlier rap on Proust was that he was little more than a social climber. When he published his first book, *Pleasures and Days* (1896), a reviewer described its contents, not mistakenly, as "little nothings about elegance." The young Proust's excessive flattery, applied not with a trowel but a backhoe, came to be known as "Proustifying."

The luster of the *gratin* would soon enough wear off for Proust. The dandiacal dilettante would soon turn into the penetrating social observer. Through his novel he would explode the pretensions of a society that would rank a young duc higher in importance than an octogenarian Victor Hugo. Weber writes that her three disdainful subjects would live to see the day that their prestige-laden but utterly artificial world would "fall to pieces under the deft, merciless touch of a (half-) Jew" named Marcel Proust.

MARCEL PROUST, who began life as a snob, soon became the great anatomist and equally great contemner of snobbery. "The juxtaposition of surface elegance and hidden corruption," as Caroline Weber writes, "would become a defining feature of his portrayal of the *monde.*" Princesse Bibesco takes the Duchesse de Guermantes to be the heroine of Proust's novel. She turns out to be quite the reverse. Proust's narrator begins "genuinely in love with" the Duchesse. As the novel proceeds, her flaws are ticked off and their number mounts. In the third volume, *The Guermantes Way*, Proust writes that she "despised rank in her speech while ready to honor it by her actions." Her put-downs of others, famous in her circle as evidence of wit, he, the narrator, views as fired by "genuine malice" by which "I was revolted." Her pretense to culture turns out to be just that—pretense, little more. This noble soul, human poem, rare flower, the Duchesse de Guermantes, with her taste for provocation, can say of the Dreyfus Affair: "I think you're all equally tiresome about this wretched case. It can't make any difference to me as far as the Jews are concerned, for the simple reason that I don't know any of them and I intend to remain in that state of blissful ignorance." In *Time Regained*, his novel's final volume, Proust describes the Duchesse as having "more head than heart," which is distinctly no compliment. "You're entirely wrong," Proust once told an admiring reader, "if you think the Duchesse de Guermantes a good-hearted woman."

All paradises, as Proust taught, are lost paradises. Many among them are mistaken for paradise to begin with. That of the *belle époque*, as every reader of *In Search of Lost Time* discovers, and will now have reinforced by Caroline Weber's excellent book, was prominent among the latter.

Denis Diderot

(2019)

VOLTAIRE, ROUSSEAU, MONTESQUIEU are the names most readily associated with the eighteenth-century French Enlightenment. Denis Diderot, though less well known than the members of this intellectual triumvirate, may ultimately have had a greater effect on the formation of Enlightenment than any of them. *Philosophe* is the rubric under which Diderot's name generally falls, never to be confused with the title philosopher. "In the eighteenth century," writes James Fowler, editor of *New Essays on Diderot*, "the word *philosophe* connoted a man of ideas but also a man of action, a would-be agent of social and political change, a champion of progress."

Which is what Denis Diderot thought himself and which he was. A literary man of all work—author of novels, plays, philosophical dialogues, art and theater criticism, and more—Diderot was the intellectual *par excellence*. His most substantial work was that on what has come to be known as the great French *Encyclopédie*. As its chief editor over the course of a quarter of a century Diderot saw its seventeen volumes containing 71,818 articles and eleven further volumes containing 2,885 plates through to publication against the always looming threat of censorship and continuous financial struggle. Among the *Encyclopédie's* 150 contributors were D'Alembert, Helvitius, d'Holbach,

Turgot, Quesnay, Rousseau, Montesquieu, Buffon, Condorcet, and Voltaire, an eighteenth century all-star literary and philosophical vaudeville. Diderot himself wrote, among others, the articles "Nature," "The Will," "The Soul," "Political Authority," "Eclectism," "Dictonary," and "Encyclopedia."

The *Encylopédie* was read and discussed both abroad and in Paris, where, in the words of Harold Nicolson, "in the drawing rooms of Madame de Lambert, Madame de Tencin, Madame du Deffand, Madame Geoffrin, and Madamoiselle de l'Epinasse the intellectuals discussed little else." More than a source of information, the work was a *sub rosa* political document, and as such a significant agent of change. The purpose behind it, as Diderot wrote, was "*changer la facon commune de penser,*" or to change the manner in which people thought. In his article "Encylopedia," Diderot wrote that "this is a work that cannot be completed except by a society of men of letters and skilled workmen, each working separately on his own part, but all bound together solely by their zeal for the best interests of the human race and a feeling of mutual good will."

The *Encylopédie* was perforce "a *sub rosa* political document" because its true intention was to secularize thought during a time when the Church and monarchy were supreme in France and in much of Europe. What Diderot and his confreres thought "the best interests of the human race" were not shared by the Church, monarchy, and much of the aristocracy. To make their views prevail the latter had the weapon of censorship on their side. Censorship in that day had real muscle behind it; prison, even execution, could accompany it. Before he took up editorship of the *Encylopédie,* Diderot served three months in prison for an early essay called "Letter on the Blind for the Use of Those Who See," and never afterward wrote without looking over his shoulder.

Born in 1713 in the town of Langres in Burgundy, Denis Diderot was the son of a cutler who specialized in knives and surgical instruments. His father was set on Denis one day joining the priesthood, and at ten years old he was sent off to a Jesuit *collége.* At twelve he went through the ceremony of tonsuring. But the anti-authority impulse in the youthful Diderot was too strong for him ever to become a priest, and, though he completed the education required for the priesthood, he dropped away before taking final vows. He next took up the study of law, but with similarly incomplete results. When asked what he wanted to do with his life, Diderot is supposed to have replied, "Nothing, nothing at all. I like to study; I am very happy, very content; I don't ask for anything else." He was, as the future would bear out, the ultimate freelance.

As a freelance, the young Diderot scrabbled out a living. He did translations from the Greek and English (among them Shaftesbury's *An Inquiry Concerning Virtue or Merit*), a bit of writing of his own (his essay on Blindness, his book, contra Pascal, *Philosophical Thoughts*), tutored the children of the rich, and read widely in literature and philosophy and science. Isacc Newton, with his emphasis on experimentation, the figure from whom it is sometimes said the European Enlightenment begins, was a potent influence on him.

Diderot claimed that the two great mistakes of his life were his marriage and the twenty-five years he gave to steering the *Encylopédie* to completion. His marriage at the age of thirty to Anne-Antoinette Champion was opposed by both their parents, and eventually, alas too late, came to be opposed by each of them. A harridan, relentless in her complaints, jealous, with a violent temper, she was, to put it gently, no comfort at all. They had four children, three of whom died; the one surviving child, their daughter Angelique, Diderot loved dearly.

Mistresses in eighteenth-century France were nearly as common as cellphones in twenty-first; everybody seemed to have one. Diderot was no exception. Some of his love affairs lasted longer than others. One, begun when he was forty-two with a thirty-eight-year old spinster named Sophie Volland, who was said to have been the love of his life. Not notably attractive physically, she had a lively and penetrating mind. In his recent biography, *Diderot and the Art of Thinking Freely*, Andrew S. Curran writes that Diderot "cherished the fact that he could treat her as he might another (male) *philosophe*: she was honest and brainy, and blessed with, as one of Diderot's *Encyclopédie* colleagues put it, 'the quick wit of a demon.'" So much did Sophie Volland meet the desideratum of a male mind in a woman's body that she was known, as Curran reports, as "the hermaphrodite." The relationship, he adds, was stronger on the spiritual than on the physical side. Diderot was haunted by the possibility that the woman he loved more than any other might have been in a lesbian relationship with her younger sister. He would go on to other love affairs, his relationship with Sophie Volland cooling and settling into the platonic. But their love for each other never died out. In her will she left him her eight-volume set of the *Essays* of Montaigne and a ring she loved.

In the early pages of his *Catherine & Diderot* Robert Zaretsky calls Diderot a *mensch*, a Yiddish word with richly complex meanings. Deriving from the German *mentsch* for man, in Yiddish *mensch* becomes a clear approbative, a man of honor and integrity, but it also means a real, a genuine person, someone who is even possibly flawed but has known travail, yet has come through not only intact but all the better, all the more human, for it. And so it seems with Denis Diderot, who most of his days feared censorship, underwent financial struggle until Catherine the Great bailed him out by buying his library and appointing him its salaried librarian, returned at night to a complaining wife. Diderot was indeed a *mensch*, something one would never think to call Voltaire or Rousseau.

Diderot had his enemies, personal, institutional, ideological. He loathed superstition, under which category he placed much of the religion of his time. "Religion," he declared, "is a buttress which always ends up bringing down the house." He went from seminarian, to deist, to atheist, though he was never a proselytizing atheist. (The word "agnostic," it turns out, did not enter the language until 1869, when it was coined by T. H. Huxley.) Diderot was an early opponent of colonization and of slavery in all its forms, from Russian to American. He thought liberty a gift bestowed upon all; unlike Voltaire who didn't mind a benign monarch, Diderot was opposed to monarchy *tout court*, certainly all monarchy justified by the divine right to kingship. "No man has by nature been given the right to command others," he wrote. "Liberty is a gift from heaven, and every member of the same species has the right to enjoy it as soon as he is in possession of reason."

In his even-handed and well-written biography, Andrew Curran portrays a tireless Diderot, a battler under the flag of reason, carrying lifelong a torch for freedom. He accounts for Diderot's uneven fame, even in our time, through his strangely erratic publishing history. Diderot wrote no

one great book—no *Social Contract,* no *Spirit of the Laws*, no *Candide*—
that might ensure his popular or permanent reputation. Much of what he
did write, out of worry about the persecution that might come his way
through censorship, was published posthumously. "Diderot's unedited
books, essays, and criticism," Curran writes, "far surpassed what he had
published during his lifetime." Many of these, Curran adds, only "trick-
led out over the course of decades." *Rameau's Nephew,* doubtless his best-
known work, made its first public appearance in German, translated by
Goethe in 1804, well before it appeared in its original French, and even
then the true manuscript in Diderot's hand wasn't recovered until 1891
and printed as he intended it until much later.

Many of these writings were censorable in Diderot's day, and a few
would get an R-rating in ours. All three of his novels are of interest, yet
none is quite a success. The first, *The Indiscreet Jewels,* is a fantasy about
a prince in the Congo given a magic ring that, when aimed at a woman,
grants her vagina (her jewel) uninhibited speech. An amusing idea, but
the problem is that it turns out the jewels haven't all that much interesting to say. Some jewels decry being overused, some underused. Muzzles
for jewels are soon invented to prevent their indiscretions. Diderot later
inserted a few further chapters to give the novel philosophical weight:
one in which the prince's consort dwells on the question of the residence of the soul in the body; another in which the ring is turned on
the prince's favorite mare, which presents a problem in translation from
animal to human language. Loftier critics than I see in *Indiscreet Jewels* a fable about hermeneutics, or interpretation, but as fiction the book
doesn't quite really come off.

Diderot's next two novels, *Jacques the Fatalist and His Master* and *The
Nun* could scarcely be more different from each other. The latter was
written under the influence of Samuel Richardson's *Clarissa,* the former
under that of Laurence Sterne's *Tristam Shandy.* Diderot's fiction was
more strongly influenced by English than French literature; and Goethe
thought his true affinity was with German literature.

The Nun, written in the mode of naturalism, is about a young woman
forced to live her life in a convent, presumably to expiate her mother's
sin in having her out of wedlock, and is grimly anti-theological in its

message. *Jacques the Fatalist* is, like *Tristam Shandy*, a satire on the very notion of storytelling. In the novel characters' stories are always being interrupted, most never get finished, to remind the reader how arbitrary the telling of any tale is. Diderot pops in from time to time to remind his reader that he neglected to inform him of important details, or one character will ask another why he loathes character studies. At one point the reader (addressed as You) is told that he is "the one with the dirty mind"; at another the Master tells Jacques that "I doubt if there is another head under the vast canvas of heaven that's stuffed as full of paradoxical notions as yours."

If Diderot's fiction has a central flaw, it is that it is too obviously driven by ideas. In the best fiction, ideas arisen naturally out of the moral conflict, out of the development of fictional characters and their tribulations and victories and defeats and what they learn from them. With Diderot's fiction one has the sense that ideas not story is driving the bus.

Which is perhaps why those of Diderot's compositions known as dialogues often show him at his best. In these dialogues—among them are *Rameau's Nephew, Supplement to Bougainville's Voyage, D'Alembert's Dream, A Conversation between a Father and His Children*—Diderot often plays the mischievous intellectual, questioning such fundamental beliefs as the necessary outlawing of incest, the importance of living up to the law, the superiority of the virtuous life. *Supplement to Bougainville's Voyage*, Diderot's addition to the travelogue of Louis-Antoine de Bougainville who circumnavigated the globe from 1766–1769, for example, is a conversation between a Tahitian wise man and the chaplain from Bougainville's ship. When the chaplain tells the Tahitian, whom Diderot gives the name Orou, about the nature of the European God, Orou answers, "He sounds to me like a father that doesn't care very much for his children. . . ." In *Rameau's Nephew*, the ne're-do-well nephew of the famous musician, who openly avows a life given over to pleasure, says to his Diderot-like inerlocator in the dialogue, "Imagine the universe good and philosophical, and admit that it would be devilishly dull" and posits that the point of life was "to keep emptying one's bowels easily, freely, copiously, every night." In *A Conversation between a Father and His Children*, the father reports discovering a long lost will that deprived poor relatives of an inheritance and does the conventionally correct thing by turning it in to the authorities, which gets from his son—called in the dialogue Diderot the Philosopher—the response that "philosophy is silent when the law is absurd." At the dialogue's close Diderot whispers in his father's ear that "the point is that when you come right down to it, there are no laws for a wise man." This is the subversive Diderot, always interesting, never easily dismissed.

Did Diderot think himself primarily an artist, a philosopher, a social scientist *avant la lettre?* We cannot know. We do know that toward the end of his life he thought himself, in the tradition of Plato and Seneca, a counselor to sovereigns. (Recall that Plato's mission to Syracuse to advise the tyrant Dionysius II ended in failure and Seneca's to advise Nero ended in Seneca's being commanded to take his own life.) Diderot's mission was to Catherine the Great, empress of all the Russias, described with great economy and ironic penetration by Robert Zaretsky in *Catherine & Diderot,* is another record of the failure of philosophy to alter the path of power.

Catherine assumed the throne of Russia in 1762 after the suspicious death of her husband Peter III. The initial reason given for the altogether inadequate Peter's death was hemorrhoidal colic. We learn from Robert Zaretzsky, though, that Peter was in fact assassinated by Alexei Orlov, one of Catherine's lovers, and the castle guards. Catherine was thirty-three at the time, and—well-read, thoughtful, and not in the least shy of power—ready to rule.

Francophile in her intellectual interests, Catherine had earlier established connections with Voltaire and the sculptor Pierre-Etienne Falconet (who did the grand equestrian sculpture of Peter the Great that stands in Saint Petersburg); she was an admirer of the writing of Montesquieu. She knew Diderot through his art criticism, and commissioned him to buy many of those paintings that would later become some of the central works of the Hermitage.

Diderot recommended Falconet to Catherine, and so when in 1776 she called on him to visit her in Saint Petersburg it was not altogether a surprise invitation. She had earlier bought his personal library, which she allowed him to keep in Paris until his death. Diderot viewed the invitation as an opportunity to put his own ideas into action through an already half-enlightened monarch. In his relation with Catherine, Zaretzsky writes, "Diderot sought the role not of Solon, but of Socrates." He also assumed powers of persuasion and charm he ultimately did not possess.

The reviews on Diderot's charm are mixed. The *salonnière* Madame Geoffrin, who eventually outlawed Diderot from her salon, reported to a friend that "he is always like a man in a dream, and who believes everything he has dreamed." The playwright and literary critic Jean-Francoise de La Harpe found Diderot altogether too delighted with his own conversation and, in Robert Zaretzsky's paraphrase, "he was his own most ardent and attentive listener." This view seems to have been partially seconded by Diderot, who of himself said, "I'm high-minded and, on occasion, come across great and powerful ideas that I convey in striking fashion." Note the "on occasion."

Once arrived in Saint Petersburg, Diderot met each afternoon from 3:00 to 5:00 with Catherine. She was initially much taken with him. "Diderot's imagination, I find," she told Voltaire, "is inexhaustible. I place him among the most extraordinary men who have ever lived." He in turn described her as possessing "the soul of Caesar and all the charms of Cleopatra." During their sessions together he in his intellectual passion often grabbed her arms, slapped her legs, and she soon complained that "I cannot get out of my conversations with him without having my thighs bruise black and blue. I have been obliged to put a table between him and me to keep myself and my limbs out of range of his gesticulation." In his rambles, she reported, "at times he seems to be one hundred years old, but at others he doesn't seem to be ten."

About what did Diderot harangue the Empress? About the evils of serfdom, the need to do away with censorship, the centrality of law, the baleful effects of religion, the importance of education, in short, the standard enlightenment program. He felt his message was getting across. The empress, he noted "loves the truth with all her soul, and although I have at times told truths that rarely reach the ears of kings, she has never been wounded." Fascinated by him Catherine may have been, but he sensed that, as Andrew Curran puts it, "she was not taking his ideas to heart." When he queried her about not having put any of what he told her in effect, she replied: "In your plans for reform, you forget the difference between our two roles: you work only on paper, which consents to anything: it is smooth and flexible and offers no obstacles either to your imagination or to your pen, whereas I, poor empress, work on human skin, which is far more prickly and sensitive." After a visit of five months, between October 1773 and March 1774, Diderot departed Russia, writing to his friend Mme. Necker that "I would be an ingrate if I spoke ill of it, and I would be a liar if I spoke well of it."

Diderot seems to have spent his final decade under the shadow of failing health. This, though, did not greatly reduce his high literary productivity. He wrote a 500-odd page study of Seneca; he is said to have contributed substantially to Guillaume Thomas Raynal's *History of the Two Indies*. He held out hope that his ideas would find seed in America. He connected with Benjamin Franklin, though it is less than clear that the two men ever met. He allowed that he had failed to produce a single masterwork, yet, according to Andrew Curran, held out the hope that his ideas "would change society for the better." Toward the end his summed up his final views: "There is only one virtue, justice; one duty, to make oneself happy; and one corollary, not to exaggerate the importance of one's life and not to fear death." Earlier he had written: "I will be able to tell myself that I contributed as much as possible to the happiness of my fellow men, and prepared, perhaps from afar, the improvement of their lot. This sweet thought will for me take the place of glory. It will be the charm of my old age and the consolation of my final moment."

Toward the very close of *Catherine & Diderot* Robert Zaretzsky notes that Montesquieu portrayed society as it was, Diderot as it ought to be. Diderot, his mind always on the future, may be said to have lived in the *ought*. He died five years before the French Revolution, which subscribed to many of his central ideas, yet he could hardly have approved of the mass killings known as The Terror that followed that cataclysmic event. What would he have made of the fate of these same ideas in the centuries since his death, centuries that featured the demise of monarchy, the lessening of the power of religion, the rise of democracy, but also the eruption of world wars, the emergence of murderous totalitarianism, the invention of weapons of mass destruction? Would he have recognized that his beloved reason alone, as far as it goes, never goes far enough?

Diderot's daughter remembers the last words she heard from her father: "The first step toward philosophy is incredulity." Were Denis Diderot alive to consider the world of our day, he might wish to add that the final step toward philosophy also happens to be incredulity.

Isaiah Berlin

(2016)

What are you? You call yourself a thinker, I suppose.

R. H. S. Crossman to Isaiah Berlin

PROLIXITY, THY NAME IS ISAIAH, last name Berlin. So one feels
on coming to the last letter in the four-volume collection of the
letters of Isaiah Berlin, edited with sedulousness and unstinting devotion by Henry Hardy. A former editor at Oxford University
Press, Hardy, not long after meeting Berlin in 1972, took it upon himself to gather together Berlin's various writings, which today, nearly two
decades after his death, fill up no fewer than seventeen books, including
ten reissues of his older books. He has now come to the end of editing
these letters. No writer or scholar has ever been better served by an editor
than Isaiah Berlin by Henry Hardy.

I write "writer or scholar," but it is less than clear whether Berlin was
one or the other, or for that matter if he were either. Berlin began his
university life as a philosopher, in the age of British analytic philosophy, which, though he recognized its usefulness, he found too arid for
his tastes, altogether too dead-ended. He gradually came to the conclusion that he wanted a subject "in which one could hope to know more at
the end of one's life than when one had begun." He turned to traditional
political philosophy, which led him to his ultimate general subject, his
passion: the history of ideas.

As for his own contribution to this history, Berlin is credited with formulating the useful distinction between negative and positive liberty. Negative liberty covers that part of life—private life, chiefly—not covered by coercion or interference by the state, allowing freedom to act upon one's desires so long as they don't encroach upon the freedom of others. Positive liberty is that entailed in choosing one's government, which in turn determines in what parts of life interference and coercion ought to be applied to the lives of citizens in pursuit of what is deemed the common good. Much has been written about this distinction by contemporary philosophers, not a little of it disputatious.

The other idea associated with Berlin's political thought is pluralism, sometimes denoted "value pluralism," holding that useful values can be, and often are, in conflict. Berlin was opposed to the notion that the central questions of human life can have one answer. Wallace Stevens's "lunatic of one idea" was not for him. In a talk called "Message to the Twenty-First Century," read on his behalf at the University of Toronto in 1994, three years before his death, Berlin wrote:

> if these ultimate human values by which we live are to be pursued, then compromises, trade-offs, arrangements have to be made if the worst is not to happen.... My point is that some values clash: the ends pursued by human beings are all generated by our common nature, but their pursuit has to to some degree controlled—liberty and the pursuit of happiness ... may not be fully compatible with each other, nor are liberty, equality, and fraternity.

"The Hedgehog and the Fox" is Berlin's most famous essay, taking off from an epigraph supplied by the 7th-century BCE Greek poet Archilochus: "The fox knows many things, but the hedgehog knows one big thing." The essay is on the intellectual travail of Leo Tolstoy—a natural fox in Berlin's reading, who, in his search for the unifying principle controlling the multiplicity of human actions, longed to be a hedgehog. The temptation of hedgehoggery was never one to which Berlin himself succumbed.

Fructifying as these ideas have been, it is not as a political philosopher that Berlin is chiefly of interest. He was instead that less easily defined phenomenon, a *flâneur* of the mind, an intellectual celebrity in three different nations, England, America, and Israel, a personage, no less—yet perhaps not all that much more. As for his reputation in England, the twenty-seven-year-old Berlin, anticipating his own career, recounts telling Maurice Bowra "that in Oxford and Cambridge only personalities counted, and not posts, and that striking and original figures always overshadowed dim professors etc." He was himself nothing if not striking; it is only his originality that is in question.

In many ways Berlin, as he would have been the first to say, led a charmed life. Born in 1909 in Riga, Latvia, the only surviving child of a successful Jewish lumber merchant, he and his family, after a brief stay in the Soviet Union, departed in 1921 for England. A tubby boy, with a lame arm caused at birth by an obstetrician's ineptitude, a foreigner in a land not without its strong strain of xenophobia and anti-Semitism, the young Isaiah Berlin carefully negotiated his way up the slippery slope to eminence. He gained entrance to St. Paul's School in London, thence to Corpus Christi, Oxford, and thence to an early fellowship at All Souls, the first Jewish fellow in the history of that college. He waited until his mid-forties to marry Aline Halban, *née* Gunzbourg, a woman whose substantial wealth allowed him to live out his days in great comfort, amidst costly paintings and servants, and putting him permanently out of the financial wars.

Gregarious and charming, Berlin met everyone: Sigmund Freud, Chaim Weizmann, Winston Churchill, David Ben-Gurion, Felix Frankfurter, Igor Stravinsky, Jacqueline Kennedy, Anna Akhmatova, Boris Pasternak . . . the list goes on. Less a Casanova than a Mercurio, he found his way into the select circles of such women as Marietta Tree, Sibyl Colefax, and Emerald Cunard. Before long Berlin himself became a name others wished to add to their own lists of social and intellectual collectibles.

Awards and honors rained down upon him: the presidency of the British Academy, honorary degrees, festschrifts, doctoral dissertations written about his works, an Order of Merit, international prizes, headship of Wolfson (a new Oxford college), all this and more—and yet none of it was sufficient to convince Berlin that he was a figure of the first quality. Self-deprecation is a *leitmotif* that plays throughout his letters over nearly seventy years. "I am quite clear that such career as I have had was securely founded on being overestimated," he wrote toward the end of his life to the archeologist John Hilton.

One might suspect this to be false humility on Berlin's part. From the evidence abundantly supplied by his letters, however, he genuinely felt himself, as a thinker, a scholar, a writer, and a Jew in England, a nowhere man. Berlin kept no diary; he wrote neither autobiography nor memoirs, though he produced a book, *Personal Impressions* (1980), of portraits of friends and famous men he had known. His letters are the closest thing of his we shall have in the line of introspection. They are a gallimaufry, a jumble, an extraordinary mixture of attack, sycophancy, resentment, confessions of weakness, gossip, exaggeration, generosity, kindliness, superior intellectual penetration, and character analysis.

Although the four volumes of Berlin's letters run to more than 2,000 pages, these published letters, Mr. Hardy informs us, are a selection merely and scarcely all of his letters. These letters give us insight into Berlin's character that Michael Ignatieff's biography, *Isaiah Berlin* (1998)—researched while its subject was alive and published at his request posthumously—fails to give. The letters emphasize Berlin's doubts and failings and are far removed from Ignatieff's hero worship.

The letters make plain why Berlin never wrote the great book every serious intellectual with scholarly pretensions hopes to write. "I really must try and achieve one solid work—say a study of [Vissarion] Belinsky [the 19th-century Russian literary critic]—and not scatter myself in all these directions all over the place," he wrote. In 1981 to Joseph Alsop he confesses: "Occasionally I wonder how many years I have left," and "will I be able to write a big book in the years left to me, and does it matter whether I can or not?" He never did.

Other impressive intellectual figures in Berlin's generation failed to write the masterwork everyone thought was in them, Hugh Trevor-Roper, Maurice Bowra, Arnaldo Momigliano, and Edward Shils among them. Why these extraordinary men failed to do so remains a mystery, but in Berlin's case it is clear that he talked and dawdled and scribbled it away in correspondence. Even his prodigious letter writing, he claimed, was a form of stalling. "Answering letters, in fact, is a kind of drug," he wrote to one of his stepsons, "great relief from real work."

The letters themselves tend to be vast rambles. To a lifelong correspondent named Rowland Burdon-Muller, Berlin writes: "Forgive me if I do not write you a long letter," and then proceeds to write him a long letter. To Margaret Paul, an economics tutor at St. Hilda's College, he writes: "By nature I like to say too much, to exaggerate, embellish, inflate." In this same letter he goes on to do just that. To the novelist Elizabeth Bowen he writes: "Please forgive me. I write on and on as I talk, and how tiresome that must often be. . . . I really must not go on and on." To Felix Frankfurter: "God knows why I go on—maundering like this."

Everyone who ever met Isaiah Berlin remarked on his rapid-fire, glittering, torrential talk. Edmund Wilson, in his journal, writes that Berlin showed up at his, Wilson's, London hotel and talked uninterruptedly for nearly two hours. "He won't, where the competition is easily overpowered and he can get the bit between his teeth, allow anyone else to talk; you have to cut down through his continuous flow determinedly, loudly and emphatically, and he will soon snatch the ball away from you by not waiting for you to finish but seizing on some new association of ideas to go off on some new line of thought." Later in his journal Wilson added: "His desire to know about everybody and everything seems to become more and more compulsive." Coming from Edmund Wilson, himself a famous monologist, this is strong criticism.

Berlin's loquacity was transformed into verbosity in his writing. Had the government ever declared a tax on adjectives, he would have had to declare bankruptcy. Triplets in adjectives, nouns, clauses were his specialty. Here is a sample sentence from "The Hedgehog and the Fox," a splendid essay that would nonetheless gain from being cut by at least a third: "With it [Tolstoy's attitude toward history] went an incurable love of the concrete, the empirical, the verifiable, and an instinctive distrust of the abstract, the impalpable, the supernatural—in short an early tendency to a scientific and positivist approach, unfriendly to romanticism, abstract formulations, metaphysics." Berlin was a man to whom it was not unnatural to append a postscript three times the length of the letter itself. From Harvard he writes to his wife about his being asked at a dinner party to say "a few words" about the current political situation, to which he responded: "'No, no, I cannot make a short statement. Are you asking me to say a few words?' Everyone laughed, I hope happily."

T. S. Eliot somewhere notes that every good letter should contain an indiscretion. Berlin's letters score high on this criterion. "Plauderei [chatty gossip] is my natural medium," Berlin writes in one of them. A sideline interest in these letters is Berlin's take-downs of people to whom he writes with great intimacy in other letters. Of the aforementioned Rowland Burdon-Muller, a wealthy homosexual with radical political views, he writes to Alice James, daughter-in-law of William James, that he "gets me down no less than you," and that he is, though "genuinely civilised, not a little snobbish and talks too much." To this same Burdon-Muller, he writes of the philosopher Stuart Hampshire, whom he genuinely liked, that he is about to deliver a lecture "suitably enough on 'Emotion and Expression,' or something of the kind, which sounds more like his own personality than like philosophy." Of Noel Annan, one of his intimates, he writes to Marion Frankfurter, "I am glad you like Annan—who hasn't much substance but a certain amount of sensibility and is the Bloomsbury (official) dauphin and, they hope, commentator." Of the Schlesingers, Arthur and his first wife, Marian, he writes: "She is much more intelligent and a better man in all ways."

Several of the figures in *Personal Impressions* whom he elevates in his high panegyrical style are taken down in his letters. Aldous Huxley, for example, is "enormously unsympathetic, I think." The saintly Albert Einstein of *Personal Impressions* is in the letters "a genius but surely a foolish one with the inhumanity of a child." Maurice Bowra, whom he elsewhere lauds for his nonconformist spirit and role as "a tremendous liberator in our youth," is in the letters this "pathetic, oppressive, demanding, guilt inducing, conversation killing, embarrassing, gross, maddening, at once touching and violently repellent, paranoiac, deaf, blind, thick skinned, easily offended presence." He thanks Felix Frankfurter for sending him a copy of his memoirs, and tells him how much he looks forward to reading it—then writes to Rowland Burdon-Muller that "the vulgarity of the whole thing is exceedingly depressing . . . the book has given me nothing but acute embarrassment." F. Scott Fitzgerald wrote that it was the sign of high intelligence to be able to keep two contradictory ideas in one's mind at the same time;

but to keep two contradictory ideas of the same person is, one should think, rather a different order of business.

Henry Hardy, perpetual counsel for Isaiah Berlin's defense, contradicts the notion that Berlin was a logorrheic, social climbing time-waster, reminding readers of his letters that he published some hundred and fifty essays and gave a great many lectures. But, as Berlin himself acknowledges, he was able to produce written work chiefly under deadline pressure; he likened himself to a taxi, "useless until summoned I stay still." Lecturing was torture for him, only relieved when he lost the use of a vocal cord and had a proper excuse for turning down invitations to give further lectures.

Berlin was one of nature's true extroverts, who flourished on committees, in common rooms, at dinner parties. "I am utterly miserable if alone," he wrote to Stuart Hampshire, "and avoid it now by every possible means." As for his need to please, he allowed toward the end of his life that its source was to be found in his efforts to adapt to a new environment when, as a ten-year-old boy, he emigrated with his family from Riga. Might it also have sprung from his precarious position as a Jew in English intellectual life? In his letters, Berlin is always on the *qui vive* for anti-Semitism, which in England could be found in the highest places. "The upper classes of England, and indeed, in all countries," he wrote to Alistair Cooke, "have a large dose of anti-Semitism circulating in their veins." In England he felt it was to be found in Bloomsbury, in the form of a "club anti-Semitism," not least in Bertrand Russell, E. M. Forster, and Maynard Keynes in whom "it was at once genuine and superficial." (One recalls here Virginia Woolf, in her diary, writing about first meeting Berlin, noting, "a Portuguese Jew, by the look of him.") In government, Ernest Bevin, the trade unionist who became Secretary of State in the Labour government, was no friend of the Jews. Even Winston Churchill was not without his touches of anti-Semitism: "And Winston, too," Berlin writes, again to Alistair Cooke, "who was a stout Zionist, did not particularly like Jews. He may have liked Baruch ... but ... quite definitely thought of them as foreigners of some kind, *metiques*, resident aliens, some of them perfectly nice, but still not Englishmen, not Scotsmen, not Welshmen, not Irishmen—Jews."

Berlin never expressed shame at his Jewishness, nor attempted to hide it in the manner of Proust's character Bloch, who removed all evidence in himself of the "sweet vale of Hebron" and broke the "chains of Israel," and in later life sported a monocle. Berlin was not synagogue-going, except on high holy days; he wanted to but finally could not believe in an afterlife, though to comfort his aged father he claimed that he did. "As for my Jewish roots," he wrote, "they are so deep, so native to me, that it is idle of me to try to identify them." Another time he claimed that Jewishness "was not a burden I ever carried, and not an attribute I ever felt made a difference to my philosophical opinions, to my friendships, to any form of life that I lived."

One wonders if being Jewish didn't confer a permanent insecurity on Berlin. Touchier than a fresh burn, he seems never to have forgotten a bad review of any of his books. He held on to grudges more firmly than an Irishman (in Irish Alzheimer's, the joke goes, one forgets everything but one's grudges). He threatened to sue Robert Craft unless he removed a paragraph on Berlin's loquacity from one of his Stravinsky books, *Dialogues and a Diary* (1963). He sometimes found insult where it is unclear any was intended. When Michael Oakeshott introduced him before a lecture at the London School of Economics by saying, "Listening to him you may be tempted to think you are in the presence of one of the great intellectual *virtuosos* of our time, a Paganini of ideas," Berlin found this to be "ironic disparagement."

Oakeshott remained on Berlin's permanent enemies list. The pro-Soviet historian E. H. Carr was on it; so, too, were Harold Laski, Lillian Hellman, A. L. Rowse, C. P. Snow, and George Steiner, whom he regarded as "having too professional an interest in the Holocaust, and [to] glory in being obsessed by it." He disliked above all Hannah Arendt. "I see nothing in her writings of the slightest interest, and never have." To Derwent May he writes that "she had become conceited, fanatical, and talked terrible nonsense both about Jews and about history in general; and what a strange thing it was that all those intellectuals in New York should be taken in by all this cultural rhetoric." Arendt's *Eichmann in Jerusalem* (1963) he thought, rightly, both "heartless and wrong."

Berlin's Jewishness may also have had to do with his never finding it easy to take strong positions, at least public ones, especially if it might make him enemies. "For reasons that must have been deep in his personality," writes David Pryce-Jones in his memoir *Fault Lines* (2015), "he wanted influence without the attendant publicity. In the absence of civil courage, that necessary virtue, he preferred a strategy of backing into the limelight." In his letters he called the student rebels of the 1960s "barbarians" of little intellectual quality, stirred into action by ennui. He felt much the same about the university campaign for egalitarianism, which in intellectual matters he knew could be fatal. But he wrote or publicly said nothing about this outside his letters. "I am temperamentally liable to compromises," he writes, when what he really means is that he wavers.

Where possible, he did his best to lend respectability to his tergiversations on subjects upon which some might think it impossible to remain neutral. To Morton White, who taught philosophy at Harvard, he writes in 1966:

> You and I and Arthur [Schlesinger]—I feel we are all there, stuck together in some curious middle-of-the-road patch of territory—no clear answers about Vietnam, about Berkeley U., about any of the questions upon which it is so easy and delightful to have clear black or white positions, doomed to be condemned by both sides, accused of vices which we half acknowledge because of general skepticism and doubt about our position, or positions in general, and not because we think them just or fair.

In his eighties, he writes to Henry Hardy that his propensity to please "probably does spring from unconscious efforts to fit myself into a totally new environment in 1919. As it is successful, the need for it evaporates, I suppose, but its traces cannot but remain in all kinds of subconscious, unexpected and perhaps rather central ways." Elsewhere he writes: "I *wish* I had not inherited my father's timorous, rabbity nature! I *can* be brave, but oh after what appalling superhuman struggles with cowardice!" The question is whether Berlin's floundering on most of the key issues of the day was the result of genuine perplexities or of fear of displeasing.

In one of his letters, Berlin allows that in writing about other people he was often guilty of writing about himself. Nowhere does this come through more strongly than in his Romanes Lectures on Russian novelist Ivan Turgenev. Berlin suffered from what I think of as Turgenev Syndrome. Or perhaps Turgenev suffered, *avant la lettre*, from an Isaiah Berlin Syndrome. Each man found himself locked in the middle between radicals and rebels, bureaucrats and tsars (crowned and uncrowned). Both were chary of offending the young. Writing of Turgenev, Berlin might be writing about himself: "audacity was not among his attributes"; he was "by nature cautious, judicious, frightened of all extremes, liable at critical moments to take evasive action"; and "all that was general, abstract, absolute repelled him."

At the center of Berlin's lecture on Turgenev is the reaction aroused against the novelist by the publication of *Fathers and Sons* in 1862, and especially by his portrait of the character Bazarov, the new man of 19th-century Russia, the nihilist, who in his ruthless scientism some claimed to be the first Bolshevik. Those on the right thought Turgenev was glorifying Bazarov; those on the left, that he was ridiculing him. Berlin, in what might again be autobiography, writes:

> It was his irony, his tolerant skepticism, his lack of passion, his 'velvet touch,' above all his determination to avoid too definite a social or political commitment that, in the end, alienated both sides. . . . But, in the end, he could not bring himself to accept their [the radicals'] brutal contempt for art, civilized behavior, for everything that he held dear in European culture.

Berlin closes his Romanes Lectures by defending those, like Turgenev and like himself, who are caught in the middle, arguing that wishing "to speak to both sides is often interpreted as softness, trimming, opportunism, cowardice." He enlists in defense of Turgenev admirable middle-of-the-roaders of whom this accusation was untrue: it "was not true of Erasmus; it was not true of Montaigne; it was not true of Spinoza . . . ; it was not true of the best representatives of the Gironde." He neglects only to say that it is also not true of himself.

In his anti-Communism, Berlin was stalwart. The Communist question was never troubling, for as a young boy he had experienced the levelling brutality of Russian Communism at firsthand. Explaining his anti-Communism to Arthur Schlesinger, Jr., he writes: "No doubt inoculation by the

1917 Revolution was in my case a dominant fact." He considered Stalin's murderousness not a departure but a natural continuation of the policies of Lenin. He considered Stalin even more monstrous than Hitler. To his friend Shirley Anglesey he wrote that the fall of the Soviet Union "is much the best thing that has happened in our lifetime."

About Zionism Berlin had few doubts, and in one of his letters to Marion Frankfurter he writes about Chaim Wiezmann wanting him to join the Israeli government "and abandon all the ludicrous efforts to teach little English boys unnecessary subjects." He was never seriously tempted, and late in life wrote to the Polish historian of ideas Andrzej Walicki that "I know it was no good my going there, that I would sooner or later, and probably sooner, be torn to pieces by contending parties and would be completely frustrated and made totally impotent."

In defense of Israel, he wrote to Karl Miller, then editor of the *London Review of Books*, calling him out for the strong anti-Zionist pieces he was publishing (and which the journal, under its new editor, continues to publish). He gave advice to Teddy Kollek, then mayor of Jerusalem, on how best to handle visiting American and English intellectual eminences, Robert Lowell among them, showing them the best of Israel in the hope of turning them into Israel's defenders.

Berlin wrote strong letters to Noam Chomsky and I. F. Stone arguing with their views on Israel published in the *New York Review of Books*. As he wrote to Mark Bonham Carter about Chomsky, "hatred of all American establishments governs him, I think, much more than thoughts about Israel as such, or fear of a world war triggered off by Israel." Then he adds: "Besides, despite his often-shocking actions, I wish to preserve my remote friendship with him." Why?, one wonders.

I used to think that Berlin's relationship with Robert Silvers, the editor of the *New York Review of Books*, resembled that of a cardinal now lost to history who was asked how he could serve under so miserable a figure as Pope Pius XII, and who answered, "You don't know what I have prevented." In 1970, as Berlin wrote to Arnaldo Momigliano, he conducted Silvers on a carefully planned tour of Israel, including a lengthy meeting with Golda Meir. As with Lowell, it didn't take, and did nothing to alter the anti-Israel line of the *New York Review of Books*, which remains firmly in place in our day. Toward the end of his life, Berlin seemed wobbly even on Israel, for he loathed the conservative Likud government of Menachem Begin and contemned the occupation of the West Bank. "Now of course," he wrote to Kyril Fitzlyon, the British diplomat, "[Israel] has an appalling government of religious bigots and nationalist fanatics, and God knows what will happen." The old Jewish leftist in Berlin, even in regard to Israel, never quite died.

To judge Berlin solely, or even chiefly, by his opinions would be reductive. His letters reveal him to be a deeply cultivated man. Music meant a great deal to him, and his knowledge of it was considerable. Like most serious historians and social scientists of any quality, he was steeped in literature, and sophisticated and subtle in his judgment of it. At another time he might have been a first-rate literary critic. He preferred Tolstoy over Dostoyevsky, remarking, "Tolstoy is always sunlight even in his most severe and tragic passages—Dostoyevsky is always night. . . . It is with relief that I stop reading him, and return to ordinary life." He notes the want of poetry in Balzac. He prefers Proust over James, adding that the former is braver, "and indeed one has to be in French which does not allow emotional timorousness to be translated into such indeterminate vagueness as English." To his friend Jean Floud he writes: "I cannot take more of the Bellow-Kazin-Malamud-Roth regional culture; it is too claustrophobic, sticky, hideously self-indulgent."

The four volumes of letters are also filled with lovely tidbits. Berlin reports Patrick Shaw-Stewart saying of Lady Diana Cooper that "she has no heart but her head was in the right place." About A.L. Rowse, he writes:

> The thing about Rowse which is not so often noticed is that underneath the nonsense, the vanity, the ludicrous and dotty and boring egotistical layers, he is quite a nasty man—very cruel to those who do not recognize his genius if they are weak and defenseless, and filled with hatred if they are in any degree formidable: a man who, I think, has some of the temperament of genius without a spark of genius, which is quite difficult to live with.

In a brilliant *aperçu*, he sets out the sonata form that after-dinner speeches take: "First light matter, allegro; then grave things which you really wish to impart, if any; then, allegro again, jokes, light matter, desire to please the audience; and in some awful cases a rondo, i.e. you go back to the beginning and start again." In a letter to Arthur Schlesinger, he offers the best short definition of democracy I know: "the government, or those in power, have systematically to curry favor with the citizens for fear of being thrown out."

It is difficult to determine how, precisely, Isaiah Berlin judged his own life. He did not have a high opinion of his writing. In a letter to Noel Annan, he remarks that after his retirement from the presidency of Wolfson College "I shall spend some time on some very obscure topics in the field of history of ideas—at once obscure and difficult without scholarly training, pedantic without being precise, general without being of interest to anyone outside a very narrow circle." Elsewhere he notes that what he has written will be little more than the stuff of other people's footnotes.

The fate of England saddened him. In one of his letters he likens the Englishmen visiting America to Greeks visiting Rome. "Ex-empires are curious places in which to live," he writes to Shirley Anglesey, "or indeed flourish." In his sixties he complained he had no one to look up to; in his early eighties he asks, "Why must the end of my life be covered in this growing darkness?" His was a remarkable generation of writers and scholars, included among them Hugh Trevor-Roper, A. J. Ayer, Evelyn Waugh, A. J. P. Taylor, Stuart Hampshire, Lewis Namier, and Elizabeth Bowen—the last gasp, really, of an English aristocratic intellectual tradition that would be replaced, dismally, by Margaret Drabble and Christopher Hitchens, A. S. Byatt and Terry Eagleton. He wrote to Stalin's daughter that "the *vieille Angleterre*, the civilized aristocrats, the marvelous novelists and poets, the urbane, cultivated statemen—that England, believe me, is no more." Berlin was lucky not to have lived on to our day, when England appears to have become the country of Sir Elton John and Sir Mick Jagger.

To the end of his life Berlin received honorary degrees—evidence, he felt, "that I am harmless." Nearing eighty-seven, he wrote to Ruth Chang, a young American philosophy professor, that he could not care less how he is remembered: "I do not mind in the least if I am completely forgotten—I really mean that." Poor Isaiah Berlin, all his life he played it safe, gave pleasure to his friends, took care to make no enemies in important quarters, and would seem to have won all the world's rewards, except the feeling of self-satisfaction that comes with solid accomplishment and courageous action.

Johnson-Boswell

(2019)

W HAT HISTORICAL ERA produced the greatest aggregate
of human intelligence? Fifth century BCE Greece provided
Socrates and Plato, Pericles and Phidias? In 18th-century
France there were the *philsophes*, among them D'Alembert, Diderot, Voltaire, Helvtius. The founding generation of the republic—Jefferson, Madison, Hamilton, and Adams—would be America's entry. My own choice
would be for the middle and late 18th-century London, where Samuel
Johnson, Edmund Burke, Edward Gibbon, Joshua Reynolds, Oliver Goldsmith, James Boswell, David Garrick, Charles James Fox, Adam Smith,
David Hume, and Richard Brinsley Sheridan walked the streets. These
men knew one another well and, with the exception of Hume, belonged
to the same club, which met on Friday evenings at the Turk's Head Tavern,
at 9 Gerard Street, off the Strand. Here was a club that even Groucho, who
claimed he wouldn't care to belong to any club that would accept him as a
member, could not have resisted joining.

The two founding members of the Club, or the Literary Club as it is
sometimes known, were Joshua Reynolds and Samuel Johnson, the always
generous Reynolds proposing it to Johnson in 1764 in the hope of helping
lift him out of one of his fairly regular bouts of depression. The original
notion was to limit the Club to nine members, though this number would

expand in later years. Convivial talk on a wide range of subjects—contentious politics only not encouraged—was the reason for the formation of the Club. (In his *Dictionary*, Johnson defined a club as "an assembly of good fellows, meeting under certain conditions.") Dinner would be served, wine drunk, wits matched. The most notable among these wits were those of Johnson and Edmund Burke, of whom Johnson said "his stream of mind is perpetual." Not all the members were of equal distinction. Boswell was not allowed membership until 1773, and this based less on his merit than on his friendship with Johnson. The prospect of women members was never up for discussion.

The Club is the ostensible subject of Leo Damrosch's excellent book. I write "ostensible" because the Club itself gets very little direct attention in Professor Damrosch's pages, despite its giving him his title. Several pages in the book are devoted to Henry and Hester Thrale, who offered Johnson a second home late in his life. The novelist Fanny Burney, who wrote trenchantly on Johnson, is included, and so, too David Hume. The real subject of *The Club* is literary life in England in the second half of the 18th century.

Leo Damrosch has written books on the Quakers, William Blake, Rousseau, Swift, Tocqueville, and others. In his career he has achieved the ideal set that many years ago by Jacques Barzun for academic publication at Columbia: that of impeccable scholarship at the service of absolute lucidity, resulting in work that can be enjoyed by thoughtful readers both inside and outside the academy. *The Club* is such a work—learned, penetrating, a pleasure to read.

As Samuel Johnson seems to have dominated every room he ever entered, so does he dominate Professor Damrosch's book, which might have been titled Samuel Johnson & Friends. One friend in particular, James Boswell, is also heavily featured. The oddest of odd couples, Boswell and Johnson, each owing his lasting fame to the other. "If Boswell found in Johnson the father he should have had," Professor Damrosch writes, "Johnson found in him the son he never had." But more than a father-and-son relation was entailed. Without his biography of Johnson, Boswell would today be regarded a third- or fourth-tier figure in English literature, his highly readable journals perhaps never having found a publisher. Without Boswell's biography, Samuel Johnson the essayist and lexicographer would not have anything like the high standing he does today. Boswell's unrelenting sychophancy paid off handsomely for both men.

Those of us who know Samuel Johnson from Boswell's *Life* and the excellent biographies of him by Walter Jackson Bate and John Wain will enounter a familiar figure in Leo Damrosch's pages. Bulky, unkempt, with a laugh, as the bookseller Thomas Davies noted, "like a rhinocerus," suffering relentless tics and twitches—Professor Damrosch speculates that he may have been obsessive-compulsive—Johnson had over a long life scrofula, nerve damage, asthma, rheumatoid arthritis, emphysema, gout, and more. Johnson was not everywhere admired. Neither Boswell's father nor his wife thought well of him, and the latter, apropos her husband's relation with Johnson, remarked that "I have seen many a bear led by a man, but I never before saw a man led by a bear."

Johnson has been accused of speaking less for conversation than for victory. This alone might seem off-putting were it not that nearly everything he said was so dazzlingly intelligent. He said that "no man but a blockhead ever wrote, except for money," yet he also said that "the only end of writing is to enable the readers better able to enjoy life, or better to endure it." His put-downs, in person or in print, were memorable. After praising *Paradise Lost*, in his *Lives of the Poets*, he added that "no one wished it longer than it is." Of a minor and now forgotten poet named George Stepney, he concluded, in a remark perhaps even more useful when contemplating many of the swollen reputations of our day, "one cannot always find the reason for which the world has sometimes conspired to squander praise." Politically conservative, he said that "most schemes of political improvement are very laughable things."

Samuel Johnson was an orthodox Christian, Church of England, down the line. "For him," Leo Damrosch writes, "every one of the doctrines of Christianity was true, confirmed by the evidence recorded in the Bible and by later fathers of the Church. But that meant that the skepticism Johnson showed in every other context had to be firmly suppressed in this one."

He was, more important to note, a genuinely good Christian, a man who took in desolate people off the streets and brought them home to live with him for extended stays at his lodgings at Bolt Court. At the same time he loathed infidels. He held David Hume's deism against him, and he never forgave his fellow clubman Gibbon his irreverent pages on the rise of Christianity in *Decline and Fall of the Roman Empire*. (Professor Damrosch defends Gibbon from the charge of being anti-Christian, noting that he much admired Jesus, but just didn't happen to believe he was the son of God.) When David Hume's serene death was reported to him by Boswell, Johnson responded that he, Hume, lied, saying that it was "a very improbable thing [that] a man should not be afraid of death; of going into an unknown state and not being uneasy at leaving all that he knew." So vehement was his response that Boswell, in his *Life,* remarks that "I seemed to myself like the man who had put his head into the lion's mouth a great many times with perfect safety, but at last had it bit off." Johnson, for all his wisdom and religious fervor, was terrified of death.

May 16, 1763 was the fateful day on which Boswell, then twenty-three, met Samuel Johnson, who was fifty-four. Johnson was already famous, Boswell aflame with unconcentrated ambition. Over the next twenty-one years of their relationship, the younger man would perfect the role of *nudje,* or relentless pest, bombarding Johnson with endless questions, goading him into conversation. On the subject of Johnson, Hester Thrale felt "curiosity carried Boswell farther than it ever carried any mortal breathing." In his biography of Johnson, John Wain wrote that "where ordinary bad taste leaves off, Boswell began."

Professor Damrosch thinks Boswell may have been bipolar, and given his impressive mood swings, from dark depression to conquistadorial enthusiasm, alternately vastly insecure and brashly confident, he may well be right. A dandy in the realm of clothes, quite possibly an alocholic, a whoremonger of some regularity, with two illegitimate children to his (dis)credit, Boswell is said to have suffered no fewer than seventeen bouts of syphilis. Syphilis and his drinking brought him to death, eleven years after Johnson, at the age of fifty-four.

"Johnson insisted on reason and self-control," writes Leo Damrosch, nicely capturing the boldface differences between the two men, "Boswell reveled in emotional 'sensibility' and seized gratification whenever he could. Johnson aspired to what he called 'the grandeur of generality" and Boswell to specificity and piquant details. Johnson crafted language in the carefully assembled building blocks of the periodic style, Boswell's style was conversational and free."

While Samuel Johnson and James Boswell are center stage in *The Club* Adam Smith, Edmund Burke, Joshua Reynolds, and David Garrick weave in and out of the story, chiefly in their relation to Johnson. Hester Thrale figures significantly, for giving Johnson safe harbor and sympathy at Streatham, her successful brewery owner husband's country estate, where he wrote his greatest work, *Lives of The Poets*. Johnson's comments on these contemporaries are often generous. Of Oliver Goldsmith, who was not especially well-spoken, Johnson said: "No man was more foolish when he had not a pen in his hand, or more wise when he had." Apart from Joshua Reynold's heavy boozing, Johnson found no flaws in him, and Boswell reports that Johnson told him that "Sir Joshua Reynolds was the most invulnerable man he knew, the man with whom if you should quarrel, you would find the most difficulty how to abuse."

Johnson was unreserved in his admiration for Edmund Burke's intellect—"you could not stand five minutes with that man beneath a shed while it rained," he said, "but you must be convinced you had been standing with the greatest man you had ever seen"—but he deplored Burke's penchant for puns. He called Adam Smith "as dull a dog as he had ever met with," but then Smith was in religion a deist, and Johnson felt deism a grievous error. As Professor Damrosch notes, "Johnson was a moralist, reflecting on how people ought to act; Smith was a social scientist, analyzing how they did act." In his *Dictionary*, Johnson defined a moralist as "one who teaches the duties of life."

The Club is filled with interesting oddments. In its pages we learn, for example, that David Garrick, the actor of the age, was 5'3" and not especially good-looking. That Hester Thrale's husband Henry died, at fifty-two, of gluttony. That the word "unclubbable," to describe an unsociable person, was first applied, by Johnson, to Sir John Hawkins, a solicitor and an original member of the Club who later wrote a biography of Johnson. That Johnson, along with the ragtag lot of lost human beings in his lodgings, kept a cat named Hodge. Then there are the illustrations, thirty-one elegant color plates and scores of black-and-white drawings of the book's *dramatis personae* and their *mises-en-scenes* scattered throughout this splendid book.

Reading *The Club* and about its illustrious members one cannot help wondering if a similar institution were possible in our country in our day. I have tried to imagine it, but, across the breadth of our vast land, can come up with only three possible members, first among them, of course, myself.

Stop Your Blubbering

(2019)

PHILOSOPHY, OR PHILOSOPHIA, from Latin via Greek, means love of wisdom, a love that seems always to have been present in human beings. Yet for all its lengthy history, philosophy appears to have achieved little in the way of settled progress. "Philosophy, from the earliest times," Bertrand Russell wrote, "has made greater claims, and achieved fewer results, than any other branch of learning." Scientists are wont to say that they stand on the shoulders of giants, their work built on the discoveries of their predecessors, but philosophers have been more likely to do their best to demolish the work of theirs. New philosophies enter the world as heresies, and heresy is at the heart of the activity of philosophy itself.

Traditional histories of philosophy tend to crush interest in the subject. Juggling all those "isms" (materialism, naturalism, idealism and the rest), distinguishing among the various "ists" (absolutists, positivists, pragmatists and the others) does not get one any closer to answering the questions that are likely to have brought one to philosophy in the first place: Why do we exist? How do we know what we know? Are there any ordering higher principles behind the discordant experiences we all undergo? What, finally, is the meaning of life?

Jonathan Ree's "Witcraft: The Invention of Philosophy in English" derives its title from a 16th-century clergyman named Ralph Lever who, in arguing for setting aside Latin as the language of the educated and replacing it with English, wrote a book about logic and dialect that he also called "Witcraft." "I hope to persuade you," Mr. Ree writes, "that philosophy in English contains far more variety, invention, originality, and oddity than it is usually credited with." In his attempt to break away from "the condescending complacency of traditional histories," he adds, "I hope my stories will bring out the ordinariness of philosophy, as well as its magnificence and its power to change people's lives. And I hope you will end up seeing it as a carnival rather than a museum: an unruly parade of free spirits, inviting you to join in and make something new."

Mr. Ree fulfills these claims through his wide learning and impressive ability to make the most abstract, not to say abstruse, philosophy intelligible to those of us not, so to say, in the business. He smoothly interweaves the lives and the thoughts of the philosophers he writes about into a continuous and lively story. Added to this is his consideration, often brief, sometimes lengthy, of writers and intellectuals—Thomas Browne, William Hazlitt, Tocqueville, Emerson, Thomas Carlyle, George Eliot, D. H. Lawrence, W. H. Auden—not normally considered philosophers, but whose concerns and in some instances temperaments were inherently philosophical. Cameo roles in Mr. Ree's pages are played by key philosophers outside the English tradition—Kant, Comte, Kierkegaard, Marx, Nietzsche, later Frege, Heidegger and Husserl, Benedetto Croce, and of course Plato and Aristotle—who are brought in for their effect on the main line of philosophy in English.

That line begins in earnest with Francis Bacon (1561–626) and runs, citing only its main figures, through Thomas Hobbes, John Locke, David Hume, Adam Smith, John Stuart Mill, Herbert Spencer, and William James. It ends with Bertrand Russell, Ludwig Wittgenstein (an Austrian who spent much the better part of his adult life in England), and the schools of analytical philosophy that swept Cambridge and Oxford in the mid-twentieth century. Mr. Rees also brings into his story many subsidiary characters, likely to be unknown to those rank amateurs, or philosophasts, among us, as Thomas Davidson. A man whose influence was greater than his written achievement, Davidson (1840–1900), through teaching and public lecturing and personal magnetism, played a serious role in the thinking of philosophers as disparate as William James and Morris Raphael Cohen, and is nicely revived here by Mr. Ree.

In this grand cavalcade of intellect, the Scottish David Hume (1711–1776) seems to have possessed the most purely philosophical mind and temperament. Schopenhauer held that one can learn philosophy but to philosophize the mind must be "truly disengaged; it must prosecute no particular aim or goal, and thus be free of enticement of will, but devote itself undividedly to the instruction which the perceptible world and its own consciousness imparts to it." Hume fits this qualification precisely. He came to think of philosophy as "a private pursuit rather than an impersonal inquiry." Hume was a sceptic who believed one must be skeptical even about skepticism.

"To Philosophize Is to Know How to Die" is the title of one of Montaigne's most famous essays, and no one appears to have died more philosophically than David Hume. Mr. Ree quotes James Boswell's famous description of Hume on his deathbed, looking lean and ghastly, but nonetheless placid and cheerful, without the least belief in, or desire for, immortality. "I could not but be assailed by momentary doubts," Boswell wrote, "while I had actually before me a man of such strong abilities and extensive inquiry dying in the persuasion of being annihilated." When Boswell reported Hume's composure on the cusp of death to Samuel Johnson, Johnson assured him that Hume had lied. But then Johnson, a true Christian, lived in terror of death, while Hume, a true philosopher, went calmly into oblivion.

Religion and philosophy have long been in open if not always acknowledged competition, a point that plays through "Witcraft." Religion by its nature precludes philosophy, making it unnecessary by confidently answering all the great philosophical questions and providing the last word about the great philosophical subjects: reality, truth, beauty, goodness. In its early years in Europe, philosophy was by its nature a radical activity, always in danger of stepping out of bounds, either by questioning religion or threatening to replace it. The early English philosophers, living in a thoroughly Christianized society, needed to tread carefully lest religious sensibilities be aroused against them, which they frequently were.

The *sub rosa* antagonism between religion and philosophy is revealed on religion's side in Martin Luther's remark that "any potter knows more than him [Aristotle]," and in John Donne, who, in Mr. Ree's words, "considered philosophy closer to music than theology. . . ." The English Puritans viewed philosophy as anti-Christian, while in Holland Spinoza was excommunicated by the Jews. Until late into the nineteenth century, religion remained firmly in command. David Hume, who was no Christian but not entirely an atheist either—Thomas Henry Huxley coined the word "agnostic" only as late as 1869—remarked that "errors in religion are dangerous; those in philosophy only ridiculous."

As religion declined from its position of pervasive dominance, philosophy did not correspondingly rise. The two, religion and philosophy, were never armies of thought openly battling to the death. Philosophy's position vis-à-vis religion was generally less a direct attack than a sniper operation. But during the twentieth century, philosophy tended to retreat—to all but vanish, some would say, up its own bottom.

This came about through philosophy's new interiority—its questioning of its own assumptions, premises, tools. Among the assumptions up for questioning were such basic items as numbers, colors and chiefly words themselves. By the close of the nineteenth century metaphysics, with its concentration on first principles and on the higher abstract concepts, had been defeated by the British empiricists, pragmatists, logical positivists and others. Then there appeared Ludwig Wittgenstein, perhaps the only authentic genius among modern philosophers.

"The difficulty in philosophy," Wittgenstein held, "is to say no more than we know." His aim, as Mr. Ree puts it, "was to trace the limits of thought, and forestall any urge to go beyond them"; or, in Wittgenstein's own admonitory words, "wherefore one cannot speak, therefore one must be silent." The silence Wittgenstein called for within philosophy was deafening—though Bertrand Russell, who in later years was often at odds with Wittgenstein, remarked that "Mr. Wittgenstein manages to say a great deal about what cannot be said."

Wittgenstein dominates the last 150-or-so pages of "Witcraft." Apart from being the most significant figure in modern philosophy, Wittgenstein is a fascinating human specimen. The scion of a wealthy family, he gave away much of his inheritance. He abandoned philosophy to fight five years on the side of Austria in World War I. For no fewer than six years, he left a fellowship at Cambridge to teach 11-year-old students in Westphalia. Wittgenstein held H. G. Wells, Albert Einstein, and Bertrand Russell to be three of the greatest vendors of nonsense of his time. As philosophy everywhere began to settle into standard university departments, he, Wittgenstein, kept to his own course, contemptuous of academic philosophy, independent until his death in 1951 at age sixty-two.

Philosophy, Wittgenstein thought, "ought to be treated as poetry, art." His own ostensibly modest view of the goal of philosophy was "to get rid of a particular kind of puzzlement"—that brought about by imprecision in language leading to muzzy thought. In one of his famous similes, he held philosophy was "more like tidying up a room" than "building a house." He believed "it is not enough to state the truth, you must find the path from error to truth." Comparing himself to Hegel, Wittgenstein remarked that "my interest is always in showing that things that look alike are really different," where Hegel was "always wanting to say that things that look different are alike."

Wittgenstein did not write books, at least not in the conventional sense of compositions in which paragraph follows paragraph, chapter follows chapter. His preferred form was the sentence. Many of these sentences are highly technical ("'pq' only makes sense if 'pvq' makes sense"), their meanings well beyond the mental grasp of this philosophast; others are in the form of questions; several feature paradox; a few attain to dazzling aphorism. In Wittgenstein's "Notebooks 1914–1916" one finds that "My method is not to sunder the hard from the soft, but to see the hardness of the soft." Or: "It is one of the chief skills of the philosopher not to occupy himself with questions which do not concern him." Or: "All theories that say: 'This is how it must be, otherwise we could not philosophize' or 'otherwise we surely could not live,' etc. etc., must of course disappear." His first work, the *Tractatus Logico-Philosophicus*, begins, "the world is all that is the case"—to which the poet Donald Hall retorted, "Now stop your blubbering and wash your face." One feels that Wittgenstein would have enjoyed the riposte.

Next to the lively periods over which, in its long history, it has passed, philosophy in English (and one gathers in every other language) is now onto dull days. At present there are no towering figures, no fruitful heresies, no new schools that command the attention of those outside the academy. Jonathan Ree does not predict its future. But he has no need to do so; his lively chronicle of philosophy in English is a splendid accomplishment sufficient onto itself. Highly intelligent, always even-handed, quietly but consistently witty, *Witocracy* is an excellent guide along the twisted path of human thought.

George Gershwin

(2009)

A

LL GENIUS IS INEXPLICABLE, with some genius more inexplicable than others. George Gershwin, a genius of the natural kind, falls into the latter category. The second son of a Eastern European Jewish family—the father, a man of all hustle, ran bakeries, Turkish baths, a cigar store and pool parlor, was briefly a bookie, the mother had no special interest in culture or talent for music—Gershwin had only to sit down at a piano in his boyhood to realize that in music lay his destiny.

Like many vastly talented people, school could not accommodate him, so he dropped out at fifteen, and went to work plugging songs. Soon he was writing them. At the age of twenty-one, he had his first hit, "Swanee," with lyrics by Irving Caesar, later to be made boringly famous by Al Jolson.

The variety of George Gershwin's music, from his early tossed-off Tin Pan Alley songs to his classical compositions, is inexhaustible yet all unmistakably his. Random and easy though he made it look, Gershwin was never without a plan. "There had been so much chatter about the limitations of jazz," he wrote. "Jazz, they said, had to be in strict time. It had to cling to dance rhythms. I resolved to kill that misconception with one sturdy blow." The blow, successfully administered, was *Rhapsody in Blue.*

Throughout his brief life—he died in 1937 at the age of thirty-eight—Gershwin had the golden touch, which never deserted him. The phenomenon of George Gershwin astonished everyone—not least Gershwin himself. He was famous for his immodesty, except in him it came off as something else, self-amazement perhaps. "You know the extraordinary thing about my mother," he once said, "she's so modest about me." When a friend in Hollywood was driving wildly, Gershwin alerted him: "Careful, man, you have Gershwin in the car." Listening for the first time to a full orchestral rendering of *Porgy and Bess,* he exclaimed: "This music is so wonderful, so beautiful that I can hardly believe I wrote it."

Not F. Scott Fitzgerald but George Gershwin may have been the reigning figure of the jazz age. Gershwin holding forth at the piano at parties in Manhattan, everyone gathered around, as if by magnetic force, were among the symbolic tableau of the 1920s. S. N. Behrman, the playwright and memoirist, described his reaction when he first heard Gershwin at one such party: "I felt on the instant, when he sat down to play, the newness, the humor, above all the great heady surf of vitality. The room became freshly oxygenated; everybody felt it, everybody breathed it."

Gershwin did everything with the throttle all the way out. As a golfer, he is said to have run between holes. He could compose intricate music in a crowded room; in fact, preferred to do it that way. His being less than conventionally handsome—he had a chosen nose and a pendulous lower lip, with an early receding hairline—did not get in the way of his notable success with women. Money from his music royalties rained down upon him, and he spent it lavishly on clothes, townhouses, dashing cars.

Walter Rimler's *George Gershwin, An Intimate Portrait* tells the story of its subject's life and career with an admirable economy and an impressive feeling for the complexities of Gershwin's character and the twists in his career. More thorough biographies exist—Edward Jablonski's *Gershwin* at 436 pages, Howard Pollack's *George Gershwin, His Life and Work* weighing in at 882 pages—but for those of us interested less in the technical details of Gershwin's music and its performance and more by the comet called George Gershwin that blazed briefly across American skies, Mr. Rimler is the astronomer of choice. He writes well, is quietly authoritative (he is also the author of *The Gershwin Companion*), and while discriminating in his selection of details never loses the larger subject, which is the trajectory of George Gershwin's extraordinary life.

Mr. Rimler remarks in an author's note at the conclusion of his book that Gershwin's was "as personal and original a musical voice as Chopin's" and the question about his career was not whether he would "choose between jazz or classical, songs or concert works"; no "the conflict, rather, was about whether he could make full use of his powers. . . ." By this he means how deeply could he develop his astonishing musical gift.

Three stories play through Mr. Rimler's book: one is Gershwin's lengthy love affair with a brilliant woman named Kay Swift; the second is his relationship, musical and personal, with his brother Ira; and the third is his travail in getting *Porgy and Bess* composed, launched and properly appreciated as a great American opera.

Kay Swift, when Gershwin first met her, was Katharine Swift Warburg, married to James Warburg, a scion of the famous banking family and a man who longed for a life in art. She was the mother of three daughters, bright, attractive, a talented musician, in fact a composer herself—she was the first woman to write a successful Broadway musical—and thus well positioned to understand Gershwin's achievement. A nice notion of the kind of woman Kay Swift was is conveyed in Mr. Rimler's quoting her on whether Gershwin knew he had a masterpiece in the works while composing *Porgy and Bess*, when she compares it to "watching a pitcher who has a no-hitter going for him. He knows it and you know it; and, in the case of George Gershwin, as in that of the pitcher, nobody mentions the fact at the time."

Their love affair was an entirely open secret, a fact far from painless to her husband. When the Warburgs divorced, Gershwin, who valued his freedom, perhaps too much, did not step forth to marry Kay, probably, Mr. Rimler suggests, a mistake. Unlike tennis, golf, and gin rummy, monogamy wasn't Gershwin's game.

Ira was George Gershwin's older brother, and in every way different from him. Where George was brash, Ira was bashful; where George was free-spirited, Ira was under the control of his strong-willed wife; where George was a full symphony orchestra of self-esteem, Ira refused to blow his own horn. Where they meshed beautifully was in the realm of talent. Ira Gershwin may have been the greatest lyricist in the history of American popular song, a man born to translate his brother's joyous music into words, which he did with an infallible touch.

Porgy and Bess was George Gershwin's great gamble, in which he set out to stake his claim to being a great American composer. With a few exceptions, Gershwin had always been treated as a bit of an interloper by contemporary classical composers. Prokofiev spoke slightingly of his *Second Concerto*. Copland excluded him from a festival of the works of modern composers at Yaddo. Virgil Thomson wrote crushingly of *Porgy and Bess* that "it is clear, by now, that Gershwin hasn't learned the business of being a serious composer, which one has always gathered to be the business he wanted to learn. . . ." though he spoke more kindly of him off the record. Ravel, one of the exceptions, delighted in Gershwin's music and recommended him to Nadia Boulanger, the great teacher of serious composers. She claimed that she had nothing to teach Gershwin, a remark that Mr. Rimler holds is "open to interpretation": did it mean he was too advanced to require her aid, or did she instead deem him hopeless?

While marking the zenith of Gershwin's musical accomplishment, *Porgy and Bess* also signaled the beginning of his fall. Confusion set in to begin with over whether the work was meant to be a musical or an opera; that it carried the subtitle "a folk opera" served only to confuse matters. The reviews, led by that of the *New York Times*'s Olin Downes, were unenthusiastic. Crowds stayed away, even when ticket prices were lowered. "There was no need," Mr. Rimler writes, "to spend one's dollars on what had been deemed a pretentious hodgepodge."

In a state of post-flop depression, Gershwin went off to Hollywood to write for Metro-Goldwyn-Mayer, though he never gave up the hope of a revival of *Porgy and Bess*. Such was the elasticity of his musical talent that he could go from writing serious formal music to movie music without a hitch. He knocked off "Nice Work If You Can Get It" soon after his *Porgy and Bess* debacle, and Mr. Rimler claims that "just about everything he had written since beginning work on *Porgy and Bess* had been a masterpiece."

With his characteristic *joie de vivre*, Gershwin enjoyed Hollywood, the weather, the golf, the women; he had an earnest flirtation with Paulette Goddard. Only the work was dreary—and foolishly unappreciated. Samuel Gershwin, that philistine of philistines, instructed Gershwin that he ought to "write hits like Irving Berlin."

All this while a tumor—technically, a "malignant glioblastoma"—was growing in Gershwin's brain. Earlier he had begun to sense the smell of burning garbage; horrific headaches soon set in. His omnipresent energy drained. Several authoritative medical misdiagnoses didn't help. Sam Behrman knew the game was up when, on a visit, he asked Gershwin if he wished to play the piano and he shook his head No.

Why a man whose music has brought so much pleasure to so many people should spend his last days in wretched pain, certain that his life had been a failure, is one of those sad puzzles for which Mr. Rimler nor anyone else has any solution.

Nelson Algren

(2019)

E RNEST HEMINGWAY ONCE CLAIMED that the writer Nelson
Algren "beat Dostoyevsky," but you wouldn't know that from
his relative obscurity today, thirty-eight years after his death in
1981 at the age of seventy-two. Whether the author of *The Man with
the Golden Arm* and *A Walk on the Wild Side* deserves to have so sadly
a faded reputation is not a question taken up by his recent biographer
Colin Asher. In a work of more than 500 pages called *Never a Lovely So
Real*, Asher never treats Algren as other than one of America's great novelists in a great tradition following Theodore Dreiser, James T. Farrell,
and Richard Wright—all of whom, like Algren, found rich soil for their
fiction in the city of Chicago.

Algren has always been identified with Chicago, where he grew up
and lived much the better part of his life. A nearly lifelong Chicagoan
myself, my only (glancing) encounter with him was as a member of the
audience in Mandel Hall at the University of Chicago for a talk he gave
one evening in 1957. All I remember of the talk is its introduction. Algren
was wearing trousers that appeared not to have seen a pressing in the past
decade, a rumbled purplish shirt with a zipper running diagonally across
it, and he looked as if he could do with a shave.

"For twenty-five-dollar talks," I remember him beginning, "I generally
wear pressed pants and a white shirt. For fifty dollars, I'll show up in a

sport jacket. A hundred-dollar talk gets a suit and tie, shined shoes. And for five hundred and above, I'll come if required in a tuxedo." He paused, then said: "I'll let you guess what my fee is for tonight's talk."

Though I can recall none of the talk itself, I believe I can reconstruct its content. I'd wager Algren set out the role of the writer as someone who is the enemy of the conformity and shallow consumerism he viewed as then swamping America. Always the enemy of the status quo, the writer, Algren held, needs to make his readers uncomfortable, dislodge them from their dullish lives with home truths about the suffering in their midst that they have trained themselves to ignore. Algren would likely have attacked American business and the middle class, noting that goals like security and personal comfort are nothing less than a denial of life. The writer must align himself with society's victims, for he is, in his innermost being, a victim himself, whose task is to shake his readers out of their complacency. He must always defend the accused.

I state this with some confidence because I have learned from Asher's biography and a re-reading of many of Algren's works that he was something of a Johnny One-Note, and the song he sang was that America is a mean and wretched place. At one point, he called the country "an imperialist son of a bitch"; he believed, for example, that the price of the Marshall Plan was acceptance on the part of those countries who partook of it of the status of an American colony. In *Conformity,* a book on the role of the writer, he claimed that "we live today in a laboratory of human suffering as vast and terrible as that in which Dickens and Dostoyevsky wrote." Among those not obviously suffering, "never has any people possessed such a superfluity of physical luxuries companied by such a dearth of emotional necessities." Degraded at the bottom, self-alienated everywhere else—such was the America of Nelson Algren's imagination.

Algren came by this song through the accident of the time of his birth. His maturity arrived just in time for the Great Depression. His family was working class, his father owning a small shop that repaired car tires. His father's father had been born in Sweden, and when a young man, under the sway of his own personal messianism, had converted to Judaism, changed his name from Nils Ahlgren to Isaac Ben Abraham, emigrated to America, thence to Israel, thence back to America. Nelson had two older sisters and a mother (*neé* Golda Kalisher) who, in violation of the cliché of clinging Jewish mothers, never thought much of her son. In his twenties Nelson changed his name from Abraham to Algren; he had long before dropped any sense of Jewish affiliation.

Under the insistence of one of his sisters, Bernice, Nelson went off to the University of Illinois, where he took a degree in journalism. The Depression still in sway, he found no work on any of the five Chicago newspapers of the day. He moved on to Minneapolis to look for a newspaper job, but without any better results. Out of work, feeling himself out of luck, he headed down south, via hitchhiking and riding the rails, to New Orleans and from there to Texas, where, apart from occasional work as a fruit picker and a few failed confidence schemes, he essentially lived the life of a drifter.

Algren had been raised to believe, as Colin Asher puts it, "that America was a place where men like him could earn degrees, find steady jobs, and buy homes using loans at a reasonable rate." But, Asher reports, "by the winter of 1933, he had become convinced that the meritocratic ideal was a fraud, that everyone who placed their [sic] faith in it had been fooled, and that he was obliged to reveal that deception." As he would later tell H. E. F. Donohue, in *Conversations with Nelson Algren*, "everything I had been told was wrong."

The lives of the underdog, America's dispossessed, would be Algren's subject. The dispossessed included, as Algren listed them at one point in *The Man with the Golden Arm*, "mush workers and lush workers, catamites and sodomites, bucket workers and bail-jumpers, till tappers, and assistant pickpockets, square johns and copper johns; lamisters and hall-room boys, ancient pious perverts, and old-blown parolees, rapoes and record men; the damned and the undaunted, the jaunty and the condemned." Toss in prostitutes and punchy boxers, junkies and pimps, drug peddlers and hustlers generally. He was interested less in the proletariat than in the *lumpen*-proletariat. What all his characters have in common, as he writes in *The Man with the Golden Arm,* is "the great, secret and special American guilt of owning nothing, nothing at all, in the one land where ownership and virtue are one."

T HROUGH THE CHICAGO CHAPTER of the John Reed Club, a
meeting place for writers, artists, and musicians of revolutionary tendencies, Algren met and befriended Richard Wright and became swept
up in the leftist political movement of the time. "I believed the world was
changing," he said in later years, "and I wanted to help change it." Asher
writes that in these early days Algren was a fairly vigilant "Communist,
pro-Soviet—and he had an unmitigated disdain for anyone who was not."
He seems to have been the type of the sentimental, rather than the rigidly
ideological, Communist. Asher is unclear about whether he was a card-
carrying member of the party. Not widely read—he allowed he much liked
Chekhov though didn't know much about him—it seems doubtful Algren
was steeped in Marxism, or even read Marx. He told H. E. F. Donohue that
"I never joined the Party, but I did a lot of work for them."

Asher goes on at some length about the FBI file on Algren, which runs
to some 886 pages, though he allows that the FBI's interest in him "was
never acute." He also feels that the FBI and the House Un-American Activities Committee played a strong part in setting back Algren's career. Algren
thought that he might have been kept from serving overseas during World
War II, which he didn't do until near the war's end, because of his Communist connections. He also believed that Doubleday, his publisher, rejected the
manuscript for *A Walk on the Wild Side* out of fear of arousing the suspicions
of the House Un-American Activities Committee, which had subpoenaed
him for an interview for which he failed to show up. Asher reports that the
FBI under J. Edgar Hoover continued to monitor Algren: "They talked regularly with his landlords, neighbors, and employers, but they never prepared
charges against him. It's likely he would have faced prison time if he had
attended his interview with HUAC and perjured himself [by denying his
Communist connections], but he remained a free man because he never did."

Through the 1950s, Algren was denied a passport out of the same suspi-
cion that he was a member of the Party. The critic Stuart McCarrell blames
the erosion of Algren's once-legendary love affair with Simone de Beauvoir on the State Department's denying him a passport, which would have
enabled him to spend more time with her. "When it finally did [allow him
a passport] in 1960," McCarrell writes, "it was too late. By then the relationship had changed subtly but decisively. . . . Surely the great love of his life,

she [Beavoir] was his best hope for the long, important, loving relationship that he wanted so much, and never had." The McCarthy era has over the years been blamed for many things, but this is perhaps the only time it has been accused of ruining a man's celebrity love life.

The Algren-Beauvoir love affair is recounted in her novel *The Mandarins*, in which Algren appears, little disguised, as the Chicago writer Lewis Brogan. The two were nicely suited to each other in their differing yet roughly equal distance from reality. He was muddled by his anger at what he took to be the world's unstinting injustice, while she was mesmerized by abstraction as only a French intellectual can be: She thought America meant the atomic bomb and Americans, when not greatly fixated on gadgets, nascent fascists. When she came calling on Algren in Chicago, he didn't at first know who she was, and only discovered her fame when he saw her name in an article in the *New Yorker*. He showed her Chicago, his Chicago, which meant the bars on the skid row of West Madison Street, police lineups, burlesque houses, slums, the epic slaughterhouse that in those years was the stockyards—everything but an execution in the electric chair.

In her novel, Beauvoir gave Algren high marks as a lover. "I used to value pleasure for what it was worth, but I never knew love could be so overwhelming," she wrote. She returned to be with him again in Chicago, he visited with her in Paris and traveled to Spain and elsewhere with her. He wanted her to stay with him, but she, with a career of her own, had *autres oeufs frire*, including an open relationship of sorts with Jean-Paul Sartre. Algren registered his disappointment in a letter in which he told her: "I began to realize that your life belonged to Paris and Sartre. . . . What I've tried to do since is take my life back from you. My life means a lot to me, I don't like it belonging to someone so far off, someone I see only a few weeks every year." In later years, he felt her writing about him was a betrayal, and subsequently, in Asher's words, "downplayed Beauvoir's importance in his life in every forum available, insulted her writing, demeaned her, and consequently made himself seem shallow and sexist."

Algren was married three times, twice to the same woman, and fathered no children. Apart from a stint with the WPA during the Depression, and a year at the University of Iowa Writers Workshop, which he detested, believing as he did that no good writing could ever come out of a university, he held no regular jobs. He lived off his writing: publishers' advances, journalist fees, the less than grand sum that the sale to Hollywood of two of his novels, *The Man with the Golden Arm* and *A Walk on the Wild Side*, brought in (a combined $40,000 for both). His diversions were poker, the race track, watching boxing and baseball. He knew no one, he was rather pleased to acknowledge, who was in business.

His book-length essay of 1951, *Chicago, City on the Make*, begins with some fairly standard colorful bits about old Chicago characters, Hinky Dink, Mickey Finn, Bathhouse John. At the outset, one might even think that, despite all its deficiencies and bad actors, Algren had a deep love for the city, which he compared to "loving a woman with a broken nose, you may find lovelier lovelies. But never a lovely so real." In so thinking, however, you would be wrong.

In Algren's rendering, Carl Sandburg's "city of the big shoulders" has developed a serious slouch, a distinct limp, blackened teeth, and the most frightful halitosis. "In Chicago," he wrote, "our villains have hearts of gold and all our heroes are slightly tainted." The city itself is "a grey subcivilization surrounded by green suburbs," where "every day is D-day under the El." The Chicago that I myself took such pleasure growing up in, with its ethnic neighborhoods, its sense of possibility and adventure open to a boy and young man, its stunning architecture, its gangsters and crooked politicians to be sure but also major cultural institutions like the Chicago Symphony, the Art Institute, the University of Chicago, the city that was in itself a great reality instructor—this Chicago fails to make an appearance in *City on the Make*.

Algren's Chicago is just another machine to grind down the defeated, a city that, in his words, "forever keeps two faces, one for winners and one for losers; one for hustlers and one for squares. . . . One for the sunlit traffic's noontime bustle. And one for midnight subway watchers when stations swing past Ferris wheels of light yet leave the moving window wet with rain or tears." In *City on the Make*, Chicago is in steep decline, a town that "grew up too arrogant, too gullible, too swift to mockery and too slow to love. So careless and so soon careworn, so challenging and yet secretly despairing—how can such a cocksure Johnson of a town catch anybody but a barfly's heart?"

B Y THE TIME OF *CITY ON THE MAKE,* Algren's personal pose had hardened into that of the poet who cannot be conned, the cynic with a heart of gold, the highly sensitive but relentlessly tough guy. His prose would become increasingly purple over the years. This empurpling is a great distraction in what he himself thought his best novel, *The Man with the Golden Arm.* Colin Asher reports that the novel was originally meant to be one of a series of four set in Chicago, one each on the city's Poles, Italians, Negroes, and Mexicans. *Golden Arm* won the first, the inaugural National Book Award for fiction in 1950, and was a best-seller. Yet more people doubtless are aware of the movie that Otto Preminger made from it with Frank Sinatra in 1956. Algren's novel ends with its main character (there are no heroes in Algren), the card dealer Francis Majcinek, better known as Frankie Machine, wanted for murder, a forty-pound monkey on his back from morphine addiction, seeing no way out, and hanging himself. In the movie, Frankie breaks his drug habit, frees himself from his irksome wife (who is assigned the killing he commits in the novel and for which she goes off to jail), and then walks off to start what is assumed to be a fine new life with a plummy Kim Novak, strains of Elmer Bernstein's jazz musical score playing in the background.

Algren said that he worked on *The Man with the Golden Arm* for two years before he came upon the idea of making Frankie Machine a junkie, when it all came together. But does it really come together? *The Man with the Golden Arm* is a novel quite without pace. Algren's lyrical flights, deployed throughout the book, ruin any narrative flow the book might have had. Throughout characters wax poetically in ways they are most unlikely to have done outside an overwritten novel. Frankie's badgering wife Sophie, for example, looks out the window of her apartment to note "moonlight that once had revealed so many stars now showed her only how the city was bound, from southeast to the unknown west, steel upon steel upon steel; how all its rails held the city too tightly to the thousand-girdered El." (Without the El, one sometimes thinks, Algren would have been out of business.) Three more paragraphs in the same vein follow: "The city too seemed a little insane. Crippled and caught and done for with everyone in it."

The milieu of *Golden Arm* is the Polish neighborhood of Chicago. The year is 1943. The characters are Blind Pig, Drunkie John, Sparrow, Meter Reader, Umbrella Man, Nifty Louie, and others—as such names suggest, they are not so much characters as caricaures. Failed similes work their way into the prose, so that "the ragged edge of that careless laughter hung like a ripped scarf upon an iron corner of his heart." Comparably disastrous flights of descriptive fancy play through the stories in *Neon Wilderness* (1947); in "Million-Dollar Brainstorm" we find the chief character, Tiny Zion, a Jewish boxer, sitting "with his head in his hands while the gutter giggled at his feet like a blowzy blonde." Details often misfire or seem incomprehensible, such as the first description of Frankie Machine as a "buffalo-eyed blond," or a "Milwaukee Avenue moon," or an "Ogden Avenue smile." Nelson Algren was not a careful writer.

The character in *Golden Arm* who carries the novel's message is a Chicago police captain named Bednar. During police lineups, he parries the alibis of the small-time crooks who pass before him with wisecracks. But in his heart lies a heavy stone of guilt. Captain Bednar thinks: "All debts had to be paid. Yet for his own there was no currency. All errors must ultimately be punished. Yet for his own, that of saving himself at the cost of others less cunning than himself, the punishment must be simply this: more lost, more fallen, and more alone than any man at all."

At one of his police line-ups, a defrocked preacher, known for cashing bad checks, answers Bednar's question about why he was defrocked by saying, "Because I believe we are all members of one another." In the words of Bettina Drew, an earlier biographer of Algren, "Clearly, we are all members of one another, and that, in a world of survival and oppression, as the critic George Bluestone put it, 'love is the only way that human beings may meaningfully relate. Nothing else is finally reliable.'"

WRITERS FALLING BACK ON THE MESSAGE of the need for universal love is an old story, and in literature never a convincing one. In W.H. Auden's poem, "September 1, 1939," there appeared the line "We must love one another or die." Auden later removed the line, explaining the deletion by remarking that while we can love one another all we want, we are going to die anyway.

Superior fiction makes the unpredictable seem probable. In Algren's fiction, the reverse occurs: The improbable seems predictable. This predictability chills and ultimately kills Algren's fiction. Ordinary people struggling to live upright ordinary lives, to raise families, to accrue accomplishments, to do the right thing often at great cost to themselves, never appear in his writing. Instead, his characters—the underdogs, the accused, the punished—come onto the scene downtrodden and depart defeated. No reversals of fortune occur. No improvement is possible. However wretched the situation, it figures to get worse. In a characteristic paragraph from his story "Design for Departure," a paragraph that could serve as a gloss on the full body of his work, Algren writes about the thoughts of a woman brought up without love and now driven into prostitution:

> For the hall [of a Chicago flop house] like their lives [those of the occupants], was equally gray by daylight or dusk. And daylight here was as gray as the sidewalks of Harrison Street; as endless as South State. Forever crowded with men and women; yet each wandering alone, all night, unwept by any and less than lost. Lost even to themselves. And there were no mourners in the world of the half-forgotten strays. Lost, by the long rain alone remembered. As she, alone, remembered the long rain.

In Algren's fiction, moral conflicts never come into play. No character seems ever to learn anything. Everyone is helpless. The cards are dealt; the game is a nightmare version of five-card stud in which no one is allowed to draw further cards. It's a dismal game, with no winners, and that, sorry to say, includes those kibbitzers hovering around the table, those unhappy few of us in the four decades since his death who have made the mistake of bothering to re-read Nelson Algren.

Essayism

(2018)

IN THE INTRODUCTION to a recent collection of his essays called "The End of the End of the Earth," Jonathan Franzen bemoans the possible end of the personal essay, which he finds currently in eclipse. More and more eschewed by general-interest magazines, "the form," Mr. Franzen writes, "persists mainly in smaller publications that collectively have fewer readers than Margaret Atwood has Twitter followers." The Internet, especially in its social-media aspect, Mr. Franzen believes, swallowed up most of the old autobiographical material of the essay and has been spitting it out in the form of tweets, Facebook entries, Instagram posts, Reddit comments and other vessels favored by those not noted for their lengthy attention spans. But might something else, something deeper, also be undermining the essay?

The essay needs talented practitioners, readers capable of the mental repose required to take pleasure in it, and connoisseurs with an understanding of the rich tradition out of which it derives. What it doesn't need is an "-ism" attached to it. An "-ism" presupposes a theoretical explanation, á la postmodernism, deconstructionism, structuralism and other dreary ismatics of recent decades. Randall Jarrell once defined the novel as "a long prose fiction with something wrong with it." So might one declare the essay a short prose nonfiction with something occasionally delightful about it? Need more be said in a general way about this literary form whose aim is never definitude and whose specialty is specificity?

In *Essayism*, the Irish writer Brian Dillon says a great deal more. He says it, moreover, essayistically, which is to say in rambling, rather disorganized, far-from-complete fashion. Mr. Dillon provides chapters of varying length on "Origins," "Lists," "Style," "Extravagance," "Taste," "Sentences," "Fragment," "Aphorism," "Detail," "Talking to Yourself," "Coherence," "Attention," "Curiosity," "Starting Again." Alas, there are also chapters on "Anxiety," "Melancholy," "Vulnerability" and no fewer than five on "Consolation." What, you might ask—I know I did—have these latter subjects to do with the essay?

In Brian Dillon's case, we soon discover, quite a lot. He is, as he has no compunction about informing us, a depressive, the illness a psychic bequest from his mother, a depressive who died at fifty, though of scleroderma, not depression, when Mr. Dillon was sixteen. His father, he also tells us, died five years later. How, as a reader, does one deal with such sentences of Mr. Dillon's as "Each day I sat at my desk in an office at the end of the garden and cried and smoked and tried to write—tried to write this book—and each day finally gave myself up to fantasies of suicide," and "I think I had learned from my mother how to long for death?" Ought one to admire the courage of a writer who works under such a psychological burden? Or ought one feel he should be charged a psychotherapist's fee for laying all his mental problems on us, strangers who happen to have come upon his book?

Mr. Dillon himself allows that "it's a cliché, of course, the intimacy of writing and depression: writing as cause, cure, or acutest expression." The standard psychological problems that writing presents—in the form of writer's block, neglect on the part of the public, rivalrousness and resentment at the (of course) undeserved success of other writers—are one thing; bringing depression to one's writing, or using writing as a method of curing depression, quite another. Depression is known for using a full-court press: In Mr. Dillon's case this means that his book turns out to be more about it, his depression, than about the essay.

When he does write about the essay, Mr. Dillon's pages on such rich subjects as "Aphorism" or "Sentence" or "Style" too frequently lapse into abstraction, opacity, obscurity. In his three pages on "Style," for example, he refers to the quality he seeks in writers as "this ruined poise." Writing about Elizabeth Hardwick, whom he greatly esteems, he exalts the prose in an essay of hers on Dylan Thomas for its "precise but unpredictable word choices, its deliberately awkward punctuation, something of the emotional intricacy and accusing ambiguity of its subject." "Ruined poise?" "Accusing ambiguity?" Your guess is as good as mine.

If I were Brian Dillon's therapist, the first thing I would tell him is that he has to change his reading habits. The majority of his chapters not devoted to his depression feature comments and quotations from essayists he admires. Almost invariably, these are writers who seek the dark or have themselves been notable for breakdown: Virginia Woolf, E.M. Cioran, Walter Benjamin, Cyril Connolly, Roland Barthes, Susan Sontag, Maeve Brennan, Joan Didion, Anita Brookner, W.G. Sebald and others. These influences are reinforced by his reading of such heavy-breathing critics as Theodor Adorno, Jacques Derrida, Michel Foucault. All have been fashionable in their day, some retain their cachet even now, but are, as Chris Rock remarked after seeing the movie *The Passion of the Christ*, not that funny.

Reading Brian Dillon, considering the writers he adores and those he ignores, one is reminded of William James's division, set out in his *Varieties of Religious Experience*, between the healthy-minded and the soul-sick, which James called "two different conceptions of the universe." The healthy-minded, whether voluntarily or involuntarily, see the world as a rich, interesting, amusing place. To the soul-sick the world "now looks remote, strange, sinister, uncanny. Its color is gone, its breath is cold."

Apart from an early mention of Montaigne, none of the healthy-minded essayists get much play in *Essayism*. Samuel Johnson, Charles Lamb, William Hazlitt, Max Beerbohm, George Orwell, in fact the main line or tradition of the essay in English—these seem not much to interest Mr. Dillon. As he writes in his opening pages, "what I desire in essays . . . is this simultaneity of the acute and the susceptible." What he seeks in his essayists is "at once the wound and a piercing act of precision."

The mention of "the wound" recalls Edmund Wilson 's essay of the 1930s, "Philoctetes: The Wound and the Bow," with its argument that art grows out of neurosis. Some does, of course, a lot doesn't. But the more powerful the neurotic writer, the more detached he becomes from his neurosis, the more impressive his art tends to be. Johnson, a man terrified of death, kept the terror out of his writing. Lamb's insane sister, whom he much loved, killed their mother, but this central event in his life does not weigh down Lamb's charming essays. Hazlitt made a great fool of himself over a chambermaid, but you would not know it from the aggressive virility of his essays. George Orwell in his private life rather specialized in gloom, but no one, reading his essays, would call him a gloomy writer.

William James's brother Henry, in an essay on Turgenev, notes that when we read a writer we want to know what he thinks of the world: "The great question as to a poet or a novelist is, How does he feel about life? what, in the last analysis, is his philosophy? . . . This is the most interesting thing their works offer us. Details are interesting in proportion as they contribute to make it clear."

If this is true of poets and novelists, it is perhaps even truer of the essayist. He, the essayist, presents himself unshielded by meter and rhyme, unclothed by the fabrications of dazzling tale telling. The essayist has only his felicity with words, his dedication to truthfulness and above all his point of view—and it is enough. Or at least it has been for the best essayists.

The essayist is allowed to be familiar, with the understanding that familiarity differs crucially from being personal. What has changed in recent years, and not in the essay alone, is the new penchant among writers for the uncomfortably personal, chiefly residing in confession. The great essayists have also been great adepts of tact, with bone knowledge of precisely how much of themselves they should reveal, how much to hold back. They did not foist their sadnesses on their readers, did not feature their weaknesses. In contemporary writing, consummate tact has been replaced by constant confession. Contemporary writers, essayists among them, provide us with accounts of their sexual kinks, their addictions, their longings, the nightmares of their childhoods, their mental illnesses. Balzac called the artist, by which he meant chiefly the writer, a prince among men; today the prince has increasingly become a patient.

Of all literary forms, this penchant for the therapeutic is most deadly for the essay. The relationship of essayist to reader has long been that of equal to equal, adult to adult, no condescension exercised, no special dispensations asked. With the triumph of the therapeutic, to use Philip Rieff's phrase, this has changed in many quarters of our culture, and the essayist has turned the reader, in effect, into silent therapist, sympathetic ear, soft shoulder upon which to cry. In the bargain writing has become therapy by other means.

In a letter of 1969 to a teacher who asked his opinion of what pedagogical method is likely to make for good writers, Lionel Trilling wrote:

> Writing well—I don't mean writing 'creatively'—has to begin as an ideal of the self: it means wanting to be a certain kind of person, the kind of person who sounds a certain way, who has a certain relation to language. If that desire isn't instilled by the general culture—if, that is, the general culture doesn't value that kind of person—no amount of pedagogy will make a student write well.

In writing this, did Trilling sense that something has happened to our culture to change the old notion of the writer as adult, strong, independent-minded, a leader in thought, into little more than someone sharing his troubles?

Brian Dillon's *Essayism* is both an exemplar and a casualty of the therapeutic culture's influence on literature in general and on the essay in particular. May his depression soon lift and depart, so that he may get up off the couch and return to the serious work of writing.

Alcibiades

(2019)

ALCIBIADES WILL ALWAYS have a prominent place in the rogues'
gallery of history. Son of Cleinias, nephew and, after his father's
death at the Battle of Coronea, ward of Pericles, he was at different times the enemy of three competing empires: the Athenian, the
Spartan, the Persian. A rogue is not necessarily villainous, but he is aber-
rant, unpredictable, often attractive, rarely dull. He is also, inevitably, in
business for himself. Alcibiades qualifies on all counts. A note of dubiety
is struck straight off by Thucydides when he first introduces Alcibiades
more than halfway through his *History of the Peloponnesian War.* There we
are told that Alcibiades was the leader of the opposition to the Athenian
treaty signed with Sparta in 421 BCE, which initiated the so-called Peace
of Nicias before being abandoned in 414. He felt his own participation
in the war leading up to the peace had been ignored because of his youth,
and that "considerations of his own dignity affected his opposition to the
peace with Sparta." History, for Alcibiades, was, in the cant phrase of our
day, all about him.

Nemesis, David Stuttard's biography of Alcibiades, sets out, in admirably clear detail, the twists and turns in the life of its subject. Stuttard, an
Englishman, is an independent scholar (someone doing serious scholarship without a permanent university affiliation) devoted to the worthy
mission of popularizing classical subjects, through books, translation,

and directing plays. *Nemesis*, as its author allows, is a book "not for the specialist but for the general reader," one that he hopes "will prove not just instructive but entertaining, too," and he is correct on both counts.

Such flaws as the book presents are minor, and chief among these is that Stuttard's prose can sometimes lapse into a purple more striking than Alcibiades' robe. He also on occasion avails himself of clipped sentence fragments: "The admiral, Astyochus, had received fresh, urgent orders. From Sparta and King Agis. To put Alcibiades to death." The device is meant to heighten the drama, but its effect is instead to divert one's attention from the action to the author. Stuttard also has what might just be the winning entry in this year's goofy acknowledgments sweepstakes, citing "the crucial role played at all times by our two cats, Stanley and Oliver, as handsome, demanding, and enigmatic as Alcibiades, but considerably more faithful."

Nemesis is a work of synthesis, but one of great scrupulosity. Scarcely a paragraph in the book is without its footnote. These notes refer to the wide literature on the Peloponnesian War generally and to Alcibiades in particular. The three great sources on the latter are Thucydides, Plato, and Plutarch; the first two knew the man; the third (CE 46-120), born nearly 600 years after Alcibiades (born 452 BCE), provides the most complete account. Among current-day writers, Stuttard leans most heavily on the Yale classicist Donald Kagan. Stuttard also mentions in one of his notes a Freudian interpretation of Alcibiades, which I've not yet but should one day be amused to read, if only to discover if Alcibiades suffered an Empire Complex, Pericles Envy, Narcissism, Sex Addiction, or all of the above. The possibilities here are boundless.

ALCIBIADES' WAS THE ART OF SEDUCTION. "As a boy, he enticed husbands from their wives," Stuttard writes, "as a young man, wives from their husbands." As he grew older, the stakes rose, and he set out to seduce entire empires—the Athenian, the Spartan, the Persian in turn— and in each instance met with more than a modicum of success. What he really wanted was dominance over the known world. When he proposed to the Athenians their expedition to conquer Syracuse, he added that, while at it, they might next go on to conquer Carthage. Alcibiades was, *avant la lettre*, an Alexander the Great, but an Alexander *manqué*.

By all accounts Alicibiades had astonishing physical beauty. According to Plutarch, this beauty "bloomed in him in all the ages of his life, in his infancy, in his youth, and in his manhood; and, in the peculiar character becoming to each of these periods, gave him, in every one of them, a grace and a charm." A detailed account of his good looks is not known, but what is certain is that he had the vanity to go along with them. As a youth, he is said to have rejected learning to play the aulos, an oboe-like instrument, because blowing on it distorted his face. He had a lisp, supplying the letter "l" when "r" was indicated. So much admired was he among the young that it is said that the aulos went out of fashion and lisps came into fashion in the Athens of his day.

Alcibiades' relationship with Socrates—they comprised the oddest of odd couples—is not the least fascinating strand of his biography. The philosopher claimed to discern great potential in Alcibiades, and put in much time attempting to bring it out while simultaneously hoping to smother his waywardness. For his part, Alcibiades esteemed Socrates above all men, recognizing his depth and his virtue. In the *Symposium*, Plato, in an ancient world version of a student evaluation, has Alcibiades remark (in Michael Joyce's translation):

> Socrates is the only man in the world who can make me feel ashamed. Because there's no getting away from it, I know I ought to do the things he tells me to: and yet the moment I'm out of his sight I don't care what I do to keep in with the mob. So I dash off like a runaway slave, and keep out of his way as long as I can; and then next time I meet him I remember all that I had to admit the time before, and naturally I feel ashamed. There are times when I'd honestly be glad to hear that he was dead, and yet I know that if he did die I'd be more upset than ever.

At an Athenian expedition to Potidaea, in Macedonia, Alcibiades fell wounded. Socrates, at risk to his own life, stood over him, saving him from the enemy. Yet it was Alcibiades, based in part on his noble birth, and in part on Socrates' recommendation, who was awarded a prize for valor at Potidaea. Later, at the Battle of Delium, Plutarch tells us, when the Athenians were routed, when Socrates with other foot-soldiers was in retreat, "Alcibiades, who was on horseback, observing it, would not pass on, but stayed to shelter him from the danger, and brought him safe off, though the enemy pressed hard upon them, and cut off many."

I N THE *SYMPOSIUM* Plato has Alcibidiades claim to have offered himself to Socrates, an exchange, as Socrates formulates it, of physical for mental qualities. Alcibiades tells of mounting Socrates' couch, wrapping his cloak around him, creeping under [Socrates'] own rather shabby mantle, and—nothing! "[B]elieve it, gentleman, or believe it not," Alcibiades tells the participants in the *Symposium*, "when I got up next morning, I had no more *slept* with Socrates, within the meaning of the act, than if he'd been my father or an elder brother." With the result, Alcibiades concludes, that he felt both humiliation and "admiration for [Socrates'] manliness and self-control, for this was strength of mind such as I had never hoped to meet."

This wasn't sufficient to cause Alcibiades to cease playing the genial screw-off, and to the highest power. Plutarch reports that he "intermingled exorbitant luxury and wantonness, in his eating and drinking and dissolute living." Thucydides, remarking on his extravagance, noted that "most people became frightened at a quality in him which was beyond the normal and showed itself both in the lawlessness of his private life and habits and in the spirit in which he acted on all occasions."

Somehow it seems foolhardy to moralize about Alcibiades. Michel de Montaigne quotes or cites Alcibiades no fewer than ten times in his *Essays*, neither praising nor condemning but largely fascinated by the grandeur and swagger of the man. In *Antiquity Matters* (2017), Frederic Raphael asks whether Alcibiades behaved any worse than other Greeks. Raphael reminds us that Themistocles went over to the Persians, the Spartan king Demaratus traveled with Xerxes, and Achilles, by petulantly withdrawing from the battlefield because Agamemnon appropriated his war trophy (the maiden Briseis), caused the death of many Greeks at Troy.

CORNELIUS NEPOS, in his *Lives of Eminent Commanders* (the Palatine Press edition), notes that Alcibiades was, "when occasion required, laborious, patient, courteous, liberal, and splendid, no less in his public than in his private life; he was also affable and courteous, conforming dexterously to circumstances; but when he had unbent himself, and no reason offered why he should endure the labor of thought, was seen to be luxurious, dissolute, voluptuous, and self-indulgent, so that all wondered there should be such dissimilitude, and so contradictory a nature, in the same man." The standard moral categories, in any case, somehow do not seem to apply to him.

The two express tickets to advancement in the ancient world were military prowess and oratory, and Alcibiades held both. Of his oratorical skills, Stuttard writes that "he would become one of Athens' leading orators," roundly admired for his abilities—"he knew exactly what to say in any situation"—and "in time the whole of Athens regarded them with awe." Oratory is of course, then as now, the art of persuasion, rarely the vehicle of truth. Alcibiades and truth didn't much mix.

Behind Alcibiades' every move—his most cunning calculation, his rashest recklessness—was the motive of personal glory. Of the democratic faction in Athens, no one was more mindful of his own personal fortunes than he. When in 415 he helped argue Athens into its fateful Sicilian expedition, against the sensible warning of the Athenian general Nicias, who saw the folly of Athens entering on two major wars at once, Alcibiades did so chiefly in the hope of self-aggrandizement. As Thucydides reports, his motives were "his desire to hold the command and his hopes that it would be through him that Sicily and Carthage would be conquered—successes which would at the same time bring him personally both wealth and honor." If Alcibiades may seem unattractive when in pursuit of power, it is worth recalling that the only parties less attractive than those pursuing power are those who have already attained it. Plutarch felt that "[c]ertainly, if ever man was ruined by his own glory it was Alcibiades."

When Alcibiades was called back to Athens to stand trial for the destruction of the herms—the statues of Hermes set in public places in the hope of protection from the god—and for his presumably mocking the religious rite known as the Eleusian mysteries, he fled instead to enemy Sparta.

While there he went native, let his hair grow out in the Spartan manner, dispensed with his ornate wardrobe, ate the drear dark porridge that was the staple of the Spartan diet. He advised, quite sensibly, the Spartans on the best military strategy to take up against the Athenians. And to pass the time he seduced and made pregnant Timaea, the wife of the Spartan King Agis. (Spartan women were notoriously free with their favors.) Plutarch reports that Alcibiades "would say, in his vain way, he had not done this thing out of mere wantonness or insult, nor to gratify a passion, but that his race might one day be kings over the Lacedaemonians." Later, when the Spartans, led by the properly resentful Agis, grew suspicious of Alcibiades, he went over to the Persian satrap Tissaphernes, whom he charmed out of his silken trousers. As he had earlier advised the Spartans about how to defeat the Athenians, he now advised the Persians how to weaken both the Athenians and Spartans by allowing them to fight out an under-financed war of attrition.

OWING TO AN ELABORATELY COMPLICATED concatenation of events, of plans made and others gone awry, Alcibiades would return to Athens in 407. This was eight years after the disastrous Sicilian expedition, which he had done so much to promote. He was forty-three. He claimed to long for his native *polis*, and held that he had never truly betrayed it but only the simulacrum of it that existed after his forced departure. When he sailed into the Piraeus, he was greeted with music and flowers as a returning hero. A much-weakened Athens looked to him to restore its grandeur. As Stuttard recounts: "They voted to make him general-in-chief, *strategos autocrator,* with supreme command on land and sea, the most powerful man in Athens . . . . In democratic Athens, it was the greatest honor he could ever hope for, the pinnacle of his ambition."

So great was the esteem in which Alcibiades was now held, so desperate were the Athenians for leadership, that some among them—"the lower and meaner sort of people," in Plutarch's phrasing—wanted to abrogate all the city's laws and allow him to govern as tyrant. Whether this would have been just fine with Alcibiades we cannot know. Cooler heads thought it best to send him on a military mission against the Lacedemonians at Andros. With a fleet of 100 triremes (ancient galleys), he was able to do this easily enough. But the difficulty came when, after this victory, he entrusted this fleet to a lieutenant, one Antiochus, who, against Alcibiades' orders not to engage the Spartans, lost much of it to Lysander at Ephesus. The loss, along with denting his newfound reputation for military infallibility, played into the hands of Alcibiades' enemies at Athens, who were able to bruit about rumors of his luxurious habits and irresponsibility causing the defeat and thus strip him of his supreme command. Once again Alcibiades was in business for himself.

Freelance now, leading a band of mercenaries, he ventured into Thrace, where he won the favor of a local governor named Seuthes, and through him of the Thracian king, Medocus. Stuttard writes that "just as in Persia and in Sparta, he had quickly adopted local customs, so, in Thrace, he effortlessly transformed into a Thracian." Which meant heavy boozing, displays of horsemanship, and whoring—at all of which Alcibiades was long proficient. But soon enough his Thracian gig was up, too, especially after the Athenian defeat at Aegospotami in 405, where the Spartans under Lysander wiped out the entire Athenian fleet of 160 triremes and put to death more than 3,000 Athenian captives. The Peloponnesian War, twenty-seven years long, ended the following year.

A FTER AEGOSPOTAMI, Alcibiades' many enemies coalesced against him: Lysander and Agis in Sparta; Critias, the dominant figure among the Thirty Tyrants put in charge of Athens by the Spartans; and finally, the Persians, who could not afford to harbor him lest doing so damage their peace pact with Sparta. He was on his own, which is to say utterly abandoned. In a house in Sardis, accompanied by two courtesans, he awoke one night to find the smell of smoke in the air and his weapons missing. Naked, armed only with a blanket and his short sword, he ran out of the burning building to meet with a cascade of arrows and javelins. "All Alcibiades could do," Stuttard writes, "was run into the night, and run, and keep on running while he could until the night engulfed him." When they discovered his body, his courtesan lovers, Timandra and Theodote, were unable to close his eyes, for his bloodless head had been lopped off and was presented as a trophy to the Persian satrap Farnavaz, as conclusive evidence of his death.

David Stuttard's biography is well titled. Nemesis, recall, was the Greek goddess who doled out happiness and misery to mortals—a cruel lady who took particular pleasure in visiting disaster on those too richly endowed by nature. She must have spit on her palms and rubbed them enthusiastically together at the prospect presented by Alcibiades. With his good looks, his several talents, his surpassing ambition, his overweening pride, Alcibiades, clearly, was her kind of guy.

Big Bill Tilden

(2016)

AT THE DEATH IN 1953 OF BILL TILDEN, generally acknowledged to have been the best tennis player in the history of the game, the sports columnist Red Smith wrote: "And so it ends, the tale of the gifted, flamboyant, combative, melodramatic, gracious, swaggering, unfortunate man, whose name must always be a symbol of the most colorful period American sports have known." That period, the 1920s and early '30s, was a time when, in their various sports, Babe Ruth, Jack Dempsey, Jim Thorpe, Bobby Jones, and Red Grange were also in their glory. While the fame of these other athletes was largely American, Tilden's was international. Great as Ruth, Dempsey, Thorpe, Jones, and Grange were, only Tilden changed the nature of the game he played. Al Laney, a sportswriter famous in his day, called Bill Tilden "our greatest athlete in any sport," *tout court*. In a 1950 Associated Press poll of the nation's top sportswriters and broadcasters, he was selected as the best tennis player of the first half of the twentieth century—and by a far wider margin than any of the athletes selected for other sports.

The reason that Red Smith, always a careful writer, ended his list of seven adjectives with "unfortunate" has to do with the scandal that marked Bill Tilden's last years and marred much he had accomplished on the courts. One likes to think that achievement outlives scandal, that the former is permanent, the latter ephemeral, but in Tilden's case it is far from certain that this has been so. In an otherwise storied life, the Fates wrote Bill Tilden a dark last chapter.

In November 1946, Tilden's 1942 Packard Clipper was pulled over by a Los Angeles policeman for zigzagging on Sunset Boulevard in Beverly Hills. The policeman discovered Tilden in the passenger seat, his arm around a fourteen-year-old boy at the wheel the four fly buttons on whose trousers were undone. Homosexuality in that less tolerant day than ours would have been troubling enough for Tilden's reputation, but sex of any kind with a minor was, then as now, unforgivable. Richard Maddox, Tilden's lawyer, said at the time that the toughest cases to defend were those that entailed crimes against dogs and children.

Tilden pled guilty not to "lewd and lascivious behavior with a minor" (a felony) but to "contributing to the delinquency of a minor" (a misdemeanor). He was sentenced to five years' probation, the first nine months of which were to be spent in jail. Not quite three years later, Tilden found himself in front of the same judge for similar charges: sex with a minor boy. This time he was sentenced to a full year in jail. All but a few of his old friends deserted him, his earnings through giving tennis lessons to celebrities were greatly curtailed, and in many of his old haunts—country clubs, Hollywood society, his birthplace of Germantown, Pennsylvania—he became *non grata*. The mighty have rarely fallen further.

As for Bill Tilden's mightiness, one need only consult the record book for certification: He is the only man to have won the American singles title six years in a row and seven times *in toto* and the US Clay Court title another seven times. He was America's top-ranked player every year between 1924 and 1934. He played in more Davis Cup matches—twenty-eight—than any other amateur player and was the first American to win at Wimbledon, which he did on three separate occasions, the last time when he was thirty-eight. His various doubles and mixed-doubles championships are nearly beyond counting as are his victories in lesser tournaments. Along the way he invented the drop shot; was the first player precisely to formulate court strategy in a book (said to be the best on its subject ever written, called *Match Play and the Spin of the Ball*); and early advocated open tennis, in which professionals and amateurs could meet in the same tournaments and which is in place today. He found tennis an upper-class, rather prissy country-club weekend activity and left it a sport that captured worldwide attention.

"Big Bill" was Tilden's sobriquet, though at 6-foot-2 and 155 pounds he wasn't as big as all that. (Roger Federer and Rafa Nadal are both 6-foot-1, and five of the currently ranked top-ten male players are 6-foot-5 or above.) The reason for the sobriquet is that Tilden's most insistent rival during his competitive years was a Californian named William Johnston, who was 5-foot-8 and 130 pounds—not as small as all that either—which nonetheless allowed journalists to confer upon him the moniker "Little Bill." Nor did Tilden play, or indeed care for, "big game" tennis, which is built on a powerful serve followed by a rush to the net for a quick kill on the volley. Tilden commanded a thunderous cannonball serve, which he used infrequently, but he much preferred to win from behind the baseline with devastatingly accurate ground strokes, which arrived with a bewildering assortment of chops, slices, spins, and blistering drives that could twist the racquet out of his opponents' hands.

Astonishing in his ability to retrieve shots that appeared to be clear winners, possessing a double-jointed wrist that gave him more than normal racquet control, Tilden was above all a brilliant strategist, able to depress opponents by demonstrating to them that against him, their best wasn't near good enough. Known for his sportsmanship, if a bad call went against the man he was playing, he would sometimes purposely lose the following point or give away the game in which the call was made. He could be gracious in (his rare) defeat. He was nevertheless, as all great athletes are, imbued with an intense desire to win. And win he did, over and over, relentlessly, almost boringly, once winning fifty-seven straight games (not sets) in tournament play, a statistic up there with Joe DiMaggio's famous fifty-six-game hitting streak.

Because not many people are alive today who saw Bill Tilden play the game at which he was supreme—a few snippets of him in action are available on YouTube—most people who remember him at all are likely to recall his scandal as the first, and thereby the primary, thing about him. That dreary scandal, coming at the close of a brilliant career, also poses a serious problem for biographers. The problem is how great an emphasis to place on his homosexual pedophilia in recounting his life. In one of the leading biographies of Tilden, Frank Deford's *Big Bill Tilden: The Triumphs and the Tragedy* (1976), sex is front and center. In the most recent biography, *American Colossus: Bill Tilden and the Creation of Modern Tennis* by Allen M. Hornblum, Tilden's pedophiliac scandal is treated as ultimately peripheral, and in fact the subject is only introduced on page 383 of the book's 405 pages of text.

Who is correct, Deford or Hornblum, and how might we judge? Before attempting that judgment, though, two questions arise: In biography, do we really need to know much of a detailed kind about the subject's sex life? And, even if we feel we do, can we truly expect to acquire such knowledge—of longings, fantasies, and above all the peculiarities of practice—with anything resembling useful precision? Homosexuality makes both questions even more complicated, for much about the nature of homosexuality, including its origin, remains unknown. What is known is that in its practice homosexuality is quite as various as heterosexuality. Bill Tilden's own homosexual practice, or what from friends, enemies, and at least one psychiatrist we have been told about it, is a case very much in point.

W ILLIAM TATEM TILDEN JR. was his parents' fifth child. The first three died of diphtheria in 1884. A fourth child, a seven-years-older brother, Herbert, was his father's favorite son. William Junior, or June as he was known when a boy, fell under the tender care of his mother, who, given the death of her first three children, worried greatly about his health. His mother was, in the old-fashioned term, musical and conferred on her son Bill Jr. a lifelong aesthetic yearning.

The Tildens were wealthy and socially prominent in Philadelphia. Teddy Roosevelt and William Howard Taft were houseguests at Overleigh, the family mansion in Germantown, then a posh suburb of Philadelphia. William Tilden Sr., the dispenser of many civic good works and often mentioned as a candidate for mayor of Philadelphia, after his death had a grammar school named for him.

After suffering with Bright's disease, Tilden's mother died in 1911, when he was eighteen. Four years later his father and older brother died, a few months apart. He was left alone in the world with an inheritance of some $60,000—a substantial sum that would have been greater but for his father's mistaken investments late in life—and no clear vocation. Tilden's first job, after dropping out of the Wharton School of Business, was working on a newspaper. He would later write plays, in some of which he acted; after establishing fame through tennis, he also occasionally acted in plays on Broadway. He wrote fiction, much of it about tennis (and moralistic in the young-adult mode), and autobiographies and was perhaps at his best writing instruction manuals about how to play tennis.

Hornblum earnestly sets out Tilden's off-the-court accomplishments in a manner that might make one think the great tennis champion, in that overused and hence much cheapened term, a Renaissance man; in fact, he comes right out and calls Tilden "as close to a Renaissance man as the American athletic community ever produced." Frank Deford, were he alive, might chime in, yeah, sure, the renaissance in the microstate of Andorra maybe. Deford has a considerably less charitable opinion of Tilden's aesthetic achievements and quotes resounding critical putdowns of his dramatic performances: A critic in the old *New York Herald-Tribune*, for example, writing of one of his acting stints on Broadway, noted: Tilden "keeps his amateur standing."

Deford writes confidently about Tilden's sex life, sometimes on matters he cannot have known with any certainty. By the time of his mother's death, Deford writes, "he understood, surely, by now, that he was a homosexual." Elsewhere he writes, again about what he could not know, that "for as much as Tilden was a homosexual, it was because he chose to be one, not because he had to." Nor could Deford know, as he writes, "that it is clear that Tilden was never an intensely sexual person."

Reporting the conversation and opinions of others about Bill Tilden's homosexuality, Deford seems on solider ground. Ty Cobb, never noted for his exquisite sensitivity, on first seeing Tilden is supposed to have said, "Who is this fruit?" Henri Cochet, one of the French tennis players, known as the Four Musketeers, who dominated tennis in the 1930s, said that Tilden "was always having difficulties with the police for soliciting little boys. But Americans are so sensitive about questions of morality. It was his business and it didn't interfere with his tennis." The journalist Adela Rogers St. Johns allowed Tilden to give lessons to her son only after he promised to keep his hands off the boy. In *Sporting Gentlemen*, his history of tennis in America, E. Digby Baltzell notes that "Tilden's effeminate mannerisms became more and more obvious as he grew older."

In Hornblum's *American Colossus*, Bill Tilden is, until the book's final pages, sexless. Relations with women are scanted; the prospect of marriage is never in question. After filling in the Tilden family's history and Bill Tilden's early years, Hornblum concentrates almost wholly on his subject's on-court accomplishments. Hornblum provides a lengthy chapter on Tilden's having lost, owing to an infection, half the middle finger on his right hand (his playing hand) and his heroic return to tennis after what many thought a permanently disabling accident. Hornblum also devotes several pages to Tilden's work developing a slashing backhand, an offensive weapon that vastly improved his game. Tilden, who barely made his college team so erratic was his play, did not attain his tennis supremacy until he was twenty-seven, late for a player in that or in any other time, and it was his deadly backhand that made this supremacy possible. "I have never regretted the hours, days and weeks that I spent to acquire my backhand drive," Tilden wrote, "for to it, and it primarily, I lay my United States and World's Championship titles."

As does Frank Deford, Allen Hornblum expends many pages on Bill Tilden's career-long battles with the United States Lawn Tennis Association. More than once, the USLTA attempted to suspend Tilden because he was earning money writing newspaper articles about tennis while himself playing it. Tilden also fought with the USLTA over expense money allowed amateurs, for he was himself always a big spender—"He traveled like a goddamn Indian prince," said Al Haney—a man who, when it came to travel and dining, knew none other than first-class. Throughout his career Tilden was a consistent opponent of the USLTA's "shamateurism," the arrangement whereby everyone but the players profited from the game.

A LEITMOTIF IN *AMERICAN COLOSSUS* is Bill Tilden's work coaching young players. Early in his career he returned to coach his old high-school tennis team. He claimed he learned much himself through teaching. Throughout his career he cultivated promising young players, attempting to imbue them with his own strategic approach to, and passion for, the game. He would have some among them while still in their adolescence—the future champion Vinnie Richards is a notable example—play as his doubles partners in major tournaments. Allen Hornblum reports all this in the most straightforward way. In doing so, he quite forgets that a dirty mind never sleeps, and readers who come to his book aware of Tilden's scandal cannot but wonder if along the way he didn't attempt to seduce these boys, or if his experiences with them aren't foreshadowings of the scandal that lay ahead.

In Frank Deford's pages we learn that Tilden did not sexually abuse any of these boys, but remained "scrupulously proper." His sexual taste, Deford reports, ran to the adolescent equivalent of "rough trade": bellhops, newspaper boys, and the like. Even here, though, perhaps owing to his fear of venereal infection, his activities, again according to Deford were restricted to fondling and being fondled. Hornblum mentions none of this.

But, then, Allen Hornblum is not greatly attentive to his reader's interest or patience. He recounts several of Bill Tilden's important five-set matches at a length that feels only slightly shorter than the matches themselves. Nor is he highly attentive to the English language. He misuses the words "enormity" and "peruse," "replicate" and "definitive," and greatly overuses "iconic." He specializes in the flaw that H. W. Fowler termed Elegant Variation—calling the same thing by several different names. So Bill Tilden is at one point the "Penn netman," at others "the long-limbed, multitalented Philadelphian," "the lanky Philadelphian," and "the tall, cocky Philadelphian." Bill Johnson, it will not surprise you to discover, was also "the diminutive Californian with the big heart." Switzerland is elegantly varied to become "the mountainous country." Whenever Hornblum encounters an infinitive, he generally pauses to split it.

Hornblum is also either inordinately enamored of, or more likely fails to recognize, clichés. William Tilden Sr. was born in a town that "nestled along the banks of the Delaware River"; after his death, his son was left in "the capable hands" of his cousin Selena. Summer matches in his pages are played in heat that is "sweltering," dies are "cast," professors "stodgy," and with rain in the offing skies, yes, you will have guessed it, "grow more ominous." Bill Tilden, meanwhile, was a man in whom "there was no quit," clearly "not one for throwing in the towel"; he was "special," and the rest, you might say—Allen Hornblum, alas, does say—"is tennis history."

In his last pages, Hornblum argues with Frank Deford's interpretation of Bill Tilden in the biography Deford published forty-two years ago. (Deford is not around to respond, having died last year.) He allows that Deford's book is "entertaining," adding "how could a book about Tilden not be," without realizing that he himself has come perilously close to bringing off this difficult task. Hornblum argues against Deford's claim that Tilden's last years, the years after his scandal, were dark and desolating. He was, Hornblum claims, nowhere near as broke as Deford reported, nor so gone to seed in appearance, nor so bereft of friends.

Allen Hornblum's real complaint is about what he calls "Deford's melodramatic psychobabble" in his interpretation of Tilden's homosexual pedophilia. Here Hornblum fails to distinguish between psychology and psychobabble, for the former does not invariably issue in the latter. Deford does not use the language of the Freudian or any psychological school. Nor are all Deford's interpretations defaming or iconoclastic. He attributes Bill Tilden's cultivating young tennis players, for example, to a fathering instinct. Tilden received very little attention from his own father, and he had no children of his own. That he wished to shower fatherly attention on younger players seems, far from psychobabblous, acting upon a generous emotion.

Lives, at least those deserving of biographies, require interpretation. Sometimes even an incorrect interpretation is better than no interpretation at all. (Freud said that biographical truth doesn't exist, by which I gather he meant we cannot finally plumb to the depth of any human soul.) But *American Colossus*, industrious though its author has been in collecting material, by forgoing serious interpretation of its subject rarely rises above the level of fan admiration.

Great athletic prowess is not so much a gift as a temporary loan from the gods—one usually called in no later than the age of forty. Greatness in any other line—art, philosophy, politics—is longer-lived. That the athletic gift is shorter-lived is what gives even the greatest of athletes, no matter how extensive their fame, how grand their emoluments, a touch of sadness. No longer to be able to do in midlife what one once did supremely is a cruel punishment.

When Don Budge, the next great American tennis player after Tilden, asked him what he would do when he was no longer able to play tennis, Tilden looked at him and replied: "Hmmmph. Kill myself." Bill Tilden did not of course kill himself. But without tennis to sustain him, he gave way to his worst and apparently long-repressed impulses and thereby came close to killing his own reputation as the greatest player in the history of tennis.

The Semicolon

(2019)

EACH OF US has his or her own history with punctuation. For the first eighteen or so years of my life I attempted get by with as little of it as possible. This meant that I availed myself of three items of punctuation, and three only: capital letters at the beginning of sentences, periods and occasionally question marks at their close. I viewed anything more exotic as a minefield of potential error, easily caught by disapproving teachers, to my embarrassment and ultimate degradation. In college, I hesitatingly began to make use of commas, chiefly after introductory clauses. I soon acquired the knowledge that the colon stood for "as follows," and would occasionally boldly slip one into one of my student compositions. Not long after college the dash came as a pleasing surprise to me—up there with the discovery of oysters, if not giving as much pleasure as that of the discovery of sex.

I don't believe I used my first semicolon until the age of twenty-four or so, and then I didn't use it confidently until a good while later, even though I had begun publishing in magazines at twenty-two. To begin with, there was the appearance of the damn creature; with its period sitting atop a comma, it looked as if it had drifted over from Japanese or some other Asian language. The short-story writer Donald Barthelme, quoted in Cecilia Watson's book *Semicolon*, described the semicolon as "ugly, ugly as a tick on a dog's body." In the standard definition a semicolon is a stop of greater emphasis and duration than that of a comma but less than that of a period. A bit vague, hazy, this, is it not? "Do not use semicolons," was Kurt Vonnegut's position on the matter. "They are transvestite hermaphrodites representing absolutely nothing. All they do is show you've been to college."

Semicolons—who needed them? In time I came to learn, I did. In my most recent composition for publication, a piece of 2,500 words, I note that I used no fewer than seven semicolons; and seven, or roughly one every 350 words, seems, if I may say so, a lot, though this is a pittance next to Herman Melville, who, according to Ms. Watson, used more than 4,000 of them in *Moby Dick*, or one every fifty-two words.

Punctuation is perhaps one-tenth rule and nine-tenths art. In that portion that is controlled by art, writers will differ, sometimes radically. The art of punctuation is the art of rhythm, for punctuation's second function, after its first function of helping to establish clarity, is to set the rhythm of sentences. Rhythm in prose, it turns out, is highly individual, for nearly everyone not only marches but writes to the beat of a different drummer.

Mark Twain, Cecilia Watson reports, went bonkers when the English proofreaders at the publishing firm of Chatto & Windus fiddled with his punctuation, and resented the time he had to spend "in annihilating their ignorant & purposeless punctuation & restoring my own." Punctuation is a highly personal matter. If a writer's style reflects how he sees the world, his punctuation records how he hears its beat.

In *Semicolon* Cecilia Watson provides a brief history of the origin and ultimate acceptance of the semicolon. She offers interesting instances of confusions caused by misplaced or misconstrued or absent semicolons. In one instance in 1900 this entailed at what times liquor may be served in Fall River, Massachusetts; and in another, in 1927 in New Jersey, a man named Salvatore Merra was wrongly executed because of the want of a semicolon in a jury's sentencing—a tragic case, as Ms. Watson writes, of punctuation as "a matter of life and death." She also provides brief accounts on the semicolonic habits of such writers as Irvine Welsh and Rebecca Solnit and Raymond Chandler as well as of Martin Luther King, Jr., and somewhat longer ones of Herman Melville and Henry James.

Cecilia Watson describes herself as a "punctuation theorist." She is enamored of what she considers the creative use of semicolons, and provides a few examples that I found less than stirring. She attacks David Foster Wallace for insisting, in an essay he wrote called "American Usage," on the necessity of using Standard Written English as a passport to negotiating and gaining acceptance in the wider world. "Where Wallace sees high moral ground lush with the fruits of knowledge," she writes, "I see a desolate valley in which the pleasures of 'speaking properly' and following rules have choked out the very basic ethical principle of giving a shit about what other people have to say."

Rules turn out to be Cecilia Watson's *béte noir*. In the middle of her book she questions the authority of the *Chicago Manual of Style,* Strunk and White, H. W. Fowler, and others, writing that "it's fair to ask why we consider these books authoritative, and if there might not be some better way to assess our writing rather than through their dicta." She finds rules inhibiting, if not binding, a brake on creativity. In an interview about her book in *Longreads* she recounts how rule-bound she herself once was, pedantic and snobbish into the bargain, and expresses her hope that those who read her book will "find themselves maybe starting to be more generous in communicating with other people. In terms of the book that would be really, in my opinion, the thing that would make me happiest."

To decry another for splitting infinitives, ending sentences with prepositions, being unaware of the distinction between "interested" and "disinterested," not knowing when to use "who" and when "whom," and much more in the same line would be, in Cecilia Watson's view, pedantic, not to say snobbishly cruel. I would myself say that it depends who is guilty of these lapses. If it is a foreign speaker of English, if it a young person without the benefit of much schooling, if it is an older person without pretensions to being cultured, she is of course correct. But if it is someone who has those pretensions, someone who earns his or her living by the use of language—a television or print journalist, a scholar or critic, an author of books—then I would disagree. I have no hesitation, for that reason, in noting that Ms. Watson doesn't seem to be aware of the distinction between the words "farther" and "further," is not as alive to cliché as a serious writer ought to be, should dispense with the useless academic phrase "in terms of." She ought also to be disabused of using the two four letter words that begin with f and s under the mistaken assumption that it makes her writing seem more attractively earthy.

As for rules, some are more valuable than others. Take that most schoolmarmish among them, that of never ending a sentence with a preposition. Winston Churchill mocked it, writing, "This is the sort of English up with which I will not put." The rule has been violated by no lesser eminences than Shakespeare, Francis Bacon, and John Milton. Yet it is not without value. A sound principle—a rule, if you prefer—in writing is to attempt to begin and end sentences on strong words, and prepositions are rarely strong words, so where possible it can only improve one's writing to avoid ending sentences with them.

On the matter of rules, here is a sentence I used to set out before students in a course I taught called Advanced Prose Composition: "Hopefully, the professor will be able to seriously take the work on which I am presently engaged, which is, I believe, rather unique." The meaning of the sentence is clear enough, though it contains four mistakes. "Hopefully" is an adverb without a verb to modify; "to seriously take" is a split infinitive"; "presently" doesn't mean "currently"; and uniqueness, like pregnancy, doesn't allow for qualification. But if the meaning is clear, I would ask students, why bother eliminating these mistakes? The answer is because not to do so is to risk offending people who know better, the educated, a small group, to be sure, some would even say an endangered species, but one that tends to be touchy about such matters. In writing as in just about everything else, while at it, what the hell, you may as well get it right.

The Meritocracy

(2019)

T HE *MERITOCRACY TRAP* is a work in the line of Thorstein Veblen's *The Theory of the Leisure Class* (1899), John Kenneth Galbraith's *The Affluent Society* (1958), and Michael Harrington's *The Other America* (1962). Combining economics and sociology, two less than promising fields of intellectual endeavor, these books attempted to describe an underlying reality of American life that at the time was not fully understood by Americans themselves. How the rich live, the disparities between wealth in the nation's private sector and poverty in its public sector, the shockingly large number of Americans living in poverty, such were the themes of these earlier books. *The Meritocratic Trap* takes for its theme another less than fully understood reality in American life: the advance of an elite class causing the submergence of the middle class, and the dispiriting effect of this on the life of the nation.

The author, Daniel Markovits, a professor at the Yale Law School, resides, so to say, in the center of his subject. The breeding grounds for the meritocracy, he contends, has been a clutch of elite universities, Harvard, Yale, Princeton, Stanford chief among them, but also notably including the University of Chicago, Duke, and MIT. Mr. Markovits allows that he owes his own "prosperity and my caste to elite institutions and to the training and employment that they confer." After graduating from a public high school in Austin, Texas, he went off to Yale College and thence to the London School of Economics, Oxford, Harvard, and Yale Law School. The religion of the Jews, it has been said, is diplomas, but apparently not, as *The Meritocracy Trap* makes clear, of the Jews alone.

Education is the lynchpin to the meritocracy Mr. Markovits describes. The trick is to get into one of the elite schools yourself, and then arrange, from pre-school on through university and post-graduate institutions, for your children to do the same. I have myself seen this from the middle distance the summer my granddaughter went to New Trier High School on Chicago's wealthy Northshore. I noted her classmates, lacrosse mallets protruding from what looked to be their eighty-pound backpacks, perhaps going off after class to work with autistic lepers (a good *curriculum vitae* entry), all part of what I learned these kids called Preparation H, or preparing for acceptance to Harvard.

Once through the brutal education tournament, with its crushing admissions tests and big-ticket school fees, the work that lures the meritocrats is in finance, management, law, and specialized medicine. The elite universities feed into these jobs. The great choice confronting graduates of the leading business schools, Mr. Markovits reports, is "Investment Banking vs. Consulting." Elite jobs pay what Mr. Markovits calls "superordinate workers" impressively high salaries. First-year associates at leading law firms earn roughly $200,000 a year, and one law firm he names "generates profits exceeding $5 million dollars per partner, and more than seventy firms now generate more than $1 million dollar of profits per partner every year." Often these lawyers and other elite workers put in sixty-, eighty-, even hundred-hour weeks.

Meritocrats work hard in school, even harder on the job, and are richly rewarded for their efforts. The best and the brightest in the meritocratic scheme thereby rise to the top. What can be wrong with that? Better this, surely, than an earlier system, approximating European aristocracy, whereby the children of the wealthy were admitted by heredity into the best schools and lived out their leisurely lives on the profits earned by the land and businesses passed on to them by parents. Meritocracy—advancement and wealth acquired strictly on merit—is surely defensible, democracy played out to the highest power, an ideal realized.

Except, according to Mr. Markovits, it turns out to be neither defensible nor democratic, and, far from ideal, it is a disaster for the country at large. The argument at the center of *The Meritocracy Trap* holds that this new meritocracy concentrates "creativity in a narrower and narrower elite, farther and farther beyond the practical and even imaginative horizons of the broad middle class." Mini-dynasties are formed within the families of the elite, who live lives unattainable by the rest of the country, and meritocracy itself "creates a caste system."

The cockroach in the caviar is that Mr. Markovits contends that whatever financial dividends the elite achieve, these do not compensate for their work-driven, otherwise barren lives. He recounts that successful lawyers, if they are to bill 2,400 hours a year, must work twelve-hour days six days a week; successful investment bankers normally put in a seventeen-hour day, not infrequently seven days a week. Meritocracy, he writes, "traps entire generations inside demeaning fears and inauthentic ambitions," imposing "spiritual affliction on superordinate workers, condemning them to existential anxiety and deep alienation" that neither income nor status can alleviate. Burn-out is not uncommon. Thinking about money all day, every day, evidently does not refresh the spirit.

Cruelest of all is the pressure meritocracy can put on kids. "Meritocracy fundamentally remakes elite life," Mr. Markovits writes, "at home, at school, and at work, beginning in childhood, and extending through retirement," adding that insecurity is the lot of the elite through life. He offers the example of Palo Alto, deep in the elite culture of Silicon Valley, where the students in its two high schools score in the top tenth of SAT scores and more than 60 percent attend elite colleges, and where the suicide rate runs to four to five times the national average. But, then, high rates of depression, anxiety, insomnia, panic attacks, and clusters of suicide tend to show up in elite high schools and universities generally.

The once predominant middle-class has meanwhile become mired in hopelessness and resentment and simmering anger. Middle-class children under this new dispensation are consigned, Mr. Markovits writes, to "lackluster schools and middle-class adults to dead-end jobs." Many of these jobs are disappearing, a large number owing to the advance of technology, others to the reorganization of work itself under elite control.

Rare in the current day is it for a young person to start at the bottom rung of a company and rise to its top, as was the case in an earlier day. Mr. Markovits divides work under the meritocracy between gloomy and glossy jobs: "gloomy because they offer neither immediate reward nor hope for promotion, and glossy because their outer shine masks inner distress."

Elites, or superordinate workers, have taken over many of the jobs once handled by middle-management, middle-class workers. The new conflict is not between capital and labor, Mr. Markovits writes, but "between super-ordinate and middle-class workers." Once a country dominated by its middle class, America's middle class is now in retreat and is in fact diminishing. The distance between the elite and the middle-class in income stretches well beyond that separating the middle class and the poor. "Meritocracy," Mr. Markovits writes, "is far from innocent in the recent rise of nativism and populism." MAGA hats need editing; they ought more accurately to read MAMCA, or Make America Middle-Class Again.

The Meritocracy Trap is a book two decades in the making, a work replete with charts, tables, graphs, and more than ninety pages of fine-print footnotes. Mr. Markovits' data is by turns impressive and depressing: the mean income of the country's two hundred highest paid CEOs is roughly $20 million while Walmart pays a mean income to its workers, according to various estimates, between $17,500 and $19,177. The chairman of JP Morgan Chase Bank last year earned with compensation $29.5 million, which is more than a thousand times the typical salary of a Chase bank teller.

Middle-class debt meanwhile accumulates. Luxury goods, including concierge medicine, are available only to the elite rich, who even live longer than those in the middle class, more and more of whose members lapse into obesity, drug addiction, early death. "The military," Mr. Markovits notes, "attracts virtually no one from the educated elite," adding that "more Yale students died in New Haven than were killed in Iraq." In 1936, in his novel *The Big Money,* John Dos Passos wrote: "All right, we are two nations." Is this even truer of America today? Mr. Markovits' book leads one to think so.

One wonders if things aren't even drearier than Mr. Markovits sets out in *The Meritocracy Trap.* They are so in that in my view he overrates the quality—the merit, you might say—of education that underlies and reinforces the new meritocracy. Mr. Markovits shows that elite education at all stages spends more per student, that it has a smaller student-teacher ratio, that it results in higher SAT scores allowing students to gain admission to elite universities. But what if much of this added expenditure is spent on recreation facilities, computer centers, so-called cultural enrichment, and counselling salaries; what does it matter if there are more teachers per pupil if the teachers themselves are not extraordinary; what does a higher SAT score mean except that one is good at taking the SAT, and in some cases preparing for it, as Mr. Markovits records, with the aid of $600-per-hour tutoring; and what, finally, if the elite schools aren't really in fact all that intrinsically splendid but flourish largely owing to snobbery.

The sadness of the snobbery behind the reputation of Harvard, Yale, Princeton, and the rest of course is that it is snobbery that works. Having gone to such schools provides a calling card, a door-opener, a substantial leg up. But are these schools, themselves heavily politicized in their humanities and social sciences departments, in reality any more than brands? Are Harvard, Yale, Princeton, that is, any more than the educational equivalent of Ralph Lauren, Prada, and Louis Vuitton? And while at it, do we really need the 100,000 new MBAs that Mr. Markovits informs us are produced every year? The emptiness of much contemporary education may be quite as grave a problem as that of the meritocracy itself.

One cannot end a book as bleak as *The Meritocracy Trap* without offering solutions. Mr. Markovits offers two: open up the elite universities to a more democratic student body and devise tax policies that restore the old position of the middle class. Neither of these watery solutions—dilute educational snobbery and soak the rich—is likely to convince, let alone excite, anyone who has read through all that has gone before in Mr. Markovits' dark pages. A great deal more, alas, will be required to spring the country free from the meritocratic trap.

Part Two

Bits & Pieces

Close Shaves

(2018)

THE STORY GOES that the head writer on *The Simpsons* television show walked into a meeting one morning, two small bandaids on the same cheek, another on his neck under his chin. "What kind of a country is this?" he exclaimed. "They can kill all the Kennedys, but they can't make a decent razor blade." A fine touch of anarchic humor, that, but with a low truth quotient.

My friend Edward Shils once asked the historian R. H. Tawney, author of *Religion and the Rise of Capitalism*, if over his long lifetime he had noted any progress. "Yes," replied Professor Tawney, "in the deportment of dogs. Dogs are much better behaved today than when I was a boy." If I were asked the same question, my reply would be, "Yes, in gym shoes and in the manufacture of razor blades."

I am not old enough to have known anyone who, death-defyingly, daily shaved with a straight razor, though over the years I have had two professional shaves administered to me with that fierce weapon. My father shaved with a single-blade "safety razor," as they were called, often singing the British music hall song "Has Anybody Here Seen Kelly?" as he did so. As a small boy, some mornings I would sit on the edge of the bathtub and watch him as he applied shaving cream out of a jar and wielded the blade, frequently running the razor under the tap and knocking it lightly against the sink to clear off the extra cream that had gathered on it. This was a manly rite, if ever there was one, and I was mildly impatient for the day when I might take part in it on my own.

That day was a touch slow in coming. On the hirsute front, I matured more slowly than some of my friends, a few of whom began shaving as early as fifteen. When I noted friends and acquaintances whose cheeks and chins began spouting hair earlier than mine, I felt a blip of envy. If there had been Rogaine for the face, I'd have dashed out to buy it. (Riddle: What do you get when you combine Rogaine with Viagra? Answer: Don King.) I had to wait until nineteen or so before I needed to shave.

When my beard did finally arrive, it turned out to be a fairly strong one—too strong for me to use an electric razor. Of the two leading razors and blades then on the market, Gillette and Schick, I went for Gillette, in part because, a good liberal in those days, I had heard that Schick, whoever he was, backed the John Birch Society. Shaving cream now came in spray cans, and men went in for aftershave colognes of various kinds, Brut and Old Spice chief among them.

For many men shaving is a burden, and they tend to knock off shaving on weekends and holidays. I happen to enjoy shaving, view it as part of my regular hygiene, like the sound of the razor scraping against my cheeks and neck, feel cleaner, fresher, revived after having shaved. In recent years I have taken to shaving in the shower, without aid of a mirror, using soap instead of shaving cream, trimming the hair growing up to my sideburns in the bathroom mirror afterwards. While doing so, I have been known to do a turn on Petula Clark's "Don't Sleep in the Subway, Darling," changing the lyric to "Don't shave in the shower, Darling."

Never for a moment has it occurred to me to grow a full beard. Any such beard I might grow now figures to come in white, and a white beard, in one stroke, adds roughly ten years to one's actual age and, à la Colonel Sanders and Santa Claus, nicely desexualizes a man. One summer, vacationing in Wisconsin, I decided to grow a mustache. I was hoping for something decidedly English—Douglas Fairbanks Jr., say, or the young Ronald Coleman. What grew in two weeks later was Guatemalan illegal alien. That moustache never crossed the border back into Illinois.

From soul patches to Fu Manchus to beards ranging in length from Hasidic to goatee, face hair for men today seems more common than not.

The latest innovation in this realm has been the unshaved look, also known as "double-stubble" and "permastubble." I say latest, but the look began as long ago as the mid-1980s in the television program *Miami Vice* with a handsome actor named Don Johnson who wore it well. Unfortunately, if one is less good-looking than Señor Johnson, permastubble merely makes most men seem unclean, grubby, badly in need of, yep, a shave.

As for me, I'm the clean-shaven guy, neat, trim, impeccably kempt, with maybe just a touch of soap clinging to the lobe of my left ear.

Location, Location, Location

(2018)

M Y MOTHER WAS FOND OF A STORY about the little boy, miffed at his parents, who informs them he is planning to run away from home. His mother tells him she won't stop him from doing so and packs a small suitcase for him. "Run away if you like," she says, "but remember you're not to leave the block."

This story came back to me the other day when it occurred to me that I, though no little boy, have no need to leave my block. Sitting in my morning reading chair, tea and toast on a table beside me, H. L. Mencken's hefty *The American Language* on my lap, looking down on the thoroughfare that is Chicago Avenue from the windows of our sixth-floor apartment, I felt that if need be I could survive nicely without ever having to leave my block. Within a hundred yards or so of our apartment are a bank, a supermarket, the main branch of the town library, the offices of my dentist and barber, a dry cleaner, two coffee shops, roughly a dozen restaurants of various ethnicities, and (though I hope to avoid inhabiting it) a retirement home.

I bought our apartment nearly thirty years ago, because it was a convenient two blocks away from Northwestern University, in Evanston, where I was then teaching. Evanston, the first suburb north of Chicago, has always been well situated, with houses large enough to be called mansions set out along Lake Michigan, perhaps the only notable topographical feature in all of the flatland of Illinois. But for years, owing to its being the site of the Women's Christian Temperance Union, which it still is, Evanston was dry, and remained so until 1972. The first consequence of being dry is to deprive a town of decent restaurants, for the profit from booze makes possible the sale of fancier viands in livelier establishments. Evanston in its dry days was the home of the blue-rinse dowager and the dullish tea-room, hold the peach cobbler, if you please. No, thank goodness, longer.

Soon after we moved into our apartment on the edge of downtown Evanston, Whole Foods—owing to its expensiveness also known as Whole Paycheck—moved in. (If ever you want to begin a Tea Party of the left, it has been said, just troll the parking lot at Whole Foods.) A branch of Peet's Coffee and Tea shop took up residence, and just to the north of it an AT&T store selling and servicing smartphones. Beyond that is a good Greek restaurant—a Grecian spoon, as I like to think of it—that was there before I arrived in the neighborhood. At the corner is a women's dress shop, which always has elegant duds attractively displayed in its windows. At the bank, Whole Foods, the Greek restaurant, the library, I have some fairly long-established acquaintanceships in which pleasing talk about sports, the Chicago weather, and general jokiness abounds. Peet's opens at 6:00 a.m. and Whole Foods closes at 10:00 p.m., so there is foot traffic on the street sixteen hours a day.

During the late spring, all through the summer, and in early autumn three of the seven restaurants on the block, along with Peet's, set out outdoor tables for diners and, in the case of Peet's, schmoozers. During the day, a twenty-three-story apartment building between Whole Foods and Peet's debouches a small but steady stream of backpack-bearing, Asian students off to Northwestern to collect yet more As. A high percentage of the pedestrians on the street are bent over: the people from the retirement home over their walkers, the university students thumb-pumping away over their smartphones. If there has ever been a mugging or robbery on the tree-lined block during all the years I've lived here, I've not heard about it. Paradise, you might say, found. If I sound smugly satisfied about landing on this block, this is only because I am. So satisfied, in fact, that if you were to offer me a month-long use of an apartment in Paris, in the Saint-Germain-des-Prés, at no charge, my first-class roundtrip airfare paid, I would tell you

I have to think about it, though I would finally refuse. Why after all would I want to leave a routine I enjoy in surroundings that comfort in an atmosphere that pleases? Such is my contentment I even no longer indulge in real-estate porn, gazing, longingly, at pictorial ads in the *New York Times* and elsewhere for Upper East Side Manhattan brownstones, rolling Virginia farms, Montana ranches, waterfront property in La Jolla. "Let your last thinks be thanks," wrote W. H. Auden in his 1973 poem "Lullaby." High on the list of my own thanks is that for my great good luck in living where I do.

Milt Rosenberg

(2018)

FIVE NIGHTS A WEEK, Sunday through Thursday, from 1973 to 2012, Milton Rosenberg elevated AM radio and the cultural tone generally in Chicago. Milt Rosenberg died on January 9 at the age of ninety-two. His two-hour talk show was nothing if not anomalous. A University of Chicago professor, his academic specialty was social psychology, though it seems strange to use the word "specialty" in connection with Milt Rosenberg, who may have been the world's greatest paid dilettante.

Dilettante need not be a pejorative word. In its archaic sense, it meant someone with an amateur interest in many things, and amateur, in its root sense, means a lover. Milt Rosenberg qualified on both grounds. As Terence said "Nothing human is alien to me," Milt might have said that nothing intellectual was without interest to him. He seemed to know a fair amount about everything. During any given week he might have on his show Kareem Abdul-Jabbar, Milton Friedman, a film actor, an astrophysicist, and a Chicago machine politician—and he would keep the conversation humming along nicely with all of them.

The name of the show was *Extension 720*, and it ran on the *Chicago Tribune*'s radio station, WGN. (The call letters WGN stand for World's Greatest Newspaper, the *Trib*'s description of itself, which needs to be taken with a stalactite of salt.) I don't know how commercially successful

Extension 720 was, but it must at least have made its nut to remain on the air all those years. The first hour of the show was given over to interviewing the guest, the second to taking calls from the audience. Each evening it ended with Milt wishing his audience "a cordial good night."

Milt could seem an odd presence on AM radio. He had a cultivated FM classical music station voice and accent. He used academic locutions—"as it weres" and "if you wills"—liberally. He hadn't any hesitation in dropping in a quotation in French ("Wasn't it Baudelaire who said, '*Plus l'homme cultive les arts, moins il bande?*'") or popping a Latin tag (*Caca bene et declina medicos*). Mass audience though his show was, Milt never made the least attempt to dumb things down to set that audience at ease.

A list of Milt's guests over the years would doubtless be the size of a substantial suburban telephone directory. The *Tribune* obituary mentions Henry Kissinger, Carl Sagan, Jimmy Carter, Norman Mailer, Bob Feller, Jane Byrne, and Barack Obama. Julia Child and Charlton Heston, Gloria Steinem, and Friedrich Hayek were also on the roster. Authors passing through the Midwest on tour flogging their new books were, as they say in the business, easy "gets." More likely Milt was the "get" for them. I was on his show five times, three times flogging books of my own. Whether being on the show greatly stimulated sales, I have no notion. I never checked my royalties—or peasantries, as I tend to think them—after my appearance on it to find out.

Being on Milt's show was rather like meeting an old friend for coffee. The interviews were like conversations. Being on *Extension 720* was as far as possible from my appearance at 6 a.m. one rainy Cleveland morning flogging a book I had written called *Divorce: Marriage in the Age of Possibility*. The host of the show was a man in flowered pants who announced, "We got Joe Epstein here to answer all your questions on divorce," put a recording of "Two Against the World" on the turntable, and off-mike moaned, "Shit, am I hung over." Milt did his homework. He knew his guest's books, his predilections political and personal, and the right questions to ask. He gave you the feeling that your subject was interesting, serious, of significance and, by extension, so were you.

During the three-minute commercial breaks when I was on the show, Milt and I gossiped about people we both knew and exchanged jokes.

After the second time I appeared on his show he invited my wife and me to join him and his wife for dinner at a restaurant called Les Nomades, notable for its good food and ban on table-hopping. Milt's wife, Marjorie, a psychotherapist who later developed an *idée fixe* about homosexuality being purely a matter of personal choice, was attractive and lively. Milt had only one voice, his radio voice, and early in the dinner he turned to my wife and in that voice said, "Barbara, tell us, what do you do with your days?" Unable to hold back, I said, "Milt, let's take a commercial break here and get back to Barbara afterwards." He took it well.

The second-half of *Extension 720*, the audience-participation part, was never awkward or difficult. Milt's audience was respectful. They tended to address him as "Dr. Rosenberg." They listened to the show in the hope of widening, possibly deepening, their knowledge and culture. Something of the earnestness of adult education lay behind most of the questions. Toward the end of Milt's run, when WGN moved his show, which had always been at 9 o'clock, to 10 p.m., they were still up listening to him at midnight.

Here I have to confess that I did not myself often listen to Milt's show, or at least not to all of it. But then I would only stay up till midnight to listen to Aristotle and Spinoza. Sometimes, getting into what the English call my "sleep costume," I would turn on *Extension 720* to see whom Milt was interviewing. If it were someone I knew, or had a previous interest in, I would stay with it for 15 or 20 minutes.

We went to dinner a second time, and I would occasionally see him at some intellectual function—a lecture, a dinner party—around town. We were never in regular touch, and I wasn't aware that in 2012 WGN retired—for which read unceremoniously bounced—him.

F. Scott Fitzgerald said there were no second acts in American lives. He was wrong, of course, not least about his own second (if posthumous) act in which he went from a man whose books were all out of print to a place as one of the great American writers. But the toughest act, in America and everywhere else, is always the last act. This turned out to be the case with Milt Rosenberg. Without his show on WGN, he seemed lost.

One day in April 2015, I had a call from one of Milt's endless string of bright young producers asking me to appear on a new afternoon show he was doing out of a modest station called WCGO-AM in Evanston, the suburb just outside Chicago where I live. I had sworn off doing interview shows, but for Milt Rosenberg I made an exception. Unlike the capacious WGN's studio out of which he broadcast in the neo-Gothic Tribune Tower on Michigan Avenue, the Evanston station was housed in a single-story building, and the interview itself took place in a modest-sized office. Milt, whom I remember previously always dressed in blazer and necktie, was in a baggy sweater. Time, as Marguerite Yourcenar wrote, is a cruel sculptor, and it had done its work on Milt, who seemed thinner, gaunter, his nose and teeth more prominent. Before our interview began, he told me that Marjorie had fallen ill and was living in a nursing home in Seattle near their only son and his family.

The interview itself was a typical Milt performance. He began by asking me how many essays I had written over my career from which he descanted on what mathematics and astronomy had to say on the subjects of finity and infinity, and we were off. During the show he may have spoken more than in the past, but I didn't mind, for much of what he said was of interest to me and, I hoped to his listeners, though the number of those listeners, now that his show was broadcast in the late afternoons over a much less powerful station, figured to be many fewer than in his WGN days.

Along with liking Milt, I found myself admiring him. Conversation was what he did; it gave him joy. Along with his WCGO-AM show in Evanston, he was making and marketing podcasts. Clearly, he planned, even in these diminished circumstances, to go down talking. Milt Rosenberg died, in the University of Chicago hospital, owing to complications from pneumonia. None of the obituaries mentioned his last words. I like to think they were, "We'll break briefly here for a commercial, and be right back."

Only a Hobby

(2018)

I HAVE NEVER HAD, nor felt the need of having, a hobby. When I was a kid, friends of mine collected stamps or miniature cars or made model airplanes. I did none of these things. When I was eleven or twelve, a shop moved into our neighborhood called Hobby Models, catering to hobbyists of all sorts. I found nothing of the least interest there. I didn't disdain or put down friends with hobbies. In fact, I rather envied them. I myself seemed to have neither the temperament nor the skill to be a hobbyist.

Something there is about a hobby that suggests handsome margins of leisure in one's life—that and interests beyond the humdrum of merely making a living. That a man or woman grows roses or keep orchids, does woodworking, searches out coins from antiquity, seeks out first editions, or collects 19th-century cookbooks gives that man or woman's life added dimension.

None of these hobbies, or any other I have been able to discover, has attracted me. Perhaps a writer, being too dreamy, doesn't require a hobby. A year or so ago, my dentist having retired, I signed on with the man who had taken over his practice and who asked me to fill out a medical-history form for him. Toward the bottom of the form, on its second page, was the simple question, "Hobbies?" Not wishing to leave a blank, I wrote in "Grievance collecting."

At one time hobbies seemed pandemic. So much so that in the early 1950s, trousers called "hobby jeans" went on the market. Hobbyless though I was, I nevertheless had a pair of these jeans, which were of light-weight cotton, baby blue, with ample pockets, and a comfortable elastic band round the waist. When the chapter devoted to jeans in the history of the decline and fall of the West comes to be written, I hope hobby jeans will at least get a footnote.

The danger in a hobby is that it can elide into an obsession. One can easily turn from a hobbyist into a collector, from a collector into a con-noisseur. (The distinction between a collector and a connoisseur is that the former wants everything in whatever he is collecting, the latter wants only the very best.) I recently read *The Wine Lover's Daughter*, Anne Fad-iman's memoir of the obsession of her father, the literary critic Clifton Fadiman, with wine. As it happens, I worked with Kip (as we called him) Fadiman on the *Encyclopaedia Britannica* in the 1960s and liked him, though I was often amused by his pretensions. At the age of sixty-three, he told a friend of mine, "What do I have left to live for? Certain wines, a few cheeses." He once wrote a rubric for that portion of the encyclo-paedia that was devoted to the movies that read: "The curious conflation of a new technology and a rising ethnic group." I recall passing a note to a friend at the conference table at which this was discussed that read: "I believe he means the Jews got there first."

The interest for me in Anne Fadiman's memoir is in how, in her father's case, a hobby, acquiring knowledge about wine, turned into a continuing act that gave meaning—or so at least he believed—to the life of this highly intelligent man. Born in Brooklyn, the son of immi-grant Jewish parents, Kip Fadiman had been exposed to anti-Semitism early in life. He once told me that he had been denied entry into grad-uate school at Columbia because the English department there had already chosen its one Jewish student, Lionel Trilling. These experi-ences caused him to attempt to shed his Jewishness, and he sought to do so in part through indulgence in expensive wine. For Kip, in his daughter's words, wine was one "of the indices of civilization." Through wine he would escape his origins. Hobbyism spun utterly out of con-trol. Sad stuff, really.

Kip Fadiman's story is a stern reminder that a hobby should stay in bounds—remain a hobby merely. Which brings to mind the one joke about hobbies I know. Two old friends in New York meet after a hiatus of some years. Both are now retired. One asks the other what he does to fill in his time.

"I have a hobby," he says. "I raise bees."

"Really," says the other, "here in New York?"

"Yes, in my apartment."

"But don't you still live in that studio apartment on West 79th Street?"

"I do." "

So where do you keep the bees?"

"In a suitcase in my closet."

"A suitcase in your closet! How can the bees breathe? They'll die."

"So if they die, they die," the man replies. "It's only a hobby."

Only a hobby—the old boy got it right, absolutely nailed it.

Hello, Dolly

(2018)

VER SINCE **MICHEL DE MONTAIGNE** noted that he couldn't be sure whether he was playing with his cat or his cat was playing with him, an essayist without a cat has seemed like a Hasid without a hat. Or so I came to conclude a month or so after our charming calico cat Hermione died one sad evening in our living room. Hermione's death was jolting, and I thought that this was it, who needs the trouble, no more pets, no more livestock *chez* Epstein. I, though, apparently need the trouble, or at least welcome it. How else explain late one afternoon finding myself turning in to the Evanston Animal Shelter in search of another cat?

The Abbé Mugnier, the *belle epoque* priest, friend to so many of the French writers of his day, was once asked how he, so gentle a man, could believe in hell with all its terrible tortures. "I believe in hell because my faith tells me I must," he replied, "but I don't have to believe there is anyone in hell." My condition as a pious agnostic is to believe in heaven if only because the people who work at animal shelters, so many of them as volunteers, deserve a place there at life's end.

At the Evanston Animal Shelter, I met one of them, a volunteer named Christine Garvey. She walked me round the back where the cats, sitting in small individual cages, were sheltered. I was taken straightaway by another calico, sitting in her cage with what seemed to me stoical patience. Ms. Garvey brought her out to what was, in effect, a visitor's room, there for me to inspect her. The cat, whose name is Dolores, had short legs, a rich thick coat, and a figure that was, to borrow from the Yiddish for curvaceous women, *zaftig*, without in Dolores's case the sensuous part. We spent ten or so minutes alone, Dolores and I, just long enough for me to note how different, physically and temperamentally, she was from the lithe and lively Hermione. I left without committing myself.

On my second visit to the shelter I decided that Dolores was the cat for me. She was eight years old, and thus not in great demand, for most people want kittens. All that is known of her history is that her previous owner left her one night in her carrier at the door of the shelter. I neglected to ask how long she had been confined in her cage at the shelter.

The first change in Dolores's life once she arrived at our apartment was, at my wife's sensible suggestion, a name change. The too dolorous name of Dolores was changed to Dolly. Much better. The two, wife and pussycat, hit it off immediately. "Sisterhood," as I have noted innumerable times seeing them companionly seated on the couch together, "is powerful." Dolly, a middle-age cat, turned out to be in every way the perfect fit for two beyond middle-age people.

When visitors remark on Dolly's girth, I tell them that she is "one of those fat cats from city hall." Owing to her amplitude, she doesn't jump any higher than our couches or our bed. A favorite spot of hers is the top of one of our couches, from where she can view the outside world, though she is otherwise curiously incurious. She spends most evenings between us on this same couch, napping off and tolerating our stroking her as various English detectives work on complicated cases on the television set before the three of us. Her influence is becalming.

In the early morning, once I settle into my chair with tea and toast and a book, Dolly comes around, signals her wish to be lifted onto my lap, and takes a 20-or-so-minute petting as we both look out onto the darkened street below. I think of various writing projects I have before me, she of—who knows?—the jungle she has never known, her good fortune at being out of the cage at the shelter, the strange grey-haired creature in his pajamas who doesn't seem to tire of petting her.

All Dolly's days are the same: beginning on the lap of the grey-haired guy, a six-or-seven-minute brushing, five morning cat treats, a bowl of ice water and another of dry food to snack on throughout the day, naps, countless naps, sometimes broken up with a brief workout with cat toys, until the day ends with five more cat treats, and then off to bed to sleep near her sorority sister as I have come to think of my wife. She's been with us seventeen months now, Dolly, and in her quiet way has so perfectly insinuated herself among us that life without her wouldn't seem anywhere near so pleasant. "So take her wrap, fellas, / Find her an empty lap, fellas / Dolly's never goin' away again."

Dirty Words

(2018)

"PROFANITY, LIKE ANY OTHER ART," wrote H. L. Mencken, "has had its ups and downs—its golden ages of proliferation and efflorescence and its dark ages of decay and desuetude." Mencken wrote that in 1945, in *Supplement One* to his *The American Language*. Whether he thought that that time, just at the close of World War II, was a high or low period, he does not say. My own sense is that we are just now in a dark and dreary period for profanity, which is a shame, for lively profanity can be a delight to both its users and its audience.

That profanity can be an art there is no doubt. I once worked with a man named Bob Larman who, when honked at in traffic, would quickly roll down his window and respond, "Blow it out your duffelbag, farthead!" I went to high school with a boy who introduced me to "Schmuckowitz," a wonderful term of contempt. Nor shall I ever forget Andrew Atherton, my sergeant in basic training at Fort Leonard Wood, Missouri, master of the art of high-low comic swearing. Upon announcing the availability of religious services, he closed by saying, "As for those of you of the Hebrew persuasion, it behooves you to get your sorry asses to Friday evening services."

I have a distinct recollection of my own initiation into profanity. It was, precisely, at eight-and-a-half years old, when I went off to Interlaken Summer Camp in Eagle River, Wisconsin. Before that summer I remember using such words and phrases as "jeez," "goledarn," "cry Pete," and "holy cow." The older boys at Camp Interlaken, widening my vocabulary in this realm, taught me more vivid language was possible.

My father never swore in mixed company, and when he did swear, he never used the f-word. Nor did he ever avail himself of below-the-belt words, those many dysphemisms for the male and female genitals. He might refer to another man as "an s.o.b."; or, when aroused to true anger, "a real bastard." But that was it. I never heard my mother, a true lady though no prude, swear at all.

Today, of course, men and women swear freely, in or out of mixed company. A contemporary movie without what is designated "adult language" is rarer than Provençal French heard in a National Football League locker-room. In postgame interviews, athletes will occasionally speak of having "kicked ass" or describe coaches or managers as "pissed off" without being bleeped. Less than a century ago the press and radio and later network television stations were not allowed such words as "prostitute" and "bordello," let alone "hooker" and "cat-house." In 1945, Mencken noted that the general tendency was "toward ever plainer speech [in what was not yet then known as the media], and many words that were under the ban only a few years ago are now used freely." Now, with cable television having swung the gates wide open to profanity, the only dirty word left is "censorship" itself.

Notable holdouts for a while there were. Under the editorship of William Shawn, no profane words were allowed in the *New Yorker*, and the description of the sex act in his pages was beyond unthinkable. If one came across a short story by those two regular *New Yorker* contributors, John Cheever or John Updike, in any other magazine, one could be sure that it included an elaborately described bonk or two.

At various times in my own life I have been more profane than others. In high school I swore no less than my friends, which was a fair amount. In the army it was no more possible to refrain from swearing than to refrain from smoking. I recall once, about to enter the mess hall at headquarters company, Fort Hood, Texas, asking a fellow trooper coming out what was for dinner, and his casually replying, "Some red shit."

While profanity is ubiquitous today, it has also lost much of its ability to shock, though Samantha Bee's recently applying that still most sulphurous of words to Ivanka Trump did get the nation's attention. But the great f-word, through overuse, has become a bit of a bore, and the too frequent, or overly dramatic, use of it shows a want of originality. (Robert De Niro, take a bow.) I try to restrict my own use of it to the exclamatory, when, say, breaking a dish or stubbing a toe, when my self-editing facility is nil.

Now an older gentleman, white hairs far outnumbering brown, I feel it unseemly to swear more than is absolutely necessary. The loss of the useful word referring to bull droppings when listening to politicians has been a genuine subtraction. Formulating insults about them in cleaner language, though, I find gives more pleasure than the easy resort to vulgar epithets. Is there life without profanity? Gosh, gee-whizz, doggone, I hope so.

See Me Out

(2018)

THE OTHER DAY at my neighborhood shoe store I bought a new pair of house-slippers. My old slippers gave out, the bottom of one of them having detached itself from the main body, causing me in the early mornings to flap my way round our apartment. I bought the same kind of slipper I had before, blue, wool-felt, clog-like, made by Haflinger, a German outfit. C. Wright Mills, a once-famous American sociologist, years ago gave a lecture in which he attacked the East and the West, all religions, the family, children, dogs, and much else. In the question session after the lecture, a student asked him if he believed in anything. "I do," said Mills, "German motors." I guess I must believe in German slippers.

When I arrived home, unpacked, and tried on my new slippers, I heard myself mutter, "These should see me out," meaning I'm unlikely to need another pair during my lifetime. I must have picked up the phrase from an old English movie. In my mind's eye I see an older actor, trying on an overcoat, adjusting his shoulders to feel the snugness of the fit, examining briefly the length of the sleeves, and announcing, "This should see me out." By "out," of course, he meant until death.

When one gets to a certain age—at eighty-one, I am there—the future becomes decidedly more finite, and one tends to view one's needs in a much different, drastically less expansive way. I have an eleven-year-old car—a black S-type Jaguar with fewer than 50,000 miles on it—that has given me no trouble, is not overly advanced technologically, is in every way comfortable, and has, as the newer Jaguars do not, the silvery figure of a jaguar on its hood above its roundish grill. The car is taking on the feel, if not quite the look, of Inspector Morse's 1960 red Jaguar, which I always thought was the true star of that English television show. Every time I get into my 2007 Jaguar, I say to myself, gently patting the false wood on the front dash, "I'm counting on you to see me out."

Here is a partial list of See Me Out items in my possession: Three blue blazers. Four Latin and three French dictionaries. One pair of tennis shoes (for a man who doesn't play tennis). Five copies of H. W. Fowler's *Modern English Usage*. Six pairs (in various shades) of gray trousers. Seventeen wine glasses. Thirty-seven shirts, long and short sleeved. Fifty-six neckties. One tuxedo. All these, I do believe, should see me out.

Not, please understand, that I am in any hurry to leave. I like it here, on earth, like it exceedingly. But a man of a certain age, an *alte kocher*, if you will (and why wouldn't you?), has to think about what he no longer needs. With advanced age, I find envy, like any interest in movies about people under forty, has departed, and with it covetousness. Villas in Tuscany, Rolls-Royces, French mistresses, who needs them? Not this dude, surely.

If all this is true, and I assure you it is, why do I find myself fairly frequently strolling into resale, consignment, thrift shops, and used bookstores? In one such store the other day I found, for $5, a small white polished clay Roman charioteer behind two rearing horses. For $10 I recently brought home a large poster of a slightly menacing elephant advertising guided tours of the Serengeti. In a clothing consignment shop near my apartment I discovered, in a perfect fit, an unsullied tan suede jacket for $24. A trip to a nearby used-bookshop yielded a copy of Lesley Chamberlain's *Nietzsche in Turin* and Barry Strauss's *The Battle of Salamis*, the two for under $10.

Now what is a man who finds himself regularly muttering about this or that item "seeing him out" doing buying tchotchkes, wall decorations, clothes, and yet more books? Is it that I cannot resist a bargain, which, when come upon, still brings a pleasing *frisson*? I prefer to think it is instead evidence that I am far from ready, without aid of stage directions, to exit at left. My friend Edward Shils, at my age, would occasionally buy a bowl or a new kitchen utensil. "Doing so," he told me, "gives me a sense of futurity." Santayana wrote that no matter what one's age, one should live as if one expected to live another ten years. I don't know at what age Santayana wrote that, but he himself lived to eighty-eight.

My new German slippers may well see me out, though I'm counting on the exact departure time being still a good way off. When that time does come, I hope that I, like the man presented with his hat by a butler in many an English movie, may be alert enough to say, "Thanks just the same, but I'll see myself out."

Shabby Chic

(2017)

A FRIEND SENT ME AN ARTICLE, accompanied by several photographs, from the July 5 *Daily Mail* about the celebration of the playwright Tom Stoppard's eightieth birthday. The photographs, chiefly of English actors whom I've watched with much admiration on PBS and in the movies over the years, confirmed my view that we are living in one of the unhappiest periods for human dress in memory, the age of shabby chic.

But for the occasion of Tom Stoppard's birthday, this afternoon party might as easily have been billed as a Worst-Dressed Man and Woman contest. Assuming it was such a contest, allow me to announce the winners. The envelopes please.

- **Worst Shoes Worn by a Middle-Age Performer**: Iain Glens of *Game of Thrones* for his leather flip-flops.
- **Most Overly Denimed, Jacket and Jeans**: Ralph Fiennes.
- **Greatest Wife-Beater Undershirt Exposure**: Jude Law.
- **Least Makeup Worn to Less Than Good Effect**: Dame Maggie Smith.
- **Most Makeup Worn to Sadly Overdone Effect**: Joanna Lumley.
- In the **Ugliest Shirt Untucked in Trousers** category: Damian Lewis.

- **General Rumpledness**: Michael Kitchen.

- **Most Impressive Pot Belly Hanging over Jeans**: Sir Tim Rice.

- **Least Ironed Chambray Workshirt**: the birthday guy himself, T. Stoppard.

- The coveted **Gabby Hayes General Fuzziness Award**: Michael Gabon.

What, one might ask, is going on here? Why are these moderately but genuinely famous people all so badly got up? At the bottom of invitations in an earlier day, a note sometimes appeared, Dress: Casual, which meant not formal. Might the invitations to Tom Stoppard's party have read, Dress: Slovenly, which in this case seems to have meant out of the dirty-laundry bag? In the days of the Hollywood studios no actor or actress would be permitted in public in other than elegant or glamorous attire. Presumably no one wishes the return of the tyrannical reign of the studios. Yet need the pendulum have swung so far to the other side?

The general populace once followed, or at least attempted to follow, the movie stars of the day in the matter of dress. No man could bring off the sartorial suavity of Cary Grant or Fred Astaire, or woman the refined elegance of wardrobe of Deborah Kerr or Audrey Hepburn, but these and other actors did provide models of sorts. Now, if the crowd at Tom Stoppard's party is any example, actors are imitating the population in its general schlepperosity.

When did this schlepperosity set in? Some people blame it on California, the home of the open-collared shirt for men, Betty Grable shorts for women. Others lay the blame on the tumultuous years of the 1960s, when student protest brought on the militantly unkempt look. (When I began teaching at a university in the early 1970s, I had the choice of doing so in tie and jacket or polo-shirt and jeans; I went for the former, in the hope of convincing my students that, should my teaching not work out, I might be able to get a job selling shoes.) In the business world, casual Friday became casual everyday, and successful CEOs took to being photographed for the business pages of the *New York Times* and *Wall Street Journal*—just regular guys, earning serious seven-figure salaries—tieless. Today men and women in their 50s, 60s, 70s walk about in crowed urban areas in outfits that most of our parents wouldn't have worn to take out the garbage.

The baseball cap, the cargo shorts, the gym shoes, the inevitable jeans—such, for men, is the uniform of the day. Many women wear it, too, should the mood strike them. Along with being close to androgynous, this outfit is certainly ageless. Achieving agelessness is one of the leading desiderata of the day. Sitting in a favorite restaurant recently, at an interval of ten or so minutes, I saw two men with grey ponytails go by on walkers. Tom Wolfe, I believe it was, said that contemporary Americans seem to be going from juvenility directly to senility, with no stops in between; their wardrobes are helping to get them there.

Capitalism, never caught napping, has long been producing expensive shabby-chic wear. One can acquire Prada pre-washed jeans for a mere $365 (pre-torn jeans may cost more), an Yves Saint Laurent work shirt for $900, fatigue jackets for upwards of $1,000.

Clothes once expressed personality; they could be cosmopolitan, garish, serious, puritanical, witty even. The effect of shabby chic, with its eschewing of style and letting-down of adult standards that it brings with it, is to divest the world of the pleasures of clothes. Under shabby chic, they are covering merely. Clothes make the man and woman, haberdashers and designers once held, which of course clothes don't. But they do make, or at least once did, life richer, more charming. The reign of shabby chic is soon enough likely to put an end to that.

Thoughts and Prayers

(2018)

DIFFICULT TO DETERMINE the exact point when a word or phrase departs reality and becomes weightless, perfunctory, without the least credibility. When, for example, was the last time you took seriously anyone's—a friend's, a sales clerk's, a begging homeless person's—exhortation to "have a nice day." Some pump it up to "a nice weekend," "holiday," "summer," "fiscal quarter," but all to little avail. Such pure verbal rubbish has the phrase become that "have a nice day" is now included as one of the country's three most common lies: The other two are "the check is in the mail" and "don't worry, sweetie, I've had a vasectomy."

Another phrase about to enter the status of verbal inanity is the response, when a death is reported, that runs, "our thoughts and prayers go out to the family." The phrase is usually uttered—often "muttered" is closer to it—by public officials. President Obama used it quite often, never very convincingly. When President Trump uses it, it is, somehow, even less convincing. I have heard sports broadcasters spray it around when a famous athlete pegs out. I should imagine it is big in show business, possibly, among actors, with a tear added at no extra charge.

The only thing more difficult than paying condolence, in my experience, is receiving it. Easily the most awkward moment at any funeral service is when one has to pass before and greet the family of the deceased. A few words of comfort, some expression of sympathy, is expected, indeed required. To say one is sorry won't do, and besides it is inaccurate, unless your failure to supply blood or donate an organ directly caused the person's death. To mention that you will miss him seems trivial next to the effect of his loss to his family. To claim one loved him and will miss him sorely is likely to call for the suspension of disbelief on the part of the bereaved.

Candor, on the other hand, though tempting, is never an alternative. "He never really got it, did he?" is not likely to go down well with a man's grieving wife. "He really could be a bit of a bore, especially toward the end" doesn't sound quite the right note, either. Nor "I never understood what you saw in him." Nor, again, "I was always impressed by the extent to which he overestimated his charm." Best, too, to hold back on, "He died owing me $500, but no hurry in repaying it." Perhaps the rule for paying condolence is that which W. H. Auden lay down for Catholic confession: "Be brief, be blunt, be gone," but without the blunt part.

Most of the condolence paid me at the death of family has been less than memorable. I had remarkable parents, but I cannot recall, at either of their funerals, anyone comforting me by saying anything remarkable about either of them. The one piece of memorable condolence I have ever received came from my friend Norman Podhoretz. When someone very dear to me died, he sent me a note saying that the only recompense I could take from this death was that nothing as sad was likely to happen to me for the remainder of my life. Turns out he was right.

The Irish have their wakes, the Jews their *shivas,* but even with the lubricants of whisky or the comforts of religious ritual, condolence remains awkward for nearly everyone. It should be more awkward for those public figures who have fastened on to that useless gurgle—"thoughts and prayers," sometimes "prayers and thoughts"—a formulation unconvincing at best, never less than glib. How much time did an Obama or does a Trump take out to devote thought (forget about prayer) to the death of a Navy Seal in Afghanistan or a Marine in Iraq. Less no doubt than a nano-second, which, at last calculation, is a billionth of a second. Out of the mouth of a politician that "thoughts and prayers" shibboleth has all the resonant sincerity of the sound made by compressing a whoopee cushion.

The larger problem, of course, is big D, not Dallas but Death itself. Everyone may know that he or she is going to die, yet, as Turgenev somewhere says, death, that most democratic of events, is itself "an old joke that strikes each of us afresh." All but the most carefully chosen, the most heartfelt, words in its presence are rendered otiose. Unspeakable in its profundity, it is scarcely a surprise that death renders us speechless.

May anyone who is reading this not be in need of condolence for years to come. But should the need arise, if anyone tells you that you are in their thoughts and prayers, my advice is to look that person straight in the eye and tell him to have a nice day.

Table It

(2018)

ORDS, LIKE CHILDREN with Attention Deficit Disorder, won't sit still. The nature and condition of language
is change, relentless, unremitting, remorseless. Verbs are
formed out of nouns, like butterflies out of caterpillars; other words, trans-
mogrified, seem more like butterflies turned into caterpillars. Neologisms,
or newly coined words, abound. A great game, the language game, one that
is played without a clock and knows no season. "The notion that anything
is gained by fixing a language in a groove is cherished only by pedants,"
wrote H. L. Mencken toward the close of the first volume of *The American
Language*. Still, sometimes so twisted in their meanings do words become
that one feels the need for a referee with a loud whistle at least to keep
things generally in bounds.

Have you noticed, for one egregious example, what has happened to the
word "surreal?" From the name of a distinct artistic and literary style featuring the fantastic and the hallucinary, it is now used to mean just about
anything the slightest bit out of the ordinary. A baseball player knocks in
the winning run of an extra-inning game, and in his post-game interview
he calls it "surreal." A woman describes having had twins as "surreal." The
experience of a car accident is, you will have guessed it, "surreal." If André
Breton, the French poet who published the first Surrealist Manifesto in

1924, were alive to see what has happened to his lovely neologist, he would, as the English say, cack his pants.

Some magical quality inheres in certain words that unduly please people who emit them. Suddenly the words "many" and "several" have everywhere been replaced by "multiple." So that not several but "multiple witnesses" saw the mugging; the teacher instructed her students on a particular point not many but "multiple times"; and "multiple stores" carry the product which attracts "multiple customers." The word nowadays pops up endlessly—you might say, though I wouldn't, with multiplicity—during television and radio news broadcasts. For those sensitive to language it is almost enough to want to change the name of the dread neurological disease from multiple- to many-sclerosis.

"Global" is of course another such word, a vogue word riding high just now. H. W. Fowler, in his *Modern English Usage*, describes the phenomenon of vogue words with a nice precision: "Every now and then a word emerges from obscurity, or even from nothingness or a merely potential and not actual existence, into sudden popularity. It is often, but not necessarily, one that by no means explains itself to the average man, who has to find out its meaning as best he can." One easily enough sees the attraction of "global." To talk about "the global economy," or about "the global effects of the Internet," or merely munch on that fat syllable sandwich "globalization," suggests you are a person interested in large views, grand connections, the big picture. Global, baby, smile when you say it.

In the vast realm of currently over-worked metaphors, "table" walks away with all the prizes. What began life as a noun, a simple enough piece of furniture, "table" is these days showing up everywhere and with fatiguing regularity. Nancy Pelosi, when she not long ago told a *Boston Globe* reporter about her intention to retain her position as Democratic congressional leader, said: "It's important it not be five white guys at the table, no offense. I have no intention of walking away from that table." Apropos of talks with North Korea, Donald Trump has said, doubtless more than once, "Nothing's off the table, nothing's on the table."

As a verb, the metaphorical table began life in England with a very different, in fact an opposite, meaning than it has in America. In the English Parliament to table something is to put it on the agenda of things to be acted upon; in the United States, of course, it means to delay, or postpone, the item. As a metaphor, table is ubiquitous and nearly all-purpose. In the news, people, negotiators especially, are always threatening to walk away from the table. The insincere refuse "to lay their cards on the table." Others are asked "what they bring to the table?" In baseball, the first and second hitters in a lineup are known as "the table-setters."

What must a person new to the United States and attempting to grasp American English think when confronted with the various uses of the word "table"? Where is this table? he must wonder? How large and strong must it be for all the things that are apparently set upon it? And how scratched up from all those taken off it! Can it be that there is more than one table being talked about? How very confusing! It's enough, really, as the Americans say, to drink oneself under the table.

Don't Hide Your Eyes,
Weaponize

(2019)

THOSE OF US WITH THE EFFRONTERY to set up as guardians of the English language find ourselves in the condition of the village idiot of the *shtetl* of Frampol, whose job it was to stand at the village gate awaiting the coming of the Messiah. The pay, the poor fellow was made to understand, was low but the work was steady. And so it is with us guardians; such are the relentless depredations upon the language, we are never out of work.

Not that our work is much appreciated. I have myself railed about the emptiness of the word "focus," a weak metaphor taken from photography, when in all cases "concentrate" or "emphasize" will do nicely and serve more precisely. Despite my admonitions, the word continues to flourish in politics, sports, and so far as I know animal husbandry. "Issue" is another word I have complained about. There are questions, problems, and issues, with questions requiring answers, problems solutions, and issues being matters in the flux of controversy. So please, I implore you, don't tell me you have "issues" with your knee or with your kids, when what you have are problems.

Then there is that hardy misplanted perennial "charisma." The word was first brought into the language by the German sociologist Max Weber to refer to authority "resting on devotion to exceptional sanctity, heroism, or exemplary character of an individual person." Moses and Christ had charisma, so, too, did Napoleon, Gandhi, perhaps Martin Luther King, Jr. Beto O'Rourke doesn't. Charisma has been steeply degraded to mean anyone with a pleasing personality; it also happens to be the name given to a perfume sold by Avon.

Language guardians have long groused about turning nouns into verbs. An early entry in this field was "prioritize" from "priority." This particular barn door should never have been left open, for from out of it most recently has debouched the hideous "incentivize" and "weaponize." The latter is especially popular just now and pops us in such sentences as "They are weaponizing the Mueller Report to use against the President" and "Weaponizing the Supreme Court against Congress is not what the Constitution intended." Seeing the word "weaponize" turn up in print or talk is enough to disincentivize a person from reading or listening further to anything he has to say.

My favorite of the new empty words is the phrase "existential threat." Existentialism, it will be recalled, was a modish philosophical school, begun, where so many intellectual modes do, in France. Existentialism is primarily about "being," for, as its proponents had it, "existence precedes essence," which leads to the notion of "not-being" or "Nothing." From this brief summary you can see why as a philosophy existentialism went out of business. But the word "existential" continues to carry a heavy load of non-meaning; to use another nonsense word, it is "fraught."

"Existential threat" is chiefly put to use as a linguistic scare tactic. So our sending American troops into Venezuela could represent "an existential threat." Climate change is an ongoing, a permanent "existential threat." And the most threatening of all "existential threats" is of course—you will have guessed it—President Donald J. Trump. The only genuine existential threat I can think of, a threat now long past, was having one's daughter sleep with Jean-Paul Sartre, the frog-faced existentialist philosopher with a taste for girls a third his age.

Weaponize, incentivize, fraught, existential threat, these are all what H. W. Fowler, that god in the pantheon of all guardians of language, called "vogue words." "Ready acceptance of vogue words seems to some people the sign of an alert mind," Fowler wrote, "to others it stands for the herd instinct and lack of individuality."

No gainsaying that people enjoy getting their tongues around vogue words and phrases. They much prefer saying "multiple" rather than "many" murders; they enjoy calling life "a journey" (in the 1960s, older players will recall, it was "a trip"); they fancy using the phrase "in terms of" lends their speech academic gravity; they feel it elegant to toss in an occasional "if you will." Such language, they think, confers depth and shows intelligence. The cheerless job of the language guardian is to assure them that they are wrong.

Does Not Hug

(2017)

POOR **DAVID COPPERFIELD,** to add to the other humiliations of his boyhood, at school is forced, for reasons too elaborate to go into here, to wear a sign that reads, "Take Care of Him. He Bites." I have been thinking of that sign in connection with a sign I should like to make for myself that reads: "Beware. He Does Not Hug Men!" For I don't. Not, that is, if I can help it, though sometimes, alas, I cannot. Being hugged by a man, you will have gathered, is not my idea of a swell time.

I don't know when, exactly, men hugging one another got going in the big-time way it has in recent years, but I suspect its origins can be found, like so many false intimacies of the age, in show business. One easily imagines two burly comedians—Shecky Greene, say, and Don Rickles—hugging on a late-night talk show. Jerry Lewis must have been a hell of a hugger. Contemporary athletes also do lots of hugging after touchdowns, home runs, overtime victories. I have seen victorious professional golfers hug their caddies.

Two famous hugs in modern history are those of Sammy Davis Jr. hugging Richard Nixon and Jesse Jackson's being hugged—and kissed at no extra charge—by Yasser Arafat. Davis, taking Nixon by surprise, hugged him, surely among the most unhuggable men in history, from behind. The hug of Arafat (Yasser, that's my baby) must be among the hugs that Jackson would like to have removed from all photo files.

Barack Obama patented, if he did not invent, the combined handshake-hug, in which while shaking hands you lean in for a half hug and lay two quick pats on the other fellow's back, while he does the same to you. I've had it used on me, and it is a slight improvement over the conventional masculine bear hug, but I could do nicely without it, too. I try to make it plain—in my posture, my facial expression, my general demeanor—that I'm not up for hugs, but that hasn't stopped a small number of men I've known or recently met from putting the clamp on me. If only I had the physique to back it up, I'd say to anyone who attempted to do so, "Hug me and I'll drop you."

In this, the age of the masculine hug, I have in my mind been compiling a list of unhuggable figures in history—men no man of good sense would ever attempt to hug. I shouldn't think Aristotle or Maimonides would welcome a hug. Had it ever, I wonder, occurred to another man to hug Stalin, or, on a somewhat lower level of monstrosity, Leonid Brezhnev? Woodrow Wilson seems impressively unhuggable, so, too, does Winston Churchill and in fact every English prime minister in history up to Tony Blair. Perhaps the most unhugsome (unhuggly?) figure of all was Charles de Gaulle, whose *hauteur*, physical and emotional, seemed to resist any possibility of a male embrace.

Some families are big on hugs, kisses, love-ya's. Mine was not among them. My mother and I rarely hugged, and I have to strain to recall our kissing. I don't have to strain to recall kissing or hugging my father, because I am certain that, past the time I reached the age of three or four, we never did either. What I do recall is my father, when I was five or six, upbraiding me for too gentle a handshake. "You call that a handshake, that fish you just put in my hand?" I remember him saying. Yet I loved both my parents, have never felt less than fortunate in being their son, and I haven't the least doubt that they loved me. We just didn't see any reason to get physical about it.

The male-on-male hug is supposed to demonstrate warmth, camaraderie, intimacy. An argument can be made that it is a perfectly natural expression of masculine ebullience, the expression of feeling much stronger than a mere handshake can convey. But I'm not buying it. I myself think it is little more than gaudy exhibitionism in a touchy-feely time. In the leaden embrace of such a hug, the grisly bearded or permastubbled cheek of another man grazing mine, I have only one feeling: sympathy for women.

The one male-to-male hug of which I thoroughly approved took place roughly twenty years ago when the two wittiest, most intelligent men I knew, Edward Shils and Hilton Kramer, neither among the obviously huggable, embraced affectionately after an evening we three had spent together, so delighted were they in each other's company. That years before I had originally introduced them pleased me to the point where I almost could have hugged myself.

In Bad Taste or Not,
I'll Keep My Comic Sans

(2019)

QUICK QUESTION: Would you rather be attacked for your opinions or your taste? I would much prefer to be attacked for my opinions. Opinions, after all, can be modified, altered, changed, dropped. Taste, on the other hand, is more an expression of one's personality, point of view, character. No doubt I hereby reveal my shallowness, but I would rather be thought wrong about Brexit than about the choice of buttons on my double-breasted blue blazer.

Tastes vary in different social and intellectual circles. Dining in one's shirtsleeves in the *haute monde*—is there, I wonder, still a *haute monde*?—would be thought vulgar. I am old enough to recall when, in highbrow circles, writing for the *New Yorker* was thought in poor taste. I myself harshly judge people who have the bad taste to use the words and phrases "impactful," "existential threat" and "in terms of." Funny thing, taste. Petty and merciless it can often be, and when one's own is under fire, it can leave a sting.

Only recently have I learned that my own taste has been called into question, and for, of all things, my choice of computer typeface. I use, and have used for at least the past twenty years, the typeface known as Comic Sans, and I use it in twelve-point type. The attack has not been personal but has come by the way of an attack on John Dowd, a former lawyer of President Trump. Dowd had the temerity to send a letter in Comic Sans explaining why he would not supply documents nor allow two of his clients to appear before the House Intelligence Committee. Comic Sans, which *USA Today* described as "the whimsical, chalkboard-like typeface that often appears in school projects and memes," apparently "has been divisive for years."

Letters castigating Dowd's choice of Comic Sans were written; the Twittersphere was abuzz with condemnations. Vincent Connare, who created the typeface in 1994, told the *New York Times*, "If you love Comic Sans you don't know much about typography. And if you hate it, you need a new hobby." He also called it "the Justin Bieber of fonts." Dowd meanwhile claimed he had been using the typeface for many years, in all sorts of correspondence, and hadn't until now received any complaints.

Comic Sans is even in bad odor internationally. In Britain, when the Conservative Party recently used the typeface in an appeal to "get Brexit done," the Tories were accused not of rotten taste but of cynically choosing Comic Sans to seem unslick and thereby of and for the people. One graphic designer argued that the use of the font "tips you to the fact they're doing this badly on purpose." Has a mere typeface before now or ever carried such heavy political significance?

I claim no expertise, but I am mindful of typefaces, especially when it comes to choosing type for my own books. Until recently, though, I had no notion that my own typeface of choice, Comic Sans, was déclassé, infra dig or in bad, make that execrable, taste. Now that I learn that I have been in wretched taste all these years, well, what the Helvetica, you could knock my serifs off, embolden my Bodoni, italicize me purple, I intend to do nothing about it.

There exists online a Ban Comic Sans manifesto, created by a couple whom I have made a mental note never to invite for dinner. Others characterize the typeface in its whimsicality as being an affront to political correctness, which would recommend it to me. Some claim it is the type favored by comic books (hence its name?) and that there is something inherently juvenile about it. Comic Sans, I have learned, is also a typeface favored by the British Dyslexia Association, and if it is favored by those with dyslexia, it is good enough for me.

Undaunted by what is apparently my ghastly taste, I plan to continue using Comic Sans. I like the spaciousness it allows between letters. I can see an entire sentence in it as I can in no other typeface. I feel it provides a clarity for me as a writer that is helpful in revising my writing—and revising, it has been noted, is what writing is really all about. For serious and trivial correspondence, letters of resignation, essays, short stories or polemics, Comic Sans remains the typeface for me, and I'm sticking with it.

Yidiosyncrasies

(2018)

NEOLOGISMS, words newly coined, are as necessary to language as water to land. New inventions, institutions, patterns of behavior require new words to describe them. Nor need all neologisms describe new phenomena. Some are required to cover long-established phenomena that have called out for but never received the word they need.

In the latter category, I hereby introduce—French horns and kettle drums, please—the neologism *yidiosyncrasy* to describe the odd behavior of my fellow Jews. "Idiosyncrasy," of course, describes the peculiar behavior, often the distinguishing oddity, of an individual, but yidiosyncrasy is meant to describe the idiosyncrasies of an entire people. By yidiosyncrasy I certainly do not include the too-long established, vicious anti-Semitic characterizations of Jews, for as a Jew I side, naturally enough, with that philo-Semite Mark Twain, who wrote that the Jew, having survived all other ancient civilizations, is "as he always was, exhibiting no decadence, infirmities of age, no weakening of his parts, no slowing of his energy, no lessening of his alert but aggressive mind." What I mean by yidiosyncrasies are those traits that give Jews their distinctive, often comic, quality.

Start with Chinese restaurants. Perhaps the most memorable thing that Justice Elena Kagan has said, or ever will say, was her reply when asked by

Senator Lindsey Graham about her whereabouts on Christmas. "Like all Jews," she replied, "I was probably at a Chinese restaurant." Walk into any Chinese restaurant in America and you are sure to find Jews. (The same cannot be said of finding Chinese in Jewish delicatessens.) Jewish civilization dates back 5,778 years and Chinese civilization roughly 4,000 years, which is why, as the Old Testament neglects to mention, the Jews went hungry for nearly 1,800 years.

Almost as strong as the penchant for Chinese food is the Jewish regard for education. Diplomas, I have heard it said, are the Jewish religion. The Jewish fetus, an old joke has it, does not become viable until it graduates medical school. My friend Edward Shils years ago told me he thought the Phi Beta Kappa Society was really formed to recognize the achievements of neurotic Jewish mothers for hounding their children to do well in school. I once sat at dinner with a Jewish woman who seemed unable to utter a sentence without the name of a prestige university in it. The greatest restraint was required for me not to remark, "Daddy, you know, went to Leavenworth."

Another yidiosyncrasy is familial argumentativeness. Rare is the Jewish family in which there has not been a fallout somewhere, so that one sibling doesn't speak to another, or a son chooses not to attend his father's funeral, or a daughter to take her mother's calls. My own parents' families were riddled with such disputes: brothers-in-law who didn't speak to each other, aunts who wore their resentments on their sleeves, cousins holding grudges that seemed to last slightly longer than the Roman republic. Sad though all this may seem, this particular yidiosyncrasy prevents Jewish family life from ever becoming dull while adding a certain spice to holiday dinners.

The want of *sitzfleisch*, otherwise known as bottom patience, is another yidiosyncrasy, one that goes by the name of *shpilkes,* or needles in the pants. Jews do not wait well, whether in queues at restaurants or in airports or even at home. Jackie Mason does a bit about gentiles at an airport calmly awaiting the late arrival of a plane while "the Jew," marching up and down, "is *shvitzin'* and *shvitzin'*" (sweating and sweating). Extended periods of calm, let alone lengthy serenity, are apparently unavailable to my co-religionists.

The phrase is Henry James's, whom no one ever accused of attempting to pass for Jewish, but Jews also have a keen "imagination for disaster." In any enterprise they enter, they may hope for the best but are haunted by the possibility of the worst resulting. Cheerfulness is possible, but optimism is utterly alien to Jews. A man with whom I went to school, a Candide among Jews, sees all of his life as upward and onward, in the best of all possible worlds, and doesn't mind saying so repeatedly. I suspect he isn't really Jewish at all but was, though never revealed to him, adopted.

Other yidiosyncrasies could be cited. Nor in this brief scribble have I attempted to account for the origin of those I mentioned in Jewish lives lived in exile, under persecution, or for scores of other historical reasons. Yidiosyncrasies, though, they remain. Doubtless every people, the French, Germans, Swedes has its own idiosyncrasies: Fridiosyncrasies, Gidiosyncrasies, Swidiosyncrasies, and more. Yet those of the Jews have an especially strong flavor, a pungency all their own. The reason I so enjoy them is that I happen to share every one.

Sinfood

(2017)

Samuel Johnson, about to tuck into a pork roast, is supposed to have said that the only thing that would make the food before him better is if he were a Jew. Voltaire called ice cream "exquisite," adding "what a pity it isn't illegal." The question both these men raise is whether the ultimate spice in food, lending it a piquancy otherwise unavailable, is sin.

The first, the ultimately most sinful of all foods of course was that apple that the devious Edenic snake encouraged Eve to taste. How good the apple tasted we are not told. Did she even get to finish the damning thing? Imagine what that core would fetch today from the kind of ditzy collector who buys the old clothes of dead celebrities!

Jewish, I did not grow up in a kosher home. Some dietary laws, though, my mother did observe, more through cultural habit than piety. We had no pork of any kind—ham, bacon, sausages—in the house. Milk and meat were not generally mixed.

My mother claimed that kosher chickens tasted better than any other and bought and cooked and served them exclusively. Shrimps, however, were also on offer *chez* Epstein, though as creatures that crawl along the earth (Leviticus 11:9), they are not kosher and known, as all non-kosher foods are, as *treyf*.

I ate my first pork in adolescence in the form of bacon-lettuce-tomato sandwiches, though so good is a well-made BLT that even the condiment of sin could not improve it. There ought to be statues raised, perhaps replacing those of Confederacy generals, to the unknown inventor of the BLT, who has brought more satisfaction into the world than the past fifty years of contemporary poetry.

One of the advantages of being a vegetarian, if you happen to be Jewish, is that you are automatically kosher at no extra charge. Isaac Bashevis Singer became vegetarian in mid-life and, when asked if he did so for the sake of religion, replied, "No, I did it for the sake of the chickens." Would a vegetarian plowing into a Big Mac or an orthodox Jew gobbling down a ham sandwich, derive sinful pleasure in doing so? Somehow, I'm not sure why, it seems unlikely.

When the great cholesterol war was being fought, a great many foods were declared medically out of bounds, and thereby sinful because thought dangerous. Perhaps the most punishing of the items on the list was eggs. I have a friend who in restaurants seemed always to be ordering egg-white omelettes, which tended to be a bit more expensive and a lot less tasty than the real thing. He was more than mildly ticked when suddenly—presto change-o—eggs were taken off the banned list. I, who followed the old ban against them, now try to eat an egg (hard-boiled) at least once a day, but at this rate may have to live well beyond 100 to make up for all the eggs I missed during the years of their having been banned.

Perhaps the largest collection of contemporary sinful foods is those declared, you should pardon the expression, "unsustainable" by the foodie division of progressives. Food is at the center of the new progressivism in its more extreme wing. Want to form a Tea Party of the left, it has been said, all one need do is troll the parking lot of Whole Foods. Want to break with a seriously progressive acquaintance, invite him over for a veal dish with perhaps chihuahua tartare as a starter.

Why does the notion of "eating healthy" sound so boring, dreary even? Perhaps, from original sin days onward, food requires just a touch of the sinful to raise it above mere fuel. At an advanced age in a perhaps too quiet life, eating sinful foods is, alas, just about all that is left to me in the way of risky behavior. Yet I may have reached the stage beyond which no foods any longer have sinful or even unhealthy significance.

I seem to have lost my taste for rare red meat, but my sweet tooth is sharp as ever. One of the favorites of the gods at least insofar as I do not seem to have to watch my weight, which does not change, I do not turn away from cheesecake and am up for a black cow if there is root beer and vanilla ice cream in the house. I order, two boxes at a time, dark-chocolate covered peanut clusters from Oaks Candy Company in Oshkosh, Wisconsin; three or four nights a week, as a late-night snack, I fill an old-fashioned sundae glass with various exotic flavors of Talenti ice cream. What the hell! I figure, to play off the old blues song, I may be beautiful, but I'm gonna die some day, so hows 'bout a box of French macaroons before I pass away?

A Nobel Prize for Marriage

(2018)

NOW THAT THIS YEAR'S Nobel Prize for Literature has been cancelled, I wonder if it wouldn't be an excellent opportunity to use the prize money to establish a wholly new but long-needed Nobel Prize—one for marriage. The Nobel Prize for Marriage would go to those men or women who have long suffered in difficult marriages and stuck it out to the lugubrious end. Certain standards would have to be met: all candidates for the prize must have been married to the same person for ten years or more; evidence of egregious behavior on the part of the offending partner to the marriage must be ample; and physical spousal abuse does not qualify, for the punishment undergone by all candidates must have been psychological.

In the nature of the case, many of the early prizes would have to be awarded retroactively—given, that is, to historical figures. Surely Socrates, married to that many-years-younger-than-he harridan Xanthippe, who regularly embarrassed him by showing up with their children to drag him home from the agora, would be in line for a Marriage Nobel. Modern feminists, perhaps, would say that not Socrates but Xanthippe is more deserving of the prize, married to a man who spent every available hour away from home attempting to teach the young men of Athens that they didn't know what they thought they did. But, then, nobody said that the

Marriage Nobels figure to be any less controversial than the Literature Nobels and those in other fields.

Countess Sophia Tolstoy is a shoo-in for the prize. Tolstoy began the marriage by giving her his diaries to read, diaries filled with accounts of his lust, whoring and toppling his own female serfs on Yasnaya Polonya, his estate 120 miles from Moscow. Then there were all those annoying Tolstoyans—vegetarians, fruit-juice drinkers, utopians of every stripe—encouraged by her husband to hang around the house, a few actually moving in. To top it all, at the close of their lives together, he, her husband, the count, Lev, runs off to die alone at the Astopov, a small railway station in the middle of Russia. Well, not quite alone, since no death before his was covered, on the scene, so thoroughly as his by journalists of nearly every nation. Yes, Countess, it may not make up for all the inconvenience, irritation, embarrassment, and sheer selfishness which you had to undergo, but the hope is that the Nobel Prize for Marriage might nonetheless be some small recognition for your suffering.

The next logical candidate for the Nobel Prize for Marriage is Leonard Woolf, husband of Virginia. This patient Jewish man, a socialist of the heart, married a woman who was not only an anti-Semite but quite nuts into the bargain. We cannot know what Leonard felt when word reached him that his wife on March 29, 1941, walked into the River Ouse near their weekend home near Lewes. Relief, though, seems a distinct possibility. Even in death she was a pain in the neck, for her body floated down river and wasn't discovered until it washed up on April 19, nearly three weeks later. Her last note to him, assuring him of his patience and goodness to her, couldn't have been much help. One likes to think a Nobel Prize would provide Leonard posthumous solace of a kind.

Some Nobel Prizes for Marriage will of course have to be split between both parties to the same marriage. One thinks of the Carlyles, Thomas and Jane, whose tempestuous and possibly never consummated marriage caused Samuel Butler to remark that "it was very good of God to let Carlyle and Mrs. Carlyle marry one another and so make only two instead of four people unhappy." The split Marriage Nobels are not likely to be few. The Trillings, Lionel and Diana, might well be in for one; devout Freudians both, they were said to be unable to go off on holiday without a therapist riding in the backseat. A pity Edmund Wilson and Mary MacCarthy's marriage didn't make the ten-year qualifying limit, for their marriage, one between two of the cruelest put-down artists in the business, would have been an odds-on favorite for the Nobel. When their divorce charges against each other were published in the *New York Times* long after their deaths, citing in detail the insults, physical violence, and general contempt each accused the other of perpetrating, my friend Hilton Kramer remarked that he was certain both parties were telling the absolute truth.

As for contemporary candidates for the Nobel Prize for Marriage, Hillary Clinton will be on everybody's list. One likes to think the Nobel for Marriage might be some small recompense for the loss of the presidency, though since that loss, putting Mrs. Clinton into a perpetual snit, it is possible that Bill Clinton's own candidacy for the prize has to be seriously considered. Mrs. Harvey Weinstein's Nobel goes quite without saying. Is Melania Trump a serious candidate for the prize? You would have to ask Stormy Daniels.

The Nobel Prize for Marriage, if established, would be the ultimate consolation prize, recognition, and reward for all those years of mental suffering. And let's not forget the money. With it in hand, the winners could cry all the way to the bank.

Hold the Memorial

(2018)

THE OTHER DAY a friend told me that my name came up at the
funeral of someone I didn't remotely know. I told her, this friend,
that I assumed that the person who brought it up was doubtless
the minister, priest, or rabbi officiating at the funeral. She said it was the
minister. I added that I knew exactly in what connection it came up and
could tell her precisely what was said. The clergyman in charge, I knew,
quoted the final paragraph from my book of 1980 called *Ambition*. Here
is the paragraph:

> We do not choose to be born. We do not choose our par-
> ents. We do not choose our historical epoch, or the coun-
> try of our birth, or the immediate circumstances of our up-
> bringing. We do not, most of us, choose to die; nor do we
> choose the time or conditions of our death. But within all
> this realm of choicelessness, we do choose how we shall live:
> courageously or in cowardice, honorably or dishonorably,
> with purpose or in drift. We decide what is important and
> what is trivial in life. We decide that what makes us signif-
> icant is either what we do or what we refuse to do. But no
> matter how indifferent the universe may be to our choices

and decisions, these choices and decisions are ours to make. We decide. We choose. And as we decide and choose, so are our lives formed.

Over the years, at least a dozen people have told me that they have heard this paragraph quoted at funerals and memorials. I didn't realize it at the time, and it was scarcely my intention, but in ending my book I had written an all-purpose funeral peroration. My paragraph may well be in a collection of useful things to quote at funerals and memorials when the clergyman in charge didn't really know the deceased. That it has been so often used reinforces me in my own resolve not to have a memorial after my own death.

So many of the memorials I have attended have been disappointing. Frequently the clergyman in charge was winging it on the thin documentation supplied by a brief interview with the dead person's family. "Jack loved golf and enjoyed reading biographies, chiefly of American political figures." Not seldom, friends called upon to speak reveal they didn't really know the dead person at all well, or else badly misperceived him. A good rule at these memorials is never to let anyone speak who volunteers to do so. He is likely to want to talk chiefly about himself. "I'll never forget the night I won my Pulitzer Prize, Jim was the first person I called to tell the news."

Some years ago, I attended the memorial for the literary critic Erich Heller, a man of great learning and no less great skeptical wit. Of the six people who spoke at his memorial, at least three that I knew of he regarded as intellectually negligible, low academic politicians, clowns. What a shame, I remember thinking, Erich wasn't there to hear their vacuous comments, and how devastatingly amusing he would have been about them.

Not all memorials are failures. I attended one a month or so ago for a friend who by most measures had had a botched life. He had been alcoholic and had a gambling problem, and the two combined to cause him to lose a fairly prosperous business. His last years were spent on a walker, his eyesight fading, living in a hotel and then a nursing home, out of money and out of luck. What could one say in memoriam about so sad a life? My friend's son and daughter, both now in their fifties, spoke about their father's love of entertaining family and friends. (My own happiest memory of him is as a young man at a party where he played ragtime piano to the delight of perhaps seventy people in the room.) They spoke so affectingly that they redeemed him, made his life seem not a failure at all but a gift—to them, to his friends—and infused it with meaning beyond that of mere success and failure. Their having done so suggested, too, that in his way my friend was a good father.

As for my eschewing a memorial of my own, I can see no point in having one, especially now that Samuel Johnson and Max Beerbohm are long gone and unable to speak on my behalf. A simple party, with family and friends, food and drink, will do nicely. Maybe someone there will recall an amusing thing or two I said or a kind or generous thing I did. But if anyone should quote the last paragraph of my *Ambition* book, let it be known now that I want him thrown out forthwith.

Part Three

Edward Redux

Edward Remembered

(2019)

Without you, Heaven would be too dull to bear,
And Hell would not be Hell if you are there.

JOHN SPARROW, epitaph for MAURICE BOWRA

I MISS MY FRIEND EDWARD SHILS, as I miss many other now dead friends. But these others are dead for me in a way that Edward isn't quite. He seems never to have left me, and I can write about him today in a way I couldn't when he died—being enabled, by the passage of time, in the phrase of the House Un-American Activities Committee, to "name names" in a way that wasn't possible then.

An academic of renown in his own time who passed away in 1995 at the age of eighty-five, Edward published four volumes of essays and papers, a book on civility, another on tradition, a selection of portraits of intellectuals and scholars, and more. But his writing, which often arrived at a high level of generality in the German social-scientific tradition of Max Weber and George Simmel, does not convey anything like the full force of his extraordinary personality—a personality that was an amalgam of Samuel Johnson and H. L. Mencken with a strong strain of Jewish wit, Yiddishisms included.

In his will, Edward left me two Jacob Epstein busts—Epstein's great bust of Joseph Conrad and his self-portrait—that sit in our dining room and a twenty-six volume collection of the essays of William Hazlitt; and to my wife he left a set of elegant Wedgwood dishes—blue and white, trimmed in gold—that we invariably refer to as "the Edward dishes." I often think of his remarks on various subjects. Along with recalling amusing things he had said, I occasionally find myself imagining things he might have said. A number of years ago, for example, when at the Ravinia Music Festival I noticed Edward's and my lawyer Martin Cohn and his wife walking down to their expensive seats, she wearing a wide-brimmed summer hat, and I thought, channeling Edward, "Marty Cohn is the kind of Jew who buys an extra seat at a concert for his wife's hat."

Soon after Edward's death, I had a call from the obituarist of the London *Times,* who, checking his facts, asked, "He came from railroad money, did he not?" No, he distinctly did not. Edward's father, a Jewish Eastern European immigrant, was a cigar-maker, a man who sat at a bench in Philadelphia and rolled cigars for a living. Other people thought Edward was English. In World War II, he was seconded to the British Army, and because of his proficiency with German was charged with interviewing prisoners of war. That led to a job at the London School of Economics. Later he become a fellow at Kings College, Cambridge, subsequently moving on to become an honorary fellow at Peterhouse at the same university.

By that point, he had acquired not so much an English as a mid-Atlantic accent, which was highlighted by his adoption of a slightly anachronistic vocabulary. He said "district" instead of "neighborhood"; he might call a woman's dress a "frock"; I had him remove the word "wireless" from an essay he wrote for *The American Scholar,* when I was that magazine's editor, and replace it with "radio." So far as I know, he owned no leisure clothes, never appearing outside his apartment without hat, suit, tie, and walking stick.

The phrase "reinvented himself" doesn't apply to Edward. Rather, he had an idea of what a serious person should look, speak, and be like, and through force of will he, more than approximated, became that person. He also internationalized himself. During the 1950s, he spent large swatches of time in India. He knew German academic life from the inside, and Isaiah Berlin, R. H. Tawney, Hugh Trevor-Roper, and most of the other leading English intellectuals and scholars of his time were personal acquaintances, in some instances friends.

He was cosmopolitan, which is to say knowledgeable about and at ease in many countries. He introduced me, usually through an invitation to meals, to a number of international scholars: Leszak Kolakowski, Arnaldo Momigliano, Francois Furet among them. After a lunch with Furet, he asked me what I thought of the man. I said that I found him most impressive, but with a slight touch of the furtive about him. "What do you expect?" Edward replied. "He's a Corsican."

The teenage Edward Shils went to the then all-boys Central High School in Philadelphia, and thence to the University of Pennsylvania, concentrating on French literature and reading his polymathic way through the library. "My teachers would ask for twenty-page papers," he once told me of his student days, "and I would present them with eighty-page ones. It could not have been easy for them." Edward had no advanced degrees. "Ph.D.," he once reminded me, "stands of course for Piled Higher and Deeper."

Early in his adult life, while living in Chicago, Edward went to work on a project led by Louis Wirth, a well-established University of Chicago social scientist. Wirth arranged a job for him in the then famous Sociology Department at the University of Chicago, and there he stayed. The University of Chicago became the center of Edward's intellectual life. He spent roughly eight of every twelve months there, the other four usually in England. His own attitude toward the school was mixed. As Churchill viewed democracy as the best of all poor forms of government, so Edward viewed Chicago as the best of all deeply flawed American universities. He pretended not to understand why people would depart it to go off to Harvard, Yale, Princeton. He of course knew they were drawn there by the magnet of Ivy League snobbery.

Under the University's presidency of Edward Levi, from 1968 to 1975, Edward's position at Chicago was akin to that of a powerful cardinal at the Vatican. The two Edwards conferred on matters large and small. When graduate students occupied the university's administration building during the 1960s student protests, Levi, on Edward's advice, told them to evacuate the building or be removed from the university. Those who chose to remain were summarily expelled, their principles intact but (in many cases) their academic careers ruined. Owing to this decisive action, the University of Chicago was spared the empty, though destructive, tumult and loss of prestige visited on Columbia and Cornell, Michigan and Wisconsin, and other schools that caved in to the student protesters.

Edward Levi departed the presidency of the university in 1975 to become Gerald Ford's attorney general. Hannah Gray, a historian on the faculty, was his successor. I remember Edward telling me that he called Hannah Gray's office to discuss some matter, and being given an appointment in October (it was then mid-September). His days as cardinal were over, and he knew it. The university was not the better for it. Edward was less than taken with Hannah Gray. "They say President Gray is tough-minded," he once told me. "I suppose that means, as I've learned, she says 'f---' in meetings."

Edward had a long connection with Chicago's Committee on Social Thought, a department invented to foster interdisciplinary study and accommodate scholars, intellectuals, and writers who didn't quite fit into traditional academic departments. Edward was himself such a figure; though thought a sociologist, he was closer to a philosopher whose main subject was the organization of society. Hannah Arendt was for a time a member of the Committee on Social Thought and so was the art critic Harold Rosenberg. Edward brought Saul Bellow onto the Committee. He was himself never chairman of the Committee on Social Thought, but always a power there.

"BIT OF A CURMUDGEON, EDWARD SHILS?" That was a common line on him. A curmudgeon is generally thought of as an ill-tempered, surly person. Edward was no such thing; rather, he was a person who knew his mind and spoke it without looking over his shoulder. He told me that at a dinner party he once queried a married woman who spoke admiringly about Philip Roth about what must be her concomitant admiration for adultery, since that was one of the specialties in Roth's fiction. When students appeared on the first day of any of Edward's classes, he declared that he admitted no one who was there for "intellectual tourism. As soon as I close the door you are enrolled in the course for good."

I was once in his apartment during the presidential campaign of 1980 when Allan Bloom came over to report, with much agitation, that Ronald Reagan's approval ratings had dropped two points in a recent poll. "Now Allan," said Edward, "it is true you have not read many books. But you have read thirty or forty of the world's greatest books. Those books should have instructed you not to give a good goddamn about two points in some opinion poll. My advice is to return home to reread those thirty or forty books some more."

Allan took this with equanimity, or at least seemed to do so. A strange figure, Allan Bloom, volative, febrile, garish. He spoke with a slight stammer, his thoughts travelling faster than his words. He smoked nervously, wore expensive clothes, not infrequently stained by his over-enthusiastic dining. He had himself been an undergraduate and Ph.D. student at Chicago, and his crucial intellectual experience had come in the classrooms of Leo Strauss, who was known for studying philosophy in a Talmudic fashion. I recall being with Edward in a stationery shop when he picked up an elegant unlined notebook and said: "Ah, Joseph, this notebook, just the gift for Leo Strauss, who believes everything of true import the great philosophers thought was to be discovered between the lines." If Edward was less than impressed by Leo Strauss, he was scarcely more so by Allan, even though he helped bring Bloom back to the University of Chicago from a job at the University of Toronto, and allowed that he was an influential teacher.

Allan cultivated the friendship of Saul Bellow, and the two team-taught classes. A few people who took these classes report that in them Bloom served as the master of ceremonies, Bellow the star performer, with the former paying heavy obeisance to the latter: "Mr. Bellow will now explain the true meaning of the Fool in *Lear*." Along with obeisance, Bellow, a novelist who invented very little, derived from Allan Bloom the character of Ravelstein, protagonist of his final novel.

The closer Allan Bloom became to Saul, the further he departed from Edward. By the time Allan arrived back at the University of Chicago, Edward and Saul had gradually but relentlessly been distancing themselves from each other. The nature of the distance is revealed in Bellow's letters, which begin with his writing "I love Edward Shils" and toward the close by his writing "Edward Shils is a boil."

I owe to Saul my friendship with Edward, because he introduced us. At that time, and for most of the 1970s, Saul and I were close friends. He was twenty-two years older than I, but we had in common the subject of the city of Chicago in all its glories and corruptions, many shared literary tastes, and racquetball, which we played together usually once a week. No surprise to anyone who has read his fiction, Saul could be charming and very funny. Of my getting to and putting away a difficult shot, he said: "Damn, you're quicker than a sperm." I once described the insecure behavior of an intellectual. "'Insecurity?'" Saul asked, "What happened to the word 'cowardice'?" He read me, in manuscript, portions of his novel-to-be, *Humboldt's Gift*. The morning he won the Nobel Prize for Literature, he called to let me know about it.

Friendship, alas, was not Saul's strongest suit. He was touchier, in his friend Isaac Rosenfeld's simile, "than a fresh burn," and always on the *qui vive* for criticism, insult, betrayal. These could come in various forms, personal and impersonal. Erich Heller once told me that, after he had written an essay on the fate of the novel, Saul told him off, taking it as an attack on him. Saul broke with me because a woman named Ruth Miller, who was then writing a book on him, told him I had misquoted him during a symposium at the Plaza Hotel in New York—which I hadn't. Saul often repaid betrayals with acid portraits of his supposed betrayers in his novels. An old boyhood friend, an attorney named Samuel Freifeld, who is said to have given him bad advice during his, Saul's, third divorce, appears in *Humboldt's Gift* as a flasher. He was famously a literary Bluebeard, killing each of his ex-wives with poison ink.

That the friendship between Edward and Saul could not endure should not have been surprising. Not only was each a powerful personality, but both were put-down artists *extraordinaire*, and so their deepening rift was perhaps inevitable. This was fueled, I believe, by Saul's feeling that Edward was always judging him and finding him wanting. He was probably not wrong. Edward did come to think Saul a less than scrupulous teacher, a poor judge of women, and a man who didn't make the most of his artistic gifts. On this last, he felt that Saul should have extended his novelistic range beyond the subject of the discontent of intellectuals; and in the editing of the one novel that he did so, *Mr. Sammler's Planet*, Edward had a large hand, according to Bellow's biographer James Atlas.

In the realm of put-downs, sometimes I would receive back-to-back calls from Edward and Saul, each taking down the other.

"Joe," Saul would ask, "what's up?" When I told him I had had dinner with Edward the night before, he asked, "Ah, does he still have a leather palette?" The joke here is that Edward was a gourmand and a superior cook.

"Joseph," Edward would ask in a phone call twenty or so minutes later, "Have you heard from Saul recently?" After I told him I had just done so, he said, "Saul is easily imagined as one of those Jews who wears his hat in the house, and prefers to talk turkey, his hat pushed back, while sitting on a kitchen chair turned backwards."

Saul once told me, which I hadn't known before, that Edward had had not one but two failed marriages, and did so with malicious pleasure. That morning in 1977 when the Nobel Prize for Literature was announced, Edward told me to be sure not to call Saul, who was likely to be sulking about not having won it for a second time.

In later years, long out of touch with Bellow, I heard only Edward's put-downs. When Saul wrote to a colleague about the conditions he met with when he lived briefly in the house once owned by Virginia and Leonard Woolf, Edward said, "You know our Saul. Houses or women, if it's for free he takes it." When Saul attempted to get jobs on the Committee for Social Thought for his former lady friends, Edward told me that he wasn't about "to let Saul turn the Committee into a rest home for his old *nafkes.*"

At the end, with Edward on his deathbed from cancer in his eighty-fifth year, Saul called to ask if it would be all right if he came over. Edward instructed the old friend who was staying with him to tell Saul he could not, for "I don't want to make it any easier for the son of a bitch." After Edward's death, Saul put an Edward-like character in *Ravelstein*, a character to whom he attributed a pretentious library, a bad smell, and probable homosexuality, none of it true.

Edward was often critical of other intellectuals and academics. "You know, Joseph, I fear that members of the Committee on Social Thought labor under the delusion that Richard Rorty is an intelligent man." Of Hannah Arendt he said, "No great *chachemess,* our Hannah." (The word roughly means "wise and learned female.") He remarked of a left-wing philosophy professor at Harvard named Morton White, "This little Abie Kabbible, he wants revolution." I once entered Edward's apartment to find him razoring an introduction by Alfred Kazin out of a copy of a book. "I don't want any part of that wretched fellow in my apartment," he said.

He mocked Daniel Bell for his pseudo-scholarship; was fond of reminding Philip Reiff, who had extravagant pretensions to being an English gent, that his father had been a kosher butcher on Chicago's south side; and said of David Reisman, who attempted to pass himself off as a WASP, that "at least he has never taken undue advantage of being Jewish." Among the living (of the day) he admired Sidney Hook, James Q. Wilson, Edward Banfield, Hilton Kramer, R.K. Narayan, Hugh Trevor-Roper, Peter Brown, Subrahmanyan Chandrashekhar, and a small number of others.

What Edward saw in me, a man in his early thirties, some twenty-seven years his junior, with no great intellectual accomplishments to his credit apart from having published in a few okay magazines, I do not know. Whatever it was, I remain thankful for it. We also quickly used our full first names with each other, Edward and Joseph, never Ed and Joe. This, too, was a rare privilege, for I knew Edward to continue to address people he had known and even much liked for decades, including former students, by their last names.

One afternoon Edward said to me, "Joseph, you and I have talked about so many subjects and so many writers, but we are both too civilized ever to talk about Shakespeare." We talked about nearly everything else. He read more widely in literature than any social scientist I have known, and the novel was one of our subjects. We were both great admirers of Joseph Conrad and Willa Cather. What we didn't talk all that much about was politics. We were both strong anti-Communists, and such left-wing days that either of us had known were well behind both of us. Intellectuals of Edward's generation did not descend to discussing American party politics.

After the student protest movement, Edward felt that the more deleterious political mischief was arriving from the left, but, then, exposure to university life will do that to one. If Edward were alive today my sense is that he would have been appalled by Donald Trump's ignorance yet mildly amused by his effrontery. He would have considered Barack Obama callow, shallow, a less than first-class graduate student.

EDWARD PHONED ME NEARLY EVERY DAY when he was in Chicago, and we met at least once a week, usually to go to dinner, though I sometimes took him (he did not drive) to the various Chicago neighborhood shops for the Lithuanian bread, Hungarian sausages, seafood, and other comestibles he favored. He admired shopkeepers, and thought well of the city's various ethnic groups—Poles, Greeks, Italians, Irish—who scrupulously maintained the small lawns before their bungalows. He enjoyed the stories I would bring him about the decidedly unintellectual members of my own family, such as my older, considerably overweight cousin Moe Mizeles, whom I had last seen sitting in his kitchen methodically devouring a pound cake, every so often looking up at a Cubs game on the small television set he had installed there, and calling out, "Give it a *zetz!*"

Discovering new restaurants in the city gave Edward especial pleasure: a chili place on the near west side, Greek restaurants on Halsted Street, two or three restaurants in Chinatown. I took much pleasure in introducing him to Ben Moy's restaurant The Bird, which served Chinese but with an elegance and unfailing subtle flavor neither of us had ever encountered. We began to go there once a week, even though it required a thirty-mile roundtrip drive from Edward's apartment in Hyde Park. Mr. Moy soon allowed Edward the run of his kitchen. Mrs. Moy, whose family before the revolution had the exclusive rights to the sale of Phillip Morris cigarettes in all of China, paid him great deference.

A meal at The Bird would occasionally stir reminiscences in Edward of Strulewitz's Restaurant on Roosevelt Road, which he had frequented during the Depression. He would recount the elaborate and heavy meals at Strulewitz's, always beginning with chopped liver and ending with strudel, and close by noting that the entire meal might have cost 85 or 95 cents. The restaurant, he noted, was open 364 days a year; he suspected that on Yom Kippur they served from the back door. He told me he asked Mr. Strulewitz how he was able to produce such splendid fare. "Simple," Strulewitz replied. "I buy fresh. My Yiddenesses cook it up." I rarely left Edward's company or hung up the phone after one of his calls without learning something new or amusing. Knowing him in the close way he allowed me to know him was, I now understand, the most fortunate intellectual event of my life. He was not formally my teacher and would have never have claimed to be my mentor. He was instead a dear friend who was also a powerful influence. My friendship with Edward broadened and deepened my outlook, helped me establish steady intellectual standards, gave the word "serious" a new meaning for me, and in countless ways enriched and made the world a more amusing place. He will soon be dead twenty-five years, and I miss him still.

Original Publication
Information for Essays
in this Book

Part One: Essays & Reviews

"The Bookish Life," *First Things*, November 2018.

"Body without Soul," *First Things*, January 2020.

"Chicago, Then and Now," *Weekly Standard*, February 25, 2018.

"Jewish Jokes," originally published as "Jews & Their Jokes," *Weekly Standard*, January 28, 2018.

"Short Attention Span," originally published as "Confessions of a Short Attention Span Man," *Commentary*, September 1, 2017.

"Intellectual Marines in Little Magazines," from a lecture given at Hillsdale College, 2008.

"The American Language," originally published as "The Music of the Grand American Show," *Claremont Review of Books*, Fall 2018.

"University of Chicago Days," *Claremont Review of Books*, Summer 2017.

"The Frittering Prizes," *Weekly Standard*, June 23, 1997.

"The Tzaddik of the Intellectuals," *Weekly Standard*, November 3, 2017.

"The Menace of Political Correctness," originally published as "Political Correctness Knows No Statute of Limitations," *National Review*, February 5, 2019.

"Theodor Mommsen," originally published as "Hail, Mommsen," *Claremont Review of Books*, Spring 2018.

"Big Julie," *First Things*, April 2019.

"Our Gladiators," *Commentary*, November 2018.

"Diamonds Are Forever," *Weekly Standard*, October 20, 2017.

"What's the Story?" *Weekly Standard*, September 15, 2017.

"University Presidents," *Academic Questions*, Spring 2019.

"Immaturity on Campus," *Academic Questions*. Spring 2020.

"Henrich Heine," originally published as "Wit, Exile, Jew, Convert, Genius," *Commentary*, June 2018.

"Joseph Roth," originally published as "Joseph Roth: Grieving for a Lost Empire," *Jewish Review of Books*, Winter 2018.

"Stefan Zweig," originally published as "Stefan Zweg, European Man," *First Things*, June/July 2019.

"Vasily Grossman," originally published as "The Achievement of Vasily Grossman," *Commentary*, June 2019.

"Evelyn Waugh," originally published as "White Mischief," *Claremont Review of Books*, Spring 2017.

"P. G. Wodehouse," originally published as "Frivolous, Empty, and Perfectly Delightful," *Claremont Review of Books*, Winter 2018.

"Tom Wolfe," originally published as "The Statustician," *Weekly Standard*, May 24, 2018.

"Susan Sontag, Savant-Idiot, *Commentary*, December 2019.

"Lionel Trilling," originally published as "Lionel Trilling Reluctant Critic," *Commentary*, March 2019.

"Proust's Duchesses," originally published as "Life Begins at Baron," *Weekly Standard,* December 9, 2018.

"Denis Diderot," originally published as "Living in the Ought," *Claremont Review of Books*, Fall 2018.

"Isaiah Berlin," originally published as "A Thinker, I Suppose," *Claremont Review of Books*, Summer 2016.

"Johnson-Boswell," originally published as "The Club Review: An Assembly of Good Fellows," *Wall Street Journal*, March 22, 2019.

"Stop Your Blubbering," *Wall Street Journal*, August 16, 2019.

"George Gershwin," originally published as "Rhapsody Imbued," *Wall Street Journal*, September 4, 2009.

"Nelson Algren," first published as "The Man with the Leaden Ear," *Commentary*, July/August 2019.

"Essayism," originally published as "Tell Me a Bit (Less) About Yourself," *Wall Street Journal,* November 30, 2018.

"Alcibiades," originally published as "Ruined by His Own Glory," *Claremont Review of Books*, February 20, 2019.

"Big Bill Tilden," originally published as "Unforgetting Big Bill," *Weekly Standard*, June 1, 2018.

"The Semicolon" originally published as "The Art of Punctuation," *National Review*, September 12, 2019.

"The Meritocracy," originally published as "Squeezing Through the Narrow Door," *Wall Street Journal*, September 20, 2019.

Part Two: Bits & Pieces

"Close Shaves," *Weekly Standard*, December 17, 2018.

"Location, Location, Location," *Weekly Standard*, May 28, 2018.

"Milt Rosenberg," originally published as "A Cordial Good Night," *Weekly Standard,* January 19, 3018.

"Only a Hobby," *Weekly Standard*, August 30, 2018.

"Hello, Dolly," *Weekly Standard*, March 26, 2018.

"Dirty Words," *Weekly Standard*, July 2, 2018.

"See Me Out," originally published as "This Will See Me Out," *Weekly Standard*, September 19, 2018.

"Shabby Chic," *Weekly Standard*, September 6, 2017.

"Thoughts and Prayers," *Weekly Standard*, August 1, 2018.

"Table It," originally published as "Sometimes the Language Game Needs a Penalty Box," *Wall Street Journal*, June 6, 2018.

"Don't Hide Your Eyes, Weaponize," originally published as "How to Weaponize an Existential Threat," the *Wall Street Journal*, April 28, 2019.

"Does Not Hug," *Weekly Standard*, November 17, 2017.

"Yidiosyncrases," *Weekly Standard*, November 5, 2018.

"Sinfood," *Weekly Standard*, October 13, 2017.

"A Nobel Prize for Marriage," originally published as "Your Spouse Is No Prize? Maybe You Deserve a Nobel," *Wall Street Journal*, May 11, 2018.

"Hold the Memorial," *Weekly Standard*, January 8, 2018.

Part Three: Edward Redux

"Edward Redux," originally published as "Remembering Edward Shils," *Commentary*, October 2019.

Index

U

V